**ORACLE**®   *Oracle Press*™

Oracle GoldenGate 11g Handbook

CW00953925

About the Author

Robert G. Freeman works for Oracle Corporation and enjoys working with the newest technologies like Oracle GoldenGate and Oracle Exadata, and exploring the latest versions of the Oracle Database software. Robert has been working with the Oracle Database product for over two decades now and hopes to be working with it for another two decades or more. Robert is the author of several Oracle Press titles, including New Features books on Oracle Database 11*g*, Oracle Database 10*g*, and Oracle 9*i*. Robert is also the author of the Oracle Press book *Portable DBA: Oracle*. He is also the co-author of the Oracle Press *RMAN Backup and Recovery* series for Oracle Database 11*g*, Oracle Database 10*g*, and Oracle 9*i*.

About the Technical Editor

Jinyu Wang is part of the Oracle Server Technology product management team. She has managed several Oracle products over the last 12 years, including Oracle XDK, Oracle XML DB, Oracle Secure Enterprise Search (SES), Oracle Text, and Oracle GoldenGate. Jinyu's current interests are in database, data replication, XML, and information retrieval technology. Jinyu frequently speaks at conferences and publishes papers in journals. She holds a number of U.S. patents. She is the author of *Oracle Database 11*g*: Building Oracle XML DB Applications* (McGraw-Hill/Oracle Press, 2011) and the co-author of *Oracle Database 10*g *XML & SQL: Design, Build & Manage XML Applications in Java, C, C++ & PL/SQL* (McGraw-Hill/Oracle Press, 2004).

Oracle Press™

Oracle GoldenGate 11g Handbook

Robert G. Freeman

New York   Chicago   San Francisco   Athens
London   Madrid   Mexico City   Milan
New Delhi   Singapore   Sydney   Toronto

Cataloging-in-Publication Data is on file with the Library of Congress

McGraw-Hill Education books are available at special quantity discounts to use as premiums and sales promotions or for use in corporate training programs. To contact a representative, please visit the Contact Us pages at www.mhprofessional.com.

Oracle GoldenGate 11g Handbook

1234567890   DOC DOC   109876543

ISBN   978-0-07-179088-8

MHID   0-07-179088-8

Sponsoring Editor Paul Carlstroem	**Technical Editor** Jinyu Wang	**Composition** Cenveo Publisher Services
Editorial Supervisor Patty Mon	**Copy Editor** Margaret Berson	**Illustration** Cenveo Publisher Services
Project Manager Sheena Uprety, Cenveo® Publisher Services	**Proofreader** Paul Tyler	**Art Director, Cover** Jeff Weeks
Acquisitions Coordinator Amanda Russell	**Indexer** Ted Laux	**Cover Designer** Pattie Lee
	Production Supervisor George Anderson	

This book is dedicated to my wife Carrie, and my five kids: Felicia, Sarah, Jared, Jacob, and Elizabeth. Also to my newly expected little girl whom we suspect we will call Amelia, and Bennett, our fun little goldendoodle. I'm also thankful to my father who has always inspired me, and even though I might not always be good at showing it, I'm thankful to God for the good life he's given me.

Contents at a Glance

1   Introduction to Oracle GoldenGate 11*g* and Replication 1

2   The Oracle GoldenGate Architecture 17

3   Installing Oracle GoldenGate 37

4   Configuring Oracle GoldenGate 71

5   Implementing Oracle GoldenGate One-Way Replication 109

6   GoldenGate Multitarget and Cascading Replication 153

7   GoldenGate Multimaster Replication 161

8   Advanced Features 175

9   Oracle GoldenGate and Oracle Real Application Clusters 219

10 GoldenGate for MySQL 231

11 Introducing Oracle GoldenGate for SQL Server 253

12 Monitoring, Troubleshooting, and Performance Tuning GoldenGate 313

13 Oracle GoldenGate Monitor and GoldenGate Director 349

14 Zero-Downtime Upgrades and Migrations Using Oracle GoldenGate 363

15 Oracle GoldenGate Veridata 369

16 Oracle GoldenGate Integration Options 377

17 GoldenGate 11.2 New Features 393

     Index 403

Contents

Acknowledgments xvii
Introduction xix

1   Introduction to Oracle GoldenGate 11*g* and Replication 1
What Is Replication and Why Use It? 2
What Kinds of Replication Are There? 2
   Disk-Based Replication 3
   Database Data Replication 4
   Database Object Replication 7
Oracle Replication: The Past 7
   Oracle Snapshots and Materialized Views 8
   Oracle Advanced Replication 8
   Oracle Streams 8
   Oracle Heterogeneous Replication 9
   Oracle GoldenGate 11
   What's Next? 15

2   The Oracle GoldenGate Architecture 17
Documentation and Information Please 19
Overview of Databases That Support Oracle GoldenGate 19
The Oracle GoldenGate Architecture and Processes 21
   The Oracle GoldenGate Manager Process 22
   The Oracle GoldenGate Extract (or Capture) Process 23
   The Oracle GoldenGate Trail Files 30
   The Oracle GoldenGate Data Pump Process 33
   The Oracle GoldenGate Server Collector 33
   The Oracle GoldenGate Apply (Replicat) Process 34
   The Oracle GoldenGate Software Command Interface (GGSCI) 34
   The Oracle GoldenGate Parameter Files 34
Data Replication and Latency 34
Compatibility Between Different Versions of GoldenGate 35

3 Installing Oracle GoldenGate **37**
  Oracle GoldenGate Requirements 39
    Oracle GoldenGate Oracle Database Platforms Supported 39
    Oracle GoldenGate Oracle Database Versions Supported 39
    Oracle GoldenGate Memory Requirements 40
    Oracle GoldenGate Disk Space Requirements 40
    Oracle GoldenGate Network Requirements 42
  The Demonstration Environments We Use in This Book 42
    Download and Set Up Oracle VirtualBox 42
    Creating the Oracle VirtualBox Images Used in This Book 46
  Download and Install Oracle GoldenGate 62
    What Do I Need to Know Before I Download GoldenGate? 62
    How Do I Download GoldenGate? 63
    Installing Oracle GoldenGate 64

4 Configuring Oracle GoldenGate **71**
  Configuring Oracle GoldenGate After the Initial Install 73
    Configuring the Operating System Environment for GoldenGate 74
    Configuring the Oracle Database GoldenGate User 76
    Configuring for DDL Replication 80
    Configuring to Support Oracle Sequences 82
    Configuring the GoldenGate Directories and Using GGSCI 83
  Information to Collect Before You Architect Your Replication Solution 84
    Information You Will Need to Collect Before You Start 84
  Preparing Your Systems for Operation 86
  Configuration of the Oracle Database for GoldenGate Operations 87
    Configure the Database for Flashback Queries 89
    GoldenGate and Primary Keys 90
    Dealing with Deferred Constraints 91
    Verify That the Database Has Supplemental Logging Enabled 92
    Configuring the GLOBALS Parameter File 96
  Configuration and Administration of the Oracle GoldenGate
    Manager Process 96
    Configuration of the Oracle GoldenGate Manager Process 97
    Administration of the Oracle GoldenGate Manager Processes 101

5 Implementing Oracle GoldenGate One-Way Replication **109**
  Preparing for Replication 110
    Introducing the HR Schema 110
    Our Selected Topology 112
    So, What Are We Doing? 113
  Preparing the Target Database for Replication 114
  Configuring the GoldenGate Manager Process 117

Configuring the GoldenGate Extract Process 121
  Creating the Extract Parameter File 121
  Registering the Extract 124
  Adding the Trail File to GoldenGate and Associating
    It with the Extract 125
  Administering the Extract Process 125
Configuring the GoldenGate Data Pump 130
  Creating the GoldenGate Data Pump Extract Parameter File 130
  Registering the GoldenGate Data Pump Extract 131
  Administering the GoldenGate Data Pump Extract Process 132
Instantiating the Target Database Using GoldenGate 136
  Configure and Register the Initial-Load Extract Process 137
  Configure and Register the Initial-Load Replicat Process 138
  Instantiate the Target Database with the Configured
    GoldenGate Processes 140
Configuring the GoldenGate Replicat Process 145
  Creating the Replicat Parameter File 146
  Registering the Replicat Process 148
  Administering the Replicat Process 148

6 GoldenGate Multitarget and Cascading Replication **153**
Configuring Multitarget Replication 154
  Configure the GoldenGate Manager Process on the
    New Target Server 154
  Add the New Target Database to an Existing
    or New Data Pump Extract 155
Configuring Cascading Replication 159

7 GoldenGate Multimaster Replication **161**
Before You Configure Bidirectional Replication 162
  The Application and Bidirectional Replication 163
  The Trusted Source 164
  Keys Are Important (Also Keeping SKs Unique) 164
  Triggers 164
  Cascaded Deletes 164
  Loops 165
  Conflict Detection and Resolution 165
  Other Bidirectional Replication Issues 168
Example of Configuring a Bidirectional Replication 169
  Configure the GoldenGate Extract Processes 169
  Configure the GoldenGate Data Pump Extract Processes 170
  Configure the Replicat Process for Both the ORCL.HR Schemas 171
  Instantiate the GOLDENGATE2.ORCL.HR Schema 172

Create a Conflict Handler 172
Start Replication in Both Directions 174

8 Advanced Features **175**
Advanced Configuration 176
Checkpoint Tables 176
Securing Your Environment 181
Filtering Your Data 191
Filtering Tables 191
Filtering Rows 194
Mapping Column Data 197
Table-Level Column Mapping 197
Global Mapping 202
Executing SQL 204
SQLEXEC as an Option for TABLE or MAP 204
sqlexec as a Standalone Statement 206
Scheduling sqlexec 206
Configuring for RAC 207
Where to Install 207
How to Capture Changes 207
Synchronizing Nodes 208
Threads 209
Connecting 209
Configuring for ASM 210
Modify the Listener 210
Modify the tnsnames.ora File 210
Modify the Extract Parameter File 211
DBLOGREADER 211
Error Handling 212

9 Oracle GoldenGate and Oracle Real Application Clusters **219**
Oracle Maximum Availability Architecture (MAA) 220
Disaster Recovery, High Availability, and Replication 223
Installing GoldenGate in a RAC Environment 225
Configuring the Application Virtual IP Address 225
Creating an Action Script 227
Clusterware Registration 229
Basic Administration of the GoldenGate Application 229

10 GoldenGate for MySQL **231**
Installing GoldenGate for MySQL 232
Preparing for the Installation of GoldenGate
on a MySQL Database Server 232
Installing GoldenGate for MySQL
on a MySQL Database Server 233

Oracle to MySQL GoldenGate Replication 233
    Setting Up the MySQL Database 234
    Creating the GoldenGate Schema on MySQL 235
    Performing the Initial Load from Oracle to MySQL 236
    Creating the Definition File 237
    Initial Loading of the MySQL Schema 238
    Creating the Oracle Extract Process and the MySQL
       Replicat Process 240
Replicating from MySQL to Oracle 244
    Defining the Objects and Generating the Definitions 244
    Initial Population of the Oracle Table from MySQL
       Using GoldenGate 246
    Configuring Replication Between MySQL and Oracle 248

11   **Introducing Oracle GoldenGate for SQL Server** **253**
Installing and Configuring Oracle GoldenGate for SQL Server 255
    Hardware Requirements 255
    Windows Server Requirements 257
    SQL Server Requirements and Supported Features 259
    Target Database SQL Server Instance Configuration 267
Installing Oracle GoldenGate for SQL Server on Windows 270
Configuration 274
    Configuring the Manager Process 274
    Manager Parameters 277
Managing Oracle GoldenGate for SQL Server 279
    Database Management Considerations
       with Oracle GoldenGate for SQL Server 279
    Configuring Basic GoldenGate Replication for SQL Server 283
Advanced GoldenGate for SQL Server 306
    Configuring Oracle GoldenGate in a Windows
       Clustering Environment 308
    Maintaining the Transaction Log Secondary Truncation Point
       When Extract Is Stopped 310
    IDENTITY Property on Columns in Multimaster Configurations 310
    Making DDL Changes to Existing Tables Configured for OGG 311
    The ALTARCHIVELOGDEST Extract Parameter 312

12   **Monitoring, Troubleshooting, and Performance Tuning GoldenGate** **313**
Monitoring Oracle GoldenGate 314
    GUI-Based Tools 314
    GGSCI 315
Troubleshooting 326
    Common Methodology 327
    Commonly Used Diagnostic Tools 327

Common Extract Performance and Error Issues 328
Common Replicat Issues 335
Hung Processes 338
Taking It Further 338
Performance Tuning 341
Tuning the Initial Load 341
GoldenGate Lag 342
Before You Begin 344
Extract Lag 345
Pump Lag 345
Replicat Lag 346
Parallelization 347

13 Oracle GoldenGate Monitor and GoldenGate Director **349**
Oracle GoldenGate Monitor 350
Oracle GoldenGate Monitor Architecture 351
Oracle GoldenGate Instance Prep 353
Using Oracle GoldenGate Monitor Server 354
Oracle GoldenGate Director 355
The GoldenGate Director Architecture 356

14 Zero-Downtime Upgrades and Migrations Using Oracle GoldenGate **363**
Zero Downtime Methodology 364
Failback Option 366

15 Oracle GoldenGate Veridata **369**
Veridata Functionality 370
Configuring and Using Oracle GoldenGate Veridata 372
Oracle GoldenGate Veridata Web 373
Running Comparisons on the Command Line 374

16 Oracle GoldenGate Integration Options **377**
Using GoldenGate to Create a File for a Database Utility to Use 378
Oracle GoldenGate for Flat File 379
Installing Oracle GoldenGate Flat File 379
The Oracle GoldenGate Flat File Infrastructure 380
Types of Flat Files That Can Be Created 380
DSV Files 380
LDV Files 381
The User Exit Properties File 381
The Writer Process 382
Defining the Writers 383
Defining the Writer Mode 383
Defining the Output File Name 384

Defining Rollover Attributes 384
Other Writer Output File Property Settings 385
Configuring File Data Content Properties 386
Including Meta File in Your Datafile Output 387
Including Statistics in Your Datafile Output 388
Including Statistics in Your Datafile Output 389
Other API Interfaces into GoldenGate 391

17 GoldenGate 11.2 New Features **393**
New and Expanded Support for Database Platforms 394
Globalization 394
Security 395
Intelligent Conflict Resolution 395
Network Performance Improvements 399
Integrated Capture 399
GoldenGate and Compressed Data 399
GoldenGate and Extract Memory 400
Downstream Capture 400
Finally: A RAC-Related Change 401

Index **403**

Acknowledgments

Writing a book is always an interesting endeavor. You learn new things, you experience new things in your life while you are writing it, and you try things that sometimes work and sometimes don't work. Of all the books I've written to date (I've lost count but it's something beyond 15 at this point), I've never had my life be more unsettled, had a book project be more complex and painful, and had such a hard time writing the acknowledgments and the introduction.

It was my intent when I started this project so long ago that this would be THE guide to Oracle GoldenGate. I wanted it to be more than just an introduction; I wanted it to be a book that you referenced all the time, with pages marked and dog-eared and worn from use. I want all my books to be that way. Even though this book has been a challenge, I believe you will find that the contents within do, in the end, meet my initial objective: This is THE guide to Oracle GoldenGate.

As such, there are many people to acknowledge, or this book would never have been written and would not be the book it is. A book this comprehensive and aggressive requires a lot of help. I've had help from so many people. So, special thanks go to the following. First, thanks most of all to the additional contributors to this work. This is a long list that includes (alphabetically): Mack Bell, Scott Black, Dennis Heisler, Venkatesh Kalipi, Paul Longhurst, Gene Patton, Amardeep Sidhu, and Eric Yen. All of these folks provided content for some portion of this book in varying amounts. If you read something you like, then they probably had some part in it. If you read something you don't like, I am probably the one who wrote that part.

Beyond contributors, there are those people in your life who just make life easier and make the writing of a book easier. The biggest credit of all goes to my wife Carrie. We got married during the course of the writing of this book and she deserves a lot of credit and probably thinks she is a book widow already (especially since I'm starting my next book on the heels of this one). Bennett, my new friend (a little white-haired goldendoodle) also deserves thanks. He's a friendly two-year-old jumping furry ball of fun.

Also, thanks to my kids, to whom I dedicated this book in part. They have always been my inspiration and support. As I look back at my life, they are the best of what my life has been.

To my technical editors, Gene Patton in the beginning and then Jinyu Wang who did the technical editing for a majority of this book, I am thankful. You caught mistakes, typos, and errors, and you made this book much better. Being a technical editor is a largely thankless job. It does not pay well, and your eyes start to bug out after reading tons of material and testing examples. Gene and Jinyu deserve a lot of thanks.

To the tons of folks at Oracle Press, I owe lots of thanks, from Paul Carlstroem, to Wendy Rinaldi, Amanda Russell, and Ryan Willard.

In writing these acknowledgments, I hope I didn't leave anyone out. I don't believe I have, but I apologize if I've missed anyone and I hope you will forgive me.

Introduction

When I think about databases, sharing data, and really analyzing enterprise data, I sometimes think of the *Rime of the Ancient Mariner* by Samuel Taylor Coleridge. I had to learn parts of this poem in junior high (which was no small feat for my little brain). As I thought about what to write in this introduction, the first part of the *Rime* came to me. I include it here, for it seems to apply to the dilemma of data, data sharing, and the question of distributed data. The first part of the *Rime* goes like this:

"Day after day, day after day,
We stuck, nor breath nor motion;
As idle as a painted ship
Upon a painted ocean.

Water, water, every where,
And all the boards did shrink;
Water, water, every where,
Nor any drop to drink."

The water to me can also represent our oceans of data, and it's everywhere. Enterprises are adrift in data, stuck in it as the hours progress. Data in different places, different platforms... data that can't truly be drunk because so often it sits inaccessible in the middle of an ocean (or if you prefer, alone on its own island) and because of its sheer volume. Day after day the data collects, and yet, we could do more with it if we were just free of the constraints that confine that data.

These constraints include physical constraints such as different database vendors with their various impedances, silos (or islands if you prefer) of data, the sheer volume of data, and distances between various data centers. Logical constraints exist, too. These include differences in how data is logically stored (such as in tables), what the data actually means (for example, in one system the volume of some item might be defined using liters, and the definition of the volume in another system might be in gallons).

There are other problems to solve, real-time data processing and data warehousing, high availability, and disaster recovery. Data swirls around all of these problems. Indeed, as with the mariner, these problems become the albatross hung around our neck, weighing us down. Often this albatross is of our own doing, a result of not thinking and planning ahead. How do we remove this albatross from our necks? How do we stop the grinding death that confronts us as data continues to grow, and how do we figure out how to make the best use of our data? Maybe we can avoid the fate of the mariner—maybe we can find a solution to solve that problem we have created for ourselves and avoid wandering the earth telling our story.

It is our hope that this book will help you in your effort to remove the albatross from around your neck. This book is about a product called Oracle GoldenGate. Oracle GoldenGate can be a very comprehensive solution to the data problems that today's enterprises face. Oracle GoldenGate offers us the ability to collect our islands of data from the still waters and pool them into places where that data can be of even greater use and effect.

With Oracle GoldenGate, you can move data between Oracle and other databases such as DB2 or Microsoft SQL Server. You can create combined data sources (that is, operational data stores), which allow you to store, aggregate, and analyze data in different ways. By bringing all this diverse data together and discovering relationships that were previously obscured, you can develop powerful solutions.

As you will see in this book, Oracle GoldenGate is about more than just moving data between disparate data sources. Oracle GoldenGate provides high availability solutions to protect your data. These solutions also make upgrades and migrations of your database software much easier. With Oracle GoldenGate's features, you can perform near zero-downtime migrations and upgrades (any downtime is dependent on the time it takes to switch your application over to another database).

In this book, you will find a wealth of information on Oracle GoldenGate, and we hope you will find it helps you to make better use of your data, and improve your uptime. You will find a good foundational introduction to Oracle GoldenGate in the first chapter. As we progress, we will lead you through using Oracle GoldenGate step by step, from installing and configuring the product, to configuring various forms of Oracle GoldenGate replication.

Toward the middle of the book, after you have learned how to really use Oracle GoldenGate in an Oracle environment, we will cover setting up and using Oracle GoldenGate in a variety of non-Oracle environments including Oracle MySQL and Microsoft SQL Server. These chapters demonstrate one of the more powerful features of Oracle GoldenGate, its heterogeneous nature.

In the later chapters we will cover topics such as performance tuning, troubleshooting, and monitoring of Oracle GoldenGate. We will also cover various GoldenGate utilities such as the GoldenGate Monitor, Veridata. Finally, we will discuss using Oracle GoldenGate for zero-downtime operations, other GoldenGate integration options (like reading flat files and writing out SQL*Loader compatible files), and then, last but not least, we provide a chapter that highlights the newest features released in Oracle GoldenGate Version 11.2.

Intended Audience

This book is suitable for the following readers:

- DBAs who need to replicate data across Oracle databases.

- DBAs who need to replicate data across heterogeneous database environments.

- DBAs and architects who need to replicate large volumes of data, between various databases, in a widely distributed environment.

- DBAs and architects who need to replicate data over large distances in a very efficient manner.

- Database architects who need to share data across real-time OLTP databases.

- Data warehouse architects who need to design low-latency replicated operational data repositories and stores.

This book is not for the Oracle Database beginner, though it is for the Oracle GoldenGate beginner. To get the most out of this book, you will need a basic understanding of how the Oracle Database software works. You will need to understand how to create basic SQL statements and how to navigate Oracle schemas and create schema objects. With these basic administration skills, you should be able to navigate this book easily.

I hope you enjoy this book and that it helps you in your efforts to improve your enterprise database architecture.

CHAPTER
1

Introduction to Oracle GoldenGate 11g and Replication

Welcome to our Oracle GoldenGate 11g book! We hope that this book will help you with all aspects of Oracle GoldenGate from installing the product to configuring and actually using it. Oracle GoldenGate is a replication tool from Oracle. It is the preferred way to replicate data between Oracle databases as well as non-Oracle databases, such as MySQL, Microsoft SQL Server, DB2, and other databases that you might find in a heterogeneous enterprise environment. Oracle GoldenGate is a very powerful product, and yet it is easy to use (though its complexity does tend to increase as the complexity of the replication needs increases).

In this chapter, we will discuss what replication is in general, and we will discuss the different kinds of replication that one might see in the enterprise.

What Is Replication and Why Use It?

If you picked up this book, then you probably have some idea of what Oracle GoldenGate is, or you might have heard about it and been curious what it is for. Oracle GoldenGate is a database data replication product. What is database data replication? We might define replication in this way:

Replication involves the sharing of information between databases. Replication tools are designed such that the results are consistent between the replication source and the various targets of the replication operation. Replication can involve different component layers including hardware and software. The purpose of replication is multifold, including improved system reliability, fault tolerance, minimum or no downtime system upgrades, performance, and accessibility. *Heterogeneous replication* involves replication between a replication source(s) and target(s) where the source and targets are significantly different, such as replication between different operating systems, different database vendors, and so on.

What Kinds of Replication Are There?

Oracle GoldenGate is interested in data (or database) replication, as opposed to other kinds of replication such as disk storage (or disk-based) replication, file-based replication, or batch storage replication. It's outside the scope of this book to dive into the depths of these other forms of replication. Sometimes people will mistake one type of replication (and its benefits) for another. Most frequently, database replication and disk storage replication are misunderstood, and it might be worthwhile to take a moment to distinguish between the two and look at what each of these types of replication is typically architected for.

Disk-Based Replication

Disk storage replication, also known as *disk-based replication*, is a macro (or high-level) architecture-based method of replicating an entire database and is not well suited to the micro-based solution requirements often related to database data replication. Disk-based replication solutions are better suited for backup and recovery of databases, making copies of an entire database (or perhaps several tablespaces) in an effort to create a new database, using various snapshot technologies to provide for database quick restores to a given point in time, and in some cases, disaster recovery solutions. Disk-based replication can also be used to perform the initial instantiation of environments that will be used during database replication, depending on how many of the source database objects you intend on replicating.

Disk-based replication is like carpet bombing. It's very fast, but unlike data replication, it is not very targeted. Disk-based replication typically comes in two flavors, but the end result is the same. In the first flavor, known as *disk cloning*, the used disk blocks from the logical device and its associated physical devices on the source are copied over to a defined logical target device and associated physical devices on the target system. This method then requires an equivalent amount of disk space for both the source and the target systems. Once the blocks are copied, then the two physical disk locations are essentially mirrored at that point. After that point, the information on the physical disks usually will diverge as separate systems will access the data on the different disk devices.

The disk cloning method becomes pretty expensive if you are making multiple copies of the same database. Each copy requires the same amount of space. So if your source database size is 2TB, and you make three copies of that database, then each of those copies will consume 2TB, for a total of 8TB used.

A solution to this high cost of disk block copying when you need to make multiple copies is the use of snapshot technologies (which is our second flavor). To use a snapshot technology, we first clone the disk blocks associated with the source system just as we did when doing disk cloning. This clone is actually a static, read-only copy of the data and is never touched by any application or presented in a file system.

Now that the static clone is created, we are ready to create an environment where we can use it. This is done through the creation of a *snapshot clone* (the actual names and implementation details will vary wildly by vendor). When a snapshot clone is created, a file system is mounted with what appears to be the cloned copy of the disk data (for example, all our database data files, control files, and online redo logs for a given database). This is a view of the cloned static copy of the disk blocks that we created earlier. Keep in mind that the blocks in this copy are static and will never be changed no matter what we do in this file system.

Of course, once we open the database, it's going to want to start changing data on this file system almost immediately, and if it can't, then the database will fail.

Snapshot clones facilitate the change of disk blocks by maintaining *snapshot copies* of changed blocks. When a disk block is changed (for example, a write to a block in a database data file occurs), the blocks that are dirtied are copied from the snapshot clone to another area of storage (this is called *copy on write*) when they are first written to. The change is then made to the block that was just copied. For the rest of the life of that snapshot, that copied block will be used instead of the block in the original snapshot copy that was made earlier. The upshot of this, then, is that as more and more blocks are touched and copied to support the divergence of the block from the static copy, the amount of disk space required as time goes on will increase.

Database Data Replication

Database data replication is more like using a cruise missile than carpet bombing. Unlike the carpet bombing–based solution of disk-based replication, database data replication provides a targeted approach to replication of enterprise data. Database data replication provides the ability to select specific items to be replicated and to control, on a much more granular basis, where that data will be replicated to, and how it will be replicated.

Features of Database Data Replication

Typically database data replication has several features and issues, which include:

- Data replication always involves latency. It is important to remember that there is always latency involved with database replication. The latency can be minimized through a number of features of the data replication product, but it will always be there. The farther away the data is from the "source" system that is the single source of truth for that data, the greater the latency will be for that data.

- The ability to replicate data at various levels:

    - Replicate table data at a row level

    - Replicate specific columns within a row

    - Replicate an individual table or tables in a schema

    - Replicate one or more complete schemas

- The ability to easily move (or *instantiate*) a complete data set from one database to another separate database.

- The ability to determine changes in the underlying data set and replicate those changes as directed to other data stores.

■ The ability to filter the data that is being replicated. Filtering gives you complete granular control over what data is being replicated to a given location. For example, you may have an employee table, and you want to replicate that table to all of your locations, but you only want the employees associated with that location replicated. Filtering would accomplish this.

■ The ability to update data changes in bulk (scheduled or on demand), or in real time.

■ The ability to recover from failures during the replication process should they occur.

■ The ability to detect and recover from "collisions" during data replication operations.

■ The ability to "cleanse" or "scrub" the data as it's moved. *Data cleansing* is a method of taking data and normalizing it such that the data meets specific data quality requirements for the system the data is being moved into. For example, data cleansing might involve standardizing address formats. The main goal with respect to data cleansing is to make the data standardized, accurate, complete, valid, and consistent.

■ The ability to "transform" data. This is the process of converting data from a format in the source system into the equivalent format in the destination system. This is typical, for example, in data warehouse systems where a number of disparate data sources are combined within the warehouse. It may be that the identifying information in these disparate systems has different values or meaning to specific data.

Data transformation occurs through the identification of the system that is the "single source of truth," and identifying the standard data mappings from that system to other systems that contain related (or even sometimes competing) data values. When transforming data from these disparate data sources, we take the mappings, transform the data being moved from the disparate systems into a common set of mappings, and write the newly "transformed" data out to the database. Thus, the warehouse has standardized our disparate data into a single view that represents one single statement of truth with respect to that data at the time it was loaded into the warehouse.

■ Replicating Data Definition Language (DDL) changes to objects.

Oracle GoldenGate is capable of all of these types of activities.

As you can see, database replication is a very powerful tool in the arsenal of the database architect/developer and DBA. It is that power, though, that sometimes causes replication to become very difficult to administer. Replication also increases security risks and leads to the proliferation of data in the enterprise, which can have its own serious problems.

Common Ways of Replicating Data

There are many different ways of replicating data, and Oracle GoldenGate supports all of these. Typically when we talk about replication, we talk about the following forms of replication:

- *One-to-one* (in only one direction), also known as *unidirectional* (see Figure 1-1). This is the movement of data from one source database (or schema) to a different target database (or schema). This is the most basic and simple form of data replication.

- *One-to-one* in both directions, also known as *bidirectional* (see Figure 1-1). This is the movement of data between two (and only two) different databases (or schemas). This kind of replication methodology requires the implementation of conflict resolution.

- *Many-to-many*, also known as *peer-to-peer* or *master-to-master* (see Figure 1-1). This is the replication of data in both directions between three or more nodes. This kind of replication offers many opportunities for data collisions, and this risk needs to be addressed when architecting such a system.

- *One-to-many*, also known as *broadcast* (see Figure 1-1). This is the movement of data from one database to more than one database at the same time (that is, in parallel).

- *Many-to-one*, also known as *consolidation* (see Figure 1-1). This is the replication of data from many disparate systems into a single system. Depending on how the replication is defined, there may or may not be concerns with data collisions that will need to be dealt with. Data collisions will be discussed later in this section.

- *Cascading* (see Figure 1-1). This is replication to one or more servers using any of the replication methods already listed. The downstream server then replicates that information to additional servers.

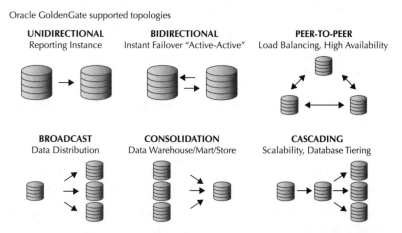

FIGURE 1-1.   *Various forms of database replication*

In addition to these basic replication methods, replication can be cascaded (see Figure 1-1) across several different databases. For example, we can have a many-to-many replication configuration between Server A and Server B, and we can also have Server B replicate its changes and the change it receives from Server A to Server C. In this way, the changes from Server A are cascaded to Server C by way of Server B.

Database Object Replication

Often we want to do more than just replicate data; we want to replicate associated schema objects such as tables and indexes, and we want to replicate any changes made to those objects. Just as with replicated data, a given schema's objects need to be instantiated in the target databases before they can be replicated. Once instantiated, the objects in the target schema will be maintained and updated as a result of any **alter, create**, or **drop** statement. Oracle GoldenGate supports database object replication.

Oracle Replication: The Past

Replication had its start long ago in Oracle. It might be helpful to take a moment and highlight the history of replication in Oracle Database. First we will start with snapshots, materialized views, and advanced replication. Then we will cover Oracle Streams and Oracle heterogeneous replication. Finally, we will introduce you to the future of Oracle replication: Oracle GoldenGate.

Oracle Snapshots and Materialized Views

Oracle Database Version 7.1 introduced snapshot replication of database data. With snapshot replication you can replicate data between a source database and a target database via database links. Initial snapshots are instantiated (or created) with the **create snapshot** command. Snapshots can be updated in two different ways.

- In bulk (reloading the whole snapshot) either using the Oracle Scheduler or on demand

- When changes occur to the source tables using a method called *fast refresh*:

    - Fast refresh can be done in bulk using the Scheduler or on demand. This method of fast refresh involves a few restrictions that must be met.

    - Fast refresh can be done at the end of every transaction (on commit) with a number of restrictions.

In Oracle Database Version 8 and later, snapshots were renamed to *materialized views*. Materialized views maintained the same functionality of snapshots and added the ability to do summarizations of data on a limited scale and with quite a few restrictions. Replication via materialized views continues to exist through the most current versions of the Oracle Database. Replication via materialized views was limited in many ways, and better and more complete solutions were needed for more complex forms of data replication.

Oracle Advanced Replication

To provide for more complex replication options, Oracle offered Oracle Advanced Replication starting with Oracle Database Version 7. Advanced Replication provided for the replication of more than just data including DDL, triggers, packages, views, and other database objects. Oracle Advanced Replication also provided for bidirectional replication, multimaster replication, conflict resolution, and cascading replication models.

Oracle Advanced Replication was really a precursor to new functionality that would arise in Oracle Database 9*i* Release 2, Oracle Streams.

Oracle Streams

Oracle 9*i* Database Release 2 introduced a new product called Oracle Streams. Oracle Streams provided a number of different features including:

- Data replication

- Message queuing

- Data cleansing

- Data transformation

- Event notifications

Oracle Streams in many ways works like Oracle GoldenGate. Oracle Streams uses a capture, propagate, and apply methodology, in much the same way Oracle GoldenGate does.

During *Streams capture*, the replication information is captured from the Redo stream at the *source database* by a Capture process. The Capture process can exist on the source database where the changes were created, or they can be captured on a different *capture database* downstream (on the same database server, or a different database server).

The Capture process takes the logical change records (LCRs) and *stages* (or queues) them in the Oracle capture database for *propagation* (or dequeuing if you prefer). The propagation process will then dequeue the stored LCRs in the appropriate order and propagate these LCRs to another system for *consumption* (or application).

At almost any point during this replication process, the LCRs can be modified as required by the process. This allows you to do any data cleansing or transformation on the data before it is actually applied on the target system.

Oracle Streams provides support for all the different forms of data replication including one-way, one-to-many, and multimaster replication methods. Cascading replication is also supported by Oracle Streams. Oracle Streams could also move data to non-Oracle databases using Oracle Heterogeneous Replication, which we will discuss next. Figure 1-2 provides a graphic of the different operational stages of Oracle Streams replication.

Oracle Streams functionality provides many benefits in addition to simple data replication. These benefits include high availability, making zero or near-zero downtime for migrations and upgrades possible. In addition, Streams provides the ability to create live reporting databases, and real-time business intelligence (BI) databases. The messaging and other features of Streams also provide for event-driven architectures in near-real-time.

Oracle Heterogeneous Replication

Before we discuss Oracle GoldenGate, let's also take a minute to talk about Oracle's heterogeneous replication features. Heterogeneous replication is the replication between differing database types, such as Oracle and DB2. Oracle provides Oracle Heterogeneous Replication Services associated with Oracle Streams to support movement of data between varying database sources. Oracle Streams seemed to be the future of Oracle replication until 2009 when Oracle bought a little company called GoldenGate.

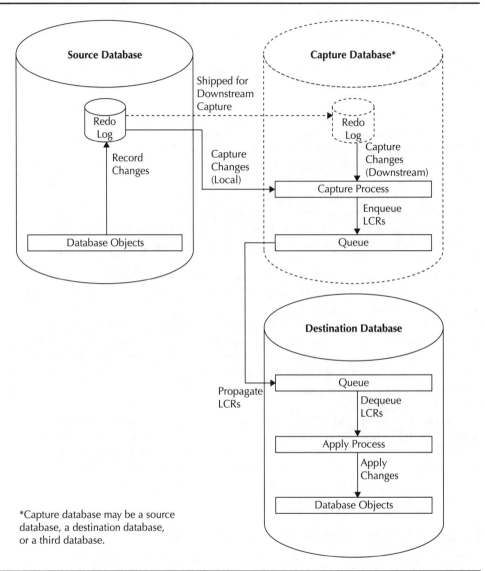

FIGURE 1-2. *Oracle Streams replication*

Figure 1-3 provides a graphic that depicts the various stages of Oracle Streams replication including the Capture, Propagate, and Apply process. It also depicts heterogeneous replication to a non-Oracle database.

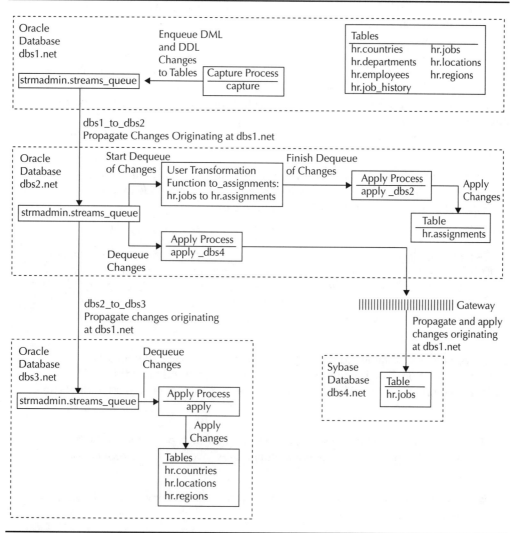

FIGURE 1-3. *Oracle Streams replication*

Oracle GoldenGate

As you have learned, Oracle GoldenGate is a database replication product, owned by Oracle. In September of 2009 Oracle bought a company called GoldenGate. GoldenGate was founded in 1995 in San Francisco. GoldenGate found its niche in the financial industry and quickly gained a name for itself in the form of stability, which is understandably important within that industry. GoldenGate's features include features that guarantee no data loss and replicated data integrity, while also being a fast way of replicating data.

When Oracle first purchased GoldenGate, there was some confusion as to where GoldenGate would fit juxtaposed with Oracle Streams. In November 2009 Oracle released a document titled "Oracle GoldenGate Statement of Direction," which clarified the position of GoldenGate with respect to Oracle Streams and the future of Oracle GoldenGate.

The main statements in the document that really define the future of Oracle GoldenGate are these:

> *Oracle GoldenGate is the strategic replication solution for Oracle Database and for heterogeneous databases, with proven success in a wide range of demanding industries and mission-critical use cases.*

and

> *Given the strategic nature of Oracle GoldenGate, Oracle Streams will continue to be supported, but will not be actively enhanced. Rather, the best elements of Oracle Streams will be evaluated for inclusion with Oracle GoldenGate.*
>
> *Current customers depending on Oracle Streams will continue to be fully supported, and Oracle Streams customers should continue using the feature wherever it is deployed today.*

As you can see, Oracle GoldenGate is going to be Oracle's strategic data replication solution. That being the case, what are some of the main things that GoldenGate brings to the replication picture? Some of the benefits that GoldenGate brings to the IT table include:

- A flexible replication architecture designed for high performance with minimal impact on the underlying databases involved in the replication process

- Real-time data transfers, reducing the overall latency experienced in your replication environment

- Support for replication between many heterogeneous database environments

- The ability to create both highly available and highly reliable replication architectures

- The ability to *support* almost real-time decision making, BI, and reporting systems

■ The ability to easily integrate your enterprise business data into a single platform for a variety of uses

Where Oracle GoldenGate Sits in the Oracle Stack

Oracle GoldenGate is part of an overall data integration solution that Oracle provides, which includes:

■ Oracle Active Data Guard

■ Oracle GoldenGate

■ Oracle Data Integrator

Each of these solutions provides different benefits that need to be considered when architecting the databases for your enterprise. When considering the different tools that are available, you will want to consider the following factors:

■ Complexity

■ Latency

■ High availability

■ Disaster recovery

■ Requirements to transform or summarize data

■ Heterogeneous processing requirements

So, when should you use GoldenGate rather than Oracle Active Data Guard? This seems to be one of the biggest questions. We would recommend looking at Oracle Active Data Guard if you have these requirements:

■ If the remote database is truly dedicated to disaster recovery duties and the database is not needed for other purposes

■ If you have a need for "reader farm" databases that are simply to be used for read-only activities

■ If you need minimal latency with respect to the time a transaction occurs on the source system and the time it's applied to the target system

■ If there is no need to transform or cleanse data in any way

Further, we would recommend Oracle GoldenGate as a solution in the following cases:

■ You wish to create an active/active data replication (DR) configuration that contains two different database types (for example, Oracle and MySQL).

NOTE
While it might seem like a good idea to have two different databases in your production environment (perhaps to prevent some database code bug from causing data loss or system outage), there are significant complexities in such architectures. For example, if you use Oracle and Sybase, you would not be able to use PL/SQL in the database, since Sybase would not support PL/SQL program units. Sometimes ideas that seem great initially are not so great once you start looking at the details.

■ There is a need for individual DR sites, but you also wish to be able to use the remote databases for active work or even testing at the same time.

■ You wish to have multiple copies of your production database, and

    ■ *The copies are* geographically spread apart.

    ■ Each database *contains* the same data.

    ■ Changes in each database are replicated to the other databases.

    ■ In the event of an isolation event (that is, network failure), the individual databases can operate independently of the rest of the database.

■ The remote databases are to be used for read and write purposes.

■ Light to moderate forms of data transformation or cleansing are required.

Oracle GoldenGate Best Practices
In this book we will offer a series of best practices associated with GoldenGate that we feel are important and should be a part of almost any Oracle GoldenGate solution. The best practices we will offer will help ensure a stable GoldenGate architecture, reduce latency, and improve performance in Oracle GoldenGate. We strongly recommend that you follow the best practices outlined in this book to ensure that you have a GoldenGate replication architecture that is as stable and performant as possible.

What's Next?

We have now introduced you to replication generally and within the context of Oracle Database. We have also introduced you to Oracle GoldenGate, the product that this book is about. So, what's next, you may be asking? Next we will discuss the Oracle GoldenGate architecture, and then we will talk about how to install and configure Oracle GoldenGate. The following chapters will then discuss how to actually replicate data with Oracle GoldenGate in many different ways.

Then we will do something really cool, as we will talk about configuring Oracle GoldenGate in other non-Oracle database environments. We will cover MS SQL, MySQL, DB2, and Teradata databases. We will continue by covering other topics such as performance tuning, the Management Pack for Golden Gate, using GoldenGate for zero-downtime operations, and also using the Oracle GoldenGate–related product called *Veridata*. Finally, in the last chapter we provide several Oracle GoldenGate–related workshops that will help you practice your newly acquired Oracle GoldenGate skills.

CHAPTER
2

The Oracle GoldenGate
Architecture

I n this chapter we will build on the basic foundation of replication that we laid in Chapter 1 and really start diving into the topic of this book, Oracle GoldenGate. Before you can truly use Oracle GoldenGate, you need to understand the architecture of the product. So, the Oracle GoldenGate architecture is what we will be tackling in this chapter.

We find that many problems experienced by customers could have been avoided if they simply had understood the Oracle GoldenGate architecture and the associated best practices and applied those best practices correctly. It's important to start at the beginning with Oracle GoldenGate. You might be tempted to skip this chapter and move on to the following chapters that cover installing GoldenGate, configuring it, and so on. However, if you do, you will be missing some important foundational information.

In this chapter we will discuss the databases that Oracle GoldenGate supports and then we will look at the Oracle GoldenGate architecture and processes. In the final section of this chapter we will discuss planning your Oracle GoldenGate implementation and share with you the "do's and don'ts" that you will want to know when it comes to making architectural decisions involving GoldenGate. In that section we will discuss best practices and decision points to be considered as you architect your Oracle GoldenGate solution.

The overall goal of this chapter is to provide you with the knowledge you need to architect an Oracle GoldenGate solution properly, in part by understanding how GoldenGate works. This way, you can do it right the first time and ensure that your Oracle GoldenGate replication architecture is performant and robust. Later chapters will then guide you through the process of actually implementing the various pieces of Oracle GoldenGate to implement the robust architecture you have designed.

Choose Wisely...

The fact is that there are many ways you can configure replication with GoldenGate. This is because GoldenGate is a robust product that allows you to configure it in various ways. As with many things in life, there is a right way and a wrong way to do things. In this book we will make recommendations, and these recommendations are made for really good reasons (which we will endeavor to explain). At the end of the day, it's up to you to choose the right architecture.

Choose wisely, for while selecting the correct GoldenGate architecture will bring you correct data and excellent performance, the wrong architecture will take them from you.

Documentation and Information Please

I often find that people newer to IT, or to a specific product, are not quite sure how to get the documentation and information on the product that they need. They may often know where the documentation lies, but they might need more information than that. In this section, I hope to provide you with some ideas on where to go to get GoldenGate help when you need it.

Oracle provides plenty of documentation on Oracle GoldenGate. I have found the easiest and most reliable way to locate Oracle GoldenGate documentation is via Google or your favorite web search engine. I usually just type in the search words **Oracle GoldenGate documentation** and voilà! I'm pointed to the location of the documentation that I seek. Of course, make sure that you are being redirected to the most current copy of the documentation and not a version that is out of date. The version that the documentation is associated with should appear on the home page of the documentation.

Besides the documentation, there are other great sources of information on GoldenGate. If you have a licensed copy of GoldenGate, you probably have a support contract with Oracle. In this case you have access to Oracle Metalink. You should reference Metalink for quick tips, how-to's, and bug reports on Oracle GoldenGate. Also, if you run into a problem with Oracle GoldenGate, Oracle Metalink is the place to report those bugs. Please, please report any bugs you find! Don't just find a workaround or a quick fix. If you find a bug, it's just a matter of time before someone else finds that same bug. Be a good GoldenGate citizen; open a service request (SR) and report the bug to Oracle.

Want more GoldenGate help, support, ideas, and a place to give your feedback? Oracle's Technology Network GoldenGate forum is the place to go. There you can find lots of other GoldenGate users, and perhaps a developer or two, ready to answer your Oracle GoldenGate questions. You can also find the answers to questions others have posed that might well answer your own questions.

Finally, you can use Google, or whatever web search engine you like, to search for and find all kinds of information on GoldenGate topics. The Web really tends to be my first line of support for information with respect to Oracle and GoldenGate. Often I find answers to questions there much faster than anywhere else.

Overview of Databases That Support Oracle GoldenGate

One of the great benefits of Oracle GoldenGate is that it supports replication to and from a number of different databases. Oracle GoldenGate Version 11g supports a number of different databases, as seen in Table 2-1.

Database	Log-Based Extraction (Capture)	Non-Log-Based Extraction (Capture)	Replication (Delivery)
c-tree	X		X
DB2 for i			X
DB2 for Linux, UNIX, Windows	X		X
DBE for z/OS	X		X
Oracle	X		X
Microsoft SQL Server	X		X
MySQL	X		X
SQL/MX	X		X
Sybase	X		X
Teradata		X	X
TimesTen			X
Generic ODBC			X

TABLE 2-1.   *Oracle GoldenGate–Supported Platforms and Supported Processing Methods*

Looking at Table 2-1, we see that Oracle GoldenGate supports capturing the transactions on almost all platforms from the native transaction logs (that is, Oracle redo logs) of those platforms. Looking further at Table 2-1, we can also see the databases that accept GoldenGate transaction record application. In general, cross-platform heterogeneous platform replication is supported by GoldenGate with few exceptions. For example, looking at Table 2-1, we could replicate transactions from Microsoft SQL Server to Oracle or from MySQL to Microsoft SQL Server. This ability to replicate across many different heterogeneous platforms is what makes Oracle GoldenGate very powerful and useful even in non-Oracle environments.

There are some restrictions to this heterogeneous architecture: for example, c-tree replication is only supported to another c-tree environment, and other platforms are only supported as target databases and cannot be source databases.

The Oracle GoldenGate Architecture and Processes

To help you as we progress to discuss the different components of the Oracle GoldenGate architecture, we provide you with the diagram shown in Figure 2-1. This diagram lists the different processes we will be discussing throughout this chapter. Note that some processes (such as the Data Pump process) can exist on one or more servers depending on how you configure GoldenGate. Figure 2-1 is not an architectural recommendation (we will get to those later in this book) but simply a diagram designed to help you see how all the pieces of Oracle GoldenGate fit together.

In reviewing this diagram, you'll see that there are three different architectural data flows demonstrated. Each of the processes or components displayed in this figure is defined in this chapter, and in later chapters you will see how to configure them. The diagram lists the principal components of the Oracle GoldenGate architecture, and the order in which they execute in the data flow process. The components and processes are as follows:

■ **The Extract process**   You can see in the diagram that the Extract process reads data from the source database. Data is read either directly from the source database itself in bulk for initial data loads or from the transaction logs when doing change synchronization. Change synchronization can be done in online mode (that is, real time) or in batch mode, depending on your architectural needs. You can also extract data from a database and replicate to a file outside of the database. We will cover each of these methods in detail in later chapters of this book.

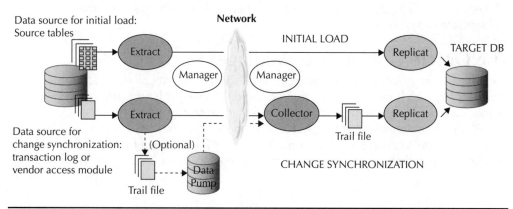

FIGURE 2-1.   *Oracle GoldenGate process data flow*

■ **The Collector process** This process accepts the change information pushed to it by the Extract process and writes that information to the remote trail file. The Collector process is only used if the Data Pump process is used and if a remote trail file is to be created.

■ **The trail files** These are physical files that store database change information collected by the Extract process. There are two different kinds of trail files:

  ■ **Remote trail files** Trail files on the target database server.

  ■ **Local trail files** Local trail files are optional trail files that exist on the source operating system. Local trail files are optional but are strongly recommended.

  Trail files are optional, and if they are not used, then the trail data is simply shipped to the target systems for processing by the remote Replicat processes. When used, trail files on the source operating system are written to by the local Extract process, and are often subsequently read by the optional local Data Pump process, which will transport the trail file data to target systems.

  The trail file data on the target system is read by the Collector process, which loads the data into remote trail files on the target operating system.

■ **The Replicat process** The Replicat process will either apply bulk data loads for instantiation of the target database, will read the incoming trail stream sent by a remote Extract process, or will read change records from the remote trail files created by the Collector process and apply those changes to the already instantiated target database.

Let's look at these processes and other architectural components of Oracle GoldenGate in more detail.

The Oracle GoldenGate Manager Process

The GoldenGate Manager process is the process that controls all other GoldenGate processes. As such it must be configured first, and then started before any other GoldenGate processes can be started. You will want to configure the Manager process to start automatically upon system startup in most cases (we provide examples of how to do this in Chapter 5). The GoldenGate Manager process can then be configured to start up the remaining GoldenGate processes as you see fit.

The Oracle GoldenGate Extract (or Capture) Process

The Oracle GoldenGate Extract process (also known as the Capture process; we will use the terms interchangeably in this book) always runs on the source database system and is responsible for two different jobs. Each GoldenGate Extract process is defined and created by the GoldenGate administrator. Each GoldenGate Extract process is named when it is created with a name of up to eight characters, and that name is referenced in many different GoldenGate operations. Because of the name size limitation and the fact that this name is referenced in many places, it's a good practice to develop a naming standard for your Extract process names.

What Is the Purpose of the Oracle GoldenGate Extract Process?

The Oracle GoldenGate Extract process (also known as the Capture process) always runs on the source database system and is really the first part of the GoldenGate architectural process flow.

The Oracle GoldenGate Extract process has two principal jobs:

- Perform the initial data load (or instantiation) from the source system objects to the target system or systems. There are other ways to instantiate your target systems such as using RMAN or Oracle Data Pump (not to be confused with Oracle GoldenGate Data Pump). We will discuss these methods in more detail in Chapter 6 (and other chapters) of this book.

- Capture the changes that occur to the database objects being replicated and forward them to a trail file or over the network for further processing. The Oracle GoldenGate Extract process is very flexible and can be configured in many different ways. The Extract process can capture or ignore specific DML and DDL operations (DDL operations are only supported on an Oracle database) on defined database tables, schemas, and other database objects. For example, for a given table being replicated to a given target database, you might want to ignore any delete operations (because you never want records removed from the target database). GoldenGate makes it easy to customize such operations.

The GoldenGate Extract process can be configured to be run in two different modes:

- **Bulk run mode**   In this mode the GoldenGate process execution is a one-time execution run. The Extract process will start, do the work the administrator has configured it to do in one single operation, dump the results into an extract file (which we will discuss later in this chapter), and then end normally. Bulk run mode is typically used for one-time operations such as instantiation of the target database from the source database. Bulk mode can also be used to process target database changes in bulk, which can be quicker than processing a large number of individual changes.

- **Online mode** In online mode, the Extract process runs continually, reading the transaction logs of the source database and processing those records to be ingested by downstream GoldenGate processes. In this mode the Extract process writes records into memory and will move committed transactions either into local trail files or across the network to be written in remote trail files.

Each GoldenGate Extract process is defined and created by the GoldenGate administrator. When the GoldenGate Extract process is created, it is named with a unique eight-character identifier. Each GoldenGate Extract process is associated with one or more parameter files, which the administrator creates. These parameter files control various attributes of that Extract process, such as what objects the Extract process will capture changes on. We will discuss the GoldenGate parameter files in more detail later in this chapter and in many chapters throughout this book.

The Extract process must be started from the GoldenGate Software Command Interface (GGSCI). Scripts can be written to interface with GGSCI to automatically start when the operating system starts. We will discuss GGSCI later in this chapter, and we will discuss the specifics of creating, administering, and removing Extract processes in later chapters throughout this book.

How Does the Oracle GoldenGate Extract Process Work in Online Mode?

An Extract process in online mode is going to capture transactional data on the source database for processing on the target database. To capture this transactional data, the Extract process uses the transaction logs of the source database (for example, the Oracle online redo logs). For the purposes of this discussion about the Extract process and how it works, we will restrict our discussion here to Oracle databases and the Oracle Database architecture. Please take a look at Chapters 11 through 14 for detailed information and exceptions with respect to the operating systems covered in those chapters. At this point, we are not trying to walk you through the configuration and startup process step by step. That will come in later chapters. Right now, we are just trying to give you a basic feel for the architecture you will be dealing with.

First: Configure, Create, and Start the Extract Process Everything has to start somewhere. Before an Oracle GoldenGate Extract process can do its thing, you will need to perform some basic configuration steps. First, you will use GGSCI to configure the Change Data Capture parameter file for that Extract process (you will also need to have configured the Manager process if you have not already, which we will discuss later in this chapter). You will then use GGSCI to create the Extract process and to start the Extract process. When configuring the parameter file for the Extract process (don't worry, we will discuss parameter files in a lot more detail throughout this chapter and in other chapters in the book), you will indicate which objects you wish to collect change information on (for example, specific tables), where the extract trail file is located, password information, and so on. Also, each Extract process has its own unique name, and this name is defined when you create the Change Data Capture parameter file. We will cover each of these steps several times throughout this book, so don't be concerned; by the time you are done with Chapter 6, you will know the configuration process really well. By the time you are done with Chapter 8, you will be an expert!

Second: Extract Reads the Redo   Most commonly the Oracle GoldenGate Extract process will read the redo stream generated by the database directly from the online redo logs. You can also configure the Extract process to read from the archived redo logs only. When the GoldenGate Extract process is configured this way, it is known as Archive Log Only (ALO) mode. When reading data from other databases, the Extract process will read that database's version of the Oracle redo logs.

When reading from the online redo log stream, it's possible that the redo that the Extract process needs will not be in the online redo log. This might happen for a number of reasons. One reason you might find a gap in the redo is that the Extract process was shut down for a period of time due to an abend or some form of maintenance. When the redo needed is not found in the online redo logs, the Extract process will attempt to access the archived redo logs to acquire and process the appropriate redo information. In the event that the redo information is not available from the online or archived redo logs, then the Extract process will abend and fail. In this case, you would need to find the archived redo logs that contain the redo required by the Extract process to continue.

Of course, if you need to process redo from an archived redo log, it's kind of hard to do that if the archived redo log is not available. It is typical for RMAN backup operations (database or archivelog) to delete the archived redo logs after they are backed up (hey, I wrote the RMAN book for Oracle Press, so I know these things!). If you are using RMAN to back up your archived redo logs (either during database backups or as separate backups), you can configure Oracle GoldenGate and RMAN to work together to control the deletion of archived redo logs. This is only available if you are using Oracle Database Version 10.2 or later, and if you are using RMAN to back up your archived redo logs (either during database backups or as separate backups).

If the GoldenGate Extract process is configured to use the archived redo logs instead of the online redo logs, then it will read the entire archived redo log file once it has been created by the ARCH process. In this case, there can be significant latency with respect to the time when transactions occur and the time when they will be read and propagated to the target systems. As with real-time Apply, if the Extract process can't find the redo records it needs, it will abend and fail. As in the previous case, you would need to find the archived redo logs that contain the redo required by the Extract process to continue.

One configuration where you might use Extract to read the archived redo logs instead of the online redo logs is when you want to minimize the impact of the Extract process on the database server. In this case, you could mirror the disks where the archived redo logs are on a different machine (or you could simply have the Oracle database create those archived redo logs in a second location for processing) and have the Extract process run on another system, reading the archived redo logs as they are created. This is helpful if you are concerned that the Extract process(es) might consume too much CPU or disk I/O on your database server.

As the Extract process reads the redo from the redo log stream, it will only extract the information that it is configured to extract. Thus, if you have configured the Extract process to track changes to the table scott.emp, then the only redo records associated with scott.emp will be extracted, converted, and stored in memory. The result is that the memory and physical disk space of the trail files that are required to store change information can be significantly less than that of the redo logs as a whole. This also means that the network bandwidth required to ship that information can be significantly less.

Third: Convert and Store the Redo in Memory   When GoldenGate reads redo from whatever source, the data is converted into a format that is unique to GoldenGate. That data is then stored in memory until the transaction is committed. This may require a great deal of memory for long-running, uncommitted transactions. If GoldenGate runs out of memory, then the contents of the memory buffer will be spilled out to disk. We will discuss GoldenGate and memory in more detail later in this chapter.

If the Extract process is configured for real-time redo log usage, the Extract process will read the online redo logs as near to real time as it can. This configuration offers the minimum latency between the completion of a transaction and the redo associated with that transaction downstream at target databases. The Extract process reads the redo log information in the order in which it is generated (that is, in the order of the system change number [SCN]) inside the database). This maintains the integrity and order of the redo that is to be replicated out to target database.

If you are running a Real Application Clusters (RAC) configuration, the Extract process will only run on one node of the cluster. You can configure GoldenGate so that the Extract processes will fail over to another node in the RAC configuration. This kind of failover consideration can reduce the impacts of a failure of a database node on GoldenGate implementations on RAC.

Fourth: Process the Committed Transaction   As GoldenGate reads the source database transaction logs, it will store the transactional data in memory until the transaction is committed or until it's rolled back. If the transaction is rolled back, then GoldenGate will simply not use that transactional data (since it has no purpose) and clear it from memory. As transactions are committed, one of two things can occur depending on whether you are using a local trail file or not:

■ If there is a local trail file (discussed later in this chapter) on the source system, then the transactions will be written to that trail file. The Extract process will then ship those transactions over the network to the target database system where the Collector process on that system (see Figure 2-1) will write them to a remote trail file on that system. We will discuss the Collector process in more detail later in this chapter.

■ If there is not a local trail file, then the Extract process will write the committed data over the network to the target database system. The Collector process on that system will receive the information and write it to a remote trail file.

This second configuration is not recommended for a number of reasons, principally because not using a trail file on the source system makes the overall architecture more prone to failure. Using only memory to store transaction records can be problematic. For example, there could be a network failure, the target system goes out of service, or other reasons. Thus it is considered a best practice to configure trail files on the source and the target system for use by the Extract process. We will discuss trail files in more detail later in this chapter.

When the GoldenGate Extract process is finished writing to a local trail file, it will by default create a recovery point record in the trail file (the Collector does this with remote trail files, too). Checkpoints are also recorded to aid in recovering in the event of an Extract process failure. Recovery points and checkpoints are used by GoldenGate for recovery purposes, and we will discuss recovery points and checkpoints in more detail later in this chapter.

Problems with the Extract Process

While you were reading the previous section, it might have occurred to you that there are a couple of potential problems that you will have to deal with. The first is memory exhaustion. Since GoldenGate uses memory to store the transactional data, if you run out of memory, you will have a problem.

When writing to memory, and before the commit, GoldenGate will spill out to a disk file if memory is exhausted until the transaction is committed and the data is transferred to a trail file on the target system. We strongly recommend that you use trail files on the source system as they provide a more robust storage solution for the processed redo.

Even trail files are not immune from problems. Since trail files require disk space, running out of disk space is decidedly a bad thing. If you do run out of disk space, the Capture processes writing to the trail file will abend. At this point you will need to address the disk space exhaustion issue, and then restart the Capture process. There are many reasons why you might run out of disk space. For example, someone might have created files on the file system where the trail file resides (as such, we recommend a dedicated file system for the trail file). Another possible reason is a slow network, or the target system(s) might be down.

How Does the Oracle GoldenGate Extract Process Work When Doing Bulk Loads?

As mentioned earlier, there are two different kinds of bulk loads that the GoldenGate Extract processes can perform: bulk loads and mass change capture loads. Let's look at each of these different types of executions in more detail.

Bulk Data Loads with the Extract Process   As we already mentioned, bulk load mode is used to instantiate target databases with the objects, and any associated data, that will be replicated to those databases. Bulk load mode is also used if you need to capture a large number of changes to be synchronized on target databases. When run in bulk load mode, the Extract process will create extract files instead of trail files. When configured for bulk data load, the Extract process will control the entire load process. While you will configure the Replicat process to accept the data being extracted, the Extract process will actually be responsible for starting and stopping the associated Replicat process.

Change Capture Data Loads with the Extract Process   Configuring the Oracle GoldenGate Extract process to do a bulk data load is quite similar to configuring a regular GoldenGate data extract. A few different parameters are configured in the Extract process parameter file, and you can also configure a Replicat process to work with the Extract process. The Extract process will then read the data directly from the database and transmit it over the network, and the Replicat process will receive the network data and write it to the database. Generally, the Extract process is responsible for managing the entire operation, including starting the remote Replicat process and stopping it. We will demonstrate this entire process in Chapter 5 of this book.

NOTE
There are data type restrictions when using the direct transmission method. For example, LOB movement is not supported with this method. The data types supported will vary based on the versions of Oracle Database and Oracle GoldenGate that you are using, so please consult the GoldenGate Administration Guide *for details on data type support.*

Oracle GoldenGate Extract Files GoldenGate extract files are the files that the GoldenGate Extract process creates when run in batch mode. Batch mode is used by GoldenGate to perform an instantiation of the target database. You also create extract files when you use GoldenGate to transitionally update a target database in batch mode. Usually you create just one large extract file, but Oracle GoldenGate will support the creation of multiple extract files should you need to do so. You will see us use extract files in many of the chapters in this book.

States of the Oracle GoldenGate Extract Process

The Oracle GoldenGate Extract process has one of four possible "states." These states can be viewed using the **info** command from the GoldenGate Software Command Interface (GGSCI), which will be discussed later in this chapter and throughout the book. The states that the GoldenGate Extract process can be in are as follows:

- **Stopped** In this state the Oracle GoldenGate Extract process is not running. Typically, this would indicate a normal shutdown, not a shutdown associated with an error condition (which would typically be an abended status). If the Extract process has a status of **stopped**, you will need to manually start the process (or perhaps develop some script that can do so). To start the Extract process, you would use the **start extract** command at the GGSCI command prompt. If you wished to stop the Extract process, you would use the **stop extract** command, again from GGSCI.

- **Starting** This state indicates that the Oracle GoldenGate Extract process is starting up.

- **Running** This state indicates that the Oracle GoldenGate Extract process is running normally.

- **Abended** This state indicates that the Oracle GoldenGate Extract process has shut down due to some abnormal condition. If you find that the Extract process has this condition, you will need to do some troubleshooting/error correction. Refer to Chapter 12 for more details on how to deal with Extract processes that are in an abended state.

Parallel Oracle GoldenGate Extract Processes

Oracle GoldenGate provides the ability to start multiple Extract processes and parallelize both the instantiation and redo log extraction process. This can be very helpful with respect to performance when you have a large database with many objects to instantiate or if you have a very busy database and you need to extract redo log data as quickly and efficiently as possible. You will also need a separate Extract process for each target database that you wish to replicate database data/DDL to.

When configuring parallel Extract processes to the same database, you will need to consider the objects being processed by that extract and whether they are child objects in a foreign key relationship. If an object is a child object in a foreign key relationship, you must ensure that the parent object is also being processed by the same Extract process. You cannot split parent/child relationships enforced by a foreign key into two or more separate Extract process definitions where those extracts are destined to the same database. For example, assume you have an EMP table and a DEPT table, and the EMP table column DEPT_ID has a foreign key relationship defined to the DEPT table primary key called DEPT_ID. If you are going to replicate the EMP table to a target database called BACKUP, you must also replicate the DEPT table in the same Extract process as the EMP table to the BACKUP database because of the defined foreign key.

RAC and the Oracle GoldenGate Extract Process

When you are running extracts on an Oracle RAC clustered database, you will only need one Extract process regardless of how many nodes there are in the cluster. That Extract process will need to run on a single node of the cluster. The Extract process will need access to all of the redo threads of the source database, as well as all the archived redo logs. Since the Extract process(es) will only run on one node, Oracle GoldenGate does provide a failover process should the node that the Extract process is running on fail. Please see Chapter 9 for full details on Oracle GoldenGate and RAC databases.

The Oracle GoldenGate Trail Files

Trail files are the persistent means that Oracle GoldenGate uses to record committed changes made to objects within the source database. As we have already discussed, the Extract process will record the change records it is configured to capture, convert those records into a proprietary format, and then store those change records in memory. When the transaction associated with those change records is committed, the Extract process will write those records to a trail file. The trail file may be on the source system (called a *local trail file*) or it might be on the target system (called a *remote trail file*). There will always be a remote trail file. The local trail file is optional. but we strongly recommend that you use local trail files as a matter of application of best practices. Using both a local and remote trail file provides the highest degree of redundancy and safety for the data that is being replicated.

The trail files are critical to the successful operation of Oracle GoldenGate, and great care should be taken when architecting trail files for your GoldenGate solution. Losing a trail file is like losing an archived redo log. Once it's gone, you have lost the transactions contained in the trail file. Losing transactions is okay if those transactions have already been processed on the target system. Losing trail files is not so okay if the transactions have not been processed on the target database. To ensure that your trail files are protected, you should store them on a disk architecture that provides some form of redundancy (such as RAID 0+1, RAID 1+0, or RAID 5).

In all the years that we have worked as Oracle DBAs, one of the more common questions goes like this: "If I lose some of my archived redo logs (such that there is a gap), how do I recover my database?" The answer is that you cannot recover your database through the archived redo gap. This is why the redo log files and the archived redo log files are so important to an Oracle database. The same is true with the GoldenGate trail files. This risk of trail file loss and data loss is one of many reasons why having trail files on both the source and target systems is considered a best practice.

Trail files are 10MB in size by default, though this size can be customized when creating the trail file. As each trail file is filled, a new trail file is created automatically, again 10MB in size (or whatever custom size you have defined). Each trail file is associated with a specific Extract process, and only one Extract process can write to a given trail file.

A unique set of trail files is identified by a two-character name that is prefixed to the trail file physical file name, and assigned when the trail file is created. Another six digits are appended to the end of the trail files to keep them unique. These six digits start with 000000 and end with 999999. At 999999, they will roll back over to 000000 and the sequence starts over again. The result is a trail file that is eight characters in length. An example naming convention for trail files might be EX000010.

NOTE
You will find this eight-character limitation on file naming a common limitation throughout Oracle GoldenGate.

What Is in the Trail Files?

We already mentioned that the Extract process copies the captured change information into memory. Once the change is committed, then the Extract process writes that information to the trail file associated with that Extract process. So, basically, the Oracle GoldenGate trail files contain all the committed transactions captured by the Extract process associated with the trail file. The changes stored in the Trail file are stored in canonical order, which is just a fancy way of saying that they are stored in the order in which they were processed in the source database. This helps avoid problems during replication, like the accidental creation of child records before the parent records are created.

Each trail file is associated with a given Extract process. Since each Extract process is assigned specific objects to track changes for, the individual trail files associated with that process will contain only the redo associated with those objects.

Where Are the Trail Files?

Depending on how you have configured GoldenGate in your environment, the trail file that the change records are *initially* loaded into may exist in one of three places:

- **On the source database**   This is known as a local trail file. Local trail files are optional, but the use of local trail files is a strongly recommended configuration for Oracle GoldenGate. If you use local trail files, then a second Oracle GoldenGate process called the Data Pump process (which we will discuss later in this chapter) will be used to move the local trail file to the remote trail files on the remote database servers that are being replicated to. In most of the examples in this book, we will configure local trail files.

- **On a secondary server dedicated to GoldenGate operations**   Typically the redo on these systems will be processed from the archived redo logs by a local Extract process and then a local trail file will be loaded.

- **On the target database server**   These are known as remote trail files. Remote trail files are always required for replication. Local trail files are optional. The use of remote trail files without a local trail file is not recommended as it is more prone to architectural failures that can negatively impact Oracle GoldenGate operations.

In all cases, by default the trail files created by the Extract process are located in the GoldenGate root install directory location under a directory called dirdat. When you configure the Extract process, you can define a nonstandard location for the trail file.

Tracking Changes in the Trail File

Inside the trail files, each record is associated with a specific number called the Commit Sequence Number (or CSN). The CSN number is a generic number assigned to transactions as they are stored in the trail files and is much like the SCN found within an Oracle database. The CSN maintains the canonical order of transactions within the trail file and is coupled with the internal change tracking number for each database supported by Oracle GoldenGate. The CSN is stored in the transaction header record of each transaction record in the GoldenGate trail files. One of the main uses of the CSN for GoldenGate administrators is to provide a marker in the transaction stream with which you can start replication. You will see examples of this in later chapters as we instantiate databases and then start replication at a specific CSN. Oracle GoldenGate Extract and Replicat processes will also use the CSN to determine at what point in time to restart database redo log extract and target database application when those processes are started.

Additionally, GoldenGate tracks the current version number of the GoldenGate version that created the trail file within the header of each trail file. This is important since all of the components of Oracle GoldenGate are pretty much decoupled, and it's quite possible that the version of GoldenGate creating the trail file will be different than the version reading the trail file. See the section on "Compatibility Between Different Versions of GoldenGate" for more information on using different versions of the product together.

The Oracle GoldenGate Data Pump Process

As you will recall, when you configure a given Extract process, you have two options. You can write the change data to a local trail file or to a remote trail file. When you write to a local trail file, then another process, the Oracle GoldenGate Data Pump process, is responsible for forwarding the contents of the local trail file to any remote Collector processes (which we will discuss next). The remote collectors will then write the remote trail files.

NOTE
Don't confuse the Oracle GoldenGate Data Pump process with the Oracle Data Pump utility, as they have completely different jobs.

The Oracle GoldenGate Data Pump process is simply an Extract process that is designed to read the contents of the local trail file (as opposed to the online redo logs) and transport that trail file content as defined in the parameter file of the Data Pump Extract process. Like a normal Extract process, the Data Pump process has an eight-character name associated with it, and again we recommend that you use a standard naming convention to keep all things straight. We will cover the use and configuration of the Oracle GoldenGate Data Pump process throughout the chapters of this book.

The Oracle GoldenGate Server Collector

What comes in must be processed. The Oracle GoldenGate Server Collector resides on the individual target system. Its job is to accept the stream of GoldenGate change data coming from the Extract process or the Data Pump process on the source system, and write it out to the remote trail file located on the target database server. This trail file data is then processed by the Replicat process and the data written to the target database. Typically there is little configuration required of the Collector process on the part of the administrator.

The Oracle GoldenGate Apply (Replicat) Process

The final step in the GoldenGate replication architecture is the Replicat process. The Replicat process is configured by the administrator, much like the Extract process. It is assigned an eight-character name to uniquely identify the process. The Replicat process will read the data in the remote trail file, and apply the changes to the target database. In the event of a bulk data load, the Replicat process will accept the input stream from the Extract process reading the data on the source database system and write that data directly to the target database system.

The Oracle GoldenGate Software Command Interface (GGSCI)

Central to controlling, managing, and reporting on Oracle GoldenGate processes is the Oracle GoldenGate Software Command Interface, also called the GGSCI. This command-line interface provides complete access to GoldenGate and is the means with which you will configure and control GoldenGate processes. Yes, it's not a nice GUI interface, but it does the trick and provides a nice robust way of controlling and monitoring GoldenGate operations. You will see many examples of the use of GGSCI throughout this book.

The Oracle GoldenGate Parameter Files

GoldenGate parameter files are at the heart of all the various GoldenGate processes. They are text files that you will configure for the specific process that the file is associated with. Often you will edit these files in the GGSCI interface, but you can also manually configure the files with your favorite editor if you prefer. Usually, if there is a problem with GoldenGate replication errors, the problem can be found within the body of the parameter file you have created.

Data Replication and Latency

Latency is the measure of time between the commit of a given transaction on the source system and the time the data becomes available for use on the target system. Latency can make or break a replication solution. Latency can be impacted by many things including the network, the hardware the database is running on, the underlying I/O infrastructure (for example, the disk drives), and the volume and nature of the data being replicated. Latency can also be seriously impacted by how Oracle GoldenGate is configured and how the replication solution is implemented.

The bottom line with GoldenGate (as with other technologies) is that just because you can do something does not mean that it is the right thing to do. Also, sometimes the simplest architecture is not always the best architecture. When configuring your GoldenGate infrastructure, make sure that you consider the latency and the time it takes for your remote systems to communicate it, and weave that knowledge into your overall replication plan.

Compatibility Between Different Versions of GoldenGate

When you are first configuring your Oracle GoldenGate replication architecture, make sure that you are replicating from and to supported versions of Oracle GoldenGate. The GoldenGate certification matrix is available on Oracle Metalink and support is changing all the time. Also, sometimes you might think that a particular platform would be supported (for example, MS SQL Server 2008 support only extends to the Enterprise Edition of the product, and support for MS SQL Server 2005 ended in August 2012).

On the other hand, you may find that your versions are supported, but that the software is not available. This is often easy to fix by simply making a support request through Oracle Metalink and asking for the specific version of the software that you need. Obviously, you need an Oracle support contract for such things. Oracle does make every effort as it releases new versions of GoldenGate to ensure forward and backward compatibility.

CHAPTER
3

Installing Oracle
GoldenGate

We have talked a lot about the architecture of GoldenGate, but now it's time to get down to business and actually get ourselves in a position to be able to use the product. This chapter is all about downloading and installing the Oracle GoldenGate product. In Chapter 4 we will talk about the initial configuration of Oracle GoldenGate, in preparation for later chapters where we will actually set up GoldenGate replication in a number of different ways.

In this chapter, and in Chapters 4 through 10, we will use Linux and Microsoft Windows as our primary operating systems for our examples. As a result, we will dedicate some time in this chapter to how we set up those environments, which we will use in the examples and the workshops throughout this book. Chapters 11 through 14 will provide insight into other platforms that GoldenGate supports. Still, the basics remain the same regardless of which platform you will be using, so there is a lot to be learned from Chapters 4 through 10, even if you are using Microsoft SQL Server, MySQL, or another platform. You can't be all things to all people, but we will try our best.

We start this chapter with a discussion on the various hardware, software, memory, and disk requirements associated with Oracle GoldenGate, confining our discussion to Linux and Windows. Next, we will introduce you to the environments that we will be using for the examples in this book and how they are set up. This way, you can set up environments exactly like the ones we have set up. After we have described our environments, we will finish the chapter by downloading the Oracle GoldenGate software from the Oracle download site and installing it on our servers.

NOTE
Anyone can download the Oracle GoldenGate software (subject to the appropriate export limitations) from the Oracle Web site and use it for trial purposes. That makes it insanely easy to learn how to use Oracle GoldenGate!

Throughout this and many of the remaining chapters of this book, you will find workshops that take you through Oracle GoldenGate step by step. In this chapter we will have workshops specifically geared toward setting up a test environment like the one we are using, and then you can download and install Oracle GoldenGate in your test environment. Of course, you don't have to use our environment, and in most cases it should be easy to follow the workshop instructions on slightly differing environments.

Oracle GoldenGate Requirements

There are a number of requirements that you will want to consider when planning for the install and use of Oracle GoldenGate. In this section we will cover the following in detail:

- GoldenGate memory requirements
- GoldenGate disk space requirements
- GoldenGate networking requirements

Oracle GoldenGate Oracle Database Platforms Supported

In Chapter 2 we provided a list of the different database versions that were supported by Oracle GoldenGate at the time this book was written. Oracle is adding support for new databases and other functionality all the time. Prior to any install, you should reference the Oracle certification matrix for Oracle GoldenGate to ensure that you are architecting a certified solution. You can find the certification matrix at the following URL: http://www.oracle.com/technetwork/middleware/goldengate/overview/index.html. The certification matrix provides a complete list of the databases supported by various versions of Oracle GoldenGate. When architecting your GoldenGate solution, you should reference the Oracle certification matrix to make sure that the version of GoldenGate, your operating system, and the version of the databases that you will be using are compatible. Sometimes Oracle will move URLs around, so it's possible that the link shown earlier in this paragraph won't work when you try it. You may need to do a Web search for Oracle GoldenGate certification matrix in order to find the most current edition.

NOTE
Make sure you check the certification matrix before you start installing GoldenGate.

Oracle GoldenGate Oracle Database Versions Supported

Oracle GoldenGate supports all Oracle versions after Oracle Database 9*i* Release 2 (specifically, 9.2.0.7 and later). DDL replication is supported for Oracle Database Versions 10*g* and later (see the product-specific chapters of this book, or the Oracle GoldenGate documentation, for information on DDL replication support to or from and between non-Oracle databases). Various versions have different limitations, so make sure you check the Oracle documentation for the version of GoldenGate you are using and what database features it supports. This information can be found in the *Oracle GoldenGate Oracle Installation and Setup Guide*. Again, reference the certification guide to determine the compatibility of GoldenGate, your database vendor and version, and operating system.

NOTE
If you are using a version of Oracle Database prior to 9.2.0.7, you will not be able to use Oracle GoldenGate.

Oracle GoldenGate Memory Requirements

The amount of memory required by Oracle GoldenGate is largely determined by the number of Extract and Replicat processes. Each of these processes, individually, will consume approximately 25 to 55MB on average. They may consume even more if the sizes of the transactions are larger. So, the real question is how many GoldenGate processes you will be running. You will need at least one Extract process on the source database, and one Replicat process on the target system. You may well find that you will be running more than one GoldenGate process on a given server, and thus the memory requirements will increase.

You will also need to ensure that sufficient swap space is available for Oracle GoldenGate. Typically, if you have a database installed, the amount of swap space should be sufficient. You can check to ensure that you have sufficient swap space by starting the GoldenGate Software Command Interpreter (GGSCI) and viewing the report file. You can also use the GGSCI command **send extract chachmgr cachestats** to review the current status of the transactions, and whether they are in memory or being swapped to disk. We will show you how to do this in more detail in Chapter 5 when we configure our first GoldenGate one-way replication.

Oracle GoldenGate Disk Space Requirements

The download image for Oracle GoldenGate is fairly small. For example, the compressed download image for GoldenGate for Windows is roughly 25MB in size. When extracted to disk, the overall install image is roughly 70MB in size. So the GoldenGate files do not require that much disk space. Allow for another 40MB in working space for each instance of Oracle GoldenGate that you wish to operate. An *instance* is essentially each occurrence of an Oracle GoldenGate home that is in use, regardless of how many databases or processes the individual GoldenGate home is supporting.

The biggest consumer of space will be the Oracle GoldenGate trail files. We discussed the Oracle GoldenGate trail files in Chapter 2, and we will certainly be discussing them in much greater detail in future chapters. The size of the trail files is defined when they are created, and they can vary in size depending on the overall number and size of database transactions. The total cumulative size of the

GoldenGate trail files can easily exceed several gigabytes, and therefore you need to make sure you allocate sufficient space to store these files in.

You can estimate the total size that you need to allocate for the GoldenGate trail files for an Oracle database by multiplying the amount of redo generated over a given period of time by 40 percent. For example, if you wanted to ensure that you had sufficient space for 24 hours' worth of trail file storage (for example, should your network between your source and target databases fail for an extended period of time), you would simply multiply the total amount of redo generated by the database over the last 24 hours by 40 percent. I always like to throw in a little extra space for such things to deal with what I call Robert's rule #10, which reads, "If something can go wrong, it will, and sooner than you think and at the most inconvenient time." As a result I'd add another 20 percent or so just to be sure. If you want to know how much redo is being generated by your database and the approximate space you need to dedicate to the trail files (40 percent), you can query the V$ARCHIVED_LOG view inside the Oracle database with a query like this one:

```
Select trunc(completion_time) date_generated,
  sum(blocks*block_size) total_redo_generated,
  sum(blocks*block_size)*.40 total_GG_Space_Needed
  from v$archived_log
  group by trunc(completion_time);
```

Since the trail files are so important, it's probably a good idea to make sure that the file system that the trail files live on is monitored to make sure that it has sufficient space. You should establish monitoring thresholds and alert when those thresholds are violated. Running out of disk space for the trail files is not a good thing, so monitoring and quick action are important. While filling up the disk will not corrupt the data being replicated, it will take down the GoldenGate Capture process and stop replication until you have dealt with the issue. This can result in your target database getting way out of sync with the source. This means it will take time to resynchronize it with the source database transactions. So you're in a real pickle if something bad should happen and you lose your source database, and all that stands between you and unemployment is the target database. Is that dramatic enough to get you to make sure you monitor the disk space for the trail files?

NOTE
The important thing to remember is that you need to allocate enough space to the trail files so that they don't fill up under abnormal operating conditions. In other words, you should figure out how long a potential network outage is likely to last, worst case, and based on that (and some good old fudge factors), size the trail file accordingly.

Oracle GoldenGate Network Requirements

Two things are critical when it comes to networking. The network can be the single most limiting factor with respect to replication. It's important to have a network that is fast and efficient. First, speed is important, but what's just as important (and sometimes seems to be forgotten in lieu of speed) is latency. Latency can be a major limiting factor of your GoldenGate architecture and various defined requirements (data replication [DR], acceptable lag time, and so on) associated with your target database. Latency can be a factor of the speed of the network, or of the volume of data being transported over that network. Latency and poor network performance can also be a factor of other things including the cabling, misconfigured equipment, broken equipment, the distance between the locations on the network, and other factors. Often GoldenGate installations, particularly DR-related locations, are distant from each other. So don't forget that you need to factor network limitations into the equation when you are architecting your application and use of GoldenGate for things like long-distance DR or geographically distant master-master replication schemes.

Another network problem we often see is the various network security measures, like firewalls, that can cause Oracle GoldenGate problems. You will need to have various TCP/IP-related ports open for GoldenGate to operate correctly. This means configuring the network so that these ports are available for use. We will cover network port-related information throughout this book as we configure Oracle GoldenGate replication.

The Demonstration Environments We Use in This Book

We will be using two environments in this book as we introduce you to Oracle GoldenGate. The first is a two-server environment using Oracle Unbreakable Linux, and the second is a two-server environment using Microsoft Windows. Both of these environments will be created on a single host OS (Windows) server using Oracle VirtualBox, Oracle's Virtual Machine technology. In the next sections we will discuss downloading and setting up Oracle VirtualBox software. Then we will provide workshops to help you set up the same environment that we will use in this book.

Download and Set Up Oracle VirtualBox

To ease your effort in learning about GoldenGate, we decided to use virtual environments created using Oracle VirtualBox. This way you don't have to have four different laptops to create the environments that you will need! This section will help you to set up the virtual environments that we will be using in this book. In this book, we will be creating our VMs using Oracle VirtualBox. In this section we will first discuss what Oracle VirtualBox is and how to install it. Then we will have a workshop that will guide you through downloading and then installing Oracle VirtualBox.

About Oracle VirtualBox

Oracle bought Sun Microsystems back in 2009. As a part of that purchase, Oracle acquired a product called VirtualBox (VB). VirtualBox is a virtualization product that runs on Windows, Linux, Mac, and Solaris hosts. VB supports a number of host operating systems including those that we will be using, Oracle Unbreakable Linux and MS Windows 7. VB is very flexible and can be used for both the enterprise and smaller applications, like the test environments for this book! Oracle actively develops and supports VirtualBox, with the most current release being version 4.1.6 as of this writing. More information on VirtualBox (including the documentation) is available at https://www.virtualbox.org.

Installing Oracle VirtualBox

Installing Oracle VirtualBox is fairly straightforward. First, you download VirtualBox and then you install it on the guest OS that it is to run on top of. Note that VirtualBox does not run on bare metal (a system without a host operating system). In all of our examples, we will be using Microsoft Windows 7 as the guest operating system that VirtualBox will run on top of. Since this is not a book on VirtualBox, we will not concern ourselves with how to run VirtualBox on other host operating systems, nor will we concern ourselves overly with describing the nature of virtual machines. We will, however, provide you with more than enough information to get the test environments set up and how to administer them (such as starting them up or shutting them down).

GoldenGate Workshop: *Downloading VirtualBox*

Workshop Notes

In this workshop we will guide you through downloading Oracle VirtualBox. We assume you are running on the Microsoft Windows 7 operating system as the guest operating system. If you are installing VirtualBox on a different guest OS, please reference the VirtualBox documentation to ensure that you are installing VirtualBox properly on that OS. Also note that we have kept screen shots to a minimum so as to save space. This is because Web pages tend to change over time.

Follow these steps to download Oracle VirtualBox. You will find the steps fairly easy and straightforward!

Step 1. Create a directory to download the VirtualBox install file into. (In our case, we used c:\downloads\virtualbox.)

Step 2. Go to the VirtualBox download site by opening your browser of choice, and surf to the following URL: https://www.virtualbox.org/.

Step 3. Click the Downloads link (it can be found on the left side of the page). This will take you to a page that offers a number of VirtualBox downloads.

Step 4. We want to download the product called VirtualBox Platform Packages (generally toward the top of the page). There will be several options to choose from. Make sure you click on the package for Windows hosts.

Step 5. When prompted, save the file to be installed to the directory created in Step 1. Before you start the download, double-check that the file name has the word "Win" contained in it. This indicates that the file is part of the Windows distribution. In our case the file is called VirtualBox-4.1.6-74713-Win.exe, though your file name may be (probably will be) different. Just make sure it has Win as a part of the file name to indicate that it is the VirtualBox image for Windows.

> **NOTE**
> *As with any other file you download, you should scan the file with a virus detection utility before opening it or using it. This is just a best practice no matter where the file originates from.*

That completes this easy workshop. In the next workshop we will actually install VirtualBox.

GoldenGate Workshop: *Installing VirtualBox*

Workshop Notes
In this workshop we will be installing VirtualBox, which we downloaded in the previous workshop. We will take the default install options during the workshop. Once the workshop is complete, we will be prepared to create the Virtual Machines for the workshops in this book.

Follow these steps to complete the workshop. Once you are done, you will have installed Oracle VirtualBox.

Step 1.   Using Windows Explorer, open the folder where you downloaded the VirtualBox install executable in the previous workshop titled "Downloading VirtualBox."

Step 2.   Click on the VirtualBox executable file that you downloaded. The VirtualBox install process will begin.

> **NOTE**
> *If Windows asks if you want to run the file, click the Run button.*

Step 3.   The VirtualBox Setup Wizard Welcome screen will appear. Click the Next button.

Step 4.   The Custom Setup screen will appear next. You should not need to change any options. You can change the install location from this setup screen if you wish. Please refer to the VirtualBox documentation if you wish to do any VirtualBox customization from this screen. Otherwise, click the Next button.

> **NOTE**
> *The initial VirtualBox will require about 130MB of hard drive space and about 10K of memory. The OS images to be installed later will have their own unique memory and disk storage requirements that will need to be met.*

Step 5.   Another screen will appear, giving you the option to create shortcuts. Take the default settings (typically with the shortcuts being created) and click the Next button.

Step 6.   On the next screen VirtualBox will warn you that, as a part of the install, there will be a network interruption. Obviously, if you are doing something important on the network, this probably isn't the right time to be installing VirtualBox. If you can afford a quick network outage, then proceed by clicking the Yes button to continue the install.

Step 7.   Oracle VirtualBox is now ready to install, as indicated by the final page of the install wizard. Click the Install button to finish the install of Oracle VirtualBox.

Step 8.   Now, you wait for the install to complete. Depending on the level of security you are running on your Windows system, you may have to give the installer permission to perform certain actions as the install progresses. On my Windows laptop the install of VirtualBox took about three minutes.

Step 9. When the install is completed, the VM Install Wizard will present the Install Completed screen. Click the Finish button to complete the install.

Step 10. The Oracle VirtualBox Manager screen will appear. For now, you can press CTRL-Q to close the VirtualBox Manager screen. You should also notice that there is an icon on the desktop called "Oracle VM VirtualBox."

You have completed the second workshop! You are on your way to becoming a GoldenGate expert, or at least an Oracle VM VirtualBox expert.

Creating the Oracle VirtualBox Images Used in This Book

Now that we have installed Oracle VirtualBox, we need to create the virtual machines (VMs) that we will be using in the examples in this book. In our case, we will be creating four separate VMs:

- **Two Linux VMs** These will be preconfigured images that we will download from Oracle.

- **Two Windows XP VMs** These will be images that we create ourselves from scratch.

First we will create the Linux VMs and then we will create the Windows VMs.

Downloading and Creating the Linux VMs

The Oracle VirtualBox community (VirtualBox is OpenSource) provides a number of "prebuilt" virtual machines that you can use once you have installed VirtualBox. These prebuilt machines can be found on Oracle's Technology Network pages at this URL: http://www.oracle.com/technetwork/community/developer-vm/index.html.

In our Linux environments we will use one of these prebuilt images to create the two Linux server VMs that we need. Next we have two workshops for you. The first is the workshop to download the VM image, and the second will be to create the two VMs that we will be using.

GoldenGate Workshop: *Downloading the Linux Virtual Machine Image*

Workshop Notes

In this workshop we will use the VirtualBox Database Application Development VM available on Oracle's Technology Network Web site. This VM contains the following Oracle components:

- Oracle Linux 5 (32-bit version)

- Oracle Database 11*g* Release 2 Enterprise Edition

- Oracle TimesTen In-Memory Database Cache

- Oracle XML DB

- Oracle SQL Developer

- Oracle SQL Developer Data Modeler

- Oracle Application Express 4.0

- Oracle JDeveloper

Obviously we don't need all these components installed, but you will find that installing these prebuilt VMs will make your work a lot easier overall, even if they have more components than you need. For example, in this case, notice that we don't need to install Linux or Oracle Database when we install this image. All we will need to do is download and install Oracle GoldenGate once we get the image installed.

> **NOTE**
> *The VM downloaded for this workshop is a 32-bit version of Linux. As a result, you will want to download 32-bit versions of any additional programs you will want to add to this image.*

Follow these steps to complete the workshop. When you are done, you will have downloaded the Oracle VMs for Linux that we will be using in this book.

Step 1. In this workshop we will download the VMs to the same directory we used in Step 1 of the first workshop in this chapter. In our case we are using a directory called c:\downloads\virtualbox.

Step 2. Go to the following URL: http://www.oracle.com/technetwork/community/developer-vm/index.html.

Step 3. Find the image called Database App Development VM on the Web page. Note that it is possible that the name of this image might have changed. You want to make sure that the image you download contains the Linux OS and Oracle Database Version 11.2 (or later) in the Enterprise Edition. Click on the link that says "Downloads and Instructions."

Step 4. Review the requirements of the install image and make sure your computer meets those requirements.

Step 5. On the setup portion of the page you loaded in Step 2, click on the image. In our case the name of the image was oracle_developer_days.ova.

Step 6. *Do not* click on the Open With option, which may be selected by default. Instead, choose the Save File option and download the image to the directory we selected in Step 1 of this workshop. Our download image was about 4.2GB in size, so the download could take a while (ours took about 40 minutes on our home wireless network).

Step 7. Once the image has been downloaded, create a copy of the original image you downloaded and name that image oracle_developer_days_01.ovm. This will be the base image for your second VM.

> **NOTE**
> *You can run GoldenGate with the other Oracle Database editions, but we recommend you use Enterprise Edition when running the workshops in this book since that is the version of Oracle Database we used when creating these workshops.*

GoldenGate Workshop: *Installing and Starting the Linux Virtual Machines*

Workshop Notes
Now that we have downloaded the Linux VirtualBox VM, we need to create two Linux Virtual Machines using this VM image. During the workshops in later chapters, we will expect that both VMs will be up and running at the same time. Thus, the

overall hardware requirements for running the VMs will be doubled. While the Web site suggests you need 2GB per VM, I was able to comfortably run two of the VMs on my laptop with 4GB of memory without having to make any changes to the memory requirements of the VMs.

If you find the requirements for running both images are too much for your individual machine (perhaps you have a laptop with only 3GB installed), you can work within each image to reduce the overall memory requirements of that image, including reducing the database memory footprint, and shutting down the Oracle TimesTen server.

NOTE
This workshop assumes that you want to use VMs to manage your GoldenGate test environments. All of the examples in this book can also be run on individual servers or even with several databases on the same server with few, if any, modifications. So, if you have a whole bunch of machines, or want to use one single test server, be our guest; it all works out fine in the end. In the workshops though, we will assume you are using VMs, as configured in the workshops in this chapter.

Follow these steps to complete the workshop. Once you are done, you will have two Oracle Unbreakable Linux virtual machines installed, each running an Oracle database!

Step 1. Start Oracle VirtualBox from the desktop icon titled Oracle VM VirtualBox. The Oracle VM VirtualBox Manager will appear.

Step 2. We now need to import the VM image you downloaded in the workshop titled "GoldenGate Workshop: Downloading the Linux Virtual Machine Image." Click File | Import Appliance from the Oracle VM VirtualBox Manager screen.

Step 3. From the Appliance Import Wizard screen, click the Choose option and you will see the Select an Appliance to Import window appear.

Step 4. From the Select an Appliance to Import window, find the Oracle VM image you downloaded in the workshop titled "GoldenGate Workshop: Downloading the Linux Virtual Machine Image." Select that image and click Open.

Step 5. From the Appliance Import Wizard screen, click the Next button.

Step 6. The Appliance Import Settings screen will appear. Click Name and change the name of the image to "Linux Database Image One." Click the Import Image button.

Step 7. You may be prompted to review the Software License Agreement. Review the terms of the agreement and if you are satisfied with them, click the button titled Agree.

Step 8. Oracle VirtualBox will begin to import the image. This should take about 10 minutes to complete.

Step 9. Once the VirtualBox image has been imported, you will see a new machine listed in the left pane of the Oracle VM VirtualBox Manager window called "Linux Database Image One." In the Oracle VM VirtualBox Manager window, you will find that the status of the "Linux Database Image One" virtual machine is "Powered Off."

Step 10. We need to make a change to the network configuration of the virtual machine so that it can communicate with the host network and also with the other VMs that will be running on your system. From the left window pane of the Oracle VM VirtualBox Manager, click on the machine titled "Linux Database Image One" to make sure that image is active. Now, from the top of the Oracle VM VirtualBox Manager window, click on the icon titled "Settings."

a. On the left side of the Settings page, click Network. The network adapter information will appear.

b. Make sure that adapter 1 is enabled and set to Bridged.

c. Click Advanced Settings.

d. Make sure that Promiscuous Mode is changed from "Deny" to one of the following settings depending on your needs:

- **At a minimum set to Allow VMs** This will allow communication between the different VMs and the host OS but will not allow network communication to the outside world from the VMs. With this configuration, you will not be able to surf to outside Web sites such as www.oracle.com from within the Virtual Machines. This is a slightly safer option than "Allow All," but it does restrict, so we prefer the "Allow All" option (mentioned next) so we can surf to support sites from within the VMs and so on.

- **Optionally set to "Allow All"** This will allow communication between the different VMs and the host OS and will also allow you to communicate with outside Web sites such as www.oracle.com from within the Virtual Machines. This setting also involves more risk as it provides more hacking opportunities from the outside. We prefer this setting for various reasons including the ability to get to support sites and download important updates.

Once you have made the changes to the networking options, click OK to save the changes you made to your networking configuration.

NOTE
If you are using a host OS that provides a firewall, you may find that the firewall will block attempts to test connectivity (such as ping). Make sure that your firewall is properly configured so that you don't mistakenly think that the networking between the VMs is not working correctly.

Step 11. Let's start the VM to test it. Click "Oracle Developer Days" in the left pane of the Oracle VM VirtualBox Manager window. Then click the Start button at the top of the Oracle VM VirtualBox Manager window. As the machine starts, you will get a warning screen about the auto capture keyboard option. Click OK to continue. You should now see the virtual machine open and you will also see the Linux OS boot.

Step 12. Once the Linux image boots, sign in as oracle, using the password oracle to fully test the VM. Note that the root account's password is also oracle.

Step 13. The Oracle database orcl should have started. You can check that this has occurred by trying to log in to the database as seen here:

```
[oracle@localhost ~]$ env|grep ORACLE_SID
ORACLE_SID=orcl
[oracle@localhost ~]$ sqlplus / as sysdba
SQL*Plus: Release 11.1.0.7.0 - Production on Wed Nov 23 09:42:40
2011
Copyright (c) 1982, 2008, Oracle.  All rights reserved.
Connected to:
Oracle Database 11g Enterprise Edition Release 11.2.0.2.0 -
Production With the Partitioning, OLAP, Data Mining and Real
Application Testing options
SQL> select open_mode from v$database;
OPEN_MODE
--------------------
READ WRITE
```

Step 14. Let's change the hostname of this server. The default hostname for the server in this image is xyz. We want to change it to goldengate1. From the Linux prompt, first make a copy of the /etc/sysconfig/network file. Then, edit the /etc/sysconfig/network file. Inside that file, find the entry that says HOSTNAME. Change this line to read as follows:

```
HOSTNAME=goldengate1
```

And then save the file. You have now changed the hostname of the first Linux machine. Perform this action on the second Linux machine, making its hostname goldengate2.

Step 15. You will need to change the listener.ora and tnsnames.ora files to reflect the new hostname of the machine. Log in as the Oracle user and change to the directory $ORACLE_HOME/network/admin. Now, edit the listener.ora and tnsnames .ora files.

This is what the resulting listener.ora should look like. Note that the changes you need to make are shown in bold:

```
LISTENER =
  (DESCRIPTION_LIST =
    (DESCRIPTION =
      (ADDRESS = (PROTOCOL = TCP)(HOST = goldengate1)(PORT = 1521))
    )
    (DESCRIPTION =
      (ADDRESS = (PROTOCOL = TCP)(HOST = goldengate1)(PORT = 80))
      (PROTOCOL_STACK =
          (PRESENTATION = HTTP)
          (SESSION = RAW)
      )
    )
    (DESCRIPTION =
      (ADDRESS = (PROTOCOL = TCP)(HOST = goldengate1)(PORT = 21))
      (PROTOCOL_STACK =
          (PRESENTATION = FTP)
          (SESSION = RAW)
      )
    )
  )
ADR_BASE_LISTENER = /home/oracle/app/oracle
```

The tnsnames.ora file should be modified to look like the following:

```
LISTENER_ORCL =
  (ADDRESS = (PROTOCOL = TCP)(HOST = goldengate1)(PORT = 1521))
ORCL =
```

```
   (DESCRIPTION =
     (ADDRESS = (PROTOCOL = TCP)(HOST = goldengate1)(PORT =
1521))
     (CONNECT_DATA =
       (SERVER = DEDICATED)
       (SERVICE_NAME = orcl)
     )
   )

TTORCL =
  (DESCRIPTION =
    (ADDRESS_LIST =
      (ADDRESS = (PROTOCOL = TCP)(HOST = goldengate1)(PORT =
1521))
    )
    (CONNECT_DATA =
      (SERVICE_NAME = orcl)
    )
  )
```

This should take care of all the configuration issues. Congratulations! You have imported your first Linux VM!

> **NOTE**
> *Because of the vast complexity, vagaries, and differences in networking, we can't address all of the things that might come between you and connecting to the network with these virtual machines. Things like firewalls (even those on your local client machine), routers, and the like can conspire to make connectivity a challenge. It is important that your VMs be able to talk to each other via TCP/IP (for GoldenGate purposes), and it's important that they be able to talk to the outside world (so they can download software). We have given you some configuration tips here, but you will probably need to customize your own install for your specific environment.*

Now, we need to do the same thing a second time to install the second Linux VM. First, I'd shut down the first VM until you get the second VM configured and started. To configure the second VM, simply follow Steps 1 through 12 earlier using the copy of the image you created in Step 7 (oracle_developer_days_01.ovm) of the workshop called "Downloading the Linux Virtual Machine Image" earlier in this chapter.

> **NOTE**
> *You can also create the second image by using VirtualBox's available cloning features. Simply press CTRL-O to start the cloning process. Follow the prompts and VirtualBox will clone the image for you.*

During and after the creation of the second image, you need to make these changes on one or both of the Linux images as indicated:

1. When the Appliance Import Settings screen appears, call this image "Linux Database Image Two." You should now have two VMs that appear in the left pane of the Oracle VM VirtualBox Manager window.

2. Open the Settings for "Linux Database Image Two." Go to the Network settings (you should already have configured the correct value for promiscuous mode). Find the MAC Address setting. You will want a unique MAC address for this machine. Click the button to the right of the MAC Address text box (it looks like a little arrow going in a circle), and VirtualBox will create a new MAC address for that network adapter. Click OK to save this change.

3. After starting the second VM, you will need to change the hostname of that Linux server. Follow Step 13 of this workshop and make the hostname of the second VM goldengate2.

4. You will want to adjust the /etc/hosts files on the VMs so that they are aware of each other's existence.

5. The VMs are set up to use DHCP-assigned IP addresses. You might want to consider hard-coded IP address assignments to these VMs so that the addresses will not change. If you do not use hard-coded IP addresses, then you will need to change the hosts file whenever the IP address of the machine changes.

Having set up the second VM, start it and ensure that it comes up correctly. Then, start the first VM and make sure that both VMs will run at the same time properly on your host OS. Also test the connectivity between the two VMs and between each VM and the host OS by using ping, ssh, or your favorite testing method.

Creating the Windows VMs

We will also be using Microsoft Windows throughout the workshops in this book, so we will want a couple of VMs for Microsoft as well. There are no prepared Windows VM environments, so in this case we will have to create our own, using the Windows XP install media. We have a workshop for you that will walk you through that process next!

GoldenGate Workshop: *Installing and Starting the Windows Virtual Machines*

Workshop Notes

This workshop will walk you through the steps of creating the Windows Virtual Machines, and then installing Windows XP onto those VMs. Note that this is not a tutorial on installing Windows; we expect you already know how to do that. We will quickly walk you through each step, but we won't spend a great deal of time describing what is going on during those steps (for example, we won't have long and involved discussions on the best disk partitioning scheme). We also assume that you have the appropriate licenses for the Windows products that you install. Make sure you have the correct licenses because we're not going to bail you out of jail if the software police come knocking!

Another assumption we make is that you have already run the previous workshops. In particular, you will need to have installed Oracle VM VirtualBox. If you have not installed Oracle VM VirtualBox, then run the workshop earlier in this chapter entitled "Installing VirtualBox." So, in sum, this workshop requires that you have the following ready to go:

- Oracle VM VirtualBox installed

- The Windows install disks available (we are using XP in our example, but Windows 7 will work just fine)

Now that we have the prerequisites done, let's proceed to the workshop!

Step 1. Click on the Oracle VM VirtualBox icon on your desktop. The Oracle VM VirtualBox Manager window will open. You can see an example of the Oracle VM VirtualBox Manager window in Figure 3-1.

Step 2. From the Oracle VM VirtualBox Manager window, click on the New icon image at the top left of the window. The Create New Virtual Machine Wizard introduction screen will appear. On this introduction screen, click Next to proceed.

Step 3. You will now see the VM Name and OS Type screen of the Create New Virtual Machine wizard as seen previously in Figure 3-1. Enter the following values in this window:

- **Name: GoldenGate Windows Image One**

- **Operating System: Microsoft Windows**

- **Version: Windows XP**

FIGURE 3-1. *The Oracle VM VirtualBox Manager window*

Click the Next button once you have entered these values. Figure 3-2 shows the screen with these values entered.

Step 4. The Memory screen appears next. This screen represents the amount of memory that you want to allocate to the virtual machine. Enter a minimum of 1024MB for this value. Then click the Next button.

Step 5. The Virtual Hard Disk screen appears next. Leave the Start-up Disk box checked, and make sure that the Create New Hard Disk button is selected. Then click the Next button.

Step 6. The Welcome to the Virtual Disk Creation Wizard screen will appear. This wizard will help you create the virtual disk for your VM. Make sure the VDI radio button is selected and click Next.

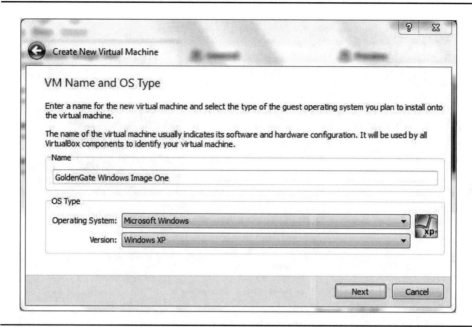

FIGURE 3-2. *VM Name and OS Type screen from the Create New Virtual Machine Wizard*

Step 7. On the Virtual Disk Storage Details screen, make sure that the Dynamically Allocated radio button is selected and click the Next button.

Step 8. On the Virtual Disk File Location and Size screen, accept the default location. Make the disk size 40GB. Note that Oracle VM VirtualBox will not allocate all 40GB of space when the image is created. Disk space will be allocated on demand. Thus, the disk space on the underlying host operating system will not be instantly consumed by this VM. Click the Next button to continue.

Step 9. Next you will see the Summary page of the Create New Virtual Disk page. Review the summary and click Create to begin the creation of the virtual image.

Step 10. The Oracle VM VirtualBox Manager screen will now appear. The VM you just created will appear on the left pane of the screen as seen in Figure 3-3. Now, it's time to install Windows on your Virtual Machine.

Step 11. This step involves installing Windows XP. We will not follow the Windows install process step by step, but in the next few steps, we will provide you with a few notes and some guidance as you perform the Windows install.

FIGURE 3-3. *The Oracle VM Virtual Box Manager with the new **GoldenGate Windows Image One** VM ready to start*

Step 12. Load your Windows XP Install media into the CD drive on your laptop. Oracle VM VirtualBox will install Windows XP from this image.

Step 13. From the Oracle VM VirtualBox Manager window, highlight the VM image you just created called "GoldenGate Windows Image One." Click the Start button at the top of the Oracle VM VirtualBox Manager window. The VM will start at this time.

Step 14. You will see the Welcome screen of the First Run Wizard. Click Next to continue.

Step 15. On the Select Installation Media window, select the location of the Windows install media that you will load from (for example, Disk f:\). Then click the Next button.

Step 16. The First Run Wizard Summary screen will appear. Review that screen and then click Start to start the new VM, and to start the Windows install process.

Step 17. The VM will start. The Oracle Windows Install screen should appear. At this time, you will begin a normal Windows XP install. It is beyond the scope of this workshop to provide you with a blow-by-blow instruction on how to install Windows. Simply follow the prompts as you would when installing Windows normally. When you create the image, make sure you name this Windows machine GoldenGate-One.

Step 18. You will want to install the Oracle VM VirtualBox Guest Additions on the Windows VMs that you are creating. This will enable copy/paste functionality between your VMs and the host OS. To enable the Guest Additions, click the Devices menu of the running Windows VM addition as seen in Figure 3-4. Then click the Install Guest Additions option. Follow the on-screen instructions to install the Guest Additions.

FIGURE 3-4. *Installing the Oracle VM VirtualBox Guest Additions*

Step 19. Following the instructions on https://download.oracle.com, extract the Oracle Database install images. At the time of this writing, you would extract the two download images into a single directory. Check the instructions on the Oracle download site to make sure that is still the method used.

Step 20. Install Oracle but do not create a database at this time. This book is not a book on installing or using the Oracle Database software. In fact, we will assume, in this book, that you have some basic administrative understanding of Oracle databases and that you know how to perform basic tasks (like installing the database, starting it, and shutting it down).

Step 21. Once you have installed Oracle, we want to clone the VM, creating our second VM. This is much easier than re-creating the VM. To clone the VM, do the following:

- Shut down the VM to be copied. To do this, simply shut down Windows XP and the VM will close once Windows has shut down.

- From the Oracle VM VirtualBox Manager screen, make sure that the GoldenGate Windows Image One that we created is highlighted. Press CTRL-O to start the clone process.

- The Welcome screen of the clone, a Virtual Machine screen, will appear. Change the name of the image to be cloned to GoldenGate Windows Image Two Clone. Click the checkbox that says Reinitialize the MAC Address of All Network Cards. See Figure 3-5 for an example of the screen after the changes are made. Click Next.

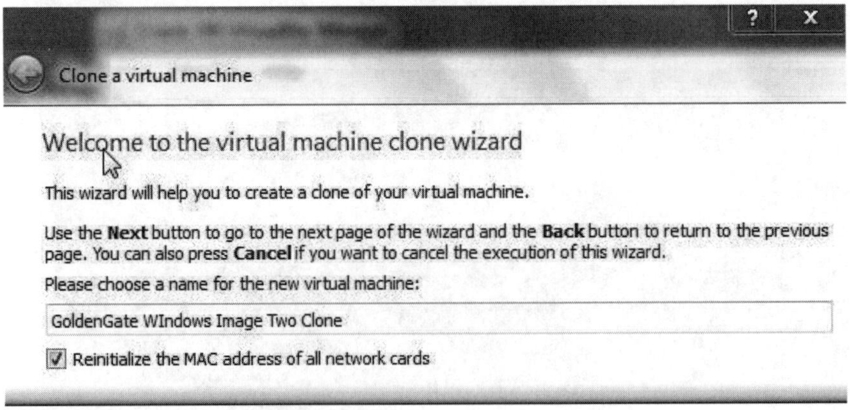

FIGURE 3-5. *Clone a Virtual Machine window options*

- The Cloning Configuration screen will appear. Here, you need to select the Full Clone option to create an actual, independent copy of the VM. Click the Clone button and the cloning operation will begin.

- Once the cloning has completed, start the newly cloned image to ensure that the cloning operation was successful and the image will start. You will want to change the machine name of the newly cloned VM. In our case, we changed the machine name from GoldenGate-One to GoldenGate-Two.

Step 22. Start each VM and install the Oracle Database Server software into each machine that you extracted earlier in Step 19 using the Oracle Universal Installer. In this book, we assume you have some basic Oracle database experience, including an understanding of how to install the Oracle Database software. You can opt to create the database when installing the Oracle Database software, or you can use the DBCA to create the database as described in Step 20. If you install Oracle Database in this step, follow the recommendations in Step 20 with respect to installing the sample schemas, the database name, and other settings.

Step 23. In each VM use the Oracle Database Configuration Assistant (DBCA) to create a database. Again, we assume you have some familiarity with Oracle databases and the DBCA. When installing Oracle Database in this step, make sure you install all of the demonstration schemas including HR, SCOTT, and so on. We will be using these schemas in later workshops throughout this book.

Step 24. Using ping, FTP, or SFTP, check the connectivity between both of the Windows VMs and between the Linux VMs and the Windows VMs. Each of the four machines must be able to communicate with the other successfully in order for you to successfully run all the workshops in this book.

NOTE
It is way beyond the scope of this book to teach you all the possible nuisances of networking and troubleshooting problems. During the course of writing this book, we were traveling a lot and found that things like hotel networks and wi-fi networks that we didn't set up ourselves often caused problems with our VM intracommunications—sometimes very frustrating problems. We suggest that you perform these installs and setups in a network environment that you are very comfortable with and that you understand.

In the workshops in the book we will be using the database names ORCL1 and ORCL2 for the Windows-based Oracle databases in this exercise. We suggest you name your databases the same to avoid confusion. Finally, you will want to put your database in ARCHIVELOG mode as we will require the archived redo logs when using GoldenGate.

Now that we have gotten our VMs installed and our databases created, we are ready to install Oracle GoldenGate.

NOTE
For the systems in most of the workshops, we will not be using Automatic Storage Management (ASM) except in Chapter 10 when we talk about Oracle GoldenGate and RAC databases. You should create the Oracle databases in these exercises using file systems as a result. Note that the Linux databases created in the earlier workshops also use file systems.

Download and Install Oracle GoldenGate

Now that we have our environment set up, we are ready to download and install Oracle GoldenGate. In this section we will first find and download the Linux and Windows versions of GoldenGate. We will then install GoldenGate on our Linux and Windows VMs. We will then be ready to configure Oracle GoldenGate, which we will do in the next chapter.

What Do I Need to Know Before I Download GoldenGate?

Before you can download Oracle GoldenGate, you will need to have some information on hand. Specifically, you will want to know:

- The operating system you are on, including the version and bit size

- The databases you will be using (that is, Oracle or otherwise) and the version of those databases (10*g*, 11*g*, and so on)

This information needs to be collected for any database that will be used as either a source or a target in Oracle GoldenGate operations. Once you have collected this information, you are ready to download Oracle GoldenGate.

How Do I Download GoldenGate?

Oracle GoldenGate, like other Oracle products, is available to download from Oracle with a free development license to pretty much anyone, subject to export restrictions. You can review the specifics of the licensing of Oracle GoldenGate when you download the product.

Oracle GoldenGate is available from a couple of different sources. First, Oracle maintains an informational page on Oracle GoldenGate, which contains many of the most popularly downloaded versions of Oracle GoldenGate. You can find these download images at the following Web URL:

http://www.oracle.com/technetwork/middleware/goldengate/downloads/index.html

Sometimes the version of Oracle GoldenGate is not available at this URL. In these cases you should go to the Oracle Software Delivery Cloud (previously called E-delivery) Web site, which can be found at this URL: https://edelivery.oracle.com/

If you download the software from the Delivery Cloud, you will need to indicate the product pack that you want to download. To get GoldenGate, you will need to select "Oracle Fusion Middleware" from the product pack select box. Then, select the correct platform (for example, Linuxx86). Once you have selected these two options, click the Go button on the form. Once you have clicked Go, various products will appear at the bottom of the screen, including several versions of GoldenGate. What you are looking for is something like "Oracle GoldenGate on Oracle v11.1.1.1.0 Media Pack for Linux x86." The "Media Pack" for GoldenGate is the main set of programs for GoldenGate. You will also find other options including the "Management Pack" and "Non Oracle Database Media Pack," and other GoldenGate software options. We will cover almost all of these options within the chapters of this book, but for now, let's concentrate on the base product.

So, what happens if you can't find the version of GoldenGate you are looking for that runs on the operating system you are using? This happens, and Oracle is ready to deal with it. In these cases you will need to open a support ticket with Oracle and request the specific version build that you need. They will then build the version and let you know where you can get it. While writing this book, we had to do just that because a new version of GoldenGate had been made available, but it was not yet available for 32-bit Linux. We put in a request to Oracle Support and they cut the version we needed very quickly.

Before you download Oracle GoldenGate, you should choose or create the directory you want to download it to. Often I like to keep my download images separate from actual programs and other kinds of operational files. In this case, I might create a directory called something like /download/GoldenGate on Linux or c:\download\goldengate on Windows to download my Oracle GoldenGate image to.

The size of the Oracle GoldenGate image varies based on the version of GoldenGate and the operating system that you have selected. On average, the image sizes are pretty small, around 50 megabytes. You will want to ensure that you have enough disk space to download the Oracle GoldenGate install image into the directory structure you create.

Installing Oracle GoldenGate

In this section we will discuss installing GoldenGate after you have downloaded the product. First we will talk about the basic requirements of GoldenGate. In this section we will discuss how to install Oracle GoldenGate on Linux and Windows platforms. Both installs are very similar, and all Oracle GoldenGate installs generally fit the same pattern.

After this section we have some workshops for you that will lead you step by step through installing Oracle GoldenGate on the Windows and Linux VMs that we created in earlier workshops. You might be wondering about things like memory, disk space requirements, and so on. We will cover those requirements in Chapter 4 when we talk about configuring Oracle GoldenGate.

NOTE
You should always read the installation guide and associated readme files before doing a production install of Oracle GoldenGate. This way you get the latest information on GoldenGate before installing it.

Installing GoldenGate on Linux

When you download the Oracle GoldenGate image for Linux, you will find that the image is a compressed tar file. The tar image in the zip file needs to be uncompressed with the **uncompress** command and then extracted from the tar file using the **tar** command (that is, `tar -xvf`). You should have already decided what directory you want to use for your GoldenGate "Home" directory. We will provide examples of the install process in the GoldenGate Linux install workshop shortly.

If you want to test that the install was successful, you can run the GoldenGate Software Command Interpreter (GGSCI) program from the GoldenGate home directory you created. You should note that if you are using the test environment we set up earlier in this chapter, the Oracle environment variables will already be set up for you. If you are setting up your own environment, you will need to make sure that the Oracle Database software is installed along with the GoldenGate software, since the GoldenGate software depends on the Oracle Database shared libraries to operate (when working with an Oracle database; requirements when working with other databases will differ). In this case, you will need to ensure that the environment variable LD_LIBRARY_PATH is configured and pointing to the shared database libraries on your database server (or intermediate server if you are configuring such an environment).

Also, note that in our test environment, we have not added the directory that contains the GoldenGate software to the PATH. Therefore we have to change into the GoldenGate software directory and start GGSCI using the ./ operator to indicate that we should start GGSCI from the local directory.

Keeping these things in mind, here is an example of testing the startup of GGSCI:

```
[oracle@localhost GoldenGate]$ . oraenv
ORACLE_SID = [orcl] ? <press enter to accept the default value>
[oracle@localhost GoldenGate]$ cd /home/oracle/app/GoldenGate
[oracle@localhost GoldenGate]$ ./ggsci
Oracle GoldenGate Command Interpreter for Oracle
Version 11.1.1.1 OGGCORE_11.1.1_PLATFORMS_110421.2040
Linux, x86, 32bit (optimized), Oracle 11g on Apr 21 2011 22:38:06
Copyright (C) 1995, 2011, Oracle and/or its affiliates. All rights
reserved.
```

NOTE
If you are setting up your own environment, you will want to make sure that the LD_LIBRARY_PATH, ORACLE_HOME, and ORACLE_SID environment variables are correctly set when using GGSCI.

Installing GoldenGate on Windows

To download the Oracle GoldenGate software for Windows, go to the following Web URL: http://www.oracle.com/technetwork/middleware/goldengate/downloads/index.html

The GoldenGate image you will download from Oracle will be a compressed zip file. Extract the zip file to the directory that will become the Oracle GoldenGate home directory. To "install" GoldenGate, simply extract the files into the directory where you downloaded the files to. We will provide an example of this in the GoldenGate workshop next.

As with the Linux installs, if you want to test that the install was successful, you can run the GoldenGate Software Command Interpreter (GGSCI) program from the GoldenGate home directory you created. Here is an example:

```
C:\app\oracle\GoldenGate>ggsci
Oracle GoldenGate Command Interpreter for Oracle
Version 11.1.1.1.2 OGGCORE_11.1.1.1.2_PLATFORMS_111004.2100
Windows (optimized), Oracle 11g on Oct  5 2011 00:50:57
Copyright (C) 1995, 2011, Oracle and/or its affiliates. All rights
reserved.
GGSCI (goldengate-one) 1> quit
```

To download the Oracle GoldenGate software for 32-bit Linux, go to the following Web URL: http://edelivery.oracle.com/.

We will discuss the additional configuration of Oracle GoldenGate in Chapter 4, including the creation of directories and other configuration tasks.

Oracle GoldenGate Workshop: *Installing Oracle GoldenGate for Linux*

Workshop Notes

In this workshop we will download and install Oracle GoldenGate for Linux onto our Linux VMs that we created earlier in this chapter. There is no special setup required for this workshop.

Step 1.   Using a Web browser, go to the following Web URL: http://edelivery.oracle .com/. This is the page for the Oracle Software Delivery Cloud. Sign in to the page with your Oracle OTN account. If you do not have one, you will need to create it.

Step 2.   Accept the OTN License Agreement on the page and the export restrictions option. Click Continue to proceed.

Step 3.   The Media Pack Search screen will appear. Under the Select a Product Pack option, select "Oracle Fusion Middleware." Oracle GoldenGate is considered part of Oracle's Fusion Middleware product offerings. Click the Platform option and select Linux X86. Now click Go. An example of the Media Pack Search screen with these options selected is shown in Figure 3-6.

Step 4.   In the Results section of the page, you will find a number of different products offered. You want to find the product that is called Oracle GoldenGate on Oracle <version> Media Pack for Linux x86. You may find more than one of these options. Choose the version that is the more recent and download it. Click the radio button next to that product pack and then click the Continue button.

Step 5.   You will now see a page with several Oracle GoldenGate Media Packs available for download. Select the Download button for the most current version for Oracle Database 11g. The most current version will say something like: "Oracle GoldenGate V11.1.1.1.0 for Oracle 11g on Linux x86." Click Download to download the image. Figure 3-7 provides an example of the download screen.

Create a folder in /home/oracle/app called GoldenGate and download the image called V26188-01.zip to this new directory. This will become our GoldenGate home directory.

Step 6.   Unzip the downloaded file using the **unzip** command as seen here:

```
[oracle@localhost GoldenGate]$ cd /home/oracle/app/GoldenGate
[oracle@localhost GoldenGate]$ unzip ./*.zip
```

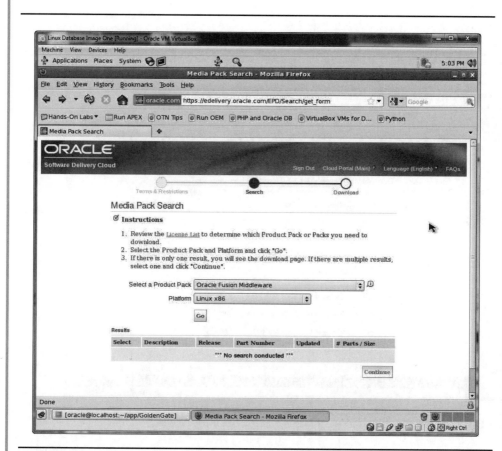

FIGURE 3-6. *The Media Pack Search window*

NOTE
We have not configured the PATH environment yet, so for now we will need to indicate that the zip file, the tar file, and GGSCI are in the current working directory by prefixing each command or file reference with ./ to indicate that the current working directory is the target directory.

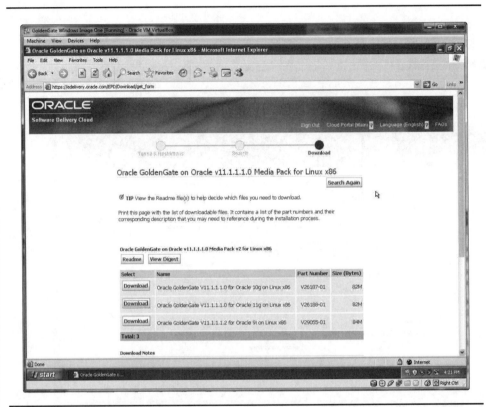

FIGURE 3-7. *Downloading GoldenGate for Linux from the Software Delivery Cloud*

Step 7. Use the **tar** command to extract the files from the tar file we uncompressed in Step 6. Here is an example:

```
[oracle@localhost GoldenGate]$ tar -xvf V26188-01.tar
```

Step 8. Test that the install was successful by starting the GGSCI executable as seen here.

```
[oracle@localhost GoldenGate]$ ./ggsci
Oracle GoldenGate Command Interpreter for Oracle
Version 11.1.1.1 OGGCORE_11.1.1_PLATFORMS_110421.2040
Linux, x86, 32bit (optimized), Oracle 11g on Apr 21 2011 22:38:06
Copyright (C) 1995, 2011, Oracle and/or its affiliates. All
rights reserved.
GGSCI (localhost.localdomain) 1> quit
```

Step 9. Repeat this exercise in the second Linux VM so that both images have GoldenGate installed.

GoldenGate Workshop: *Download and Install Oracle GoldenGate for Windows*

Workshop Notes

In this workshop we will download and install Oracle GoldenGate for Linux onto our Windows VMs that we created earlier in this chapter. There is no special setup required for this workshop, so, on we go.

Step 1. Using a Web browser, go to the following Web URL: http://edelivery.oracle .com/. This is the page for the Oracle Software Delivery Cloud. Sign in to the page with your Oracle OTN account. If you do not have one, you will need to create it.

Step 2. Accept the OTN License Agreement on the page and the Export Restrictions option. Click Continue to proceed.

Step 3. The Media Search Pack screen will appear. Under the Select a Product Pack option, select "Oracle Fusion Middleware." Oracle GoldenGate is considered part of Oracle's Fusion Middleware product offerings. Click the Platform option and select Microsoft Windows (32-bit) (or select the Windows version you installed). Now click Go.

Step 4. In the Results section of the page, you will find a number of different products offered. You want to find the product that is called "Oracle GoldenGate on Oracle GoldenGate on Oracle v11.1.1.1.0 Media Pack for Microsoft Windows (32-bit)." You may find more than one of these options. Choose the version that is the more recent and download it. Click the radio button next to that product pack and then click the Continue button.

Step 5. You will now see a page with several Oracle GoldenGate Media Packs available for download. Select the Download button for the most current version for Oracle Database 11*g*. The most current version will say something like: "Oracle GoldenGate on Oracle v11.1.1.1.0 Media Pack for Microsoft Windows (32-bit)." Click Download to download the image. Save the image to the Oracle GoldenGate home directory. I created c:\app\oracle\GoldenGate as my Oracle GoldenGate directory.

Step 6. To unzip the file you downloaded, open Windows Explorer. Right-click on the zip image and click "Extract." This will extract the GoldenGate files into their correct locations.

Step 7. Test that the install was successful by starting the GGSCI executable as seen here.

```
C:\app\oracle\GoldenGate>ggsci
Oracle GoldenGate Command Interpreter for Oracle
Version 11.1.1.1.2 OGGCORE_11.1.1.1.2_PLATFORMS_111004.2100
Windows (optimized), Oracle 11g on Oct  5 2011 00:50:57
Copyright (C) 1995, 2011, Oracle and/or its affiliates. All
rights reserved.
GGSCI (goldengate-one) 1>
```

Step 8. Repeat these steps on the second Windows VM. You have now completely set up your Windows virtual environments.

CHAPTER
4

Configuring Oracle GoldenGate

We have made good progress thus far! You have created some test environments, or you have identified the ones you want to use. You have downloaded and installed Oracle GoldenGate. Now it's time to do some configuration of Oracle GoldenGate before we can actually use it. That's what this chapter is all about. In this chapter we will provide you with the basic "getting started" information, so that when we move on to the following chapters, many of the things we will discuss will already seem familiar.

This chapter is not designed to walk you step by step through setting up any specific GoldenGate replication architecture. The following chapters in this book will provide you with step-by-step instructions on setting up a large number of replication configurations. In this chapter our objective is to look at each process in the GoldenGate stack individually. We want you to be familiar with the basics of configuring, controlling (starting/stopping), and reporting on those processes before we dive into actually doing GoldenGate replication. This way, when you start working on the next several chapters, you will already have some familiarity with GoldenGate Software Command Interpreter (GGSCI) and also a firm foundation of the parameters you will set, and what they are used for. We won't cover all the GoldenGate processes and related parameters in this chapter as there are a number of them and some of them are platform-specific. We will cover the most commonly used ones, and we will cover any "one-off" parameters in the later chapters.

NOTE
There may be some parameters that we won't cover at all in this book because they are obscure or not commonly used. As always, you should consult the GoldenGate documentation if you need further information on a given parameter and its use on your specific hardware platform.

In this chapter we will also discuss configuring automated startup or restart of Oracle GoldenGate processes. We will also show you where you can find the various files that the Oracle GoldenGate processes create, what those files are for, and why you will want to use them.

This chapter builds heavily on Chapter 2 and the Oracle GoldenGate architecture and processes that are described there. It also depends on Chapter 2 with respect to your understanding of where the different processes fit in the overall data flow associated with Oracle GoldenGate. As a result, if you have not read Chapter 2, or it's been a while, you might want to quickly review or skim Chapter 2.

So, coming up in this chapter will be

- Configuring Oracle GoldenGate after the initial install

- Information to collect before you architect your replication solution

- Configuration and control of the Oracle GoldenGate Manager process

- Configuration and control of the Oracle Extract process

- Configuration and control of the Oracle GoldenGate Data Pump process

- Configuration and control of the Oracle GoldenGate Replicat process

- Automating the startup and restart of GoldenGate processes

The task described in each of these bullet points is really a step toward getting GoldenGate up and running. They are almost checklist items that should be run on any GoldenGate instance or any database running GoldenGate.

Configuring Oracle GoldenGate After the Initial Install

In Chapter 3 we installed Oracle GoldenGate. Now we need to configure it before we can actually do some replication. In this section we will cover the configuration of Oracle GoldenGate after the initial install. First we will configure setting the operating system environment for GoldenGate operations. We will then cover the creation of the GoldenGate Oracle user, which is optional but highly recommended. Finally, we will cover the creation of the Oracle GoldenGate directories. At this time we will also introduce you to the use of GGSCI.

NOTE
It is recommended that any database that will have GoldenGate replication processes running (Extract or Replicat) have its own user configured for GoldenGate to connect to. In this chapter we will just be discussing the Oracle user. See Chapters 12 through 15 for more information on configuring GoldenGate users on the databases covered in those chapters. Also see the Oracle documentation for database user configuration on databases not covered in this book.

Configuring the Operating System Environment for GoldenGate

When installing GoldenGate on various systems, you will want to set the environment variables associated with GoldenGate correctly. In this section we will discuss configuring the operating system environment for GoldenGate. We will discuss setting what we call the GoldenGate home variable, which is something of our own making, but we think it's very important. We will then discuss setting the operating system PATH variable and, finally, the shared library path environment variable.

The GoldenGate Home Environment Variable

The GoldenGate home environment variable (I often call it GGHOME) is an environment variable I like to set that allows me to quickly navigate to the GoldenGate home directory. Note that there is no mention of a GoldenGate home (unlike, say ORACLE_HOME) in the GoldenGate documentation; it's just our contention that it's a good practice to define it. Setting this variable makes it easy to change into the GoldenGate home directory. Typically this variable would be set in the .bashrc, .bash_profile, or similar file on the Oracle owning account when using Linux. You will see us using $GGHOME often in this book as we have it set in our environments.

If you have many Oracle GoldenGate instances installed, you may want to create a script that allows you to change the setting for the GGHOME parameter, as well as the other parameters you have to set for GoldenGate operations. Another option is to create different parameters for each instance of GoldenGate, like GGHOME1 and GGHOME2. Running many instances of GoldenGate can be confusing, so you will want to be careful that your environment is pointing to the right one.

In Windows you can add environment variables by right-clicking My Computer | Properties. From there you will find the Systems Properties window. From the Systems Properties window, click the Advanced tab. From here you will see the Environment Variables window. You can add the new environment variables from the Environment Variables window.

The OS PATH Environment Variable

When configuring our system for GoldenGate operations, we also need to make sure that the system's PATH environment points to the correct location of the Oracle GoldenGate software home location where GoldenGate was installed. Typically, you would configure this path for the Oracle user. In Linux you might edit the .profile or .bash_profile files in the home of the operating system Oracle user.

In Windows you can change the path by right-clicking My Computer |
Properties. From there you will find the Systems Properties window. From the
Systems Properties window, you click the Advanced tab. From here you will see the
Environment Variables window. From the System Variables window at the bottom of
the Environment Variables window, you can find the PATH variable. You would then
click the Edit button to add the newly created GoldenGate home to the PATH and
then save your changes.

The GoldenGate Shared Library Environment Variable

If you are running on Linux, you will want to set the shared library path to the
location of the GoldenGate shared libraries. The shared library path is LD_LIBRARY_
PATH in Sun, HP Tru64, and Linux. The library path is LIBPATH in IBM variants (AIX
and z/OS) and SHLIB in HP-UX. To modify the library path, edit the profile file for
the Oracle owning account. For example, in Linux we might edit the .bash_profile
file and change LD_LIBRARY_PATH to point to the lib directory in the GoldenGate
home directory and to the ORACLE_HOME shared library locations. Setting the
shared library path, coupled with configuring the PATH environment correctly, will
allow you to execute the GGSCI command from within any directory location and
execute GoldenGate commands easily. Without setting these path variables, you
would need to change into the GoldenGate software home directory.

Configuring Memory for GoldenGate

As we have discussed in previous chapters, GoldenGate does need memory. You
need to make sure that your system has sufficient memory available for GoldenGate
to run. The more memory you have, the better GoldenGate is going to run,
especially the Extract processes. If you don't have enough memory allocated to
GoldenGate, your system will start paging to disk, which can cause all sorts of
problems.

While this is a book about Oracle GoldenGate, it's also important to make sure
that you have allocated memory to your Oracle database properly. Allocating
insufficient memory can impact database performance; almost any beginning DBA
understands that. Allocating too much memory is something that DBAs don't always
think about. When you start adding GoldenGate to your database server, make it a
habit to validate that you have not overallocated memory to your Oracle databases.
You can check this by looking at the various memory advisors that are accessed
through Advanced Workload Repository (AWR) reports or using Oracle Enterprise
Manager (OEM). You will want to check both the system global area (SGA) memory
allocations and program global area (PGA) memory allocations and make sure that
they are in-line. If you have allocated too much memory, consider releasing some of
it back to the OS so that GoldenGate can use it.

With respect to how much memory to allocate to GoldenGate processes, the basic Oracle guidelines say to plan on 25 to 55MB of memory for each Extract or Replicat process. I'd calculate on the high side just to be safe. The OS must also have sufficient swap space available for Extract and Replicat processes. In general you can expect that each process will need between 4 and 10GB of swap space available. Some will need more or less, of course. You can tell for sure by looking at the report files for each of the processes. In the report file, you will find a line that reads PROCESS VM AVAIL FROM OS (min). This is the minimum amount of swap space that is required by that specific process. You can then add up all these amounts from the different Extract and Replicat processes running on your system. I'd add a fudge factor (say, a factor of 1.20) to that amount. Of course, this last method can only be used once you have set up the Extract and Replicat processes. Kind of like closing the barn doors after the horse has gone if you ask me, but there you go.

NOTE
Keep in mind that certain kinds of operations can cause GoldenGate to use extreme amounts of memory. For example, if you have large amounts of data changes with few or no commits during those changes, then GoldenGate will store all those changes in memory until the transaction commits. This can lead to large amounts of memory being used on the operating system, and potentially large amounts of paging activity.

Configuring the Oracle Database GoldenGate User

Each GoldenGate process will need to connect to the database that it will be operating on. For example, the Extract process will need to connect to the database to manage the extraction of transactional data (though the actual extraction of redo is done via the log file), and the Replicat process will need to be able to connect to the database to manage the replication process on that database.

To create the user, connect to the database with a user that has DBA privileges, and use the **create user** command to create the GoldenGate administrative user, as seen here:

```
[oracle@goldengate1 ~]$ sqlplus / as sysdba
SQL*Plus: Release 11.1.0.7.0 - Production on Sun Dec 18 14:47:20 2011
Copyright (c) 1982, 2008, Oracle.  All rights reserved.
Connected to:
Oracle Database 11g Enterprise Edition Release 11.2.0.2.0 - Production
With the Partitioning, OLAP, Data Mining and Real Application Testing options

SQL> create user ggadmin identified by ggadmin;
User created.
```

Now, we need to grant the appropriate privileges to the user we just created. It is not uncommon for administrators to just grant DBA privileges to the GoldenGate administration account in an effort to ease the administrative burden of correctly determining the correct privileges to grant. We strongly advise against just granting DBA privileges to the GoldenGate administrative user because this is a significant security issue. We are strong believers in the minimal approach to granting privileges; only those that are needed are granted.

The privileges we will grant are determined by the Oracle GoldenGate processes (such as Extract and Replicat) that will connect to the database user. Tables 4-1, 4-2, and 4-3 provide the list of privileges that you will need to assign to the GoldenGate administration account based on the type of processes (Extract, Replicat) that will be running. Use the following lists of privileges to correctly configure security for the GoldenGate administrator.

NOTE
These privileges are specific to Oracle Database 11.2.0.2. Refer to the Oracle GoldenGate documentation for additional privileges that might be required by earlier versions of Oracle Database.

Privilege Name	Description
Alter any table	This privilege is not listed in the Oracle GoldenGate documentation but is required to execute certain operations including enabling supplemental logging.

TABLE 4-1. *Privilege Required to Enable Supplemental Logging from GGSCI*

Privilege Name	Description
Delete privilege on Oracle GoldenGate DDL objects	This would be the Delete privilege on any object that GoldenGate might need to execute DDL operations on.

TABLE 4-2. *Privilege Required by the Manager Process*

Privilege Name	Comments
Grant Oracle Streams administration privileges	Run the package dbms_goldengate_auth.grant_admin_privilege('user_name') from a DBA privileged account. The user_name is the name of the user you are creating.
Create session	Required privilege.
Alter session	Required privilege.
Resource	Required privilege.
Connect	Required privilege.
Select any dictionary	Required privilege.
Flashback any table	Alternative syntax is flashback on <owner.table_name>.
Select any table	Alternative syntax is select on <owner.table_name>.
Select on DBA_CLUSTERS	Required privilege.
Execute on dbms_flashback package	Provides access to the Oracle SCN.
Grant gss_gguser_role	Only needed if DDL replication is installed.
Access to Oracle ASM privileges (SYSDBA)	Required if you are using ASM. In this case, the Oracle GoldenGate user will need SYSDBA privileges. See Chapter 11 for more details on GoldenGate and ASM operation.
Sys.dbms_internal_clkm	Required if you want to replicate objects that are encrypted with Oracle Transparent Data Encryption (TDE).
Select any transaction	This allows the Extract process to use newer ASM APIs. See the Oracle GoldenGate documentation for more details if you don't want to grant this privilege.

TABLE 4-3. *Privileges Required by the Extract Process*

Privilege Name	Description
Grant Oracle Streams administration privileges	Run the package dbms_goldengate_auth.grant_admin_ privilege('user_name'). The user_name is the name of the user you are creating.
Create session	Required privilege.
Alter session	Required privilege.
Resource	Required privilege.
Connect	Required privilege.
Select any dictionary	Required privilege.
Select any table	Alternative syntax is select on <owner.table_name>.
Insert, delete, update on target tables	Required privilege.
Create table	Required if using add checkpoint table to enable database checkpoint feature.
Any privilege for DDL operations	Required if DDL replication is enabled.
Lock any table	Required if using GoldenGate initial load method using SQL*Loader for direct bulk load.

TABLE 4-4. *Privileges Required by the Replicat Process*

Configuring the GoldenGate User Privileges Example

The following code snippets provide an example of configuring an Oracle database for the different Oracle GoldenGate processes:

```
-- connect to a privileged DBA user
Connect / as sysdba
-- Configure for all users
Grant connect to ggadmin;

-- Configure to allow for add trandata
Grant alter any table to ggadmin;
```

```
-- Configure for Extract processes. We are going to assume you're
-- replicating the-- Scott.emp table.
Exec dbms_goldengate_auth.grant_admin_privilege('GGADMIN');
Grant create session to ggadmin;
grant alter session to ggadmin;
Grant resource to ggadmin;
Grant connect to ggadmin;
Grant select any dictionary to ggadmin;
Grant flashback any table to ggadmin;
Grant select any table to ggadmin;
-- Alternative is grant select on scott.emp to ggadmin;
Grant select on dba_clusters to ggadmin;
Grant execute on dbms_flashback to ggadmin;
-- no DDL replication at this time.

-- Configure for Replicat processes.
-- We are going to assume you're replicating the scott.emp table.
-- This would be run on the target database.
Exec dbms_goldengate_auth.grant_admin_privilege('ggadmin');
Grant create session to ggadmin;
grant alter session to ggadmin;
Grant resource to ggadmin;
Grant connect to ggadmin;
Grant select any dictionary to ggadmin;
Grant select any table to ggadmin;
Grant insert, delete, update on scott.emp to ggadmin;
Grant create table to ggadmin;
-- no DDL operations for now.
Grant lock any table to ggadmin;
```

Configuring for DDL Replication

Oracle GoldenGate will not only replicate Data Manipulation Language (DML) (data) operations but will also replicate DDL operations. This is not the default configuration for GoldenGate, and it requires additional configuration to accommodate DDL replication. In this book, we will always assume that you have configured DDL replication.

When installing Oracle GoldenGate DDL replication, there are several steps, as follows:

1. Determine the schema that you want to use to store the Oracle GoldenGate objects that will be created. GoldenGate DDL replication requires the creation of several objects (which we will discuss in the next section). We recommend that you use the GoldenGate administrator account to keep things simple.

2. Determine which tablespace to create the GoldenGate DDL replication objects in. We recommend that you create a tablespace just for the use of the GoldenGate objects. Ensure that this tablespace has sufficient space to load those objects into it. Consider that if this tablespace fills up, DDL operations in the database that are being replicated will be suspended and the applications calling them will freeze. The space required is dependent on the amount of DDL that occurs. High DDL activity will cause the GGS_ DDL_HIST table to grow in the tablespace.

In our case, we will create a tablespace called GGTBS and allocate 10MB to it initially and allow it to grow 10MB at a time up to a size of 100MB. We will then grant the GGADMIN user unlimited quota to that tablespace:

```
create tablespace GGTBS
datafile '/home/oracle/app/oracle/oradata/orcl/ggtbs01.dbf' size 10m
autoextend on next 10m maxsize 100m;

alter user GGADMIN quota unlimited on GGTBS;
```

1. Add the GSSSCHEMA parameter to the GLOBALS parameter file (you probably will need to create the file). You will use the GGSCI interface to set this parameter. The value of this parameter should be set to the schema where you will install the GoldenGate DDL replication objects. In our case we will set GGSCHEMA to a value of GGADMIN. Here is an example of starting to edit the GLOBALS parameter file and then the actual content we will add. (Note that this is a Linux example. Windows users would use a Windows editor such as Notepad.)

    ```
    GGSCI (goldengate1) 13> edit params ./GLOBALS
    <pressed i to insert>
    GGSCHEMA ggadmin
    <pressed wq! To write and exit the vi editor>
    ```

2. Change to the Oracle GoldenGate install directory.

3. If you are installing DDL replication on a version of Oracle Database 10*g* or later, you will need to disable the recycle bin. This is done by setting the parameter RECYCLEBIN to a value of OFF (this is a hidden parameter in Oracle Database Version 10.1). You can use the **alter system** command to disable the RECYCLEBIN as seen in this example:

    ```
    Alter system set recyclebin=OFF deferred;
    ```

4. There should be no activity on the database during the install process. You may want to shut down the database and reopen it in restricted mode. If you do this, you will need to grant the **restricted session** privilege to the GoldenGate administration account as seen here:

```
grant restricted session to ggadmin;
```

5. Using SQL*Plus, log in to the database using the SYSADM privilege.

```
Sqlplus sys/password as sysdba
```

6. Run the script marker_setup.sql. The script will request the name of the GoldenGate user account.

```
SQL>@marker_setup
```

7. Run the script ddl_setup.sql. You will be prompted to do the following:

   ■ Enter the name of the GoldenGate administration schema.

   ■ Enter the installation mode. For first-time installs, you will use the INITIALSETUP mode.

```
SQL>@ddl_setup.sql
```

8. Run the script role_seup.sql. You will be prompted to do the following:

   ■ Enter the name of the GoldenGate administration schema.

```
SQL>@role_setup.sql
```

9. You use the **grant** command to grant the role that was created in step 8 to all schemas that will be involved in GoldenGate Extract process operations.

```
Grant ggs_ggsuser_role to scott;
```

10. Run the script ddl_enable.sql to enable the trigger that GoldenGate uses to track DDL operations.

```
SQL>@ddl_enable.sql
```

Oracle is now ready to replicate DDL operations along with DML operations. You can now configure the Extract processes with the DDLOPTIONS parameter to control DDL replication for that Extract process. We will discuss the specifics of configuration for DDL replication, including mapping and filtering, in detail throughout the chapters of this book.

Configuring to Support Oracle Sequences

If you are running Oracle GoldenGate Version 11.1.1.1 and later, you will want to install a script that adds additional functionality with respect to Oracle sequences.

In some cases, during the initial instantiation of the target database, you will issue the GoldenGate command **flush sequence**. To support this new command and new functionality, you need to run a script called sequence.sql on both the source and target database. This sequence.sql script is available in the GoldenGate install medium or in the root GoldenGate directory.

Configuring the GoldenGate Directories and Using GGSCI

Now that we have configured the GoldenGate administrative database account, we need to finalize the Oracle GoldenGate configuration by having GoldenGate create its directories. The directories that will be created are the ones we first mentioned in Chapter 2. These are the directories that by default will store the GoldenGate trail files, log file, and other GoldenGate files. These directories will be created under the GoldenGate home for the GoldenGate instance that you are connected to. Creating the directories is as easy as logging in to GGSCI and issuing the **create subdirs** command, as seen in this example:

```
[oracle@goldengate1 ~]$ ggsci
Oracle GoldenGate Command Interpreter for Oracle
Version 11.1.1.1 OGGCORE_11.1.1_PLATFORMS_110421.2040
Linux, x86, 32bit (optimized), Oracle 11g on Apr 21 2011 22:38:06
Copyright (C) 1995, 2011, Oracle and/or its affiliates. All rights reserved.

GGSCI (goldengate1) 1> create subdirs
Creating subdirectories under current directory /home/oracle

Parameter files                  /home/oracle/dirprm: created
Report files                     /home/oracle/dirrpt: created
Checkpoint files                 /home/oracle/dirchk: created
Process status files             /home/oracle/dirpcs: created
SQL script files                 /home/oracle/dirsql: created
Database definitions files       /home/oracle/dirdef: created
Extract data files               /home/oracle/dirdat: created
Temporary files                  /home/oracle/dirtmp: created
Veridata files                   /home/oracle/dirver: created
Veridata Lock files              /home/oracle/dirver/lock: created
Veridata Out-Of-Sync files       /home/oracle/dirver/oos: created
Veridata Out-Of-Sync XML files   /home/oracle/dirver/oosxml: created
Veridata Parameter files         /home/oracle/dirver/params: created
Veridata Report files            /home/oracle/dirver/report: created
Veridata Status files            /home/oracle/dirver/status: created
Veridata Trace files             /home/oracle/dirver/trace: created
Stdout files                     /home/oracle/dirout: created

GGSCI (goldengate1) 2>
```

You can see in the preceding listing the different directories that are created, and GoldenGate even nicely tells you what those directories are for (as do we in Chapter 2 and throughout this book).

Information to Collect Before You Architect Your Replication Solution

As with anything else, the devil is in the details. Therefore, it's a really, really, really good idea to plan your GoldenGate architecture before you start building and configuring things. It's also a good idea to plan what you're going to do, when and where, before you start doing it. In this section we will discuss the following:

■ Information you will need to collect before you start

■ Things that will make your life a lot easier

Information You Will Need to Collect Before You Start

Before you start, you will want to decide several things. We actually recommend a checklist like the one seen in Table 4-5. This checklist assumes you will be following the GoldenGate best practices.

Checklist Item Number	Description	Results
1	Check basic network connectivity between the source machine and all target machines.	Success/Failure
2	List location of GoldenGate home.	
3	List source database server name and IP address(es).	
4	List source database hardware.	
5	List source database OS and OS version.	
6	Is the source database 32- or 64-bit?	
7	List the source database name.	

TABLE 4-5.   *Oracle GoldenGate Preimplementation Checklist* (continued)

Checklist Item Number	Description	Results
8	List the source database version.	
9	Is the database in ARCHIVELOG mode?	Database must be in ARCHIVELOG mode.
10	Is supplemental logging enabled?	Yes/No
11	List the number of Extract processes.	
12	List the names of Extract processes.	
13	Local trail file?	Yes/No If Yes, local trail file name:
14	List the size of the trail file.	
15	List schema/tables to be replicated (wildcards allowed).	
16	What kind of replication? (for example: basic one-way replication, cascade replication, master-master replication).	
17	Are you going to use GoldenGate Data Pump?	Yes/No
18	List the server that Data Pump will run on (typically the source database server).	
19	What will be the Data Pump process name?	
20	Will I need to replicate DDL?	Yes/No
21	Will any column mappings be required?	Yes/No
22	Will any data transformations be required?	Yes/No
23	Determine the port number to be used between the GoldenGate Database Data Pump and the different Replicat processes that will be used.	Port number:
24	Determine how you wish to instantiate the GoldenGate target database(s).	Instantiation method will be:
25	Do any tables in these schemas lack primary keys?	Yes/No
26	Are there any high-usage tables that might benefit from their own Extract/Replicat processes?	Yes/No

TABLE 4-5. *Oracle GoldenGate Preimplementation Checklist* (continued)

Checklist Item Number	Description	Results
27	If you are considering parallelism Extract/Replicat, are there any tables related by foreign keys?	Yes/No
28	Are there triggers that need to be dealt with in the schemas to be replicated?	Yes/No
29	Are there any cascading delete constraints that need to be disabled?	Yes/No
30	List target database server name(s) and IP address(es).	
31	List target database server hardware.	
32	List target database OS and OS version.	
33	Is the target database 32- or 64-bit?	
34	List the target database name(s).	
35	List the number of Replicat processes.	
36	List the Replicat process names.	
37	List the schema(s) you are replicating to.	
38	List the method you will use to instantiate the target database(s).	

TABLE 4-5.   *Oracle GoldenGate Preimplementation Checklist*

Preparing Your Systems for Operation

Before you start configuring GoldenGate, you should make sure that the systems that GoldenGate is going to operate are properly configured. You will want to make sure that you check the following:

- Check the ports you identified earlier in the section titled "Information You Will Need to Collect Before You Start" and make sure that they are not blocked by firewalls. If they are, you will need to open those ports.

- Check the network connectivity between the source and target machines and make sure that it works successfully. You can do this in various ways including using the ping utility or connecting between the various systems using telnet or ssh.

- Ensure that the source and target databases are of compatible versions.

- Ensure that all of the data types on the source database are supported by Oracle GoldenGate.

Configuration of the Oracle Database for GoldenGate Operations

Before you can start Oracle GoldenGate replication from your database, you need to ensure that your database is properly configured. In this section we will address some database configuration items you need to consider before GoldenGate replication can begin. These topics will include:

- Putting the database in ARCHIVELOG mode

- Configuring the database for flashback queries

- GoldenGate and primary keys

- Deferred constraints

- Verify that the database has supplemental logging enabled

- Configuring the GLOBALS parameter file

Putting the Database in ARCHIVELOG Mode

First, your database will need to be in ARCHIVELOG mode. When Oracle Database is in ARCHIVELOG mode, Oracle will create copies of the online redo logs, called archived redo logs. While Oracle GoldenGate Extract processes will typically read the transactional data from the online redo logs, there may be cases where Oracle GoldenGate will need to read this transactional data from the archived redo logs. You can determine if your database is in ARCHIVELOG mode by issuing the following query:

```
SQL> select log_mode from v$database;

LOG_MODE
------------
NOARCHIVELOG
```

If you find the database is in NOARCHIVELOG mode, as in this example, you will need to follow these steps to put the database in ARCHIVELOG mode:

1. Configure the appropriate parameters for ARCHIVELOG mode. In Oracle Database 11g Release 2 and later, you would typically configure the parameters for the Fast Recovery Area (FRA), which include:

   a. DB_RECOVERY_FILE_DEST

   b. DB_RECOVERY_FILE_DEST_SIZE

   You can use the **show parameter** command to check the value of these parameters. You can use the **alter system** command to change the values of these parameters if needed. Here is an example of checking the value of the parameters with the **show parameter** command:

   ```
   SQL> show parameter recover

   NAME                            TYPE         VALUE
   --------------------- ----------- -------------------------------
   db_recovery_file_dest           string       /home/oracle/
   app/oracle/flash_

                                                 recovery_area
   db_recovery_file_dest_size      big integer 3852M
   ```

2. Shut down the database with the **shutdown immediate** command. Do not use the **shutdown abort** command because Oracle will not allow you to put the database in ARCHIVELOG mode if the last shutdown was not a consistent shutdown. If you must do a **shutdown abort,** then you should perform a **startup restrict,** and then a **shutdown immediate** afterwards to ensure that your database is shut down cleanly.

3. Mount the database with the **startup mount** command.

4. Put the database in ARCHIVELOG mode with the **alter database archivelog** command.

5. Open the database with the **alter database open** command.

   Here is an example of putting our database in ARCHIVELOG mode:

```
SQL> shutdown immediate
Database closed.
Database dismounted.
ORACLE instance shut down.
SQL> startup mount
ORACLE instance started.
Total System Global Area  456146944 bytes
```

```
Fixed Size                       1344840 bytes
Variable Size                  381684408 bytes
Database Buffers                67108864 bytes
Redo Buffers                     6008832 bytes
Database mounted.
SQL> alter database archivelog;
Database altered.
SQL> alter database open;
Database altered.
```

NOTE
Yes... Technically you can run Oracle GoldenGate replication without the database being in ARCHIVELOG mode. However, this is considered a worst practice and we are not about to suggest you do it. Why? Because as soon as a gap in the redo occurs and the Extract process needs the redo that would have been in those archived redo log files, you're going to have all sorts of problems and likely you will have to reinstantiate your target databases.

Configure the Database for Flashback Queries

When you saw this section on flashback queries, you might have checked the front cover of this book wondering if you did, indeed, have a book on Oracle GoldenGate. We would not blame you if you wondered why you needed to be concerned about flashback queries when using Oracle GoldenGate. While it's true that the GoldenGate Extract process uses the redo logs of the Oracle database to collect the changes that occur in the database, there are times when GoldenGate actually queries the database to completely process the changes that have occurred. GoldenGate will access the Oracle database for the following types of data:

- Large Objects (LOBs; only with Oracle Database versions before Oracle Database Version 10g)

- User-defined tables

- Nested tables

- XMLType objects

When configuring your database for GoldenGate operations, you will need to consider that GoldenGate does use flashback query in the cases mentioned in the preceding list. The parameter UNDO_RETENTION controls how long (in seconds) undo is stored in the Undo tablespace, as long as sufficient space is available in the Undo tablespace. You should modify the parameter UNDO_RETENTION to a value that will ensure that the undo will be retained long enough for GoldenGate to use it. You can use the V$UNDOSTAT table to monitor undo utilization and adjust the UNDO_RETENTION parameter accordingly. You will also want to ensure you have allocated sufficient space to the UNDO tablespace to make sure that the UNDO records will be maintained, and will not be aged out prior to the expiration of the UNDO_RETENTION period. Here is an example of querying the database for the current value of the UNDO_RETENTION parameter, and then an example of changing the value from the default value of 900 seconds (15 minutes) to a value of 1800 seconds (30 minutes):

```
SQL> show parameter undo_retention

NAME                               TYPE         VALUE
---------------------------    -----------    ---------------------------
undo_retention
integer      900

SQL> alter system set undo_retention=1800;
System altered.
```

GoldenGate and Primary Keys

Oracle GoldenGate replication requires that individual rows in a table can be identified uniquely (sounds strangely like a ROWID, does it not?). This rule provides a way to match up the row on the source table and the row on the target tables for change application. Identification of a unique row is done in one of three ways:

- Using the primary key
- Using a unique key
- Combining all the columns of the table together to form a very large unique key

GoldenGate has a preference for the use of primary keys. So if a primary key and unique keys are both available, GoldenGate will use the primary key. GoldenGate cannot use primary keys that are defined but not enabled or not validated. In these cases, GoldenGate will try to use a unique key, or it will generate a pseudo-primary key from all the columns of the table.

If a primary key has not been created at all, GoldenGate will use a defined unique key. If there are multiple unique keys, GoldenGate will use them in alpha order with a preference for unique keys that do not contain NULLable columns in them.

GoldenGate cannot use unique keys that contain function-based indexes, virtual columns, or user-defined types (UDTs).

Finally, if the table lacks any kind of primary or unique key, GoldenGate will happily use all the columns (with some exceptions such as columns with LOBs) of the table to create one big huge primary key. Just the idea of this should make you cringe. Using all the columns of the table as the key is definitely not preferred and should be avoided for many reasons. Combining all the columns of a table into one large key can significantly increase the size of the data being replicated over the network significantly. This can result in degraded performance and increases in latency between the time the change takes place on the source system and the time it's actually applied on the target system.

So, the bottom line of all of this information is that it's best if your tables have validated primary keys associated with them. In some cases you might have a table to be replicated that does not have a primary key or unique key defined for a specific reason. These kinds of situations are sometimes found in operational data stores or data warehouses. Often in these cases there may well be a natural key available for GoldenGate to use. In these cases you should use the KEYCOLS parameter to define the natural key that GoldenGate should use. The KEYCOLS parameter is used along with the TABLES parameter in the Extract process. The KEYCOLS parameter and the MAP parameter are used in the Replicat process. We will show you examples of how to do this in later chapters of this book.

If a target table truly does not have a primary or unique key defined, then it's possible that duplicate rows will exist. In this case, a given change from the source database may impact many rows, causing possible performance problems. You can use the Replicat parameter DBOPTIONIS with the LIMITROWS option to limit the total number of rows that will be changed in the target when a change is processed.

NOTE
We have mentioned some GoldenGate parameters in this chapter before we have really discussed what the parameters are, how they are changed, or what they are for. This is kind of a chicken-and-the-egg sort of thing, but we really needed to add the references to parameters here. We will discuss setting parameters for the various Oracle GoldenGate processes later in this chapter and others in great detail.

Dealing with Deferred Constraints

Normally, database constraints are checked when a SQL statement is executed. Take a case where we issue an **insert** statement to insert data into a child table called

EMP_PAYROLL. Assume that the employee ID (EMPID) column of EMP_PAYROLL has a foreign key constraint referencing the EMPID column in a parent table called EMP. Because the constraint is there, whenever someone inserts a value into the EMPID column of the EMP_PAYROLL table, Oracle will make sure that there is a matching value in the EMPID column of the EMP table. This check, by default, takes place immediately when the **insert** occurs. This might be a problem for an application that will insert the child records before it inserts the parent records in a given transaction.

To deal with the problem of out-of-order parent/child record inserts, you can define constraints as deferred. Deferred constraints will not be validated until the transaction is committed. Thus, within the transaction you can freely insert child records first and then parent records, assuming that the constraints associated with those tables and columns are set to be deferrable.

If you are using deferred constraints on the source system, typically they are set to a state of deferrable. This means the constraint will not automatically be deferred, but you have to set it to be deferred with the SQL command alter session set constraint deferred. GoldenGate can deal with deferred constraints in a few ways. First you can configure the Replicat process so that it will set all constraints to a status of deferred by using the **sqlexec** command along with the appropriate **alter session** command to set constraints as deferred, as seen in this example:

```
SQLEXEC ("alter session set constraint deferred")
```

You can also use the DBOPTIONS parameter with the DEFERRCONST option in the GoldenGate parameter file if you prefer.

Verify That the Database Has Supplemental Logging Enabled

As you know, the Oracle database logs all changes that occur in the database in the online redo logs. Normally the things that are stored in the online redo logs are the ROWID of the row being changed, and the new values for the column or columns (there is other information stored, of course, but this is the important part!). This level of change-related redo information is all Oracle needs to be able to reconstruct a database during recovery since the database ROWIDs on a database being restored remain consistent.

Because the Oracle ROWIDs in the source and target databases are going to be different, additional redo log information is required to be able to match up the rows being changed in the source and target databases. The additional information that is required in the online redo logs is the values of a column or set of columns that uniquely identify the row being changed, such as the primary key of the table. You enable the recording of these values in the Oracle redo logs by enabling a feature called supplemental logging. You only need to enable supplemental logging on a database where the Extract processes will be running (source databases).

When supplemental logging is enabled, then Oracle will record one of the following values within the online redo logs along with any column that has been changed:

- The primary key of the table

- A unique key of the table

- All columns of the table (with some exceptions)

Within Oracle GoldenGate, there are two different kinds of supplemental logging that we will be configuring. Note that these are kinds of GoldenGate supplemental logging, not Oracle Database Supplemental Logging Groups. When we enable these types of GoldenGate supplemental logging methods, GoldenGate will interact with the database and enable the required table-level supplemental logging as required. The following types of GoldenGate supplemental logging are available:

- Schema-level supplemental logging

- Object-specific supplemental logging

Note that Oracle GoldenGate does require that database-level supplemental logging be enabled at the database level in addition to enabling the GoldenGate supplemental logging of specific objects. Let's look at these two different requirements: enabling database supplemental logging from the Oracle database and then enabling either schema-level or object-level logging from GoldenGate.

Enable Minimal Database Supplemental Logging

You can determine if the database is configured for supplemental logging by querying the V$DATABASE database view column SUPPLEMENTAL_LOG_DATA_MIN, as seen here:

```
SQL> select supplemental_log_data_min from v$database;

SUPPLEME
--------
NO
```

In this case, supplemental logging is not enabled. We need to enable supplemental logging at the database level, which we will do using the **alter database add supplemental log data** command, as seen in the following example:

```
SQL> alter database add supplemental log data;

Database altered.

SQL> select supplemental_log_data_min from v$database;

SUPPLEME
--------
YES
```

Enable Schema-Level or Object-Level Supplemental Logging

In addition to database-level supplemental logging, Oracle also has Supplemental Logging Log Groups. These logging groups are recorded in the database as constraints and are created on a table-by-table basis. Oracle GoldenGate uses Oracle Supplemental Logging Log Groups to support GoldenGate replication. Each object, or the schema that the object resides in, will have to be configured within GoldenGate for supplemental logging either at a schema level or at an object level. Schema-level supplemental logging is required if you will be doing DDL replication. If you will not be doing DDL replication, then object-level supplemental logging may be used instead. Oracle recommends that you enable schema-level logging as a best practice as long as the additional data being put into the redo logs does not impact the replication process.

NOTE
At the time that this book was written, the most current version of Oracle GoldenGate required that you install a patch to Oracle Database (patch number 10423000) before you use schema-level logging (see the documentation for your version of GoldenGate for more information). If you do not have Oracle support, then you will not have access to the patch to download it.

*The use of **schematrandata** is a best practice when using DDL logging. Because of the requirement for the database patch, and the possibility that you will not be able to download or install the patch on your system, most of our examples in this book will use object-level logging via the **add trandata** command instead of the **add schematrandata** command.*

Enabling schema- or object-level supplemental logging is done from GGSCI using the GoldenGate commands **add schematrandata {schema_name}** for schema-level supplemental logging or **add trandata {schema_name.object_name}** for object-level supplemental logging. For example, if we wanted to replicate the EMP table in the SCOTT schema, we would start GGSCI, and log in to the database using the **dblogin** command. We could then decide to use either the **add schematrandata** command or the **add trandata** commands to enable supplemental logging of objects. Here is an example of using the **add schematrandata** command to enable supplemental logging on the SCOTT schema:

```
#need to set your Oracle environment first. ORACLE_SID, etc...
[oracle@goldengate1 ~]$ cd /home/oracle/app/GoldenGate
[oracle@goldengate1 GoldenGate]$ ggsci
Oracle GoldenGate Command Interpreter for Oracle
Version 11.1.1.1 OGGCORE_11.1.1_PLATFORMS_110421.2040
Linux, x86, 32bit (optimized), Oracle 11g on Apr 21 2011 22:38:06
Copyright (C) 1995, 2011, Oracle and/or its affiliates. All rights
reserved.

GGSCI (goldengate1) 1> dblogin userid ggadmin password ggadmin
Successfully logged into database.
GGSCI (goldengate1) 2> add schematrandata SCOTT
```

Here is an alternative example where we use the **add trandata** command (**add trandata scott.emp**) to enable supplemental logging on the SCOTT.EMP table:

```
#need to set your Oracle environment first. ORACLE_SID, etc...
[oracle@goldengate1 ~]$ cd /home/oracle/app/GoldenGate
[oracle@goldengate1 GoldenGate]$ ggsci
Oracle GoldenGate Command Interpreter for Oracle
Version 11.1.1.1 OGGCORE_11.1.1_PLATFORMS_110421.2040
Linux, x86, 32bit (optimized), Oracle 11g on Apr 21 2011 22:38:06
Copyright (C) 1995, 2011, Oracle and/or its affiliates. All rights
reserved.

GGSCI (goldengate1) 1> dblogin userid ggadmin password ggadmin
Successfully logged into database.
GGSCI (goldengate1) 2> add trandata scott.emp
Logging of supplemental redo data enabled for table SCOTT.EMP.
```

NOTE
*If you get an error when running the **add trandata** command, make sure that you have the correct permissions set including permissions to issue the **alter table** command.*

The **add trandata** command when used against an Oracle database is the equivalent of issuing the following **alter table** command:

```
Alter table scott.emp add supplemental log group ggs_emp_12345 (empid)
  always;
```

Obviously the command will have different implementations on non-Oracle database platforms.

Note that with the GGSCI command **add trandata**, you could use a wildcard character * (we affectionately call this one "splat") to cover a number of different objects. For example, if we wanted to enable supplemental redo logging for all tables in the SCOTT schema, we could have issued the GGSCI command this way:

```
GGSCI (goldengate1) 3> add trandata scott.*
```

NOTE
Don't forget that object-level and schema-level supplemental logging are not the same thing. You must use schema-level supplemental logging if you will be doing DDL replication.

Configuring the GLOBALS Parameter File

It is not often that you need to configure the GLOBALS parameter file within GoldenGate. The GLOBALS parameter file controls various settings across the entire GoldenGate instance. You might use the GLOBALS parameter file if you are configuring the GoldenGate Manager process as a Windows service (which we will discuss later in this chapter) or to change various default, instance-related, values.

The GLOBALS parameter file is contained in the GoldenGate home directory. You can edit the GLOBALS parameter file with a regular text file or with the GGSCI command-line interface to GoldenGate using the **edit params ./GLOBALS** command or with your favorite text editor. As we said, there are few times you need to actually have a GLOBALS parameter file. As we come across those cases in this book, we will configure the GLOBALS parameter file as a part of the text.

Configuration and Administration of the Oracle GoldenGate Manager Process

In the process of designing the outline of this book, we debated where to discuss the configuration of the GoldenGate Manager process. Generally the GoldenGate Manager process is almost global in nature, and in this respect it seemed to belong in this chapter. However, there are specific occasions where you might need to modify the Manager process configuration as a part of implementing a specific replication topology. In these cases it made sense to put it in the later chapters of the book as we demonstrate the implementation of the various forms of GoldenGate replication.

So...We discussed the Oracle GoldenGate Manager process in Chapter 2. Recall that the Oracle GoldenGate Manager process is responsible for managing all the GoldenGate processes and operations within a given GoldenGate instance, so it's a pretty important process. This includes the Extract, Data Pump, and Replicat processes. In this section we will discuss the configuration of the Oracle GoldenGate Manager process. Next we will discuss the administration of the GoldenGate Manager process, which is just a fancy way of saying we will show you how to stop and start the process. Then we will do something, and you will think we read your mind. At some point in time as you start to deploy Oracle GoldenGate, you're going to ask, "How do I get this thing to start automatically when the server reboots?" Well, we answer that question at the end of this section with some example scripts for Linux that will start up all Oracle GoldenGate processes configured for automatic startup, and also we will discuss the creation of a Windows service that will manage the automatic startup of GoldenGate on Windows!

Configuration of the Oracle GoldenGate Manager Process

To configure the various GoldenGate processes, you will configure the individual parameter files for that process. Each Oracle GoldenGate process has a configuration file that controls the operation of that process. The configuration file is a plain text file that contains the various parameters that are used to configure the process associated with that configuration file. The parameter file is located in the GoldenGate home directory in a subdirectory called dirprm. You can edit these files with the text editor of your choice, but the most common way of editing these files is with the GGSCI command **edit params** followed by an option such as MGR (which opens the Manager process configuration file), or the name of the unique parameter file you want to edit. Don't forget to make sure you are in the GoldenGate home directory of the instance you are configuring the parameter file for!

Table 4-6 lists the different GoldenGate parameter files that you will typically be configuring for a GoldenGate instance, and the different processes that you will configure within that instance.

In configuring Oracle GoldenGate, we would typically want to configure the GoldenGate Manager process after installing Oracle GoldenGate. We will discuss

Parameter File Name	Purpose	GSSCI Command to Edit
GLOBALS	Used to manage the entire GoldenGate instance. Only required in limited cases such as defining a default checkpoint table (see Chapter 2). The globals file exists in the GoldenGate home directory.	**Edit params ./GLOBALS**
Mgr	Used to configure the GoldenGate Manager process. There is one GoldenGate Manager process associated with each GoldenGate instance. See Chapter 2 for more information on GoldenGate instances and the GoldenGate Manager process.	**Edit params mgr**
Group name	Used to configure Extract, Data Pump, and Replicat processes. Each process has its own unique group name assigned to it when the parameter file for that process is created. The group name assigns an identifier to each individual process to make it unique within that GoldenGate instance. See Chapter 2 for more information on the individual processes and group names assigned to those processes.	**Edit params {group_name}**

TABLE 4-6.   *Oracle GoldenGate Parameter Files*

the configuration of the other parameter files in the following chapters as we configure the different replication topologies that Oracle GoldenGate supports.

When configuring the Manager process, you must define the one required parameter, which is the PORT parameter. The PORT parameter is used to assign a TCP/IP port to the GoldenGate Manager process on the local system. Oracle GoldenGate defaults to using port 7809, but you must define the port in the Manager process configuration file even if you are using the default value. Each GoldenGate Manager process on a given machine (one per GoldenGate instance) must have its own unique port number. This port will also be defined in each Extract process parameter file as you define different Extract processes. Thus, if you have two instances of Oracle GoldenGate on a given machine, you will have to define two unique port numbers for the Manager processes on those machines.

Like the other GoldenGate processes, each Manager process has its own assigned name. If you are running a single instance of Oracle GoldenGate, the default name for the Manager process is GSSMGR. Since this is the default name, if you are just running one instance of GoldenGate, you won't need to include this in the Manager process parameter file. If you will be running more than one instance of Oracle GoldenGate, then you will need to define the name of one or both Manager processes in the parameter file using the MGRSRVNAME parameter.

There are a number of optional parameters that you can configure in the Manager process parameter file. You can find more details on these parameters and the various configuration options that can be used with them in the Oracle GoldenGate Reference Guide. Table 4-7 shows the different parameters that Oracle recommends that you configure.

Parameter Name	Purpose	Example
USERID	Required if you are going to configure Oracle GoldenGate DDL support. Note that the password can be encrypted. See Chapter 9 for more detailed information on using encrypted passwords.	USERID Ggadmin,password
DYNAMICPORTLIST	You can use up to 256 unreserved/unrestricted ports for dynamic TCP/IP communications between the source and target systems. The Collector process, Replicat process, and GGSCI will use these ports. Oracle GoldenGate, by default, will start trying to use port 7840 and will increment the ports by one until an available port is discovered.	DYNAMICPORTLIST 7900-7910, 7920
DYNAMICPORT-REASSIGNDELAY	Indicates how long you want to wait (in seconds) for GoldenGate to assign a port that had been previously assigned.	DYNAMICPORT-REASSIGNDELAY 5

TABLE 4-7. *Common GoldenGate Manager Process Parameters* (continued)

Parameter Name	Purpose	Example

AUTOSTART	Automatically starts Extract and Replicat processes when the Manager process starts. Note that wildcarding is supported. See the section on configuring automated startup of GoldenGate for more information.	`-- Starts all extracts`
		`AUTOSTART extract *`
		`-- Starts all Replicat processes that have a group name that starts with rep.`
		
		`AUTOSTART replicat rep*`
		
		`-- Starts all extract and all Replicat processes`
		`AUTOSTART ER *`

AUTORESTART	Causes the Extract and Replicat processes to be restarted if they terminate abnormally.	`AUTORESTART extract *, retries 10, WAITMINUTES 5, RESETMINUTES 60`
PURGEOLDEXTRACTS	Purges the trail files after they are no longer needed. The use of the PURGEOLDEXTRACTS parameter in the Manager process parameter file is considered a best practice.	`PURGEOLDEXTRACTS`
USECHECKPOINTS	This causes the purge of the trail files (via PURGEOLDEXTRACTS) to not occur until all the data in those trail files has been consumed by all processes that need it.	`USECHECKPOINTS`

TABLE 4-7. *Common GoldenGate Manager Process Parameters* (continued)

Parameter Name	Purpose	Example
MINKEEP rules	This is a set of rule-based parameters that indicate how long the trail file data should be maintained, even if it's been consumed. Includes options such as minkeephours, minkeepdays, and minkeepfiles. Only one parameter can be used in a given parameter file.	Minkeepdays 5

TABLE 4-7. *Common GoldenGate Manager Process Parameters*

NOTE
If you have configured PURGEOLDEXTRACTS in the GoldenGate manager parameter file, you should not manually delete trail files as this could cause problems for the Manager process. Note that we have to use the PURGEOLDEXTRACTS parameter with the USECHECKPOINTS parameter.

Here is an example of a GoldenGate Manager process parameter file:

```
-- This is a Manager process file
PORT 7809
PURGEOLDEXTRACTS, USECHECKPOINTS
AUTOSTART ER *
AUTORESTART extract *,retries 10, WAITMINUTES 5, RESETMINUTES 60
```

Administration of the Oracle GoldenGate Manager Processes

In this section we will review starting and stopping the GoldenGate Manager process. First we will discuss starting the GoldenGate Manager process, and then we will talk about stopping the GoldenGate Manager process. This is pretty basic stuff, but important nonetheless.

Starting the GoldenGate Manager Process

Starting the GoldenGate Manager process can be done either from the operating system prompt using the **mgr** command, or it can be done from the GSSCI command-line interface (either by issuing a command or calling an obey file). If you are running GoldenGate on Windows, and you have installed GoldenGate as a service, you can also start up the Manager process from the Services window. See Chapter 9 for more information on setting up GoldenGate using Windows services.

Here is an example of using the **mgr** command to start the Oracle GoldenGate Manager process. Note that we have started the process as a background process and used **nohup** so that it will continue to run even if we log out of the system. This would be the way to start the Manager process from an auto-startup job, as we demonstrate later in this chapter.

```
nohup mgr paramfile ./dirprm/mgr.prm &
```

Here is an example of using GSSCI to start the Manager process:

```
[oracle@goldengate1 ~]$ cd /home/oracle/app/GoldenGate
[oracle@goldengate1 GoldenGate]$ ggsci
Oracle GoldenGate Command Interpreter for Oracle
Version 11.1.1.1 OGGCORE_11.1.1_PLATFORMS_110421.2040
Linux, x86, 32bit (optimized), Oracle 11g on Apr 21 2011 22:38:06
Copyright (C) 1995, 2011, Oracle and/or its affiliates. All rights
reserved.

GGSCI (goldengate1) 1> start manager
```

Stopping the GoldenGate Manager Process

You won't often need to stop the GoldenGate Manager process. Typically it should be running all the time. If you do need to stop it, you can use the **stop manager** command in the GGSCI command-line interface as seen in this example:

```
[oracle@goldengate1 ~]$ cd /home/oracle/app/GoldenGate
[oracle@goldengate1 GoldenGate]$ ggsci
Oracle GoldenGate Command Interpreter for Oracle
Version 11.1.1.1 OGGCORE_11.1.1_PLATFORMS_110421.2040
Linux, x86, 32bit (optimized), Oracle 11g on Apr 21 2011 22:38:06
Copyright (C) 1995, 2011, Oracle and/or its affiliates. All rights
reserved.

GGSCI (goldengate1) 1> stop manager
```

If you have GoldenGate configured as a service on Microsoft Windows, you can also stop that service to stop the Manager process.

Status of the GoldenGate Manager Process

If you want to know the status of the GoldenGate Manager process, you can use the GGSCI command **info all** as seen in this sample output:

```
GGSCI (goldengate1) 1> info all
  Program        Status       Group         Lag              Time Since Chkpt
  MANAGER        STOPPED
```

In this case the GoldenGate Manager process is stopped. Let's see what happens when we start it and issue the **info all** command again:

```
GGSCI (goldengate1) 2> start manager
  Manager started.

  GGSCI (goldengate1) 3> info all
  Program        Status       Group         Lag              Time Since Chkpt
  MANAGER        RUNNING
```

In this case we see that the Manager process is running.

Automating the Startup of the Oracle GoldenGate Processes

Now, for something really exciting! To truly "productionize" Oracle GoldenGate, we need to be able to start up the GoldenGate processes automatically when the system reboots. It's either that or calls at 3 a.m. in the morning after the server reboots. Personally, I prefer the automation. It's fairly simple actually, because all you need to do is configure the Oracle GoldenGate Manager process correctly, and then find a way to start that process up when the system boots, and there you go, automated startup of GoldenGate. In this section, we will provide you with a guide to starting Oracle GoldenGate on Windows and then on Linux.

Auto Startup of GoldenGate in Windows Environments   The easiest and best way to get Oracle GoldenGate to start up automatically in Windows (and to keep running) is to create a service in Windows that does just that. Oracle GoldenGate provides the **install** command to help you create the service. Here are the steps to configuring the GoldenGate Manager process and then using the install program to create the service so GoldenGate will start automatically.

1. This is going to be one of those times when we will need to configure the GLOBALS parameter. Open a command prompt and navigate to the Oracle GoldenGate home directory. Start the GSSCI command interpreter and edit the GLOBALS parameter with the **edit params ./GLOBALS** command. Add the following to any existing GLOBALS parameter file:

   ```
   MGRSERVNAME OracleGGSMGR1
   ```

   Note that OracleGGSMGR1 is going to be the name of the new service. Also, note that if you don't already have a GLOBALS parameter file, you will be prompted to save the file. Make sure you call it GLOBALS and save it to the GoldenGate home directory of the instance you are configuring.

2. Now, create the GoldenGate Manager process parameter file using GSSCI as shown previously in this chapter. The GoldenGate Manager process parameter file should look something similar to this:

```
-- This is a Manager process file
PORT 7809
PURGEOLDEXTRACTS, USECHECKPOINTS
AUTOSTART ER *
AUTORESTART extract *,retries 10, WAITMINUTES 5, RESETMINUTES 60
```

What is key here is the AUTOSTART parameter. In this case, AUTOSTART ER * indicates that all Extract processes and Replicat processes should be started when the Manager process for that GoldenGate instance is started. If you have specific Extract or Replicat processes you want to start, you can name them explicitly instead of using the wildcard feature of GoldenGate, though only one Extract or Replicat process can be listed per AUTOSTART line. GoldenGate supports the use of multiple AUTOSTART parameters in the Manager process parameter file.

3. Now that you have configured the GoldenGate Manager process, make sure you test it, making sure that when you start the Manager process, the Extract, Data Pump and Extract processes all start automatically, as shown here.

```
[oracle@goldengate1 ~]$ cd /home/oracle/app/GoldenGate
[oracle@goldengate1 GoldenGate]$ ggsci
Oracle GoldenGate Command Interpreter for Oracle
Version 11.1.1.1 OGGCORE_11.1.1_PLATFORMS_110421.2040
Linux, x86, 32bit (optimized), Oracle 11g on Apr 21 2011 22:38:06
Copyright (C) 1995, 2011, Oracle and/or its affiliates. All rights reserved.

GGSCI (goldengate1) 1> start manager
```

Wait a few seconds so all the processes can start successfully. You can then run the **info all** command to determine that the processes all started successfully, as seen here:

```
GGSCI (goldengate1) 1> info all
```

4. Now, let's use the install program to create the service. From the Windows command prompt: Change to the GoldenGate home directory, then run the install program, passing it the name of the service that you defined in the GLOBALS parameter. In this example, we are going to use the **install adsservice** command to add the service. In this case, the install program will look in the GLOBALS file for the service name we added in step 1. If the GLOBALS file does not exist, a default service called GGSMGR will

be created. Here is an example of running the install program, which will create the service OracleGGSMGR1 that we defined in the GLOBALS parameter earlier in this section:

```
Install adsservice
```

5. Repeat this process for each unique GoldenGate instance.

6. Test the automated startup by booting the server when possible, and then running the **info all** command from GGSCI. All the processes configured to start automatically should be started.

NOTE
*More detailed information on the **install** program (should you need it) is contained in the Oracle GoldenGate Oracle Installation and Setup Guide.*

Auto Startup of GoldenGate in Linux   The steps that you will generally follow to configure GoldenGate to automatically start up in the various versions of Linux are as follows:

1. From each individual GoldenGate home for which you wish to automate the startup of GoldenGate, create the GoldenGate Manager process parameter file using GSSCI as shown previously in this chapter. The GoldenGate Manager process parameter file should look similar to this:

```
-- This is a Manager process file
PORT 7809
PURGEOLDEXTRACTS, USECHECKPOINTS
AUTOSTART ER *
AUTORESTART extract *,retries 10, WAITMINUTES 5, RESETMINUTES 60
```

What is key here is the AUTOSTART parameter. In this case, AUTOSTART ER * indicates that all Extract processes and Replicat processes should be started when the Manager process for that GoldenGate instance is started. If you have specific Extract or Replicat processes you want to start, you can name them explicitly instead of using the wildcard feature of GoldenGate, though only one Extract or Replicat process can be listed per AUTOSTART line. GoldenGate supports the use of multiple AUTOSTART parameters in the Manager process parameter file.

After creating this parameter file, you should test it and ensure that it starts the processes as you expect.

2. Now, create a shell script that will use the **mgr** command to start the Manager process. Note that this script will run from the Oracle owning account. Here is an example (I like Korn shell, but you can use the shell script language of your choice) that we will call start_GoldenGate.ksh. We are creating it in the GoldenGate home directory on our system, which is $ORACLE_BASE/GoldenGate:

```
#!/bin/ksh
#Set the Oracle environment
# This should set the following parameters
# ORACLE_BASE, ORACLE_HOME, LD_LIBRARY_PATH, ORACLE_SID (the default)
# ORACLE_TERM, PATH, CLASSPATH
export GGATE_HOME=$ORACLE_BASE/GoldenGate
./.bash_profile
./.bashrc
cd $GGHOME
#Use a here document to start the Manager process.
# we could also use the mgr command if we wanted.
ggsci<<WEOF
start manager
exit
WEOF
```

As usual you will want to test this script after creating it.

3. Make the start_GoldenGate.ksh script you created executable using the **chmod** command as seen here:

```
chmod a+x $GGHOME/start_GoldenGate.ksh
```

4. Now, we also want to create a shutdown script for GoldenGate. Note that this script will run from the Oracle owning account. Here is an example (I like Korn shell, but you can use the shell script language of your choice) that we will call stop_GoldenGate.ksh. We are creating it in the GoldenGate home directory on our system, which is $ORACLE_BASE/GoldenGate:

```
#!/bin/ksh
#Set the Oracle environment
# This should set the following parameters
# ORACLE_BASE, ORACLE_HOME, LD_LIBRARY_PATH, ORACLE_SID (the default)
# ORACLE_TERM, PATH, CLASSPATH
# We assume GGHOME is configured in the .bash files too
./.bash_profile
./.bashrc
cd $GGHOME
#Use a here document to stop the Manager process.
ggsci<<WEOF
```

```
stop manager
y
exit
WEOF
```

Test this script, of course!

5. Make the kill_GoldenGate.ksh script you created executable using the
   chmod command as seen here:

```
chmod a+x $GGHOME/kill_GoldenGate.ksh
```

6. Now, we want to create the wrapper script that we can call during system
   startup or shutdown that will start up, shut down, or restart the GoldenGate
   services. We will call this script GoldenGate_Boot_StartStop.ksh and store it
   in the GoldenGate home directory. Here is our script:

```
#!/bin/ksh
# Remember - this runs as root!
# description: startup and shutdown the Oracle 11g GoldenGate Manager process

echo "Goldengate start/stop"
ORA_OWNER=oracle
# You will need to manually put in your GG_HOME directory here.
# Note - this script only supports one GG instance.
GG_HOME=/home/oracle/app/GoldenGate
#
case "$1" in
'start')

# Start GoldenGate
echo -n "Starting goldengate : "
su - $ORA_OWNER -c $GG_HOME/start_GoldenGate.ksh
echo
;;

'stop')
# Stop GoldenGate
echo -n "Shutting down goldengate : "
su - $ORA_OWNER -c $GG_HOME/kill_GoldenGate.ksh
echo
;;

'restart')
# Restart GoldenGate:
echo -n "Restart GoldenGate : "
$0 stop
$0 start
echo
;;
*)
echo "Usage: GoldenGate_Boot_StartStop.ksh [ start | stop | restart }"
exit 1
esac
exit 0
```

7. Make the GoldenGate_Boot_StartStop.ksh script you created executable using the **chmod** command as seen here:

```
chmod a+x $GGHOME/GoldenGate_Boot_StartStop.ksh
```

8. Use the su command to access the root account and copy the GoldenGate_Boot_StartStop.ksh script to the /etc/rc.d/init.d directory structure.

```
su - root
cp $ORACLE_BASE/GoldenGate/GoldenGate_Boot_StartStop.ksh /etc/
rc.d/init.d
```

9. From root, test the script to make sure that it works as expected. The commands you would use to test the script are:

```
./GoldenGate_Boot_StartStop.ksh
./GoldenGate_Boot_StartStop.ksh start
./GoldenGate_Boot_StartStop.ksh stop
./GoldenGate_Boot_StartStop.ksh restart
```

10. Now we need to add the GoldenGate_Boot_StartStop.ksh script to the Linux boot configuration with the **chkconfig** command. These steps are shown here to add the script to the bootup process, list the status, and then enable the bootup script:

```
/sbin/chkconfig -add GoldenGate_Boot_StartStop.ksh
/sbin/chkconfig -list GoldenGate_Boot_StartStop.ksh
/sbin/chkconfig GoldenGate_Boot_StartStop.ksh on
```

CHAPTER
5

Implementing Oracle GoldenGate One-Way Replication

We have spent several chapters introducing you to GoldenGate. In Chapter 2 we introduced you to the GoldenGate architecture. In Chapter 3 you installed Oracle GoldenGate, and in Chapter 4 you configured Oracle GoldenGate. These chapters prepared you for this chapter and the next several chapters where we will put Oracle GoldenGate to work actually *doing* something. Chapters 5 through 8 will hold your hand and work with you to actually implement various GoldenGate topologies from basic replication to multimaster and cascading replication. After these chapters, you will almost be able to do GoldenGate in your sleep.

In this chapter we will get you started with basic one-way replication with Oracle GoldenGate. The mantra of this chapter is "keep it simple," so in this chapter we will hold your hands as we proceed to configure the Extract process, the Data Pump process, and the Replicat process. We will assume in this chapter that you have installed and configured Oracle GoldenGate as described in Chapters 3 and 4. However, this chapter is also a bit of a "quick-start" chapter. In that vein, we will review a few important configuration issues as we proceed through the chapter, just to make sure we cover all the bases and get you to replicating data as fast as possible.

Then we will start preparing to set up GoldenGate replication. This will involve things like reviewing the schema, determining if there are issues with the schema and any GoldenGate restrictions, and generally laying out the GoldenGate topology we will use.

Preparing for Replication

It's time to put GoldenGate to use. You should have configured the Manager process on both the source and target databases as described in Chapter 4. If you have not done that, then shoot back to Chapter 4 and configure the Manager process. Remember that the Manager process manages everything else with respect to GoldenGate. It keeps an eye on the Extract, Data Pump, and Replicat processes and makes sure that they are running correctly. So, it's important to get the Manager process up and running.

Introducing the HR Schema

In this chapter we will be replicating several objects from the HR schema. This is the HR schema that is created as a part of the sample schemas that you can create in an Oracle database. Figure 5-1 provides the data model for the HR schema that we will be using.

Notice that we have a lot going on in this data model. First, we have seven tables that we are replicating. What this data model does not show is that there are also 19 indexes associated with these tables. We also have all sorts of foreign key

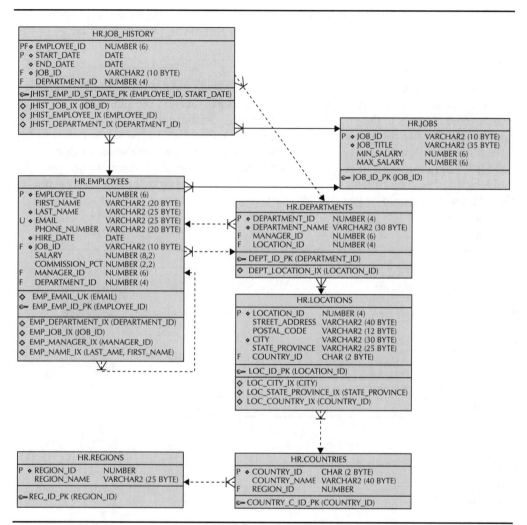

FIGURE 5-1. *HR schema data model*

relationships going on in our schema, including parent-child relationships and even a self-referential relationship! This is a pretty busy schema for only seven tables.

Looking at this schema, we know a few things. First, we know that we can only use a single Extract process because of all the foreign key relationships. This is because tables that have foreign key relationships must be replicated together. Second, note that each table has a primary key associated with it. This is a good thing because we don't need to be concerned about replicating all the columns of a given row in the table every single time a change to a column occurs. For any given column change, GoldenGate will only need to record the primary key column and the changed value.

Our Selected Topology

Let's also take a quick look at the GoldenGate topology that we will be configuring. Figure 5-2 provides a picture of the overall architecture. Overall, our plan is to replicate the changes in the HR schema of the ORCL database on the server Goldengate1, or the HR schema on a database also called ORCL on a server called Goldengate2. Let's be clear; the names of the databases and even the schemas don't need to be the same here—they just happen to be. The name of the database on Goldengate1 could be called LIFE and the database on Goldengate2 could be called DEATH, and that would be just fine. We could even replicate to a different schema

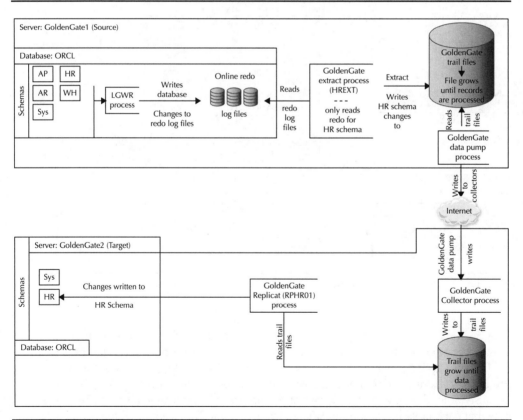

FIGURE 5-2. *GoldenGate topology*

name if we wanted to, but that adds a layer of complexity that we don't want to deal with just yet. Again, the mantra of this chapter is: keep it simple.

As you can see from Figure 5-2, we will be using one Extract process on our host server called Goldengate1. That Extract process (which we will call HREXT) will write the changes from only the HR schema in the ORCL database to a local trail file, again on the Goldengate1 server. We will have a Data Pump process running on the Goldengate1 server that will then send the contents of the trail file to the Collector process running on Goldengate2. The Collector process on Goldengate2 will write the data received to the trail file on the Goldengate2 server. Finally, the Replicat process on the Goldengate2 server will write these changes to the database.

While we don't need to have the middle layer of the local trail file and the GoldenGate Data Pump process, we are concerned with protecting the data being replicated and following best practices. Because of this, and because we recommend always following established best practices, we will create the local trail file, and use the Oracle GoldenGate Data Pump to move the trail data across to the target system. Again, using local trail files and the GoldenGate Data Pump process is optional, but this practice is highly recommended.

So, What Are We Doing?

Reviewing everything, then, it appears that this particular replication solution will be pretty straightforward. Before we get started, you should review Chapters 3 and 4 and review this checklist to make sure that you have finished the following:

- Completed the install of GoldenGate on servers Goldengate1 and Goldengate2 as outlined in Chapter 3.

- Configured the GoldenGate directories on both servers as demonstrated in Chapter 4.

- Configured your environment as outlined in Chapter 4. We will use the GGHOME environment variable throughout this chapter, so you will want it set correctly. Also make sure the PATH and Library path variables are set correctly on both servers.

- Configured the GoldenGate administrative user on both databases. You should have granted the GoldenGate administrative user on the Goldengate1 server the privileges needed for the Manager process and the Extract process. You should have granted the GoldenGate administrative user privileges for the Manager process and the Replicat process as shown in Chapter 4.

- The ORCL database on Goldengate1 should be in ARCHIVELOG mode. Make sure that it is successfully generating archived redo logs in the Fast Recovery Area as shown in Chapter 4.

- Enabled database-level supplemental logging as shown in Chapter 4.

Having completed our preliminary checks, it seems we are ready for liftoff. The next steps to getting GoldenGate replication going are as follows:

■ Prepare the Target database for its initial load.

■ As described in Chapter 4, configure the Manager process.

■ Use a single Extract process to replicate the data.

■ Configure the Extract process to write to a local trail file.

■ Use the GoldenGate Data Pump utility to write from the source database server to a trail file on the target database server.

■ Configure the Replicat process to read from the remote trail file and write the changes in the trail file to the target database.

■ Since we are replicating a single schema, and in this case, limited amounts of data, we will instantiate the database using GoldenGate itself.

■ Start the actual replication process.

Note that we are setting up the replication process before we actually get the source database instantiated. This is very typical of Oracle GoldenGate operations in that we want to have the Extract process tracking changes before we actually instantiate the database. You will understand the reasons for this better (and we will discuss it more) as we move along in this chapter. For now, just understand that we want to set up the change capture infrastructure first, then we instantiate the database, and then we start replicating!

Let's get started!

Preparing the Target Database for Replication

Before we can start replication, we need a location to replicate to, of course. Recall that in Chapter 4 we installed two Linux server images and two Windows server images. The first Linux server is called Goldengate1 and the second Linux server is called Goldengate2. The first Windows server is called WinGoldengate1 and the second is called WinGoldengate2. Recall that the databases on each of these servers are called ORCL.

In this chapter we will be replicating the HR schema from ORCL on Goldengate1 to ORCL on Goldengate2. Since the database on Goldengate2 already has an HR schema in it, we will drop that schema, and then use Oracle Database Data Pump to re-create the schema and the objects in that schema. We could use Oracle Database Data Pump to instantiate (or populate) the Goldengate2 ORCL database, but we have decided to use GoldenGate to do that instead. Using GoldenGate instead of Oracle Data Pump to populate the schema does require that the schema and schema objects be created before they can be instantiated. If we were to use Oracle Data Pump, then that utility would create the objects for us too.

The following workshop will help you prepare the ORCL database on Goldengate2 for the later operations in this chapter.

GoldenGate Workshop: *Configure the ORCL Database on the Goldengate2 Server*

Workshop Notes

This workshop will guide you through removing the HR schema on the ORCL database on the Goldengate2 server. In it you will do the following:

- Create an Oracle Database Data Pump backup of the HR schema (without data) on the ORCL database on the Goldengate1 server

- Log in to the ORCL database on the Goldengate2 server

- Drop the HR schema on the ORCL database on the Goldengate2 server

- Re-create the HR schema on the ORCL database on the Goldengate2 server

Step 1.   Log in to the server Goldengate2 as the Oracle OS user.

Step 2.   Check the Oracle environment, ensuring that it's set to ORCL.

```
[oracle@goldengate2 ~]$ oraenv
ORACLE_SID = [orcl] ?
The Oracle base has been set to /home/oracle/app/oracle
```

Step 3.   Log in to the ORCL database as sys using the SYSDBA privilege. Note that the password, by default, will be oracle.

```
[oracle@goldengate2 ~]$ sqlplus sys/oracle as sysdba
SQL*Plus: Release 11.2.0.2.0 Production on Mon Jan 9 16:44:59 2012
Copyright (c) 1982, 2010, Oracle.  All rights reserved.

Connected to:
Oracle Database 11g Enterprise Edition Release 11.2.0.2.0 - Production
With the Partitioning, OLAP, Data Mining and Real Application Testing
options
SQL>
```

Step 4. Now, drop the HR user using the **drop user** command. Make sure you include the **cascade** command.

```
SQL> drop user hr cascade;
User dropped.
```

Step 5. Log in to the Goldengate1 server as the Oracle user.

Step 6. From the current working directory, create a directory named export. Change into the export directory you just created and check the entire directory path. Our path is /home/oracle/export.

```
[oracle@goldengate1 ~]$ mkdir export
[oracle@goldengate1 ~]$ cd export
[oracle@goldengate1 export]$ pwd
/home/oracle/export
```

Step 7. Log in to the ORCL database on the Goldengate1 server using sys as sysdba:

```
[oracle@goldengate2 ~]$ sqlplus sys/oracle as sysdba
SQL*Plus: Release 11.2.0.2.0 Production on Mon Jan 9 16:44:59 2012
Copyright (c) 1982, 2010, Oracle.  All rights reserved.

Connected to:
Oracle Database 11g Enterprise Edition Release 11.2.0.2.0 -
Production
With the Partitioning, OLAP, Data Mining and Real Application
Testing options
SQL>
```

Step 8. We need to create a directory from the Oracle SQL*Plus prompt. This directory will be used in Step 9 by the Oracle Database Data Pump utility.

```
SQL> create directory export as '/home/oracle/export/';
Directory created.
```

Step 9. Exit SQLPlus. Run the Oracle Database Data Pump and start the export of the HR schema (without data) as seen in this example (use sys/oracle as sysdba when prompted for the username):

```
expdp schemas=HR directory=export dumpfile=expdpHR.dmp
logfile=expdpHR.log exclude=table_data
```

Step 10.   Go to the Goldengate2 server. Log in as the Oracle user. Under the Oracle home directory, create a directory called export.

```
[oracle@goldengate1 ~]$ mkdir export
[oracle@goldengate1 ~]$ cd export
[oracle@goldengate1 export]$ pwd
/home/oracle/export
```

Step 11.   Now, log in to the ORCL database on Goldengate2 and create the export directory:

```
SQL> create directory export as '/home/oracle/export/';
Directory created.
```

Step 12.   Log out of the ORCL database on the Goldengate2 server. Make sure you are in the /home/oracle/export directory. Using the **scp** command, move the Oracle Database Data Pump file from the /home/oracle/export directory on the Goldengate1 server to the /home/oracle/export directory on the Goldengate2 server. Here is an example:

```
scp root@goldengate1:/home/oracle/export/expdpHR.dmp.
```

Step 13.   From the server Goldengate2, start the data pump import of the HR schema, using the dump file you just copied from the Goldengate1 server. Using **impdp**, issue the following command:

```
impdp directory=robert dumpfile=expdpHR.dmp logfile=impdphr.log
```

Step 13 will re-create the HR user/schema and ensure it has the right privileges. It will then re-create the objects in the HR schema and make sure that the appropriate constraints, grants, and so on are created.

Configuring the GoldenGate Manager Process

Chapter 4 covers configuring the GoldenGate Manager process in detail. However, replication really starts with the Manager process, we think, so we will discuss configuring the Manager process for both GoldenGate servers here and then we will have a workshop that will walk you through the process.

NOTE
We covered checkpoints in detail in Chapter 2.

Both Manager processes will have the same parameter file, which will be pretty simple. Here it is:

```
-- This is a Manager process file
PORT 7809
PURGEOLDEXTRACTS, USECHECKPOINTS
-- AUTOSTART ER *
-- AUTORESTART extract *,retries 10, WAITMINUTES 5, RESETMINUTES 60
```

This is almost the same parameter file we showed you in Chapter 4, and it will work just fine for our needs at the moment. The PORT parameter indicates that the GoldenGate Manager process will be communicating between the two GoldenGate servers via port 7809. The PURGEOLDEXTRACTS and USECHECKPOINTS parameters indicate that we will purge the trail files after the data has been consumed, and we will be using checkpoints to try to reduce the time it will take to recover the replication process should we have a failure. Note that we have commented out the AUTOSTART and AUTORESTART parameters with the double dashes (--). We don't want to have the Extract or Replicat processes automatically starting on us just yet.

We will create these parameter files on both servers using the GGSCI interface. Once we have done that, we will start the Manager processes with the **start manager** command and then check the status of the Manager process with the **info all** command. Now that we have said all that, let's do a workshop where we actually *do* all of that! Time to get our hands dirty!

One note about the workshops before we get started. In many cases we have combined the Linux and Windows tasks into one workshop, because many times the operations are exactly the same in both environments. In cases where there are slight differences, we will point those out.

GoldenGate Workshop: *Configure the Manager Processes on Goldengate1 and Goldengate2*

Workshop Notes

We are getting ready to do our first GoldenGate replication! Before you get started you might want to stand up and stretch or take a short break, because the entire configuration process will take a little while. In this workshop we are going to set up the Manager process on the Goldengate1 and Goldengate2 database servers.

Step 1. Start by logging in to the server Goldengate1 as the Oracle OS user. Open a command-line window.

Step 2. CD to the $GGHOME directory.

In Linux:

```
cd $GGHOME
```

In Windows:

```
cd %GGHOME%
```

Step 3. Now, open the GGSCI command-line interface.

In Linux:

```
[oracle@goldengate2 GoldenGate]$ ggsci
```

In Windows:

```
C:\app\oracle\goldengate>ggsci
```

Step 4. Edit the GoldenGate manager parameter file with the command **edit params mgr**.

```
GGSCI (goldengate1) 1> edit params mgr
```

Step 5. Configure the parameter file as seen here:

```
-- This is a Manager process file
PORT 7809
PURGEOLDEXTRACTS, USECHECKPOINTS
-- AUTOSTART ER *
-- AUTORESTART extract *,retries 10, WAITMINUTES 5, RESETMINUTES 60
```

Step 6. Save the parameter file (it should already default to the name mgr.prm).

Step 7. From the GGSCI interface, start the Manager process with the **start manager** command.

```
GGSCI (goldengate1) 3> start manager
Manager started.
```

Step 8. Check the status of the Manager process from the GGSCI interface using the **info all** command.

```
GGSCI (goldengate1) 4> info all
Program      Status       Group       Lag         Time Since Chkpt
MANAGER      RUNNING
```

Step 9. If you want to see the actual parameter file, exit GGSCI with the **exit** command. Then use the **cd** command to change to the dirprm directory and look for the file called mgr.prm.

Step 10.

In Linux:

```
GGSCI (goldengate2) 5> exit
C:\app\oracle\goldengate> cd dirprm
C:\app\oracle\goldengate> dir
total 12
drwxrwxr-x  2 oracle oracle 4096 Jan  3 13:08 .
drwxrwxr-x 15 oracle oracle 4096 Dec 30 19:17 ..
-rw-rw-rw-  1 oracle oracle  163 Jan  3 13:08 mgr.prm

[oracle@goldengate2 dirprm]$ cat mgr.prm
-- This is a Manager process file
PORT 7809
PURGEOLDEXTRACTS, USECHECKPOINTS
-- AUTOSTART ER *
-- AUTORESTART extract *,retries 10, WAITMINUTES 5, RESETMINUTES 60
```

In Windows:

```
GGSCI (goldengate2) 5> exit
C:\app\oracle\goldengate>cd dirprm
C:\app\oracle\goldengate\dirprm>dir
 Volume in drive C is System
 Volume Serial Number is FE19-F8F2

 Directory of C:\app\oracle\goldengate\dirprm
01/03/2012  01:15 PM    <DIR>          .
01/03/2012  01:15 PM    <DIR>          ..
01/03/2012  01:15 PM               166 mgr.prm
               1 File(s)            166 bytes
               2 Dir(s)   3,656,355,840 bytes free
```

```
C:\app\oracle\goldengate\dirprm>type mgr.prm
-- This is a Manager process file
PORT 7809
PURGEOLDEXTRACTS, USECHECKPOINTS
-- AUTOSTART ER *
-- AUTORESTART extract *,retries 10, WAITMINUTES 5, RESETMINUTES 60
```

Step 11.   Repeat these steps on the server Goldengate2.

> **NOTE**
> *I confess that I have a tendency to put semicolons after each GoldenGate command. I suppose that it's a SQL habit that I have. Don't make the same mistake!*

Configuring the GoldenGate Extract Process

We have talked about the Extract process and now we are going to use it! The Extract process is going to keep track of the changes that are made in the database by combing through the redo logs. As such, the Extract process only will need to run on one server, Goldengate1. As the Extract process finds the changes that we have told it to replicate, it will write those out to the local trail file that we will define.

Configuring the Extract process involves several steps:

- Creating the extract parameter file

- Adding the Extract process to GoldenGate

- Defining the trail file that is associated with the Extract process

- Administering the Extract process

Let's look at each of these steps in more detail, leading up to our next workshop.

Creating the Extract Parameter File

Of course, we need to configure the Extract process parameter files. We will use GGSCI to create and save the Extract process parameter file. To create the file in GGSCI, we would use the **edit params** command (**edit params exhr01**). This file will be called EXHR01.prm, and it will be stored in the directory $GGHOME/dirprm in

Linux or %GGHOME%\dirprm in Windows. We will walk you through this whole process process within the workshops contained in this chapter.

This is the first time we have seen one of these babies in this book, so let's take a look at the Extract process parameter file we will create:

```
-- Extract name. Up to 8 characters
EXTRACT EXHR01
-- Optional - This ensures that the database environment is
-- configured correctly. Using it is a best practice.
SETENV (NLS_LANG=AMERICAN_AMERICA.AL32UTF8)
-- Login and password to the administrator account in the source
-- database.
USERID ggadmin@orcl_one, PASSWORD ggadmin
-- Defines the location and prefix of the trail files
EXTRAIL ./dirdat/hr
-- This defines what we are replicating.
-- In this case, all tables in the HR schema.
-- Note the use of the wildcard character.
TABLE HR.*;
-- Note - there is no DDL capture in this extract. Only DML.
```

In the EXHR01 extract parameter file we have just created, we have used several parameters to configure the EXHR01 extract. First we used the Extract process to name the Extract process EXHR01. We will use this name throughout the extract configuration process, so it's important to get it typed in correctly here. Also, it's a good idea to come up with a good naming convention for your Extract, Data Pump, and Replicat processes. Keep in mind that the name for any of these processes can only be eight characters in length, so be careful when you define these naming conventions. In this case we used EX to indicate that this is an Extract process. We used HR to indicate the schema we are replicating and 01 to allow for more than one Extract process of the same type.

Next, we used the USERID parameter to define the userid and password of the GoldenGate administrator account. Also, in this account we used the TNS service name of the source database to indicate the database that we should connect to. There are many different ways to point the extract to the correct database. For example, we could have used the SETENV parameter to set the ORACLE_SID parameter, as seen in this alternative extract parameter file:

```
-- Extract name. Up to 8 characters
EXTRACT EXHR01
-- Optional - This ensures that the database environment is
-- configured correctly. Using it is a best practice.
SETENV (NLS_LANG=AMERICAN_AMERICA.AL32UTF8)
SETENV (ORACLE_SID=ORCL)
-- Login and password to the administrator account in the source
-- database.
USERID ggadmin, PASSWORD ggadmin
```

```
-- Defines the location and prefix of the trail files
EXTRAIL ./dirdat/hr
-- This defines what we are replicating.
-- In this case, all tables in the HR schema.
-- Note the use of the wildcard character.
TABLE HR.*;
-- Note - there is no DDL capture in this extract. Only DML.
```

Note here that we have removed the TNS identifier in the USERID parameter and added the SETENV parameter, setting the value of ORACLE_SID.

Also, did you notice that we used the SETENV parameter to set the NLS_LANG environment variable? We set the parameter NLS_LANG to the Natural Language Support (NLS) language of the database that the data is being extracted from. We determined the NLS_LANG language setting by quickly querying the V$NLS_PARAMETERS dynamic view, as seen here:

```
SQL> Select * from v$nls_parameters where parameter='NLS_CHARACTERSET';

PARAMETER                        VALUE
------------------------------   ------------------------------
NLS_CHARACTERSET                 AL32UTF8
```

Setting the NLS_LANG parameter in the extract ensures that the data that is read in the redo logs and written to the trail files is consistent with the NLS language of the database. By default the extract will use the NLS language setting that is already set in the environment or, if none is set, it will be set to US7ASCII. Often this is not sufficient if you are using a multibyte character set such as AL32UTF8 or WE8ISO8859P1, and data can be lost. Therefore we consider it a best practice to set the NLS_LANG parameter in the Extract process and in the Replicat process.

So, what if you are using different character sets in the source and target databases? The best practice is for both databases to be the same character set and set NLS_LANG to that character set. If the character sets of the source and target databases are different, then you may lose or corrupt data on the target database, and unfortunately there isn't any way around that fact unless the character set on the target database is a superset of the character set of the source database. In that case, you should be fine.

If you need to run your source and target databases using different character sets (this tends to be fairly rare), ensure that they are compatible, or that the character set on the target database is a superset of the character set of the source database.

If you are using the wrong NLS character set, you may see errors such as the following:

1. Data loss or corruption

2. ORA-12705 or ORA-01461 Oracle errors

3. Various ORA-00600 errors

There are several good Metalink documents that talk about the impacts of different character sets on Oracle GoldenGate. If you find you must run your source and target databases using different character sets, we would point you towards Metalink and Oracle Support to ensure that you did not put your data at risk.

Registering the Extract

Once we have created the GoldenGate extract parameter file, we need to perform a few more actions. First, we need to register the Extract process as seen here:

```
GGSCI (goldengate1) 5> dblogin userid ggadmin, password ggadmin
Successfully logged into database.

GGSCI (goldengate1) 6> add extract exhr01, tranlog, begin now
2012-01-03 13:57:52  INFO    OGG-01749  Successfully registered
EXTRACT
XHR01 to start managing log retention at SCN 10796294.

EXTRACT added.
```

NOTE
*If you do not log in to the Oracle database before issuing the **add extract** command, you will need to register the Extract process with the database at a later time using the **register extract** command as seen in this example:*
register extract exhr01 logretention

Note what we have done in the previous code example. First, we logged in to the database through GGSCI using the **dblogin** command. Then we registered the new Extract process using the **add extract** command from GGSCI. The TRANLOG parameter indicates that the source of the extraction will be the transaction logs of the database (as opposed to, say, a flat file). The BEGIN parameter basically indicates at what point you want the extract to start tracking changes. In this case we use the NOW option, which says to start tracking changes at the point that the command was executed. It's important to understand that **begin now** does not mean that the Extract process itself is starting now; you still need to do that. It's just telling the Extract process that you are responsible for tracking all changes after this moment. You can optionally provide a different timestamp for the **begin** command if you choose.

Adding the Trail File to GoldenGate and Associating It with the Extract

We are still not done. Now we need to add GoldenGate trail files to the mix and associate them with the EXHR01 Extract process we have already defined. This is done through the GGSCI **add exttrail** command as seen here:

```
Add exttrail ./dirdat/hr, extract EXHR01, megabytes 100
```

In this example (which is the one we will use in our workshop), we have defined (or registered if you prefer) the trail files for the extract EXHR01 that was created earlier. In this case, we told GoldenGate to put the trail files in the directory dirdat (which is one directory below GGHOME) and to prefix all the trail files with the name hr. Note that the length of the trail file prefix can only be two characters long. GoldenGate will create many trail files, of course, and as we described in Chapter 2, it will append an eight-digit number to the trail files as they are created, keeping them unique. Notice also that we have defined the size of the trial files as being 100 MB in size.

One thing to mention at this point is that we have configured our EXHR01 Extract process to write to a local trail file. As we have mentioned before, this is very much a recommended best practice. We could have configured the EXHR01 Extract process to write directly to the remote trail file on the target database server. If you did not want to configure the GoldenGate Data Pump, then your EXHR01 Extract process parameter file would need to have additional information in it to identify the source system that the Extract process should send the trail file data to. Additional parameters would include (at a minimum) the RMTHOST parameter, which indicates the target database server name and the port number that the collector will be listening on. Another parameter would be the RMTTRAIL parameter, which indicates the name of the remote trail file that the trail data will be written to. These parameters are used by the GoldenGate Data Pump process, and you can see examples of their use later in this chapter in the section where we describe the configuration of the Oracle GoldenGate Data Pump Extract process.

Now, all that is left to do with the Extract process is to start it and monitor its operation. Let's discuss that in the next section.

Administering the Extract Process

Now that we have the Extract process and its trail files defined, we need to start the Extract process so it will begin capturing changes. Remember, there is no actual end-to-end replication going on yet, so the trail files at this point will start growing without constraint. Since this is a test database, and we are pretty sure the HR schema isn't going to be that busy, we doubt there will be a problem. In this section we will discuss the following:

- Starting the Extract process

- Stopping the Extract process

- Monitoring the Extract process

Starting the Extract Process

If you thought all that configuring and adding extracts and trail files was a lot of work, you will like how easy it is to start the Extract process. You simply use the **start extract** command from the GGSCI interface as seen here where we will start our EXHR01 extract:

```
Start extract EXHR01
```

Stopping the Extract Process

Stopping the Extract process is as easy as starting it. Simply use the **stop extract** command from the GGSCI interface and the Extract process will be shut down normally. Here is an example:

```
Stop extract EXHR01
```

Monitoring the Extract Process

Once you start the Extract process, there are a couple of principal ways to monitor it. First, you can use the **info all** command, which we have already seen. It will show us the different Extract processes that are configured and their status. Here is an example:

```
GGSCI (goldengate1) 12> info all
Program      Status       Group        Lag            Time Since Chkpt
MANAGER      RUNNING
EXTRACT      RUNNING      EXHR01       00:54:23       00:00:05
```

Notice that in this case, we see that the Manager process is running and one Extract process is running, which happens to be the EXHR01 process! Notice the Lag column. In this case, the lag time is how far behind the Extract process is in processing redo log information and sending it to the trail file. In this case, we just started our Extract process. The Extract process needs to process 54 minutes of records to get caught up. In this case, the 54 minutes represents the time since we added the extract (with the **start now** parameter—remember that one?) and the time that we actually started the Extract process. The GoldenGate Extract process will quickly churn through those records and the lag will quickly drop to zero (in fact it did before I finished writing this paragraph).

The second way (and a way to get more detailed information) is by using the **info** command with the EXTRACT parameter as seen here:

```
GGSCI (goldengate1) 10> info extract EXHR01
EXTRACT     EXHR01     Last Started 2012-01-06 00:35    Status RUNNING
Checkpoint Lag          00:00:00 (updated 00:00:01 ago)
Log Read Checkpoint  Oracle Redo Logs
                        2012-01-06 01:33:42   Seqno 474, RBA 18662400
```

Note that this tells us the status of the extract, the checkpoint lag, and that at the last checkpoint, it was reading from the online redo logs, along with the time of the checkpoint and the log sequence number it was on. You can get even more information by adding the DETAIL parameter to the **info** command with the EXTRACT parameter as seen here:

```
9> info extract EXHR01, detail
EXTRACT     EXHR01     Last Started 2012-01-06 00:35    Status RUNNING
Checkpoint Lag          00:00:00 (updated 00:00:11 ago)
Log Read Checkpoint  Oracle Redo Logs
                        2012-01-06 01:32:55  Seqno 474, RBA 18651648

  Target Extract Trails:
  Remote Trail Name                          Seqno      RBA      Max MB
  ./dirdat/hr                                  1        1037       10
  Extract Source                     Begin            End
  /home/oracle/app/oracle/oradata/orcl/redo03.log 2012-01-03 23:10 2012-01-06
01:32
  /home/oracle/app/oracle/oradata/orcl/redo02.log 2012-01-03 14:07 2012-01-03
23:10
  /home/oracle/app/oracle/oradata/orcl/redo01.log 2012-01-03 14:07 2012-01-03
14:07
  Not Available                      * Initialized *   2012-01-03 14:07

Current directory     /home/oracle/app/GoldenGate
Report file           /home/oracle/app/GoldenGate/dirrpt/EXHR01.rpt
Parameter file        /home/oracle/app/GoldenGate/dirprm/exhr01.prm
Checkpoint file       /home/oracle/app/GoldenGate/dirchk/EXHR01.cpe
Process file          /home/oracle/app/GoldenGate/dirpcs/EXHR01.pce
Stdout file           /home/oracle/app/GoldenGate/dirout/EXHR01.out
Error log             /home/oracle/app/GoldenGate/ggserr.log
```

This report output shows us additional information such as the source online redo logs and the various directories that the Extract process is using for things such as the Extract process report file, and the location of the error logs of the extract.

You can also view a report on the individual Extract processes with the GGSCI **view report** command. This will cause Oracle GoldenGate to open the current output file associated with the Extract process (this command can also be used to view reports on Replicat processes). This report is very handy to have in the event that the Extract process abends, as you can see the errors it reported before the process failure. These reports are stored in the directory $GGHOME/dirrpt and they are renamed (appending a sequence number to the end of them) and maintained for the duration in this directory. So, you can go look at them manually at any time if you desire.

GoldenGate Workshop: *Configure the Extract Process on Goldengate1*

Workshop Notes
We are now ready to configure the Extract process on the Goldengate1 server. The Extract process will be responsible for collecting changes on the ORCL database on Goldengate1. It will write those changes to a local trail file, which the GoldenGate Data Pump Extract process will later read from and ship to the ORCL database on the server Goldengate2. So, let's configure that extract.

Step 1. Start by logging in to the server Goldengate1 as the Oracle OS user. Open a command-line window.

Step 2. Change to the $GGHOME directory (%GGHOME% in Windows).

```
[oracle@goldengate1 GoldenGate]$ cd $GGHOME
```

Step 3. Start the GGSCI interface.

```
[oracle@goldengate1 GoldenGate]$ ggsci
Oracle GoldenGate Command Interpreter for Oracle
Version 11.1.1.1 OGGCORE_11.1.1_PLATFORMS_110421.2040
Linux, x86, 32bit (optimized), Oracle 11g on Apr 21 2011
22:38:06
Copyright (C) 1995, 2011, Oracle and/or its affiliates.
All rights reserved.
```

Step 4. Now that we have started GGSCI, we need to edit the parameter file for the Extract process we are going to create. We will name this extract EXHR01. Use the GGSCI command edit param EXHR01 and then create the parameter file. The following code shows examples of what you will do. The editor that is used in the Linux version of GoldenGate is the vi editor by default, so you will use the appropriate keystrokes for the vi editor when creating the parameter file.

```
GGSCI (goldengate1) 4> edit param exhr01
-- Extract name. Up to 8 characters
EXTRACT EXHR01
```

```
-- Optional - This ensures that the database environment is
-- configured correctly. Using it is a best practice.
SETENV (NLS_LANG=AMERICAN_AMERICA.AL32UTF8)
SETENV (ORACLE_SID=ORCL)
-- Login and password to the administrator account in the
-- source database.
USERID ggadmin, PASSWORD ggadmin
-- Defines the location and prefix of the trail files
EXTRAIL ./dirdat/hr
-- This defines what we are replicating.
-- In this case, all tables in the HR schema.
-- Note the use of the wildcard character.
TABLE HR.*;
-- Note - there is no DDL capture in this extract. Only DML.
```

Step 5. Save the parameter file once you have created it.

Step 6. Now, you will need to log in to the database as the GoldenGate administrator using the **dblogin** command, and then register the extract with GoldenGate using the **add extract** command as seen here:

```
GGSCI (goldengate1) 5> dblogin userid ggadmin, password ggadmin
GGSCI (goldengate1) 6> add extract exhr01, tranlog, begin now
```

Step 7. Now we need to add the local trail file. This is done with the GGSCI command **add exttrail**. In our case, we are creating a trail file in the directory $GGOME/dirdat and the trail file will be prefixed with hr, followed by a numerical sequence number. We are also associating the extract with the EXHR01. Finally, in this example we are making the file 100 MB in size. Here is the command you will want to issue:

```
GGSCI (goldengate1) 7>Add exttrail ./dirdat/hr, extract
EXHR01, megabytes 100
```

Step 8. Start the extract from the GGSCI command line as seen in this example:

```
GGSCI (goldengate1) 8>Start extract EXHR01
```

Step 9. Use the **info all** command from GGSCI to determine that the extract has started without error.

```
GGSCI (goldengate1) 5> info all
Program       Status      Group      Lag          Time Since Chkpt
MANAGER       RUNNING
EXTRACT       RUNNING     EXHR01     00:00:00     00:00:07
```

Configuring the GoldenGate Data Pump

Recall that Oracle GoldenGate Data Pump is kind of a middleman, if you will. It is responsible for reading the trail file on the source, and shipping the contents of the trail file over to the Collector process on the source database server. The benefit of using the GoldenGate Data Pump, along with a local trail file, is that if there is some failure between the source database server and the target database server(s) (for example, network communications are interrupted), the Extract process can continue to write records to the local trail file and, once the failure is corrected, the GoldenGate Data Pump process can resume shipping records to the target database server.

Recall from Chapter 2 that the GoldenGate Data Pump is essentially an Extract process, much like the one we created earlier in this chapter. The main difference is that instead of extracting information from the online redo logs, it is extracting information from the local trail file. This implies that the local Extract process must be configured to create local trail files, rather than ship the trail file data directly to the target database server.

Since the GoldenGate Data Pump is really just an Extract process, configuring the GoldenGate Data Pump will be similar to the way we configured the Extract process earlier. We will follow these steps, which should seem familiar:

- Creating the GoldenGate Data Pump extract parameter file
- Adding the GoldenGate Data Pump Extract to GoldenGate
- Administering the Extract process

Let's look at each of these steps in more detail, leading up to our next workshop.

Creating the GoldenGate Data Pump Extract Parameter File

The GoldenGate Data Pump parameter file is created much as the extract parameter file was earlier. We use GGSCI to create and save the Data Pump parameter file. To create the file in GGSCI, we would use the **edit params** command (**edit params dphr01**). This file will be called DPHR01.prm and it will be stored in the directory $GGHOME/dirprm in Linux or %GGHOME%\dirprm in Windows. We will walk you through this whole process within the workshops contained in this chapter.

Note that we have again used a naming standard for the Data Pump process. In this case, we prefix it with DP instead of EX. We keep the remaining part of the name, HR01, the same so that we can maintain a relationship between the HR01 extract and the associated EXHR01 extract. Here is a listing of the EXHR01 parameter file:

```
-- Data Pump name. Up to 8 characters
EXTRACT DPHR01
-- PASSTHRU indicates that the data does not need any kind of filtering
-- or mapping of any kind. It implies that the schemas on both the
-- source and target systems are exactly alike.
PASSTHRU
-- RMTHOST points to the remote system.
-- You will see in later chapters that there can be more than one
-- RMTHOST entry.
RMTHOST goldengate2, MGRPORT 7840
-- RMTRRAIL is the remote trail that we will define shortly on the
-- target database server. In this case we kept the prefix
-- (max 2 characters) the same as the local trail file.
RMTTRAIL dirdat/hr
-- This defines what objects we are replicating to the target system.
-- In this case, all tables in the HR schema.
-- Note the use of the wildcard character.
TABLE HR.*;
```

We have created comments on the parameters for you to reference, and many of them you have already seen. In the cases of the RMTTRAIL and TABLE parameters, they reference the objects on the target database server and not the source database server. We have also added the parameter RMTHOST. This is the name of the target database server, and we have also defined the TCP/IP port that the Manager process on the source database will use to communicate with the Manager process on the target database (7840).

Registering the GoldenGate Data Pump Extract

As with the extract we created, we need to perform a few more actions after creating the GoldenGate Data Pump parameter file. First, we need to register the GoldenGate Data Pump process as seen here:

```
GGSCI (goldengate1) 5> dblogin userid ggadmin, password ggadmin
Successfully logged into database.

GGSCI (goldengate1) 6> add extract DPHR01, EXTTRAILSOURCE dirdat/hr
EXTRACT added.
```

We have pretty much done the same thing that we did when we registered the EXHR01 Extract process earlier, with a few differences. As before, we first logged in to the database through GGSCI using the **dblogin** command. Then we added the new GoldenGate Data Pump process to the GoldenGate metadata using the **add extract** command from GGSCI. The EXTTRAILSOURCE parameter indicates the location of the trail file that the Data Pump process will be reading from. Again, this does not start the GoldenGate Data Pump Extract process; we need to do that next.

One last thing we need to do is add the remote trail file on the target database server, Goldengate2 in this case. The size of the remote trail file should be the same size as the local trail file. In this example we use the **add rmttrail** command to add the remote trail file:

```
Add rmttrail dirdat/hr, extract DPHR01, megabytes 100
```

Administering the GoldenGate Data Pump Extract Process

Now that we have added the Data Pump Extract process, we need to start the Extract process so it will start capturing changes from the local trail file and writing them to the remote trail file on the target database server. In this section we will discuss the following:

- Starting the Data Pump Extract process

- Stopping the Data Pump Extract process

- Monitoring the Data Pump Extract process

Starting the Data Pump Extract Process

Starting the Data Pump Extract process is just like starting the EXHR01 Extract process earlier. You simply use the **start extract** command from the GGSCI interface, as seen here where we will start our DBHR01 extract:

```
Start extract DPHR01
```

Stopping the Data Pump Extract Process

Stopping the Extract process is as easy as starting it. Simply use the **stop extract** command from the GGSCI interface, and the Extract process will be shut down normally. Here is an example:

```
Stop extract DPHR01
```

Monitoring the Data Pump Extract Process

As with the earlier EXHR01 Extract process, you can use the **info all** command to monitor its operation. Here is an example:

```
GGSCI (goldengate1) 18> info all
    Program      Status       Group        Lag          Time Since Chkpt
```

```
MANAGER      RUNNING
EXTRACT      RUNNING     DPHR01       00:00:00     00:00:16
EXTRACT      RUNNING     EXHR01       00:00:00     00:00:08
```

Now we have the Manager process and two Extract processes running (DPHR01 and EXHR01).

You can get more detailed information by using the **info** command with the EXTRACT parameter as seen here:

```
GGSCI (goldengate1) 10> info extract DPHR01
EXTRACT      EXHR01     Last Started 2012-01-06 00:35   Status RUNNING
Checkpoint Lag          00:00:00 (updated 00:00:01 ago)
Log Read Checkpoint  Oracle Redo Logs
                        2012-01-06 01:33:42  Seqno 474, RBA 18662400
```

As with the Extract process before, you can get even more information by adding the DETAIL parameter to the **info** command with the EXTRACT parameter, as seen here:

```
9> info extract EXHR01, detail
EXTRACT      EXHR01     Last Started 2012-01-06 00:35   Status RUNNING
Checkpoint Lag          00:00:00 (updated 00:00:11 ago)
Log Read Checkpoint  Oracle Redo Logs
                        2012-01-06 01:32:55  Seqno 474, RBA 18651648

   Target Extract Trails:
   Remote Trail Name                           Seqno        RBA      Max MB
   ./dirdat/hr                                    1         1037         10
   Extract Source                    Begin              End
   /home/oracle/app/oracle/oradata/orcl/redo03.log  2012-01-03 23:10  2012-01-
06 01:32
    /home/oracle/app/oracle/oradata/orcl/redo02.log  2012-01-03 14:07  2012-01-
03 23:10
    /home/oracle/app/oracle/oradata/orcl/redo01.log  2012-01-03 14:07  2012-01-
03 14:07
   Not Available                            * Initialized *   2012-01-03 14:07

Current directory    /home/oracle/app/GoldenGate
Report file          /home/oracle/app/GoldenGate/dirrpt/EXHR01.rpt
Parameter file       /home/oracle/app/GoldenGate/dirprm/exhr01.prm
Checkpoint file      /home/oracle/app/GoldenGate/dirchk/EXHR01.cpe
Process file         /home/oracle/app/GoldenGate/dirpcs/EXHR01.pce
Stdout file          /home/oracle/app/GoldenGate/dirout/EXHR01.out
Error log            /home/oracle/app/GoldenGate/ggserr.log
```

This report output shows us additional information such as the source online redo logs and the various directories that the Extract process is using for things such as the Extract process report file, and the location of the error logs of the extract.

You can also view a report on the individual Extract processes with the GGSCI **view report** command. This will cause Oracle GoldenGate to open the current output file associated with the Extract process (this command can also be used to view reports on Replicat processes). This report is very handy to have in the event that the Extract process abends, as you can see the errors it reported before the process failure. These reports are stored in the directory $GGHOME/dirrpt and they are renamed (appending a sequence number to the end of them) and maintained for the duration in this directory. So, you can go look at them manually at any time if you desire.

GoldenGate Workshop: *Configure the Data Pump Extract Process on Goldengate1*

Workshop Notes
We are now ready to configure the Data Pump Extract process on the Goldengate1 server. The Data Pump Extract process will be responsible for collecting changes in the local trail file on the Goldengate1 server. It will write those changes to the remote trail file on the Goldengate2 server. This will stage the changes for the Replicat process on the Goldengate2 server. The Replicat process on the Goldengate2 server will then write the updates to the ORCL database on the Goldengate2 server.

Step 1. Start by logging in to the server Goldengate1 as the Oracle OS user. Open a command-line window.

Step 2. Change to the $GGHOME directory (%GGHOME% in Windows).

```
[oracle@goldengate1 GoldenGate]$ cd $GGHOME
```

Step 3. Start the GGSCI GoldenGate interface.

```
[oracle@goldengate1 GoldenGate]$ ggsci
Oracle GoldenGate Command Interpreter for Oracle
Version 11.1.1.1 OGGCORE_11.1.1_PLATFORMS_110421.2040
Linux, x86, 32bit (optimized), Oracle 11g on Apr 21 2011
22:38:06
Copyright (C) 1995, 2011, Oracle and/or its affiliates. All
rights reserved.
```

Step 4. Now that we have started GGSCI, we need to edit the parameter file for the Data Pump Extract process we are going to create. We will name this extract DPHR01.

Use the GGSCI command **edit param DPHR01** and then create the parameter file. The following code shows examples of what you will do. The editor that is used in the Linux version of GoldenGate is the vi editor by default, so you will use the appropriate keystrokes for the vi editor when creating the parameter file.

```
GGSCI (goldengate1) 4> edit param dphr01
-- Data Pump name. Up to 8 characters
EXTRACT DPHR01
-- PASSTHRU indicates that the data does not need any kind of
-- filtering or mapping of any kind. It implies that the
-- schemas on both the source and target systems are exactly
-- alike.
PASSTHRU
-- RMTHOST points to the remote system.
-- You will see in later chapters that there can be more than
-- one RMTHOST entry.
RMTHOST goldengate2, MGRPORT 7840
-- RMTRRAIL is the remote trail that we will define shortly on
-- the target database server. In this case we kept the prefix
-- (max 2 characters) the same as the local trail file.
RMTTRAIL dirdat/hr
-- This defines what objects we are replicating to the target
-- system.
-- In this case, all tables in the HR schema.
-- Note the use of the wildcard character.
TABLE HR.*;
```

Step 5. Save the parameter file once you have created it.

Step 6. Now, you will need to log in to the database as the GoldenGate administrator using the **dblogin** command, and then register the Data Pump extract with GoldenGate using the **add extract** command, as seen here:

```
GGSCI (goldengate1) 5> dblogin userid ggadmin, password ggadmin
GGSCI (goldengate1) 6> add extract DPHR01, EXTTRAILSOURCE
dirdat/hr
```

Step 7. Now we need to add the remote trail file. This is done with the GGSCI command **add rmttrail**. In this case, we are creating a trail file in the directory $GGOME/dirdat on the server Goldengate2. The resulting trail file will be prefixed with hr, followed by a numerical sequence number. We are also associating the remote trail file with the DPHR01 Data Pump extract. Finally, in this example we are making the file 100 megabytes in size. Here is the command you will want to issue:

```
Add rmttrail dirdat/hr, extract DPHR01, megabytes 100
```

Step 8. Start the extract from the GGSCI command line as seen in this example:

```
GGSCI (goldengate1) 8>Start extract DPHR01
```

Step 9. Use the **info all** command from GGSCI to determine that the extract has started without error.

```
GGSCI (goldengate1) 1> info all
Program      Status      Group      Lag          Time Since Chkpt
MANAGER      RUNNING
EXTRACT      RUNNING     DPHR01     00:00:00     00:00:02
EXTRACT      RUNNING     EXHR01     00:00:00     00:00:04
```

Instantiating the Target Database Using GoldenGate

At this point we are now capturing changes on the source database and creating a trail file. We have also configured the GoldenGate Data Pump Export process. Now we can choose to first configure the Replicat process on the target database (but not start it), or we can go ahead, instantiate the target database, and then configure and start the Replicat process. The important thing to note is that we can't start the Replicat process until we instantiate the database. It is generally a best practice to instantiate the database, configure the Replicat process, and then start the Replicat process, so that is what we are going to do.

In this section we cover the instantiation of the target database. You might want to review the topology that we defined earlier in this chapter if you are not clear on where the data is coming from and where it's being replicated to.

There are many different ways to instantiate a target database, preparing it for replication. You can use RMAN, Oracle Database's Data Pump utility (not to be confused with the GoldenGate Data Pump process). You can even use GoldenGate itself to instantiate the database, and that is exactly what we are going to do in this chapter! This will require the configuration of a special initial-load Extract process and then registering that load process to GoldenGate with the **add extract** command. Then we will configure the initial-load Replicat process to the target database server and register it with the **add replicat** command. After we have configured these two processes, we will start the process of actually instantiating the target database schema. We are close to getting replication running, so hang on, the fun is close to beginning!

Configure and Register the Initial-Load Extract Process

By this time, you have probably guessed that for this initial-load Extract process that we will build, we will need to create yet another parameter file. If you guessed that, congratulations and go to the head of the class! As with the other Extract processes, we will build the parameter file and then register the Extract process with GoldenGate.

To begin with, here is the parameter file that we will use. As always, we will use GGSCI to create and edit the parameter file (of course, you can use a regular text editor too). The name of the file will be $GGHOME/dirprm/slhr01.prm. Here is the file that we will use; note that there are a number of comments in the body of the parameter file that point out the different parameters being used:

```
-- This is the initial load extract parameter file. We use IL for the
-- prefix for all initial load extracts. Note the HR01 remains the same.
-- This is created on the source database server (Goldengate1)
EXTRACT SLHR01
-- Optional - This ensures that the database environment is
-- configured correctly. Using it is a best practice.
SETENV (NLS_LANG=AMERICAN_AMERICA.AL32UTF8)
-- Login and password to the administrator account in the source database.
USERID ggadmin, PASSWORD ggadmin
-- RMTHOST points to the remote system.
-- You will see in later chapters that there can be more than one RMTHOST
-- entry.
RMTHOST goldengate2, MGRPORT 7840
-- RMTTASK indicates that a remote task (in this case the remote
-- Replicat process by virtue of the replicat option) will be started
-- by the Extract process. The GROUP parameter indicates the name of the
-- Replicat process (which we will create shortly).
-- Note that we prefixed the initial-load extract with the letters SL (Source
-- Load) and Replicat process is prefixed with TL (Target Load).
RMTTASK replicat, GROUP TLHR01
-- There are a couple of constraints we need to disable here.
SQLEXEC "alter table HR.EMPLOYEES disable constraint HR.EMP_DEPT_FK"
-- This defines what objects we are replicating to the target system.
-- In this case, all tables in the HR schema.
-- Note the use of the wildcard character.
TABLE HR.JOBS;
TABLE HR.REGIONS;
TABLE HR.COUNTRIES;
TABLE HR.LOCATIONS;
TABLE HR.EMPLOYEES;
TABLE HR.DEPARTMENTS;
TABLE HR.JOB_HISTORY;
```

This parameter file has many parameters you are already familiar with. The new one, RMTTASK, indicates that the source Extract process should start the remote Replicat process automatically, and tells GoldenGate what the name of that process is. Of course, we have to configure that Replicat process first, which we will do in the next section.

One thing to note is that we didn't use wildcards for the TABLE parameters, but rather listed each of the tables. The reason for this was the foreign key constraints present in the schema. We could have disabled the constraints and then later on enabled them. GoldenGate will load the tables in the order listed, though, and since we only had seven tables to deal with, we just opted to list them in the order in which they should be loaded to avoid constraint violations.

Having created the parameter file and saved it, we need to register the Extract process with GoldenGate just as we did with the Extract process earlier in this chapter. We simply use the **add extract** command as we did before and as seen here:

```
Add extract SLHR01, SOURCEISTABLE
```

Note that we have used a new parameter, SOURCEISTABLE. This indicates to GoldenGate that this particular Extract process will not be reading the online redo logs, but will instead be reading data directly from the database. SOURCEISTABLE will cause the Extract process to read all the records in the table(s) defined in the parameter file we just created (in our case, all tables in the HR schema) and ship them over to the remote database server, where a Replicat process will write them to the target database. As we mentioned earlier when we configured the Extract process, when we start that process, it will automatically communicate with the Manager process on the target database server and start the Replicat process there.

As you might expect, there are many different options that we could have taken when configuring the SLHR01 Extract process. For example, we could have opted to transfer all the data to a physical file on the remote database server as opposed to just pumping it over the network and having the Replicat process write it directly into the database. To do this we would have used the RMTFILE parameter and we would remove the RMTTASK parameter (starting the Replicat process manually on the remote server after the Extract process was complete). As you can see, there are many different ways to do the same thing in GoldenGate!

Now it's time to configure and register the Replicat process on the target database server!

Configure and Register the Initial-Load Replicat Process

As with the Extract process we just configured on the source server Goldengate1, you will find the configuration of the Replicat process also looks familiar because it is similar to the Replicat process we configured earlier in this chapter. Here is the parameter file we will create, again using the GGSCI command-line interface. Note that this is created on the target server, Goldengate2:

```
-- This is the initial load Replicat parameter file. We use TL for the
-- prefix for all initial load extracts. Note the HR01 remains the same.
-- This is created on the target database server (Goldengate2).
REPLICAT TLHR01
-- Optional - This ensures that the database environment is
-- configured correctly. Using it is a best practice.
SETENV (NLS_LANG=AMERICAN_AMERICA.AL32UTF8)
-- Login and password to the administrator account in the source database.
USERID ggadmin, PASSWORD ggadmin
-- The ASSUMETARGETDEFS parameter indicates that the source and target database
-- tables are the same. Of course, there are many times when this is not the
-- case and we will cover those situations in later chapters.
ASSUMETARGETDEFS
HANDLECOLLISIONS
DBOPTIONS SUPPRESSTRIGGERS
-- There are a couple of constraints we need to disable here.
SQLEXEC " alter table HR.EMPLOYEES disable constraint EMP_DEPT_FK ";
-- This defines what objects we are replicating to the target system.
-- In this case, all tables in the HR schema.
-- Note the use of the wildcard character.
MAP HR.*, TARGET HR.*;
-- END RUNTIME indicates that the Replicat process should terminate
-- once the batch job is done.
-- There are a couple of constraints we need to enable here.
SQLEXEC " alter table HR.EMPLOYEES enable constraint EMP_DEPT_FK " ONEXIT
END RUNTIME
```

This replicat parameter file has a lot going on here. There are some familiar things as well as a number of new things that we want to discuss. The new things are

- The ASSUMETARGETDEFS parameter

- The HANDLECOLLISIONS parameter

- The DBOPTIONS SUPPRESSTRIGGERS parameter

- The SQLEXEC parameter

- The MAP parameter

- The END RUNTIME parameter

The ASSUMETARGETDEFS parameter indicates that the source and target database tables/schemas are the same. If we needed to do some special mapping, because there were differences, we would need to generate a data definitions file. We will cover this situation in Chapter 6 of this book, when we look at cascading GoldenGate replication configuration.

We added the HANDLECOLLISIONS parameter so that we could rerun this load without having to remove the data in the tables first. HANDLECOLLISIONS indicates to GoldenGate that it's possible there will be primary key conflicts and to ignore those errors and continue processing.

The DBOPTIONS SUPPRESSTRIGGERS parameter turns off the triggers that are on the target database being loaded. In most cases, all Replicat processes should have this parameter included in their parameter files as triggers in the target databases should usually be disabled during GoldenGate replication. Exceptions to this rule would be multimaster topologies.

We added the *sqlexec* command here to disable a perky foreign key and then re-enable it after the replication was complete. This will avoid constraint errors during inserts by the Replicat process.

The MAP clause is basically a mapping clause and it tells the Replicat process how the data that is being transferred from the source database should map to the schema(s) in the target database. This mapping criteria can get fairly complex (though we really like to keep things as simple and basic as possible), but fortunately in our example it's pretty straightforward (Chapter 6 will show you a more sophisticated example of schema mapping). Here we simply indicate that we are mapping the HR schema from the source database to the HR schema on the target database. The table names are all the same.

The END RUNTIME parameter tells the Replicat process that when it's done with its work, it should terminate normally rather than continue to run.

Pop quiz! Now that we have created the replicat parameter file, what do we need to do? If you said, we need to register it on the target database server with the **add replicat** command, you were correct! Here is an example of registering the SLHR01 Replicat process with GoldenGate:

```
Add replicat TLHR01, SPECIALRUN
```

Notice that we used the SPECIALRUN option of the **add replicat** command. This indicates that this Replicat process is a one-time, initial load and not a normal, change processing, Replicat process. Now we have created parameter files, registered everything, and if we have done everything perfectly, we are ready to load data into our target database!

Instantiating the Target Database with the Configured GoldenGate Processes

Starting the initial data load is as easy as calling the **start extract** command from the GGSCI prompt on the source database server (Goldengate1) as seen here:

```
Start extract SLHR01
```

This will start the SLHR01 Extract process on the source database server (Goldengate1) and that extract will automatically start the ILHR01 Replicat process on the target database server (Goldengate2). The SLHR01 will then start sending data directly to the ILHR01 Replicat process, which will write that data to the target database. Once the initial data load is complete, both the Replicat process and the Extract process will exit normally (assuming no errors, of course!).

You can validate the successful run (or abend) of the initial database load process by using the **view report** command on the target database server to view the results of the ILHR01 Replicat process, as seen in this example:

```
View report ILHR01
```

You can also log in to the target database schema and see the new HR schema populated there. It's a best practice to compare row counts in both the source and target database servers to further ensure that the data load was successful without errors.

GoldenGate Workshop: *Instantiate the ORCL Database on Goldengate2 from ORCL on Goldengate1*

Workshop Notes

We are almost ready to start replication from the ORCL database on Goldengate1 to the ORCL database on Goldengate2. In this workshop we will first drop the existing HR schema on Goldengate2. We will then create a metadata export of the HR schema that exists in the ORCL database on Goldengate1. We will move that export over to Goldengate2, and then re-create the HR schema. We will then use GoldenGate to instantiate this new schema on Goldengate2 using the data in the ORCL database on Goldengate1. Then we will be ready for our last workshop of this picture, where we will start our replication.

Step 1. On the Goldengate2 server, log in to the ORCL database as sys using the sysdba authentication.

Step 2. Use the **drop user** command with the CASCADE option to drop the HR user.

Step 3. On the Goldengate1 server, log in to the Oracle OS account and start a command-line window. Make sure the environment is set for the ORCL database.

Step 4. Log in to the ORCL database on the Goldengate1 server as the SYS user using the SYSDBA privilege. Ensure the export directory has been created using the following query:

```
[oracle@goldengate1 GoldenGate]$ sqlplus / as sysdba
SQL>Select * from dba_directories where directory_name='EXPORT';
```

If no rows are returned by the query, execute the following command:

```
Create directory export as '/home/oracle/export';
```

Step 5. On the Goldengate1 server, use the **expdp** command to create an object-only export of the HR schema.

```
expdp schemas=HR directory=export dumpfile=expdpHR.dmp
logfile=expdpHR.log exclude=table_data
```

Step 6. Go to the Goldengate2 server. Log in as the Oracle user. Change to the /home/oracle/export directory (create it if required). Using the **scp** command, copy the expdpHR.dmp file from Goldengate1 to Goldengate2 as seen in the following example. Note that you have to use the root account on Goldengate1 to successfully copy the file with the **scp** command.

```
Cd /home/oracle/export
scp root@goldengate1:/home/oracle/export/expdpHR.dmp  .
```

Step 7. Log in to the ORCL database on the Goldengate1 server as the SYS user using the SYSDBA privilege. Ensure that the export directory has been created using the following query:

```
[oracle@goldengate1 GoldenGate]$ sqlplus / as sysdba
SQL>Select * from dba_directories where directory_name='EXPORT';
```

If no rows are returned by the query, execute the following command:

```
Create directory export as '/home/oracle/export';
```

Step 8. Now, using **impdp**, create the HR schema. It will be created with no data. Here is an example:

```
impdp directory=robert dumpfile=expdpHR.dmp logfile=impdphr.log
```

Step 9. On the Goldengate1 server, make sure you are still logged in using the Oracle OS account. From a command line, change to the GoldenGate home directory.

```
[oracle@goldengate1 GoldenGate]$ cd $GGHOME
```

Step 10. Start the GoldenGate command-line interface (GGSCI). Using the **edit param** command, we are going to create the extract parameter file that will be used to initially populate the HR schema on the ORCL database on the Goldengate2 server. Here is the parameter file you should create:

```
[oracle@goldengate2 ~]$ ggsci
Oracle GoldenGate Command Interpreter for Oracle
Version 11.1.1.1 OGGCORE_11.1.1_PLATFORMS_110421.2040
Linux, x86, 32bit (optimized), Oracle 11g on Apr 21 2011 22:38:06
Copyright (C) 1995, 2011, Oracle and/or its affiliates. All
rights reserved.
GGSCI (goldengate2) 1>edit param slhr01
-- This is the initial load extract parameter file. We use IL
-- for the prefix for all initial load extracts. Note the HR01
-- remains the same.
-- This is created on the source database server (Goldengate1)
EXTRACT SLHR01
-- Optional - This ensures that the database environment is
-- configured correctly. Using it is a best practice.
SETENV (NLS_LANG=AMERICAN_AMERICA.AL32UTF8)
-- Login and password to the administrator account in the
-- source database.
USERID ggadmin, PASSWORD ggadmin
-- RMTHOST points to the remote system.
-- You will see in later chapters that there can be more than
-- one RMTHOST entry.
RMTHOST goldengate2, MGRPORT 7840
-- RMTTASK indicates that a remote task (in this case the
-- remote  Replicat process by virtue of the replicat option)
-- will be started by the Extract process. The GROUP parameter
-- indicates the name of the Replicat process (which we will
-- create shortly).
-- Note that we prefixed the initial-load extract with the
-- letters SL (Source Load) and  Replicat process is prefixed
-- with TL (Target Load).
RMTTASK replicat, GROUP TLHR01
-- There are a couple of constraints we need to disable here.
SQLEXEC "alter table HR.EMPLOYEES disable constraint
HR.EMP_DEPT_FK"
-- This defines what objects we are replicating to the target
-- system. In this case, all tables in the HR schema.
-- Note the use of the wildcard character.
TABLE HR.JOBS;
TABLE HR.REGIONS;
TABLE HR.COUNTRIES;
TABLE HR.LOCATIONS;
```

```
TABLE HR.EMPLOYEES;
TABLE HR.DEPARTMENTS;
TABLE HR.JOB_HISTORY;
```

Step 11. On the Goldengate1 server, from the same GGSCI interface, register the extract using the **add extract** command. We will add the SOURCEISTABLE parameter to indicate that we are sourcing the extract using tables in the database. Here is an example:

```
Add extract SLHR01, SOURCEISTABLE
```

Step 12. On the Goldengate2 server, make sure you are still logged in using the Oracle OS account. From a command line, change to the GoldenGate home directory.

```
[oracle@goldengate1 GoldenGate]$ cd $GGHOME
```

Step 13. Now, on the Goldengate2 server, we need to create the Replicat process parameter file. Use the **ggsci** command-line interface to GoldenGate and create the parameter file using the **edit param** command as seen here:

```
[oracle@goldengate2 ~]$ ggsci
Oracle GoldenGate Command Interpreter for Oracle
Version 11.1.1.1 OGGCORE_11.1.1_PLATFORMS_110421.2040
Linux, x86, 32bit (optimized), Oracle 11g on Apr 21 2011 22:38:06
Copyright (C) 1995, 2011, Oracle and/or its affiliates. All
rights reserved.
GGSCI (goldengate2) 1>edit param tlhr01
-- This is the initial load Replicate parameter file. We use
-- TL for the prefix for all initial load extracts. Note the
-- HR01 remains the same.
-- This is created on the target database server (Goldengate2).
REPLICAT TLHR01
-- Optional - This ensures that the database environment is
-- configured correctly. Using it is a best practice.
SETENV (NLS_LANG=AMERICAN_AMERICA.AL32UTF8)
-- Login and password to the administrator account in the
source database.
USERID ggadmin, PASSWORD ggadmin
-- The ASSUMETARGETDEFS parameter indicates that the source
-- and target database tables are the same. Of course, there
-- are many times when this is not the case and we will cover
-- those situations in later chapters.
ASSUMETARGETDEFS
HANDLECOLLISIONS
DBOPTIONS SUPPRESSTRIGGERS
-- There are a couple of constraints we need to disable here.
SQLEXEC " alter table HR.EMPLOYEES disable constraint
```

```
EMP_DEPT_FK ";
-- This defines what objects we are replicating to the target
-- system. In this case, all tables in the HR schema.
-- Note the use of the wildcard character.
MAP HR.*, TARGET HR.*;
-- END RUNTIME indicates that the Replicat process should
-- terminate once the batch job is done.
-- There are a couple of constraints we need to enable here.
SQLEXEC " alter table HR.EMPLOYEES enable constraint
EMP_DEPT_FK " ONEXIT
END RUNTIME
```

Step 14.   Now, register the Replicat process in the same GGSCI command-line interface window as seen here:

```
Add replicat TLHR01, SPECIALRUN
```

Step 15.   Now, return to the Goldengate1 server. Having configured the Extract and Replicat processes, proceed to start the Extract process and instantiate the HR schema on the ORCL database on the Goldengate2 server as seen here:

```
Start extract SLHR01
```

Configuring the GoldenGate Replicat Process

We have talked about the Replicat process and now we are going to use it! The Replicat process is going to keep track of the changes that are made in the database by combing through the redo logs. As such, the Replicat process only will need to run on one server, Goldengate1. As the Replicat process finds the changes that we have told it to replicate, it will write those out to the local trail file that we will define.

Configuring the Replicat process involves several steps. These are

- Creating the replicat parameter file

- Adding the replicat to GoldenGate

- Defining the trail file that is associated with the replicat

- Administering the Replicat process

Let's look at each of these steps in more detail, leading up to our next workshop.

Creating the Replicat Parameter File

We are close now. We have the target database seeded with data. Now we need to configure the final process, which is the Replicat process. As with the Extract process, we will use GGSCI to create and save the Replicat process parameter file. To create the file in GGSCI, we would use the **edit params** command (**edit params rphr01**). This file will be called rphr01.prm and it will be stored in the directory $GGHOME/dirprm in Linux or %GGHOME%\dirprm in Windows. We will walk you through this whole process in the "Creating the Replicat Process" workshop later in this chapter.

> **NOTE**
> *The name of the various parameter files is not case sensitive. If you use edit param rphr01 or edit param RPHR01, it will still edit the same file. The parameter files are all saved in lowercase on the $GGHOME/ dirprm directory.*

Note that we have used a naming convention of RP for the Replicat process parameter files. The rest of the convention is just like the Extract process. This way, it's easy to match the Extract and Replicat processes that go together.

Let's take a look at the Replicat process parameter file we will create:

```
-- Replicat name. Up to 8 characters
REPLICAT RPHR01
-- Optional - This ensures that the database environment is
-- configured correctly. Using it is a best practice.
SETENV (NLS_LANG=AMERICAN_AMERICA.AL32UTF8)
-- Login and password to the administrator account in the
-- source database.
USERID ggadmin, PASSWORD ggadmin
-- This will cause the Replicat to handle row collisions
-- without abending.  Typically we don't want this in a
-- Replicate file but it's not a bad idea to have it in
-- there during the first runs, while GoldenGate catches
-- up the target database with the source database.
-- So, add it now, and remove it after we have gotten the
-- Target database caught up.
HANDLECOLLISIONS
-- Need to disable triggers.
DBOPTIONS SUPPRESSTRIGGERS
-- ASSUMETARGETDEFS is used here to indicate that the source
-- and target database schemas are basically the same.
ASSUMETARGETDEFS
```

```
-- The MAP clause essentially says that all HR.* tables on the
-- source database map to the same schema/object on the target
-- database.
MAP HR.*, TARGET HR.*;
-- Note - there is no DDL capture in this extract. Only DML.
```

In the RPHR01 extract parameter file we have just created, we have used several parameters that you should already be familiar with such as the SETENV, USERID, ASSUMETARGETDEFS, and MAP parameters. In fact, we really have not introduced a new parameter in this parameter file! There are a couple of items to note:

■ We added the HANDLECOLLISIONS parameter, which was previously used and discussed when we did the initial target database load replicat parameter file earlier in this chapter. We need this parameter, especially if the source database is going to be in use while the initial target database data load is occurring. Since it's possible that change will occur, we need to initially have a way to deal with possible conflicts that may occur during the initial "catch-up" of the target database.

For example, an insert into a table might occur before the initial load, but during the capture of change in the database. During the initial load, this new record will be loaded into the target database schema. When we start applying change, after the initial data load, we will have a collision because the record has already been created on the target database, but that insert was also captured in the change capture process. Thus we have a collision. In this case, we expected the possibility of collisions, and therefore we configure the Replicat process to handle them for us gracefully and not error out.

Once the Replicat process has caught up and the source and target databases are no longer divergent (with respect to the time of the initial data load), you can shut down the Replicat process, and remove the HANDLECOLLISIONS parameter. Another option, if you don't want to shut down the Replicat process, is that you can use the GGSCI **send** command to communicate with the running Replicat process and tell it to no longer handle collisions. Here is an example of using the **send** command to perform this function:

```
send replicat RPHR01 NOHANDLECOLLISIONS HR.*
```

Note that if you do this, you will still need to modify the parameter file.

■ Notice that we used the SETENV parameter again to set the NLS_LANG environment variable. This is still an important thing to do, so don't forget!

Registering the Replicat Process

Once we have created the GoldenGate extract parameter file, we need to perform a few more actions. First, we need to register the Replicat process using the **add replicat** GGSCI command as seen here:

```
GGSCI (goldengate1) 5> dblogin userid ggadmin, password ggadmin
Successfully logged into database.

GGSCI (goldengate1) 6> add replicat RPHR01, NODBCHECKPOINT, exttrail
dirdat/hr
2012-01-03 13:57:52  INFO    OGG-01749  Successfully registered EXTRACT
XHR01 to start managing log retention at SCN 10796294.

REPLICAT added.
```

NOTE
*If you do not log in to the Oracle database before issuing the **add extract** command, you will need to register the Extract with the database at a later time using the **register extract** command.*

Note what we have done in the previous code example. First, we logged in to the database through GGSCI using the **dblogin** command. Then we registered the new Replicat process using the **add replicat** command from GGSCI. Note that we indicated the location of the trail file on the target database server using the EXTTRAIL parameter. This is the same trail file we defined when we created the GoldenGate Data Pump Extract process earlier in this chapter.

Administering the Replicat Process

Now that we have defined the Replicat process, we need to start it so it will start applying changes. Therefore, in this section we will discuss the following:

- Starting the Replicat process

- Stopping the Replicat process

- Monitoring the Replicat process

Starting the Replicat Process

To start the Replicat process, use the **start replicat** command from the GGSCI interface, as seen here where we will start our EXHR01 extract:

```
[oracle@goldengate1 GoldenGate]$ ggsci
Oracle GoldenGate Command Interpreter for Oracle
Version 11.1.1.1 OGGCORE_11.1.1_PLATFORMS_110421.2040
Linux, x86, 32bit (optimized), Oracle 11g on Apr 21 2011 22:38:06
Copyright (C) 1995, 2011, Oracle and/or its affiliates. All rights
reserved.
```

The Replicat process should start normally (you can monitor it as described later in this section). You should now see changes on the source database being replicated to the target database. You can log in to the HR schema on the target database and verify that those changes are occurring if you are so inclined. Congratulations, you have just started your first GoldenGate replication!

NOTE
You should not start the Replicat process until you have instantiated the target database!

Stopping the Replicat Process

Stopping the Replicat process is as easy as starting it. Simply use the **stop replicat** command from the GGSCI interface and the Replicat process will be shut down normally. Here is an example:

```
Stop replicat RPHR01
```

Monitoring the Replicat Process

Monitoring the Replicat process (and the overall replication process really) is like monitoring the Extract processes. You can use the **info all** command, which we have already seen. It will show us the different Replicat (and Extract and Manager) processes that are configured and their status. Here is an example:

```
GGSCI (goldengate1) 12> info all
```

You can get more detailed information by using the **info** command with the REPLICAT parameter as seen here:

```
GGSCI (goldengate1) 10> info replicat RPHR01
```

You can get even more information by adding the DETAIL parameter to the **info** command with the EXTRACT parameter as seen here:

```
9> info replicat RPHR01, detail
```

You can also view a report on the individual Replicat processes with the GGSCI **view report** command. This will cause Oracle GoldenGate to open the current output file associated with the Replicat process. This report is very handy to have in the event that the Replicat process abends, as you can see the errors it reported before the process failure. These reports are stored in the directory $GGHOME/dirrpt and they are renamed (appending a sequence number to the end of them) and maintained for the duration in this directory. So, you can go look at them manually at any time if you desire.

GoldenGate Workshop: *Configure the Replicat Process on Goldengate2*

Workshop Notes
We are now ready to configure the Extract process on the Goldengate1 server. The Extract process will be responsible for collecting changes on the ORCL database on Goldengate1. It will write those changes to a local trail file, which the GoldenGate Data Pump Extract process will later read from and ship to the ORCL database on the server Goldengate2. So, let's configure that extract.

Step 1. Start by logging in to the server Goldengate2 as the Oracle OS user. Open a command-line window.

Step 2. Change to the $GGHOME directory (%GGHOME% in Windows).

```
[oracle@goldengate1 GoldenGate]$ cd $GGHOME
```

Step 3. Start the GGSCI GoldenGate interface.

```
[oracle@goldengate1 GoldenGate]$ ggsci
Oracle GoldenGate Command Interpreter for Oracle
Version 11.1.1.1 OGGCORE_11.1.1_PLATFORMS_110421.2040
Linux, x86, 32bit (optimized), Oracle 11g on Apr 21 2011
22:38:06
Copyright (C) 1995, 2011, Oracle and/or its affiliates.
All rights reserved.
```

Step 4. Now that we have started GGSCI, we need to edit the parameter file for the Replicat process we are going to create. We will name this extract RPHR01. Use the GGSCI command **edit param RPHR01** and then create the parameter file. In the following code, you will find examples of what you will do. The editor that is used in the Linux version of GoldenGate is the vi editor by default, so you will use the appropriate keystrokes for the vi editor when creating the parameter file.

```
GGSCI (goldengate1) 4> edit param rphr01
-- Replicat name. Up to 8 characters
REPLICAT RPHR01
-- Optional - This ensures that the database environment is
-- configured correctly. Using it is a best practice.
SETENV (NLS_LANG=AMERICAN_AMERICA.AL32UTF8)
-- Login and password to the administrator account in the
-- source database.
USERID ggadmin, PASSWORD ggadmin
-- This will cause the Replicat to handle row collisions
-- without abending. Typically we don't want this in a
-- Replicate file but it's not a bad idea to have it in
-- there during the first runs, while GoldenGate catches up
-- the target database with the source database.
-- So, add it now, and remove it after we have gotten the
-- Target database caught up.
HANDLECOLLISIONS
-- Need to disable triggers.
DBOPTIONS SUPPRESSTRIGGERS
-- ASSUMETARGETDEFS is used here to indicate that the source
-- and target database schemas are basically the same.
ASSUMETARGETDEFS
-- The MAP clause essentially says that all HR.* tables on the
-- source database map to the same schema/object on the target
-- database
MAP HR.*, TARGET HR.*;
-- Note - there is no DDL capture in this extract. Only DML.
```

Step 5. Save the parameter file once you have created it.

Step 6. Now, you will need to log in to the database as the GoldenGate administrator using the **dblogin** command, and then register the extract with GoldenGate using the **add extract** command as seen here:

```
GGSCI (goldengate1) 5> dblogin userid ggadmin, password ggadmin
GGSCI (goldengate1) 6> add replicat RPHR01, NODBCHECKPOINT,
exttrail dirdat/hr
```

Step 7. Start the extract from the GGSCI command line as seen in this example:

```
GGSCI (goldengate1) 8>Start replicat RPHR01
```

Step 8. Use the **info all** command from GGSCI to determine that the extract has started without error.

```
GGSCI (goldengate2) 6> info all
Program      Status       Group     Lag          Time Since Chkpt
MANAGER      RUNNING
REPLICAT     RUNNING      RPHR01    00:00:00     00:00:01
```

At this point, we should have all the replication processes running. The EXHR01 and DPHR01 Extract processes should be running on Goldengate1 and the RPHR01 Replicat process should be running on Goldengate2.

Step 9. If you wish to test the replication process, log in to the ORCL database on Goldengate1 and run the following test PL/SQL script, which will create a number of new records in the HR schema of the ORCL database on Goldengate1:

```
[oracle@goldengate1 GoldenGate]$ sqlplus / as sysdba

Declare
v_emp_id    number;
v_email     varchar2(30);
begin
v_emp_id:=300;
v_email:='ROBERT'||to_char(sysdate, 'hh:mm:ss');
for tt in 400..1000
loop
    insert into employees
    (employee_id, last_name, email, hire_date, job_id)
    values
    (tt, 'FREEMAN','ROBERT'||tt||' '||to_char(sysdate,
hh:mm:ss'),sysdate,'AC_ACCOUNT');
    commit;
end loop;
end;
/
```

This script will create 600 test records in the ORCL database. If replication is successfully running, they should quickly be replicated to the ORCL database on the Goldengate2 server. You can check that these records were successfully replicated by issuing the following query on the ORCL database on the Goldengate2 server:

```
select * from employees where employee_id between 400 and 1000;
```

Once the replication has successfully occurred, you should see about 600 records returned by this query.

CHAPTER

6

GoldenGate Multitarget and Cascading Replication

T he last chapter contained a great deal of information, but it was a very
important chapter. In it you really got a taste for the GoldenGate basics. This
chapter will not be as long or as involved. In this chapter we are going to
discuss configuring multitarget and cascading replication using GoldenGate.

In Chapter 5 we replicated changes between a single-source database and a
single-target database. In this chapter we will first discuss multitarget replication.
Building on the configuration we created in Chapter 5, we will configure the
ORCL database on the GoldenGate1 server so that it not only replicates to the ORCL
database on the GoldenGate2 server, but we will also configure it to replicate to the
Microsoft Windows GGWINONE server we configured in Chapter 3.

Next, we will introduce you to cascading replication with GoldenGate. In
cascading replication, you replicate between two databases (in our case GoldenGate1
.ORCL and GoldenGate2.ORCL), and the target database (GoldenGate2.ORCL)
replicates those changes to one or more databases. In this chapter we will configure
cascading replication from GoldenGate2.ORCL to the GGWINONE.ORCL Windows
server that we configured earlier in Chapter 3.

This chapter assumes that you have read Chapter 5 and that you have completed
the workshops and have GoldenGate replication working between GoldenGate1
.ORCL and GoldenGate2.ORCL. So we won't repeat things you have already learned
unless it seems important.

Configuring Multitarget Replication

Configuring multitarget replication is really quite straightforward, and most of the
steps you will need to complete you already have experience with when you
configured replication in Chapter 5. To configure replication to a new target
database, you will perform the following operations:

- Configure the GoldenGate Manager process on the new target server

- Add the new target database to an existing or new Data Pump Extract

Configuring the GoldenGate Manager
Process on the New Target Server

Configuring the GoldenGate Manager process on the new GGWINONE server is
just like the configuration we did for the Manager processes in Chapter 5. In this
case, the fact that the GoldenGate process is running on a Windows server has no
real impact on how you configure the Manager process. Simply go to the GoldenGate
home directory and use the GGSCI command-line interface to create the parameter

file as shown in Chapter 5. Here is a quick example, just so you don't have to turn back to Chapter 5:

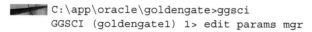

```
C:\app\oracle\goldengate>ggsci
GGSCI (goldengate1) 1> edit params mgr

-- This is a Manager process file
PORT 7809
PURGEOLDEXTRACTS, USECHECKPOINTS
-- AUTOSTART ER *
-- AUTORESTART extract *,retries 10, WAITMINUTES 5, RESETMINUTES 60
```

Adding the New Target Database to an Existing or New Data Pump Extract

Now we need to start sending the trail files from the source system to the new target system. We can do this either by adding a new Data Pump Extract process on the source system much as we have already outlined in Chapter 5, or we can modify the existing Data Pump process to simply ship the trail files to two different target sources. Let's look at each of these options in a bit more detail.

NOTE
Best practice would be to create a new Data Pump.

Creating a Brand New Data Pump Extract Process

To start replicating to the new server with GoldenGate Data Pump, we can simply configure a new Data Pump Extract process as detailed in Chapter 5. Of course, when creating a new Data Pump Extract, you will need to give it a unique name (like DPHR02). Here is an example of what the resulting parameter file might look like (remember, we would use the **edit params dphr02** command from GGSCI to start the editing process). For brevity, we have removed comments from this parameter file example:

```
EXTRACT DPHR02
PASSTHRU
RMTHOST goldengate3, MGRPORT 7840
RMTTRAIL dirdat\ha
TABLE HR.*;
```

In this case, we are going to start replicating the trail file contents to a new server called Goldengate3.

After you've created the new parameter file, simply follow the steps outlined in Chapter 5 to add the extract and add the remote trail. You would then start the

Extract process. Here is a quick-and-dirty example without all the discussion that we provided in Chapter 5:

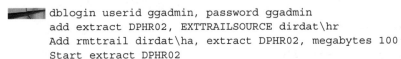

```
dblogin userid ggadmin, password ggadmin
 add extract DPHR02, EXTTRAILSOURCE dirdat\hr
 Add rmttrail dirdat\ha, extract DPHR02, megabytes 100
 Start extract DPHR02
```

Modifying the Existing Extract Process

You can choose to use add new target databases to an existing Extract process (like the DPHR01 process we created in Chapter 5). If you choose to modify an existing extract, you will need to do the following:

1. Modify the extract and add a new RMTHOST, RMTTRAIL, and TABLE clause to the extract. Thus, you will now have two of each. The resulting parameter file might look like this:

    ```
    EXTRACT DPHR01
    PASSTHRU
    RMTHOST goldengate2, MGRPORT 7840
    RMTTRAIL dirdat\hr
    TABLE HR.*;
    -- Second target database added
    RMTHOST goldengate3, MGRPORT 7840
    RMTTRAIL dirdat\ha
    TABLE HR.*;
    ```

2. Now, you will need to stop the extract. This is the downside to adding to a new extract because you cannot add a remote trail file while the extract that trail file is going to be associated with is running.

    ```
    Stop extract DPHR01
    ```

3. Now you simply need to add the new remote trail file (the extract is already registered) and restart the extract.

    ```
    dblogin userid ggadmin, password ggadmin
    Add rmttrail dirdat\ha, extract DPHR01, megabytes 100
    Start extract DPHR01
    ```

Before we can start the Replicat process on the target database server, we need to instantiate the database. We have already seen how you can instantiate a database using Oracle GoldenGate; let's look at how you can instantiate a database with Oracle Database Data Pump.

Instantiating the Target Database with Oracle Database Data Pump

We have already given you an introduction to Oracle Database Data Pump in Chapter 5 when we had you re-create the HR schema. Instead of using GoldenGate to instantiate objects in the database to be replicated to, we can use Oracle Database Data Pump to do that instantiation. Instantiating a schema or set of schemas with Data Pump is probably easier in some respects than doing so with Oracle GoldenGate replication, as we showed you in Chapter 5.

If you are a DBA, then you are probably already familiar with Oracle Database Data Pump. It is a set of tools (impdp and expdp) that allows you to logically back up your Oracle Database and then restore that backup image to the same or a different database. The database can be on any platform, and there is no conversion of the Data Pump required to cross platforms or versions of Oracle Database. As such, Data Pump is often used to move data between Oracle databases (especially across platforms).

When instantiating the target database with Oracle Database Data Pump, you will follow a two-step process:

- Export the schema/data from the database that you will be replicating from with the Data Pump export utility (expdp).

- Import the source schema/data that you backed up into the target database using the Oracle Database Data Pump import utility (impdp).

In the next few sections we will quickly give you an example of using Data Pump to extract data from our target database, and then, using the resulting dump file, we will instantiate the data into our target database.

Exporting the Source Schema for Instantiation   We will be using the Oracle Database Data Pump Export (expdp) utility here much as we did in Chapter 5, except this time we will be exporting the HR schema objects and their data. Before you can do the export, you will need to create a directory in the database that points to the location where the Data Pump dump files will be created, as seen in this code example, which creates a directory called "directory" that points to a local file system location, /home/oracle/export:

```
create directory export as '/home/oracle/export/';
```

Now that the directory is created, we are ready to perform the Data Pump export using the expdp utility. Here is the syntax we would use to perform the export. Note that the syntax is only slightly different from what we did in Chapter 5:

```
expdp schemas=HR directory=export dumpfile=expdpHR.dmp
  logfile=expdpHR.log
```

This will create an export dump file called expdpHR.dmp. This time the export file will contain all the objects, data, and metadata needed to re-create the HR schema.

Instantiating the Target Database with Oracle Database Data Pump Import

You will need to copy the dump file (expdpHR.dmp) from the source to the target database server. This is demonstrated in Chapter 5, but here is an example of using the **scp** command to make this copy (you will need to create the /home/oracle/ export directory first, of course):

```
scp expdpHR.dmp root@goldengate3:/home/oracle/export/expdpHR.dmp
```

On the target database, you will again need to use the Oracle **create directory** command to create a directory in the Oracle database. This is the directory that you copied the Data Pump dumpfile into. If you were on a UNIX system, you could use the same **create directory** command that we used in the previous step, pointing the directory called "directory" to a file system /home/oracle/export.

The import command, seen next, is exactly the same as the one used in Chapter 5.

```
impdp directory=robert dumpfile=expdpHR.dmp logfile=impdphr.log
```

This will cause the dumpfile to be imported into the target database including the actual creation of the HR schema, if required.

Configuring the Replicat Process on the Target Database Server

Now that we have instantiated the schema, we can configure and start the Replicat process on the target database server. In Chapter 5 we discussed configuration of the Replicat process, and in reality, the configuration of the Replicat process on the new target server is just the same as in Chapter 5. Here is our replicat parameter file.

```
REPLICAT RPHR01
    SETENV (NLS_LANG=AMERICAN_AMERICA.AL32UTF8)
    USERID ggadmin, PASSWORD ggadmin
    HANDLECOLLISIONS
    DBOPTIONS SUPPRESSTRIGGERS
    ASSUMETARGETDEFS
    MAP HR.*, TARGET HR.*;
```

Note that this Replicat process parameter file is exactly the same as the one in Chapter 5. We didn't even change the name of the Replicat process (since this was on a different physical server, we didn't need to).

Now that we have gotten everything configured, let's get this new replication process started.

Starting the Newly Configured Replication Process

We have gotten everything configured and ready to go. We already have the new Data Pump process (or the modified process) running and ready to go. We simply need to start the Replicat process on our target system using the **start replicat** command from the GGSCI interface, as seen here:

```
Start replicat rphr01;
```

This will start the replication process. You can now make changes on the source system and they will be replicated to both target systems.

Configuring Cascading Replication

Cascading replication is a situation where you replicate from one box to another, and then once that replication is complete, the system you replicated to will proceed to replicate those changes to one or more other systems. This topology is often used if you want to replicate to multiple systems, but you also want to reduce the overhead of the replication on the system where the production database resides.

Configuring replication is actually quite a simple process. All you need to do is configure an Extract process on the system that is accepting changes from the source database, such that the Extract process then forwards the changes in the database to the system(s) that you want it to be forwarded to.

In our example, we will assume that we are replicating changes as configured in Chapter 5. Thus GoldenGate1 is our source database, and GoldenGate2 will be the target database. Our job then is to configure GoldenGate2 to replicate the changes it receives to an additional server, GoldenGate3. Notice that the end result is not unlike the topology we configured earlier in this chapter, except that GoldenGate2 is passing changes to GoldenGate3, rather than GoldenGate1 passing changes to GoldenGate2 and GoldenGate3.

To configure our cascading replication setup, then we would

1. Configure the Manager process to run on GoldenGate3, if it was not already configured. We discuss this step earlier in this chapter.

2. Configure an Extract process to run on GoldenGate2. We would configure this extract's parameter file just as we configured the new DPHR02 extract earlier in this chapter, except it would be configured on GoldenGate2, not on GoldenGate1. We would then register the Extract process, create the remote trail file, and then start the extract. All of these steps are demonstrated in Chapter 5 and earlier in this chapter.

3. We would instantiate the database on GoldenGate3, as we did earlier in this chapter, using the Oracle Data Pump utility.

We would then create and start a replicat on the GoldenGate3 server. This would start the replication of records from GoldenGate2 to GoldenGate3.

You can, of course, have the GoldenGate2 server replicate changes to any number of servers. So, for example, if you wanted to replicate data to a test, development, and QA database, you could replicate from production on GoldenGate1, to the interim database on GoldenGate2. That database could then be used to replicate to the test, development, and QA databases, wherever those databases might be.

This was a short chapter (and after Chapter 5, you probably needed the break). In the next chapter we will configure GoldenGate for multimaster replication, which allows you to change the data on any node, and replicate that change to the remaining nodes in your architecture.

CHAPTER
7

GoldenGate Multimaster
Replication

One of GoldenGate's most powerful features may well be its ability to do bidirectional (or active-active) replication. Bidirectional replication allows you to have two or more databases, make changes in each of those databases, and then replicate those changes to the other databases. With bidirectional replication, each database essentially becomes both a source and a target database. Bidirectional replication is a powerful way of maximizing availability, balancing database load, and building a heterogeneous database infrastructure. You can also use multimaster replication to provide a method of zero-downtime migration. (We discuss zero-downtime migrations in Chapter 14 in much more detail.)

In general, you can configure GoldenGate bidirectional replication between all of the databases that have support for both GoldenGate Extract and Replicat processes. Bidirectional replication can be somewhat more complex to implement than normal replication, as sometimes there are application-related considerations you need to be aware of. In this chapter we will first cover the basics of configuring two Oracle databases for bidirectional replication, including restrictions you will need to be aware of. We will then discuss some things to be careful and aware of when it comes to bidirectional replication.

Before You Configure Bidirectional Replication

In the following sections we will be discussing some of the considerations that you might need to make when developing applications for a bidirectional GoldenGate configuration. In these sections we will discuss:

- The application and bidirectional replication
- Determining the "trusted" source database
- Dealing with primary or unique keys
- Triggers
- Constraints with cascading deletes
- Looping issues
- Detecting and resolving conflicts
- Other bidirectional issues

The Application and Bidirectional Replication

Perhaps the biggest impediment to using GoldenGate bidirectional (or peer-to-peer) replication is the application itself. Because the application would now be actively creating records in more than one database, conflicts could occur. One such conflict might occur if the application uses sequences to assign values to souragate keys; those sequences will be individually created on each individual database. As a result, duplicate sequence numbers would be issued in each database.

For example, assume you have two databases called HR and in them you have an EMPLOYEE table with a primary key column called EMPID. In this example, assume that EMPID is a souragate key whose value is derived from a sequence called SEQ_EMPID. That sequence would be created on both databases, using the **create sequence** command. After the application is started, the first new employee that is created on the first database will be assigned an EMPID, from the sequence on that database, of 1. The problem occurs the first time a new employee is created on the second database. In this case, the sequence in the second database is used, not the first database, and the EMPID of this new employee record would be assigned a value of 1. This would cause an Oracle error since there is already a value of 1 assigned to a record in the EMPLOYEE table because EMPID must be unique.

As you can see, this can be quite the issue. If you are using a packaged application, you might not be able to change the logic of the application in such a way as to solve this problem. If you have an application that was developed in-house, you might have to make changes to that application to avoid these kinds of conflicts. If you are developing new applications, your architects and developers will need to design the schemas and application code, understanding that the application will be running on a database that is using an active-active GoldenGate database implementation.

There are other considerations when it comes to applications and bidirectional replication, such as these:

- The application may execute DDL, which is not supported in a bidirectional GoldenGate solution.

- The application might execute automated DML, which might cause issues with GoldenGate replication.

- The application might use data types that are not supported by GoldenGate.

If you're considering bidirectional replication with a vendor-supplied application, you should consult with the vendor of the software, if possible, and determine whether they have any other customers who have implemented a peer-to-peer GoldenGate solution and whether that solution is supported by the vendor.

The Trusted Source

When developing the topology for bidirectional replication with GoldenGate, you should always designate one database as the trusted source database. The trusted source will be the database from which we will build the other databases in the bidirectional architecture. Also, any resynchronizations in the future will occur from the trusted source database.

Keys Are Important (Also Keeping SKs Unique)

We have already discussed the importance of having a primary or unique key (not nullable) defined on the objects that are to be replicated via Oracle GoldenGate. With bidirectional replication, the use of keys is even more important in that these keys are used during conflict resolution. If you do not have keys, then, as with regular GoldenGate replication, the entire row of the table will be used to determine whether there is a conflict. As we mentioned earlier, if you let GoldenGate use all the rows of a table to determine uniqueness, there can be significant performance problems.

Within the context of bidirectional replication, if a table contains rows that truly are not unique, the records that are truly duplicate records will cause conflict detection to occur. As a result, errors will occur, as will loss of data. In such cases, bidirectional replication just isn't going to work.

Triggers

Triggers often execute DML operations (for example, they might modify data via an **update** or **insert** command). The problem is that the DML that causes the triggers to fire in the first place is replicated to the other servers in the architecture. In such cases, we want the triggers to fire only on the database where the initial change occurs. We do not want the triggers to fire on any database where the changes are made via replication. As a result, you will need to modify any triggers to determine if the action is a replication action or an original action.

Cascaded Deletes

Cascaded delete operations are much like triggers, in that they are automatic. Again, you would want these operations to occur only on the database where the actual transaction occurred, allowing replication to carry the results of those cascaded deletes to the other databases in the replication configuration. If your application uses cascaded deletes, you will want to disable the constraints that cause the cascaded deletes and replace those with triggers that follow the rules we have already discussed in the "Triggers" section.

Loops

Without the controls that are in place in GoldenGate, each source transaction would just replicate over and over across the architecture. GoldenGate, by default, will not include any DML operations received by a Replicat process in any subsequent Extract process. Thus, the DML is not further replicated to machines on which the operation has already occurred. GoldenGate does provide certain parameters that you can use if you have a need for the Extract process to forward on change records that were processed by a Replicat process. This should be a very rare occurrence.

Conflict Detection and Resolution

When configured properly, Oracle GoldenGate will automatically detect conflicts as they occur. The following situations will cause a conflict to occur:

- A replicated insert tries to insert a row that already exists on the target database system.

- The before image of a row that is updated does not match the image of the row on the target database.

- A **delete** command that is replicated tries to remove a row that does not exist on the target database system.

- A column that is updated on the host system is missing on the target system.

Normally you hope that there will be no conflicts as database operations occur. However, they are possible—and sometimes they are unavoidable. As a DBA with exceptional skills, you know you should prepare for the possibility of conflicts. GoldenGate provides an interface that you can program to that will provide the capability to deal with conflicts.

The method of developing conflict rules boils down into these steps:

1. Create the conflict resolution procedure (for example, this might be in PL/SQL).

2. Call the conflict resolution routine using the SQLEXEC parameter in your **map** statements.

    a. You can use a FILTER clause to filter for a specific condition based on the output of the SQL, as needed.

    b. You can use multiple **map** statements in this manner to create different rules for different tables, and these rules can be as simple or as complex as needed.

    c. Use the REPERROR parameter to assign error-handling rules to specific error numbers. You can assign default rules and/or error-specific rules.

3. (Optional) If you specify a response of EXCEPTION for REPERROR, you can use an exceptions **map** statement to log operations that caused conflicts to an exceptions table. Within the same transaction that triggered the conflict, you can query the data from the exceptions table to calculate adjustments to the outcome of the transaction, to process the conflict manually, or to use a custom program to resolve the conflicts.

Here is an example of a conflict handler process. In this case, we want the most current record to survive. It's possible that the update is newer, or it's possible that the record on the existing system is newer. Whoever is newer is the winner, in this case.

```
MAP hr.jobs, TARGET hr.jobs,&
REPERROR (21000, DISCARD),&
SQLEXEC (ID lookup, ON UPDATE,&
QUERY "select count(*) conflict from jobs where &
last_update_date = :p1 and &
t_timestamp > :p2",&
PARAMS (p1 = last_update_date, p2 = t_timestamp), BEFOREFILTER, ERROR
REPORT,&
TRACE ALL),&
FILTER (lookup.conflict = 0, ON UPDATE, RAISEERROR 21000);
```

NOTE
*We discuss the more exotic statements that you are seeing here, like **reperror**, **sqlexec**, **query**, and **filter**, in much more detail in Chapter 8. In this chapter, we will briefly discuss the mechanics of these statements as they apply to conflict resolution, but you will find much more complete coverage of these options in Chapter 8.*

This **map** statement might seem daunting at first, but like everything else, when we break it down, it's not that bad. Let's break this **map** statement down a little bit. First we have this bit:

```
MAP hr.jobs, TARGET hr.jobs,&
```

This part should already look familiar to you from parameter files we have created in previous chapters. Here we are mapping the source schema.target (HR.JOBS) to the target database schema.target, which in this case happens to be the same.

Next we have a new statement, the **reperror** statement, as seen here:

```
REPERROR (21000, DISCARD), &
```

Even though the **reperror** statement appears at the front of this statement, it really will not be used until after the rest of the mapping statement has been applied. In this case, the **reperror** statement will discard the record should an error 21000 be raised within the body of this mapping statement (or occur naturally out of some result of the mapping statement like a SQL query).

Next we have the heart of the conflict handler, which starts with the **sqlexec** statement as seen here:

```
SQLEXEC (ID lookup, ON UPDATE,&
QUERY "select count(*) conflict from jobs where &
last_update_date = :p1 and &
t_timestamp > :p2",&
PARAMS (p1 = last_update_date, p2 = t_timestamp), BEFOREFILTER, ERROR
REPORT,&
TRACE ALL),&
```

First, note that the **sqlexec** statement has many different parameters. The first is the identifier for the lookup value that will be generated. In this case, the result of the SQL query will be assigned to this ID, and the column names queries in the **sqlexec** statement. We will explain this in more detail in just a second.

Next, note the ON UPDATE clause. This indicates that this mapping only applies to replication that involves updates to records. Therefore this mapping and its directives will never apply to an **insert** or **delete** replication event.

Then we have the query itself, which is a simple **select count** SQL statement. This statement will return a count (in this case, a 0 or a 1) of records in the table where the row's timestamp is greater than the timestamp being updated. In our case, the business rule is that if the row that is on the target database is more current than the row update that is to occur, then the update should not occur. So, a value of 1 would indicate that the record should be discarded. Note the use of the question marks to indicate the placement of variables (or parameters) to be used. These variables are defined in the next section of the code, the params section.

In the params section, each individual parameter for the SQL statement is defined. You start defining them using a value (in this case p1 and then p2) and assigning those values to the column name of the column being replicated. So, in our example, p1 is assigned the value of the replicated t_id column value and p2 is assigned the value of the replicated t_timestamp value. These replicated values are then used, much like bind variables, in the SQL statement. The result is the comparison of the existing data to the replicated data.

The SQL statement will return a 0 in this case if there are no records that are greater than the newly replicated t_timestamp value, which indicates that the record being updated is the newest record. If the SQL statement returns a 1, then the record in the target database is newer than the replicated record, and we will want the record discarded. Note that no action is taken at this point; only the results from a query are returned.

The BEFOREFILTER clause indicates that the SQL statement should execute before any filter is applied. This is important because it is the **filter** statement to come that will control what happens as a result of the query.

We now move to the FILTER clause, which really is the mechanism that determines whether the newly replicated update gets applied. Here is that statement again:

```
FILTER (lookup.conflict = 0, ON UPDATE, RAISEERROR 21000);
```

In this case, the **filter** statement (recall that it is executed after the **sqlexec**) is looking back to the values queried by the **sqlexec** statement and determining if the result was a 0. This is known as the *filter condition*. If the value of lookup.conflict is 0, then the filter passes. And the filter will do nothing, allowing the update to proceed. However, if the result is anything other than 0, then the filter fails and an error (21000) is raised. Recall the earlier **reperror** statement. It will now intercept this 21000 error, and discard the resulting replicated update in favor of the existing row.

You should note that if you have more than one rule you wish to apply, you could create more than one **filter** statement. Each **filter** statement is checked independently of the other. They are checked in the order in which they appear in the parameter file.

We will provide an example of the use of conflict filters later in this chapter when we demonstrate the setup and configuration of a multimaster replication site.

NOTE
The newest version of GoldenGate provides even more features for conflict resolution. See Chapter 17 for more information on these new features!

Other Bidirectional Replication Issues

There are some other considerations that you need to be aware of when implementing bidirectional replication. These considerations are:

- DDL replication is not supported when you are using bidirectional replication. For example, the **truncate** command is DDL and therefore cannot be replicated in an active-active bidirectional configuration.

- Try to keep the number of databases in a bidirectional topology to a minimum. As you add more databases, the complexity increases quickly. Adding more databases has these consequences:

  - The complexity of resynchronization is increased in the event of an outage of one or more databases.

  - Conflict resolution becomes more complex.

  - More moving parts add additional layers of complexity and points where performance can be impacted.

- Using sequences can cause problems if each sequence is unique at each site and is unaware of the other sequences, or the values that they have assigned.

We strongly suggest that you create your sequences to generate values that will always be unique to the site that they run on. There are a number of ways in which you can do this, including having them skip values. For example, you could have site #1 always generate even sequence numbers and site #2 always generate odd sequence numbers, or you could assign each site a range of sequence numbers to each site. Each of these solutions has its own drawback that you will need to consider: the first potentially limits the number of sites you can have, and the second could lead to sequence collisions if you're not careful.

Example of Configuring a Bidirectional Replication

In this section we will actually be configuring a Data Guard bidirectional replication setup. In this case, we will replicate the ORCL.HR schema on the goldengate1 server to the ORCL.HR schema on the goldengate2 server, and back of course. We will assume that you have already configured the Manager processes as described in Chapter 5.

In this section we will perform the following actions during this setup:

1. Configure the GoldenGate Extract processes.

2. Configure the GoldenGate Data Pump Extract processes.

3. Configure the Replicat process for both the ORCL.HR schemas.

4. Instantiate the GOLDENGATE2.ORCL.HR schema.

5. Create a conflict handler.

6. Start replication in both directions.

7. Test the replication.

NOTE
To save time and space and to avoid repeating ourselves, we will refer you to Chapters 5 and 6 often for the materials that were already covered in depth within those chapters.

Configure the GoldenGate Extract Processes

Configuring the Extract process is no different than configuring the Extract processes as demonstrated in Chapter 5 or Chapter 6—except for one thing. The exception is that we will configure two Extract processes instead of one. One process will be configured on the goldengate1 server, and the second will be created on the goldengate2 server.

You should already be familiar with the process of creating the parameter files. If not, please review Chapter 5. Here are the parameter files that you will want to use when configuring the ORCL databases on the goldengate1 and goldengate2 servers.

```
-- Extract name. Up to 8 characters
EXTRACT EXHR01
-- Optional - This ensures that the database environment is
-- configured correctly. Using it is a best practice.
SETENV (NLS_LANG=AMERICAN_AMERICA.AL32UTF8)
-- Login and password to the administrator account in the source
-- database.
-- Note the @orcl_one net connection string should change to @orcl_two
-- on goldengate2.
USERID ggadmin@orcl_one, PASSWORD ggadmin
-- Defines the location and prefix of the trail files
EXTRAIL ./dirdat/hr
-- This defines what we are replicating.
-- In this case, all tables in the HR schema.
-- Note the use of the wildcard character.
TABLE HR.*;
-- Note - there is no DDL capture in this extract. Only DML.
```

At this point, you should go ahead and register the Extract process. We need to wait to start this Extract process until a later step.

Configure the GoldenGate Data Pump Extract Processes

As with the Extract processes in the previous section, the Data Pump Extract processes that we need to create are pretty much the same. Again, we have the one exception that we need to create these processes on both servers this time, instead of just one. Here is the parameter file for the Data Pump Extract processes:

```
-- Data Pump name. Up to 8 characters
EXTRACT DPHR01
-- PASSTHRU indicates that the data does not need any kind of filtering
-- or mapping of any kind. It implies that the schemas on both the source
-- and target systems are exactly alike.
PASSTHRU
-- RMTHOST points to the remote system.
-- Note that the RMTHOST will be goldengate1 on the parameter file
-- created on the goldengate2 server.
```

```
RMTHOST goldengate2, MGRPORT 7840
-- RMTRRAIL is the remote trail that we will define shortly on the target
-- database server. In this case we kept the prefix (max 2 characters)
-- the same as the local trail file.
RMTTRAIL dirdat/hr
-- This defines what objects we are replicating to the target system.
-- In this case, all tables in the HR schema.
-- Note the use of the wildcard character.
TABLE HR.*;
```

Go ahead and register the Data Pump Extract processes, but we will need to wait to start these Extract processes.

Configure the Replicat Process for Both the ORCL.HR Schemas

As with the Extract processes we discussed earlier, we will also want to create two Replicat processes, one on each server. Here are the parameter files you would use for these Replicat processes:

```
-- Replicat name. Up to 8 characters
REPLICAT RPHR01
-- Optional - This ensures that the database environment is
-- configured correctly. Using it is a best practice.
SETENV (NLS_LANG=AMERICAN_AMERICA.AL32UTF8)
-- Login and password to the administrator account in the source database.
-- Note the @orcl_one net connection string should change to @orcl_two
-- on goldengate2.
USERID ggadmin@orcl_one, PASSWORD ggadmin
-- Need to disable triggers.
DBOPTIONS SUPPRESSTRIGGERS
-- ASSUMETARGETDEFS is used here to indicate that the source and target
-- database schemas are basically the same.
ASSUMETARGETDEFS
-- The MAP clause essentially says that all HR.* tables on the source
-- database map to the same schema/object on the target database
MAP HR.*, TARGET HR.*;
-- Note - there is no DDL capture in this extract. Only DML.
```

Now we have created our Replicat processes, and we are close to being ready to start the machine, but not quite yet. Register the Replicat processes, but don't start them yet! Oh yes, one more thing. We are really not quite done with the Replicat processes. We still need to modify the Replicat process so that it has a conflict handler. We will do that later in this chapter!

NOTE
Don't forget that after you create each Extract or Replicat process, you will need to register that process and any trail files (local or remote) too. See Chapter 5 for more information on this. Be careful that you use different names for each trail file (it can be easy to accidentally use the same name on a local/remote trail file on the same server).

Instantiate the GOLDENGATE2.ORCL.HR Schema

In Chapters 5 and 6 we discussed different ways that you can use to instantiate a schema for GoldenGate usage. With bidirectional replication, it's important to get good, consistent copies of the database on each node of the bidirectional configuration. We would recommend a cold backup of the primary target database, restored on the other servers of the configuration, as the easiest method to instantiate the other databases. You could also use a warm backup of the primary database (allowing it to be used during the instantiation) and then just allow Oracle GoldenGate time to get the other databases up to date after the various GoldenGate processes have been started. The process of instantiating databases with GoldenGate using GoldenGate or using Oracle's Database Data Pump tool is covered in Chapter 5 and 6. Recall from those chapters that you might have to make temporary adjustments to the parameter files in the new databases to deal with duplicate records (using the HANDLECOLLISIONS parameter in the replicat parameter file).

Create a Conflict Handler

We have already discussed conflict handlers and how they are important when implementing bidirectional replication. In our example, we are replicating the HR schema that is included in the example schemas that Oracle supplies, and that we have been using throughout this book. Looking at the entity-relationship diagram (ERD) that we provided in Chapter 5, we discover a minor problem; we really have no way of knowing when a record is modified, so we really have no way to determine if a given update is conflicting with another update.

This is one of the primary problems in bidirectional replication. The schemas of a given application may well not be architected to be able to deal with possible conflicts that might arise during replication. In our case, we will opt to make an architectural change to one of the tables that will provide the information we need to create a conflict handler. In real life, we would need to make these changes on all of the tables, but for the sake of example, we will stick with modifying one table, the HR_JOBS table.

The adjustment we will need to make is the addition of one column, which we will call LAST_UPDATE_DATE, which will be a type of timestamp. We will follow the same rules that we followed in the earlier conflict handler in that the timestamp of the record that is being replicated will be checked against the LAST_UPDATE_DATE column. If LAST_UPDATE_DATE is newer on the table we are replicating to, we will reject the update.

Of course, this is a pretty simple conflict rule, and in real life, application-related conflict resolution rules can get quite complex. When implementing any kind of peer-to-peer replication configuration, you will need to carefully consider the various conflict possibilities and deal with them programmatically.

So, first, let's modify the HR_JOBS table with the new column called LAST_UPDATE_DATE, and we will also add a trigger that always updates the column in the event of an **insert**, **update**, or **delete** statement. Note that these changes will be made on every database in the peer-to-peer configuration:

```
Alter table hr.jobs add (last_update_date timestamp default
systimestamp);

Create or replace trigger hr.tr_jobs
Before insert or update or delete on hr.jobs
For each row
Begin
     :New.last_update_date=systimestamp;
End;
/
```

Now, we need to modify the parameter file for the Replicat processes so that it checks the date on the table in the event of an update, and updates, or does not update, the record as required. Here is the new Replicat process parameter file that you will create for each Replicat process:

```
-- Replicat name. Up to 8 characters
REPLICAT RPHR01
-- Optional - This ensures that the database environment is
-- configured correctly. Using it is a best practice.
SETENV (NLS_LANG=AMERICAN_AMERICA.AL32UTF8)
-- Login and password to the administrator account in the source
-- database.
-- Note the @orcl_one net connection string should change to @orcl_two
-- on goldengate2.
USERID ggadmin@orcl_one, PASSWORD ggadmin
HANDLECOLLISIONS
-- Need to disable triggers.
DBOPTIONS SUPPRESSTRIGGERS
-- ASSUMETARGETDEFS is used here to indicate that the source and
-- target database schemas are basically the same.
ASSUMETARGETDEFS
```

```
-- The MAP clause essentially says that all HR.* tables on the source
-- database map to the same schema/object on the target database.
MAP HR.*, TARGET HR.*;
MAP hr.jobs, TARGET hr.jobs,&
REPERROR (21000, DISCARD),&
SQLEXEC (ID lookup, ON UPDATE,&
QUERY "select count(*) conflict from jobs where &
last_update_date = :p1 and &
t_timestamp > :p2",&
PARAMS (p1 = last_update_date, p2 = t_timestamp), BEFOREFILTER, ERROR
REPORT,&
TRACE ALL),&
FILTER (lookup.conflict = 0, ON UPDATE, RAISEERROR 21000);
```

NOTE
Be careful about spaces in the parameter file,
especially spaces between a given command
parameter (like ERROR REPORT,) and any trailing
continuation character (&).

In a real-life situation, you would probably need conflict handlers on each table, to institute specific rules that apply for each table. Notice that we included the HANDLECOLLISIONS parameter in this parameter file so that GoldenGate would automatically handle primary key collisions for us.

If an error occurs and one of the Replicat or Extract processes fails, we could use the **view report** command to review the report file output of the process that failed.

Start Replication in Both Directions

Now that we have configured everything, starting replication is as simple as starting each of the various processes from the GGSCI interface. In this case you would start

- The Manager process on each server

- Each Extract process on each server

- Each Data Pump Extract process on each server

- Each Replicat process on each server

See Chapter 5 if you need more guidance in executing these steps. Once you have started each of the GoldenGate processes, replication should be started. Your conflict handler should properly control the data being updated in the JOBS table.

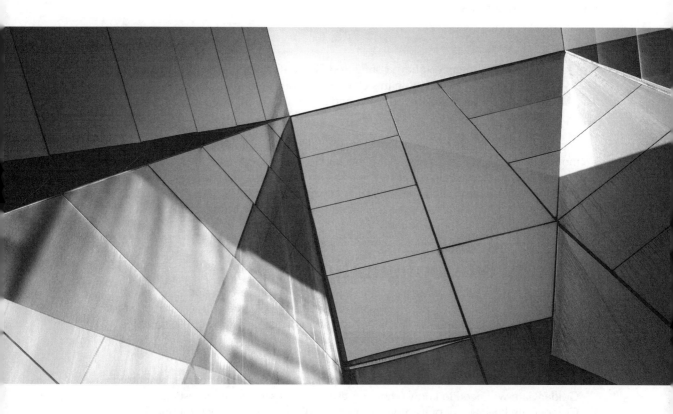

CHAPTER
8

Advanced Features

I n previous chapters you have configured GoldenGate and used basic features to do a simple replication. In this chapter we will present GoldenGate's advanced features, which you may need to use in a more complex real-world replication.

In this chapter you will learn about configuration options to make your replication more robust and secure; features that allow you to control and manipulate your data, preventing some errors and resolving the errors that do occur; and how you will need to configure your replication for Real Application Clusters (RAC).

Once you have mastered these advanced features, you will find it much easier to manage and monitor your replication.

Advanced Configuration

This section starts with adding a checkpoint table to enhance your ability to restart your replication with no gaps. Next, you will see how to secure your environment to prevent unauthorized access. Finally, this section covers purging your old trail files.

Checkpoint Tables

If the various Extract or Replicat processes stop for any reason, expected or unexpected, GoldenGate will need to know where to resume processing when it restarts. GoldenGate keeps track of its progress with checkpoints, which record critical points in time, such as the position of the last record read in the data source. Each type of process has its own checkpoint requirements. For example, an Extract process checkpoint records database redo log reads and trail file writes, while a Replicat process checkpoint records trail file reads.

By default, GoldenGate process checkpoints are written to a physical file that is located in the directory $GGHOME/dirchk. In the default configuration, there is one file for each Extract or Replicat process. The checkpoint file contains binary data, but you can view your checkpoints using the SHOWCH option of the GGSCI **info** command.

You may have noticed a potential vulnerability with writing a delivery checkpoint to file. The current checkpoint is updated when a record is read from the trail file and is not synchronized with the database transaction. If the database fails after the checkpoint is written but before the transaction is committed, you run the risk of losing that data.

Oracle GoldenGate provides a solution to this problem by allowing you to configure the use of a checkpoint table instead of a checkpoint file. The checkpoint tables use a table within a database, instead of a physical file. Using this method, the backup/recovery facilities of the database are used to maintain the transactional checkpoints in a safe and consistent way, which would be much safer instead of writing them to file. It should be clear, then, that it is a best practice to use a GoldenGate checkpoint table.

The checkpoint table can be created in any schema, but we strongly recommend creating the checkpoint table in your GoldenGate administrator account or a separate account dedicated to GoldenGate to keep things simple. There are two principal steps that you will follow to create a checkpoint table. First, you will use the **add checkpointtable** command to create the checkpoint table in the target database:

```
GGSCI (goldengate2) 1> DBLOGIN USERID ggadmin, PASSWORD ggpwd
GGSCI (goldengate2) 2> ADD CHECKPOINTTABLE ggadmin.chkpt

Successfully created checkpoint table ggadmin.chkpt.
```

You will also need to define the table as the default checkpoint table by adding it as a parameter in the GLOBALS file in the GoldenGate home directory.

```
GGSCI (goldengate2) 3> edit params ./GLOBALS
GGSCHEMA ggadmin

#Default Checkpoint table
CHECKPOINTTABLE ggadmin.chkpt
```

Now, when you create a new Replicat group with the **add replicat** command, you will use the default checkpoint table for the recovery and current checkpoints unless you specify otherwise. Startup checkpoints will still be written to file. You can add as many checkpoint tables as you want, but it's not necessary to create more than one. Checkpoint tables will remain small because rows are deleted as they are no longer needed.

NOTE
*Once you create a Replicat process, you cannot change the checkpoint properties with **alter replicat**. You must drop and re-create the Replicat process with the new checkpoint definition.*

GoldenGate Workshop: *Use Checkpoint Tables*

Step 1. Use the **add checkpointtable** command to create the checkpoint table in the target database.

```
GGSCI (goldengate2) 1> DBLOGIN USERID ggadmin, PASSWORD ggadmin
GGSCI (goldengate2) 2> ADD CHECKPOINTTABLE ggadmin.chkpt

Successfully created checkpoint table ggadmin.chkpt.
```

Step 2. Next, define the table as the default checkpoint table by adding it as a parameter in the GLOBALS file. New Replicat groups will automatically use that table unless you specify otherwise.

```
GGSCI (goldengate2) 3> edit params ./GLOBALS
GGSCHEMA ggadmin

#Default Checkpoint table
CHECKPOINTTABLE ggadmin.chkpt
```

Step 3. Create a Replicat process called RPHR02 (we covered creating Replicat processes in Chapter 5). We can't use RPHR01 for this workshop (which we created in previous chapters) because RPHR01 was created with the NODBCHECKPOINT option. Our options are to drop and re-create RPHR01 to use checkpoints or to create a new Replicat process, so we will just create a new Replicat process. Now that we have CHECKPOINTTABLE defined in GLOBALS, this Replicat will use the default checkpoint table.

```
GGSCI (goldengate2) 1> dblogin userid ggadmin, password ggadmin
Successfully logged into database.

GGSCI (goldengate2) 2> ADD REPLICAT rphr02, EXTTRAIL dirdat/hr
REPLICAT added.
```

Step 4. Create a parameter file for the Replicat process RPHR02. The options for this parameter file will use the same options as Replicat process RPHR01.

```
-- Replicat name. Up to 8 characters
REPLICAT RPHR02

-- Optional - This ensures that the database environment is
-- configured correctly. Using it is a best practice.
SETENV (NLS_LANG=AMERICAN_AMERICA.AL32UTF8)
```

```
-- Login and password to the administrator account in the source
-- database.
USERID ggadmin, PASSWORD ggadmin

-- This will cause the Replicat to handle row collisions
-- without abending.
-- Typically we don't want this in a Replicat file but it's
-- not a bad idea to have it in there during the first
-- runs, while GoldenGate catches up the target database
-- with the source database.
-- So, add it now, and remove it after we have gotten the
-- Target database caught up.
HANDLECOLLISIONS

-- Need to disable triggers.
DBOPTIONS SUPPRESSTRIGGERS

-- ASSUMETARGETDEFS is used here to indicate that the source
-- and target database schemas are basically the same.
ASSUMETARGETDEFS

-- The MAP clause essentially says that all HR.* tables on the
-- source database map to the same schema/object on the
-- target database
MAP HR.*, TARGET HR.*;

-- Note - there is no DDL capture in this extract. Only DML.
```

Step 5. Make sure the Extract process EXHR01and the Data Pump process DPHR01 (both of which were created in Chapter 5), as well as the new Replicat process RPHR02, are running. Also, you should stop the Replicat process RPHR01. If you're not sure how to start and stop Replicat processes, please see Chapter 5.

```
GGSCI (goldengate1) 1> info all

Program      Status      Group      Lag at Chkpt   Time Since Chkpt

MANAGER      RUNNING
EXTRACT      RUNNING     DPHR01     00:00:00       128:38:48
EXTRACT      RUNNING     EXHR01     00:00:00       00:00:01
GGSCI (goldengate2) 3> info all

Program      Status      Group      Lag at Chkpt   Time Since Chkpt

MANAGER      RUNNING
REPLICAT     STOPPED     RPHR01
REPLICAT     RUNNING     RPHR02     04:01:47       00:00:01
```

Step 6. From SQL*Plus, log in to the HR schema and create a transaction in the source database.

```
insert into hr.employees
(employee_id, last_name, email, hire_date, job_id)
values
(9990, 'FREEMAN', 'ROBERT9999', sysdate, 'AC_ACCOUNT');
commit;
```

Step 7. Still using SQL*Plus, log in to the GGADMIN schema and view the current checkpoint information.

```
-- Current checkpoint
select group_name, seqno, rba, audit_ts
from    ggadmin.chkpt
where   group_name = 'RPHR02';

GROUP_NA      SEQNO         RBA AUDIT_TS
--------- ---------- ---------- ----------------------------
RPHR02              0         1569 2012-07-21 15:47:36.169104
```

Step 8. Compare the output from Step 7 to the checkpoint information you get when you use the **info** command from the GGSCI command-line interface. Note that we use the SHOWCH option of the **info** command to get the checkpoint information:

```
GGSCI (goldengate2) 4> info rphr02, showch
...
  Current Checkpoint (position of last record read in the data
source):
    Sequence #: 0
    RBA: 1569
    Timestamp: 2012-07-21 15:47:36.169104
    Extract Trail: dirdat/er
...
```

Step 9. Return to SQL*Plus and issue the following query to view the Commit Sequence Number (CSN). See Chapter 2 for more information on the CSN, but recall that the CSN helps GoldenGate to determine where the Extract or Replicat process is in the transactional stream of the database.

```
-- CSN state information
select group_name, log_csn, log_xid,
log_cmplt_csn, log_cmplt_xids
from    ggadmin.chkpt
where   group_name = 'RPHR02';
```

```
GROUP_NA   LOG_CSN    LOG_XID   LOG_CMPLT_CSN  LOG_CMPLT_XIDS
--------   -------  -----------  --------------  ---------------
RPHR02     3623932  6.10.2375       3623932 6.10.2375
```

Step 10. Compare it to the CSN state information you get when you do it through GGSCI.

```
GGSCI (goldengate2) 4> info rphr02, showch
...
CSN state information:
  CRC: C4-61-B8-18
  Latest CSN: 3623932
  Latest TXN: 6.10.2375
  Latest CSN of finished TXNs: 3623932
  Completed TXNs: 6.10.2375
...
```

As you have seen in this section, checkpoint tables are a good option for maintaining consistency between your delivery process and your database. Since the checkpoints are stored in a database table, you will be able to write scripts to keep track of the delivery process.

Securing Your Environment

Security has become more and more important over the last several years, and GoldenGate has features that will help to make your GoldenGate replication processes more secure. First, we will discuss protecting access to your database account by securing the passwords used to connect to those databases. Next, we will show you how to encrypt the data stored in the trail files. Finally, we will show you how to implement command security to control access to GoldenGate commands.

Encrypting Passwords

You should encrypt your passwords in any secure environment. GoldenGate gives you the option of using the Blowfish encryption algorithm with a default key or using the more secure AES algorithm and specifying your own key. If you use AES, you can choose from AES-128, AES-196, or AES-256, depending on your environment and needs.

```
GSCI (goldengate1) 1> encrypt password ggpwd encryptkey default
  Using default key...

  Encrypted password:  AACAAAAAAAAAAAFAUCZCCEQCZDRJOFMH
  Algorithm used:  BLOWFISH
```

You just encrypted your password using the Blowfish encryption algorithm. Blowfish is weaker than AES and should not be used in a production system. The AES encryption algorithm is more robust, so let's use that instead of the weaker Blowfish. You use the **keygen** utility to create one or more keys, depending on your needs. In the next example you will generate five keys using the AES-128 encryption algorithm.

```
$ ./keygen 128 5
0x98ACD4374A63DF5E6970BE7DC46EB155
0x1DCFFE42ADFFFA131E15CE05FE25EC64
0xA2F1284E0F9C1649D2B9DD0D38DD2674
0x271453597138327E865EED1573946103
0xAC367D64D4D44D333A03FD1DAD4B9C12
```

After you generate the keys, create a file named ENCKEYS in the GoldenGate home directory. The name of the file is case sensitive. Give each key a unique name. You can store keys of varying lengths in the ENCKEYS file, but each time you use them, you have to be using the corresponding encryption algorithm.

```
key128_1  0x98ACD4374A63DF5E6970BE7DC46EB155
key128_2  0x1DCFFE42ADFFFA131E15CE05FE25EC64
key128_3  0xA2F1284E0F9C1649D2B9DD0D38DD2674
key128_4  0x271453597138327E865EED1573946103
key128_5  0xAC367D64D4D44D333A03FD1DAD4B9C12
```

Now you can copy the ENCKEYS file to the target computer and use these keys for encrypting passwords or encrypting data.

Now that the encryption keys are defined, you can use one to encrypt your database password. In this example you encrypt your password, ggpwd, using the AES-128 algorithm and the first key in the file, key128_1.

```
GGSCI (goldengate1) 1> encrypt password ggpwd aes128 encryptkey
key128_1
Encrypted password:  AADAAAAAAAAAAAFAJDJBZHZFPIXERDYCJIJCYHDCZBCIOH
KENFTGFGSGNAAISCEDXFADEAECQJODEJGG
Algorithm used:  AES128
```

You have just produced an encrypted password using the AES-128 encryption algorithm. Let's verify that the password works by logging in to the source database.

```
GGSCI (goldengate1) 2> dblogin userid ggadmin, password
AADAAAAAAAAAAAFAJDJBZHZFPIXERDYCJIJCYHDCZBCIOHKENFTGFGSGNAAISCEDX
FADEAECQJODEJGG,
 encryptkey key128_1
Successfully logged into database.
```

You can now store the password hash in parameter files instead of using a plain text password that anyone might see. Since you encrypted your password with the AES-128 algorithm, anyone wanting to compromise your system will need access to two files—the ENCKEYS file and the parameter file.

You can also use one of the encryption keys to protect your data in the trail files.

Encrypting Data in Trail Files

If it is not encrypted, your data inside a trail file can be vulnerable to hacking while it is being replicated. In fact, GoldenGate makes it easy to view the trail file contents using the logdump utility. Additionally, any data in transit over the network can be intercepted and viewed with a packet sniffer.

You can make your replication more secure by adding the **encrypttrail** and **decrypttrail** commands to your parameter files. Encrypting a trail will protect your data in the file, and this protection will continue while the data is in transit over the network. Trail file encryption offers the same AES algorithms as password encryption. You can also use the default 256-key byte substitution, but it is not secure and should not be used in production.

Encrypt Extract Trail   You will use one of the keys you generated earlier to encrypt the trail data. Although you can use the same key that you used for encrypting the password, it's not necessary. Let's use a different key for encrypting the trail files.

```
EXTRACT exhr01
...
ENCRYPTTRAIL, AES128 KEYNAME key128_2
EXTTRAIL ./dirdat/en
...
```

Using Data Pump with Encrypted Trails   Data written to the extract trail file will now be encrypted. Since you are using Data Pump (after all, it is a best practice), you must add the decryption and encryption parameters to the Data Pump Extract. The **decrypt** statement must use the same key that was used to encrypt the extract trail, but you don't have to use the same key to encrypt it again.

```
EXTRACT dphren01
...
PASSTHRU
DECRYPTTRAIL, AES128 KEYNAME key128_2
# Note that we don't have to use the same key to encrypt again
ENCRYPTTRAIL, AES128 KEYNAME key128_3
RMTHOST goldengate2, MGRPORT 7809
RMTTRAIL dirdat/en
...
```

Decrypt Replicat Trail The Data Pump Extract now transmits the encrypted trail data over the network to the remote host. The final step is for the replicat to decrypt and process the trail file. Use the same key you used for the Data Pump **encrypttrail** command.

```
REPLICAT rphren01
...
DECRYPTTRAIL, AES128 KEYNAME key128_3
...
```

Using Multiple Trails If your Extract process will write to more than one EXTTRAIL files, you can encrypt some trails while leaving others unencrypted by adding NOENCRYPTTRAIL before the EXTTRAIL parameter.

```
EXTRACT dphren01
...
ENCRYPTTRAIL, AES128 KEYNAME key128_1
EXTTRAIL ./dirdat/en
TABLES hr.*;

NOENCRYPTTRAIL
EXTTRAIL ./dirdat/un
TABLES hr.*;
...
```

You will specify the tables you want to extract with each EXTTRAIL. If you wish, you can encrypt sensitive data while leaving the nonsensitive data unencrypted.

Viewing Trail File Contents Suppose you are having problems with your replication and you need to do some troubleshooting. If you use the logdump utility, you will see the encrypted data.

```
Name: HR.EMPLOYEES
After  Image:                                            Partition 4   G  s
  0471 b1f5 aa29 8ebf 0d2a 514e 8650 f2c2 1878 c663 | .q...)...*QN.P...x.c
  6a0c 55be f073 4158 e02d d483 299d 5a3f 6012 4363 | j.U..sAX.-..).Z?`.Cc
  e45a 2b26 3945 e27a 4274 5a45 c247 c430 7ad4 d4f9 | .Z+&9E.zBtZE.G.0z...
  20fe 14aa c355 40f3 ceb3 5249 8ae6 9cf8 8739 196b |  ....U@...RI.....9.k
  fca9 39f9 7889 af41 64b1 f993 3529 0cb7 4666 5e98 | ..9.x..Ad...5)..Ff^.
  ac2c 62f1 1ca7 faf1 858d 0099 8875 5d40 bc5d a5f3 | .,b..........u]@.]..
  bdcb dce1 db7c 0a94 3b53 15fe de3a beee 029f e420 | .....|..;S...:.....
```

The encrypted trail file is impossible to read. You can make the trail file readable by directing logdump to decrypt the data. Note that you must use the same key that was used to encrypt the data.

```
Logdump 2 >decrypt on keyname key128_1
...
Name: HR.EMPLOYEES
```

```
After  Image:                                            Partition 4   G  s
0000 000a 0000 0000 0000 0000 2708 0001 0004 ffff | ............'.......
0000 0002 000b 0000 0007 4652 4545 4d41 4e00 0300 | ..........FREEMAN...
0e00 0000 0a52 4f42 4552 5439 3939 3200 0400 04ff | .....ROBERT9992.....
ff00 0000 0500 1500 0032 3031 322d 3037 2d32 313a | ........2012-07-21:
3134 3a35 333a 3034 0006 000e 0000 000a 4143 5f41 | 14:53:04........AC_A
4343 4f55 4e54 0007 000a ffff 0000 0000 0000 0000 | CCOUNT..............
0008 000a ffff 0000 0000 0000 0000 0009 000a ffff | ....................
```

Now you can view your trail file's contents to help with troubleshooting any problem you may be having.

Command Security

The third step in securing your environment is to control the access users have to GoldenGate commands. You may wish to allow some users to start and stop Extract or Replicat processes, while others should only be granted the ability to view the status. Security levels are defined by operating system users or groups.

Command security is configured by creating a file named CMDSEC in the GoldenGate home. Security rules are processed from the top of CMDSEC downward. The first rule satisfied is the one that determines whether access is allowed. Go from the most specific (those with no wildcards) to least specific when setting up the rules.

```
#<command name> <command object> <OS group> <OS user> <YES | NO>
#Grant STATUS to all members of mig group
STATUS * mig * YES
#
#Grant START to all members of mig group except robert
START * * robert NO
START * mig * YES
#
#Deny START to all other users
START * * * NO
#
#Grant all commands to members of ggusers group
* * ggusers * YES
#
#Deny all commands to all users
#It's best practice to put this as the last line
#It covers everything not explicitly covered before this
* * * * NO
```

The last line denies all commands to all users. Putting this at the end of the file is a best practice, because if there is no earlier rule that defines security access, the user will be granted full access.

GoldenGate Workshop: *Secure the Replication*

Workshop Notes

You are now ready to set up a secure replication. You will create a set of encryption keys, encrypt your database password, and then create capture, pump, and delivery processes that encrypt your data.

Step 1. Generate the encryption keys. Use AES-128 encryption for this workshop—you don't need the added security of AES-256 right now.

```
$ ./keygen 128 5
0x98ACD4374A63DF5E6970BE7DC46EB155
0x1DCFFE42ADFFFA131E15CE05FE25EC64
0xA2F1284E0F9C1649D2B9DD0D38DD2674
0x271453597138327E865EED1573946103
0xAC367D64D4D44D333A03FD1DAD4B9C12
```

Step 2. Add the keys to the ENCKEYS file on goldengate1.

```
key128_1 0x98ACD4374A63DF5E6970BE7DC46EB155
key128_2 0x1DCFFE42ADFFFA131E15CE05FE25EC64
key128_3 0xA2F1284E0F9C1649D2B9DD0D38DD2674
key128_4 0x271453597138327E865EED1573946103
key128_5 0xAC367D64D4D44D333A03FD1DAD4B9C12
```

Step 3. Create and test an encrypted password hash.

```
GGSCI (goldengate1) 1> encrypt password ggpwd aes128 encryptkey
key128_1
Encrypted password:
AADAAAAAAAAAAAFAJDJBZHZFPIXERDYCJIJCYHDCZBCIOHKENFTGFGSGNAAISCE
DXFADEAECQJODEJGG
Algorithm used:  AES128
GGSCI (goldengate1) 2> dblogin userid ggadmin, password
AADAAAAAAAAAAAFAJDJBZHZFPIXERDYCJIJCYHDCZBCIOHKENFTGFGSGNAAISCE
DXFADEAECQJODEJGG, encryptkey key128_1
Successfully logged into database.
```

Step 4. Copy the ENCKEYS file to goldengate2.

```
key128_1 0x98ACD4374A63DF5E6970BE7DC46EB155
key128_2 0x1DCFFE42ADFFFA131E15CE05FE25EC64
key128_3 0xA2F1284E0F9C1649D2B9DD0D38DD2674
key128_4 0x271453597138327E865EED1573946103
key128_5 0xAC367D64D4D44D333A03FD1DAD4B9C12
```

Step 5. Create an extract parameter file with an encrypted trail and an unencrypted trail. The unencrypted trail is for demonstration purposes.

```
-- Extract name.  Up to 8 characters
EXTRACT EXHR02

-- Optional - This ensures that the database environment is
-- configured correctly.  Using it is a best practice.
SETENV (NLS_LANG=AMERICAN_AMERICA.AL32UTF8)

SETENV (ORACLE_SID=orcl)

-- Login and password to the administrator account in the
-- source database.
userid ggadmin, password
AADAAAAAAAAAAAFAJDJBZHZFPIXERDYCJIJCYHDCZBCIOHKENFTGFGSGNAAISCE
DXFADEAECQJODEJGG  AES128, encryptkey key128_1

-- Encrypt the trail file.
ENCRYPTTRAIL, AES128 KEYNAME key128_2
EXTTRAIL ./dirdat/en

-- This defines what we are replicating with the encrypted trail.
TABLE HR.*;

-- Define an unencrypted trail
-- We're not going to use it at this time -
-- it's just for demonstration
NOENCRYPTTRAIL
EXTTRAIL ./dirdat/un

-- This defines what we are replicating with the unencrypted trail
TABLE HR.*;

-- Note - there is no DDL capture in this extract, only DML.
```

Step 6. Create a Data Pump parameter file. Note the use of DECRYPTTRAIL and ENCRYPTTRAIL.

```
-- Data Pump name.  Up to 8 characters
EXTRACT DPHREN01

-- PASSTHRU indicates that the data does not need any kind of
-- filtering or mapping of any kind.  It implies that the
-- schemas on both the source and target systems are
-- exactly alike.
PASSTHRU
```

```
-- Encrypted trail
DECRYPTTRAIL, AES128 KEYNAME key128_2
-- Use the same key to encrypt the data going out
ENCRYPTTRAIL, AES128 KEYNAME key128_2

RMTHOST goldengate2, MGRPORT 7809
RMTTRAIL dirdat/er

TABLE HR.*;
```

Step 7. Create Extract and Data Pump processes.

```
GGSCI (goldengate1) 1> dblogin userid ggadmin, password
AADAAAAAAAAAAAFAJDJBZHZFPIXERDYCJIJCYHDCZBCIOHKENFTGFGSGNAAISCE
DXFADEAECQJODEJGG  AES128, encryptkey key128_1

GGSCI (goldengate1) 2> add extract exhr02, tranlog, begin now
EXTRACT added.

GGSCI (goldengate1) 3> add exttrail ./dirdat/en, extract EXHR02,
 megabytes 100
EXTTRAIL added.

GGSCI (goldengate1) 4> add exttrail ./dirdat/un, extract EXHR02,
 megabytes 100
EXTTRAIL added.

GGSCI (goldengate1) 5> add extract dphren01, exttrailsource
dirdat/en
EXTRACT added.

GGSCI (goldengate1) 6> add rmttrail dirdat/er, extract dphren01,
 megabytes 100
RMTTRAIL added.

GGSCI (goldengate1) 7> start exhr02
Sending START request to MANAGER ...
EXTRACT EXHR02 starting

GGSCI (goldengate1) 8> start dphren01
Sending START request to MANAGER ...
EXTRACT DPHREN01 starting

GGSCI (goldengate1) 5> info all

Program     Status     Group     Lag at Chkpt   Time Since Chkpt
MANAGER     RUNNING
```

```
EXTRACT       RUNNING    DPHREN01   00:00:00       00:04:23
EXTRACT       RUNNING    EXHR02     00:00:00       00:00:09
```

Step 8. Create a replicat parameter file.

```
-- Replicat name. Up to 8 characters
REPLICAT RPHREN01

-- Optional - This ensures that the database environment is
-- configured correctly. Using it is a best practice.
SETENV (NLS_LANG=AMERICAN_AMERICA.AL32UTF8)

-- Login and password to the administrator account in the
-- source database.
userid ggadmin, password
AADAAAAAAAAAAFAJDJBZHZFPIXERDYCJIJCYHDCZBCIOHKENFTGFGSGNAAISCE
DXFADEAECQJODEJGG  AES128, encryptkey key128_1

-- This will cause the Replicat to handle row collisions without
-- abending. Typically we don't want this in a Replicat file
-- but it's not a bad idea to have it in there during the
-- first runs, while GoldenGate catches up the target database
-- with the source database.
-- So, add it now, and remove it after we have gotten the
-- Target database caught up.
HANDLECOLLISIONS

-- Need to disable triggers.
DBOPTIONS SUPPRESSTRIGGERS

-- ASSUMETARGETDEFS is used here to indicate that the source
-- and target database schemas are basically the same.
ASSUMETARGETDEFS

-- Decrypt the trail.  The key will be the same
-- as the key for the Data Pump's RMTTRAIL.
DECRYPTTRAIL, AES128 KEYNAME key128_2
MAP hr.*, TARGET hr.*;
```

Step 9. Create a replicat. Use the encrypted password to log in to verify that your encrypted password hash is correct.

```
GGSCI (goldengate2) 2> dblogin userid ggadmin, password
AADAAAAAAAAAAFAJDJBZHZFPIXERDYCJIJCYHDCZBCIOHKENFTGFGSGNAAISCE
DXFADEAECQJODEJGG  AES128, encryptkey key128_1
Successfully logged into database.
```

```
GGSCI (goldengate2) 3> add replicat rphren01, exttrail dirdat/er
REPLICAT added.

GGSCI (goldengate2) 1> start rphren01
Sending START request to MANAGER ...
REPLICAT RPHR02 starting


GGSCI (aquarius.the-heislers.com) 2> info all

Program     Status    Group     Lag at Chkpt  Time Since Chkpt

MANAGER     RUNNING
REPLICAT    RUNNING   RPHREN01  01:16:16        00:00:00
```

Step 10. Insert a row into the EMPLOYEES table.

```
insert into hr.employees
(employee_id, last_name, email, hire_date, job_id)
values
(9992, 'FREEMAN', 'ROBERT9992', sysdate, 'AC_ACCOUNT');
commit;
```

Step 11. Verify that the row was replicated to the target database.

```
SQL> select employee_id, first_name, last_name
  2  from hr.employees
  3  where employee_id = 9992;

EMPLOYEE_ID FIRST_NAME          LAST_NAME
----------- ------------------- --------------------------
       9992                     FREEMAN
```

Step 12. Use the logdump utility to view the trail file contents without decrypting the trail. As you can see, the data is unreadable.

```
Name: HR.EMPLOYEES
After  Image:
Partition 4   G  s
 e039 0735 1ecc e640 c362 de7c 38c2 b650 d85a d906 |
.9.5...@.b.|8..P.Z..
 1164 d9de 0b51 6273 e47c 2c64 707c 5515 f2b6 4e2b |
.d...Qbs.|,dp|U...N+
 07cf 2378 73fc 8c35 d768 36f7 37d1 8ada 5b75 ba94 |
..#xs..5.h6.7...[u..
 8f21 8721 3e59 7278 ade0 30e3 dd7e 092f defa de8d |
.!.!>Yrx..0..~./....
```

```
 9509 6321 bb76 72a9 3051 7087 0382 2059 18ff 6b3e |
..c!.vr.0Qp... Y..k>
 8162 2ce3 07ab d851 5135 c2a0 6157 e3a7 c60b f7ab |
.b,....QQ5..aW......
 fd80 08e3 2ffa 3797 2cd7 3272 aada 2579 391d a117 |
..../.7.,.2r..%y9...
Bad compressed block, found offset of -8135 (xe039)
```

Step 13. Enable logdump decryption.

```
Logdump 2 >decrypt on keyname key128_1
```

Step 14. View the trail file contents after decrypting the trail. Now you are able to read the record's data.

```
Name: HR.EMPLOYEES
After  Image:
Partition 4    G  s
 0000 000a 0000 0000 0000 0000 2708 0001 0004 ffff |
.............'.......
 0000 0002 000b 0000 0007 4652 4545 4d41 4e00 0300 |
..........FREEMAN...
 0e00 0000 0a52 4f42 4552 5439 3939 3200 0400 04ff |
.....ROBERT9992.....
 ff00 0000 0500 1500 0032 3031 322d 3037 2d32 313a |
.........2012-07-21:
 3134 3a35 333a 3034 0006 000e 0000 000a 4143 5f41 |
14:53:04........AC_A
 4343 4f55 4e54 0007 000a ffff 0000 0000 0000 0000 |
CCOUNT..............
 0008 000a ffff 0000 0000 0000 0000 0009 000a ffff |
....................
```

Filtering Your Data

Suppose you do not need to replicate all of your source data to a target database. GoldenGate gives you the option to filter your data by table, column, or row. Additionally, you can choose to filter your data during extraction or replication and further limit your filtering to specific operations (insert, update, delete).

Filtering Tables

So far, you have used GoldenGate to replicate the entire HR schema. You used wildcards to replicate all tables in extract EXHR01, and in extract SLHR01 you listed all tables separately but accomplished the same goal for replicating all tables. We will now look at replicating a subset of tables.

You can filter tables during capture, delivery, or both, depending on your needs. For example, you may have a requirement to replicate a single schema. In this case it may make sense to use your extract to select the tables you need. On the other hand, you may need to replicate some tables to one database and other tables to another database. In this case, it may be better to extract all tables and use multiple replicats to filter the tables as needed.

NOTE
One important consideration when you are developing a filtering plan is that tables that have a referential integrity relationship must be included in the same extract or replicat as their parent tables.

Filtering Tables at the Source

As you have seen in previous chapters, you direct GoldenGate to include tables by using the TABLE parameter in an extract parameter file. You can list each table individually, or you can use wildcards to specify multiple tables, as seen here.

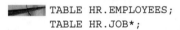

```
TABLE HR.EMPLOYEES;
TABLE HR.JOB*;
```

In this example you are replicating the EMPLOYEES, JOBS, and JOB_HISTORY tables. The EMPLOYEES table is explicitly defined, and JOBS and JOB_HISTORY are chosen by using the wildcard JOB*.

If you want to replicate all but a few tables, you may find it easier to list the tables you do not want to replicate instead of listing the ones you do want. You will still have to include a TABLE parameter to specify the range of tables you wish to include, but specifying tables to exclude may make your list shorter and easier to manage.

```
TABLEEXCLUDE HR.EMPLOYEES;
TABLEEXCLUDE HR.JOB*;
TABLE HR.*;
```

This time you are replicating all tables except EMPLOYEES, JOBS, and JOB_HISTORY. Note the location of the TABLEEXCLUDE parameter in relation to the TABLE parameter. Parameters are processed from top to bottom, and the first parameter that satisfies a given condition will be used. Because of this, the TABLEEXCLUDE parameters must be listed before any TABLE parameter that would otherwise include that table.

Filtering Tables at the Target

You can choose to filter your tables on the target database instead of the source database by using the MAP and MAPEXCLUDE parameters in a replicat parameter file. The MAP and MAPEXCLUDE parameters are used by Replicat processes in the same manner that TABLE and TABLEEXCLUDE are used in Extract processes. Once again, the MAPEXCLUDE parameters must come before all MAP parameters that contain the objects you want to exclude.

```
GGSCI (goldengate2) 1> dblogin userid ggadmin, password ggpwd
GGSCI (goldengate2) 2> add replicat RPAT01, exttrail dirdat/hr
GGSCI (goldengate2) 3> add replicat RPAT02, exttrail dirdat/hr
REPLICAT RPAT01
...
MAPEXCLUDE hr.job*;
MAP hr.*, TARGET hr.*;
REPLICAT RPAT02
...
MAP hr.job*, TARGET scott.job*;
```

The example is a demonstration of how you can use multiple Replicat processes with a single trail file. In the example you created two Replicat processes that read from the same trail file. In the first replicat, you are processing all HR tables except JOBS and JOB_HISTORY. In the second replicat, you are processing only the JOBS and JOB_HISTORY tables from the HR schema, moving them into the SCOTT schema.

Filtering Columns

If you do not need all of your source table's columns for your target, you can filter the columns by including the COLS option of the TABLE parameter in your extract parameter file to select the columns you want. Alternatively, you have the option of specifying the columns you don't need by using the COLSEXCEPT option of the TABLE parameter in your extract file.

```
TABLE hr.employees, COLS (employee_id, first_name, last_name, email);
TABLE hr.jobs, COLSEXCEPT(job_title);
TABLE hr.*;
```

In the example you first listed the tables for which you are specifying the columns that will be replicated, and then the tables that are being migrated with no changes.

There are some requirements you must consider when designing a replication that filters columns.

- If you filter columns using COLS, you should include key columns in the extract. If you don't, you must define a substitute key using the KEYCOLS option of the TABLE parameter. Likewise, don't include key columns with the COLSEXCEPT option.

■ If you use COLS or COLSEXCEPT in a Data Pump Extract, you cannot use the PASSTHRU mode. This is intuitive—if you are using PASSTHRU, the Extract process does not look up table definitions. If you specify columns, it requires the Extract process to look up table definitions.

■ COLSEXCEPT does not exclude unsupported data types.

■ Consider using the FETCHCOLS or FETCHCOLSEXCEPT options of the TABLE parameter. These options query the database to fetch the values if they are not in the transaction log.

■ If you will be filtering rows, include the FETCHBEFOREFILTER option in the table statement before the WHERE or FILTER clause. Alternatively, you can test for a column's presence first using the functions @PRESENT or @ABSENT.

Filtering Rows

After the initial data load, you can use WHERE or FILTER to filter your rows. Both can be used as options in an extract or replicat. You have a third option, SQLPREDICATE, for use during the initial data load. Unlike the other two filtering options, SQLPREDICATE can only be used in extracts.

Using the WHERE Option

The WHERE option is the simpler of the two filtering methods. You use it the same way you would use it in a conventional SQL statement. WHERE selects or excludes records based on a conditional statement, such as equals, greater than, or less than. You can use WHERE with numeric or string columns. This example shows how to use the WHERE clause with a numeric column to select the rows you want to replicate.

```
TABLE hr.employees, WHERE (employee_id < 1000);
```

The next example shows how to use a WHERE clause with a string column to select the rows you want to replicate. It will return all records for which the COUNTRY_ID is "US":

```
TABLE hr.locations, WHERE (country_id = "US");
```

Note the use of the double quotes ("") for the literal string "US". Literal strings must be enclosed in double quotes by default. If you wish to use single quotes for literal strings and double quotes for case-sensitive column names, add the USEANSISQLQUOTES parameter in the GLOBALS file.

Now let's implement the filter on the replicat. As you can see, your WHERE clause is identical to the one you used in the extract.

```
MAP hr.employees, TARGET hr.emp, WHERE (employee_id < 1000);
  MAP hr.locations, TARGET hr.loc, WHERE (ccountry_id = "US");
```

FILTER Option

The other option you have for choosing rows to replicate is FILTER. While WHERE works with numerics and strings, the FILTER option includes or excludes rows based on a numeric value. This does not mean that FILTER cannot be used to filter strings. You can use GoldenGate's column-test functions to turn a string into a numeric function.

This example demonstrates that the syntax for the FILTER clause is the same as for the WHERE clause when working with numeric columns.

```
TABLE hr.employees, FILTER (employee_id < 1000);
```

As we mentioned, you can use FILTER with string columns even though FILTER requires a numeric return value. The return value for the expression can be transformed from a string to a number by using a column-test function such as @STRFIND, which returns the starting position of a string within a string column. If ROBERT is not in the EMAIL column, the function will return 0 and the row will not be extracted.

```
TABLE hr.employees, FILTER (@STRFIND (email, "ROBERT") > 0);
```

Using the FILTER option in the replicat is identical to using it in the extract.

```
MAP hr.employees, TARGET hr.employees, FILTER (employee_id < 1000);
MAP hr.employees, TARGET hr.employees, FILTER (@STRFIND (email,
"ROBERT") > 0);
```

You can refine your FILTER even more by specifying the operation (insert, update, delete) for which the filter will be executed.

```
MAP hr.employees, TARGET hr.employees, &
    FILTER (ON INSERT, ON UPDATE, salary >= 10000);
MAP hr.employees, TARGET hr.employees, &
    FILTER (IGNORE DELETE, salary >= 10000);
```

The first FILTER clause is directing the extract to process all inserts and updates for employees who have a salary of $10,000 or more and to ignore all other inserts and deletes for employee records. All deleted records will be processed.

The second FILTER clause is directing the extract to ignore deletes for employees with a salary of $10,000 or more and to process deletes for employees whose salary is less than $10,000. All inserts and updates will be processed.

Avoiding Column Errors

All the column filtering examples shown have assumed there will be no errors and the example will always work as expected. In a real-world replication, data will not always be clean, and errors are inevitable. There are some steps you can take to avoid errors.

If you have configured your replication for compressed updates, the transaction log contains the only values for columns whose values have changed. You can ensure that the column you are using for your filter condition is always included in your extract transaction log by using the FETCHCOLS option of your table statement. If the list is too long, you can use FETCHCOLSEXCEPT instead.

```
TABLE hr.employees, FETCHCOLS(department_id), FILTER(department_id < 10);
```

If you don't care whether a column included in the filter condition is in the transaction log, you can first test whether the column is present using the @PRESENT column-test function before applying the filter. Likewise, you can apply the filter only when column data is missing by including the @ABSENT column-test function.

```
TABLE hr.employees, FETCHCOLS(department_id), &
    FILTER(@PRESENT (department_id), department_id < 10);
  TABLE hr.employees, FETCHCOLS(department_id), &
    FILTER(@ABSENT (department_id), department_id = 10);
```

In the first example you used @PRESENT to test whether the department_id column is present in the current record of the transaction log. If it is present, the filter is applied before writing the transaction to the trail file.

Initial Data Load

During the initial data load you have a third option available for filtering your data, SQLPREDICATE. SQLPREDICATE affects the SQL statement used by the extract directly, and therefore is a better choice than the WHERE or FILTER options. SQLPREDICATE does not require the extract to fetch all records, unlike the other two options.

You use SQLPREDICATE to include a conventional WHERE clause in the SQL statement that your extract uses to fetch records for the initial data load, as seen here.

```
TABLE hr.locations, SQLPREDICATE "WHERE region_id = 1";
```

WHERE vs. FILTER

Although you can generally choose either WHERE or FILTER for filtering, there are some restrictions for each.

- WHERE does not provide support for arithmetic operators and floating-point data types.

- FILTER is not supported for columns that have a multibyte character set or a character set that is incompatible with the character set of the local operating system.

■ The maximum size for a FILTER clause is 5000 bytes.

■ Don't use FILTER in a Data Pump Extract where tables are being processed in PASSTHRU mode.

Mapping Column Data

If you don't specify otherwise, all columns in the source table will be implicitly mapped to corresponding columns in the target table. If your tables do not have an identical structure, you can explicitly define the relationship for the source and target columns. Column mapping can be defined in either the Extract or the Replicat process, and you can map columns as long as the column names and data types can be identified by using DDL or definition files.

Table-Level Column Mapping

Table-level column mapping is controlled by COLMAP, which is an optional clause for the table and map statements. The use of COLMAP determines whether column mapping will be implicit or explicit. So far, we have used implicit mapping for our replications.

In this simplified example you implicitly map all columns from HR.DEPARTMENTS in the source database to HR.DEPARTMENTS in the target database. The source and target table structures are identical, and the replicat will get the columns from the data dictionary. There is no need to define each column in the map statement.

```
MAP hr.departments, TARGET hr.departments;
```

In the next example the source table is not identical to the target table. We explicitly map all columns from HR.DEPARTMENTS in the source database to HR.DEPT in the target database.

```
MAP hr.departments, TARGET hr.dept,
  COLMAP(dept_id=department_id,
         dept_name=department_name,
         mgr_id=manager_id,
         loc_id=location_id);
```

The behavior of COLMAP is determined by three options: ASSUMETARGETDEFS, SOURCEDEFS, and the default option USEDEFAULTS. We recommend that you specify one of these three options each time you use COLMAP.

USEDEFAULTS

USEDEFAULTS is responsible for mapping compatible, same-named columns and is always on if you do not specify COLMAP. If COLMAP is specified, USEDEFAULTS is turned off unless you add it as an option to the COLMAP clause.

We do not specify USEDEFAULTS in this example. The only columns that will be mapped are MGR_ID and DEPT_ID.

```
MAP hr.employees, target hr.emp2,
  COLMAP (mgr_id=manager_id,
         dept_id=department_id);
```

We do specify USEDEFAULTS in this example. All columns will be implicitly mapped except MGR_ID and DEPT_ID, which are explicitly mapped.

```
MAP hr.employees, target hr.emp2,
  COLMAP (USEDEFAULTS,
         mgr_id=manager_id,
         dept_id=department_id);
```

As you can see from the previous two examples, the outcome was much different when we included the USEDEFAULTS option. The first example replicated three columns, while the second example replicated all columns.

ASSUMETARGETDEFS

The ASSUMETARGETDEFS option directs GoldenGate not to look up the table structure in a definition file because the table structures are identical. We can repeat the last example, using the ASSUMETARGETDEFS option instead of USEDEFAULTS. The results are the same.

```
MAP hr.employees, target hr.emp2,
  COLMAP (ASSUMETARGETDEFS,
         mgr_id=manager_id,
         dept_id=department_id);
```

SOURCEDEFS

If the source and target tables are not identical or if you are using GoldenGate in a heterogeneous environment, such as migrating from SQL Server to Oracle, you must add a source-definition file and include the SOURCEDEFS option to tell your Replicat file which file to use.

In addition to using the SOURCEDEFS option you will need to create the source-definition file on the source database using the defgen utility. The defgen utility is used to create a definitions file that is used to map the table and column definitions on the source server to the tables and columns on the target server. The definitions file is created on the source server and then the definitions file is copied to your target server(s).

GoldenGate Workshop: *Create Source-Definition File*

Workshop Notes

In this workshop we'll replicate the HR.DEPARTMENTS table to the HR.DEPT2 table. The table structures are listed in the following code. We will use the defgen utility to create the source-definition file, then transfer it to the target server.

```
SQL> desc departments
 Name                                      Null?     Type
 ----------------------------------------- --------  -----------
 DEPARTMENT_ID                             NOT NULL  NUMBER(4)
 DEPARTMENT_NAME                           NOT NULL  VARCHAR2(30)
 MANAGER_ID                                          NUMBER(6)
 LOCATION_ID                                         NUMBER(4)
SQL> desc dept2
 Name                                      Null?     Type
 ----------------------------------------- --------  -----------
 DEPT_ID                                             NUMBER(4)
 DEPT_NAME                                 NOT NULL  VARCHAR2(30)
 LOC_ID                                              NUMBER(4)
```

Since we like to have everything scripted, we will put all options in a parameter file. Note the order for the parameters. The DEFSFILE parameter must be listed before the TABLE parameter.

```
GGSCI (goldengate1) 1> edit params d_dept
userid ggadmin, password ggadmin
#
#defsfile parameter must be before the table parameter.
defsfile ./dirsql/departments.sql
table hr.departments;
```

Step 1.   Generate the definition file.

```
$ ./defgen paramfile ./dirprm/d_dept.prm


*******************************************************************
     Oracle GoldenGate Table Definition Generator for Oracle
   Version 11.2.1.0.1 OGGCORE_11.2.1.0.1_PLATFORMS_120423.0230
Linux, x64, 64bit (optimized), Oracle 11g on Apr 23 2012
05:08:19
```

```
Copyright (C) 1995, 2012, Oracle and/or its affiliates. All
rights reserved.


                    Starting at 2012-07-08 13:19:46
*****************************************************************


Operating System Version:
Linux
Version #1 SMP Tue Apr 17 17:49:15 EDT 2012, Release
2.6.18-308.4.1.el5xen
Node: goldengate1
Machine: x86_64
                        soft limit    hard limit
Address Space Size   :    unlimited    unlimited
Heap Size            :    unlimited    unlimited
File Size            :    unlimited    unlimited
CPU Time             :    unlimited    unlimited


Process id: 4361


*****************************************************************
**             Running with the following parameters          **
*****************************************************************
userid ggadmin, password ******
table hr.departments;
Database type: ORACLE
Character set ID: UTF-8
National character set ID: UTF-16
Locale: neutral
Case sensitivity: 14 14 14 14 14 14 14 14 14 14 14 14 11 14 14 14
Retrieving definition for HR.DEPARTMENTS
*
Definition for table HR.DEPARTMENTS
Record length: 72
Syskey: 0
Columns: 4
DEPARTMENT_ID     134    8    0  0  0 1 0     8    8  8 0 0 0 0 1
  0 1 3
DEPARTMENT_NAME    64   30   12  0  0 1 0    30   30  0 0 0 0 0 1
  0 0 0
MANAGER_ID        134    8   48  0  0 1 0     8    8  8 0 0 0 0 1
  0 0 3
LOCATION_ID       134    8   60  0  0 1 0     8    8  8 0 0 0 0 1
  0 0 3
End of definition
```

```
defsfile ./dirsql/departments.sql

Definitions generated for 1 table in ./dirsql/departments.sql
```

Step 2. Take a look at the definition file.

```
*+- Defgen version 2.0, Encoding UTF-8
*
* Definitions created/modified  2012-07-08 13:33
*
*  Field descriptions for each column entry:
*
*     1     Name
*     2     Data Type
*     3     External Length
*     4     Fetch Offset
*     5     Scale
*     6     Level
*     7     Null
*     8     Bump if Odd
*     9     Internal Length
*     10    Binary Length
*     11    Table Length
*     12    Most Significant DT
*     13    Least Significant DT
*     14    High Precision
*     15    Low Precision
*     16    Elementary Item
*     17    Occurs
*     18    Key Column
*     19    Sub Data Type
*
Database type: ORACLE
Character set ID: UTF-8
National character set ID: UTF-16
Locale: neutral
Case sensitivity: 14 14 14 14 14 14 14 14 14 14 14 14 11 14 14
 14
*
Definition for table HR.DEPARTMENTS
Record length: 72
Syskey: 0
Columns: 4
DEPARTMENT_ID     134    8     0 0  0 1 0     8     8    8 0 0 0 0
  1    0 1 3
```

```
DEPARTMENT_NAME   64  30   12  0  0 1 0   30   30   0 0 0 0 0
1    0 0 0
MANAGER_ID       134   8   48  0  0 1 0    8    8   8 0 0 0 0
1    0 0 3
LOCATION_ID      134   8   60  0  0 1 0    8    8   8 0 0 0 0
1    0 0 3
End of definition
```

Step 3. Copy the definition file to the target.

```
$scp ./dirsql/departments.sql oracle@goldengate2:/oracle/
GoldenGate/dirsql
```

Step 4. Add the definition file to the replicat.

```
#Source-definition file
SOURCEDEFS ./dirsql/departments.sql

#For the COLMAP parameter the target column name is first,
#the source column name is second
MAP hr.departments, hr.dept2,
COLMAP (dept_id=department_id,
        dept_name=department_name,
        loc_id=location_id);
```

Global Mapping

Global mapping is controlled with the **colmatch** statement. The rules you define will be applied to all subsequent **table** or **map** statements. You enable these rules with the NAMES option and turn off the rules with the RESET option.

In this example, we define matches for dept_id and mgr_id for all tables in the target database. This time when we map hr.departments to hr.dept, we only have to specify two column names: DEPT_NAME and LOC_ID.

```
COLMATCH NAMES dept_id=department_id
COLMATCH NAMES mgr_id=manager_id

MAP hr.departments, TARGET hr.dept,
COLMAP(dept_name=department_name, loc_id=location_id);

COLMATCH RESET
```

COLMATCH has two additional options: PREFIX and SUFFIX. You can specify a prefix or suffix, which COLMATCH will ignore. Using PREFIX to remove P_ will cause target column P_DEPT_ID to map to source column name DEPT_ID, and using SUFFIX to remove _NBR will cause target column name EMP_ID_NBR to map to source column name EMP_ID.

```
COLMATCH PREFIX p_
  COLMATCH SUFFIX _nbr
```

Testing and Transforming Data

GoldenGate supports transforming data during replication. You can manipulate your data by using one or more of GoldenGate's column-conversion functions. In addition, GoldenGate has built-in functions for testing your data or adding conditions before filtering or transforming it.

Let's start with a simple manipulation. EMPLOYEES and EMP3 are identical, but EMP3 has one additional column: BONUS. You want to give each of your employees a bonus equal to 5 percent of the annual salary.

```
ASSUMETARGETDEFS
  MAP hr.employees, target hr.emp3
  COLMAP (bonus = @COMPUTE((salary * 12) * 0.05));
```

In this example, you multiplied the monthly salary by 12 to get the annual salary, then multiplied the result by 0.05 to calculate the value of the bonus. Finally, you used @COMPUTE to execute the expression and return the result so it can be assigned to BONUS.

You can omit @COMPUTE if the value of the expression will be passed to another GoldenGate function. These two expressions return the same value. The result of the COMPUTE clause is passed to the @STRNUM function, where the numerical value is converted to a string.

```
@STRNUM (@COMPUTE ((salary * 12) * 0.05))
  @STRNUM ((salary * 12) * 0.05)
```

You can transform data other than numbers. For example, the source table may have columns ORDER_YEAR, ORDER_MON, and ORDER_DAY, but you need a date value for the target table. You can use the @DATE function to build a date.

```
order_date = @DATE ("YYYY-MM-DD", "YYYY", order_year, "MM", order_
  year, "DD", order_day)
```

The first expression, "YYYY-MM-DD", gives the output format for the date. The remaining expressions are grouped in pairs, with the first representing the input format ("YYYY") and the second specifying the column from which the data is taken (ORDER_YEAR).

Let's calculate another bonus, this time based on monthly salary. We'll add a little complexity—any employees earning $5,000 or more per month will receive a $500 bonus, while everyone earning less than $5,000 will receive a $300 bonus.

```
ASSUMETARGETDEFS
MAP hr.employees, target hr.emp3
COLMAP (bonus = @IF (salary >= 5000, 500, 300));
```

You used the @IF function to perform the conditional test for salary. If the condition is true, the function will return 500, and if the condition is false, it will return 300. You can also test for multiple conditions. If you are in the Americas region and you want to separate North America from South America, you could do one of the following.

```
continent = @CASE (country_id, "AR", "South America", "BR",
"South America", "North America")

continent = @IF (@VALONEOF (country_id, "AR", "BR"), "South America",
"North America")
```

The two examples return the same results. The @CASE function evaluates country_id. It then returns a result to the CONTINENT column based on the value of country_id. If none of the conditions are met, the default value of "North America" is returned. The @VALONEOF function evaluates country_id as well, but it compares the value to the list enclosed in parentheses. If country_id is in the list, @VALONEOF will return TRUE. The @IF function will then return "South America" to continent_id. If it is not TRUE, @IF will return "North America".

As you can see, GoldenGate has included many functions to allow you to manipulate data during your replication. You can find a complete list of GoldenGate's functions in the *Oracle GoldenGate Windows and UNIX Reference Guide*.

Executing SQL

You can use the SQLEXEC parameter in your extract or replicat to communicate directly with the database to run queries, perform DML operations, execute stored procedures, or execute a database command. SQLEXEC can be used as an option in a table or map statement, or it can be executed as a standalone statement. You can even tell it when to run.

SQLEXEC as an Option for TABLE or MAP

When you use SQLEXEC as an option within a table or map statement, you can execute queries and procedures and pass and accept parameters, but you cannot execute database commands. Let's take a look.

The columns in the HR.COUNTRIES table in the source database are as follows.

```
COUNTRY_ID
COUNTRY_NAME
REGION_ID
```

We have created a new table, HR.CTRY, in the target database. It has the same structure as HR.COUNTRIES in the source database, but we have added REGION_NAME.

```
COUNTRY_ID
COUNTRY_NAME
REGION_ID
REGION_NAME
```

First you will use SQLEXEC in the replicat parameter file to get data for a column that is not in the transaction log.

```
MAP hr.countries, TARGET hr.ctry, &
    SQLEXEC (ID lookup, &
    QUERY "select region_name from regions where region_id =
:v_region_id", &
    PARAMS (v_region_id = region_id)), &
    COLMAP (USEDEFAULTS, region_name = @GETVAL
(lookup.region_name));
```

In this example, you created a SQL statement to retrieve a value for REGION_NAME. You told SQLEXEC that it will be executing a query instead of a stored procedure by using "ID" as the first option for the SQLEXEC clause and gave it a logical identifier of "lookup". The PARAMS clause set the v_region_id variable to the value of the current row's REGION_ID column. Finally, the COLMAP clause defines how columns will be populated. USEDEFAULTS directs the replicat to map all target columns to the corresponding source columns for this map statement only, overriding the replicat's global setting. The second part of the COLMAP clause directs the map statement to execute the built-in function @GETVAL for the SQL statement "lookup" to get the region name.

Next you will use SQLEXEC to call a stored procedure to perform the same lookup.

```
create or replace procedure get_region_name
    (v_region_id IN varchar2, v_region_name OUT varchar2) is
begin
  select region_name into v_region_name
  from    regions where region_id = v_region_id;
end;
/
MAP hr.countries, TARGET hr.ctry, &
```

```
SQLEXEC (SPNAME get_region_name, &
PARAMS (v_region_id = region_id)), &
COLMAP (USEDEFAULTS, region_name = @GETVAL (get_region_name.region_
name));
```

Note that in the second example SQLEXEC is followed by "SPNAME get_region_name". This tells SQLEXEC that it will be executing a stored procedure named "get_region_name".

sqlexec as a Standalone Statement

When you use **sqlexec** as a standalone statement, you can execute queries, procedures, and database commands. You can specify that you want to repeat the **sqlexec** statement at fixed intervals or direct it to execute the statement only when the extract or replicat exits.

It is not tied to any specific table and you cannot pass and accept parameters. As a standalone statement, **sqlexec** can only be used to perform general SQL operations and execute the given command.

You have already used **sqlexec** as a standalone statement to execute a database command. In Chapter 5, you used **sqlexec** to change the status of several constraints, including this one to disable a constraint.

```
SQLEXEC " alter table HR.EMPLOYEES disable constraint EMP_DEPT_FK ";
```

Scheduling sqlexec

There are three options for when **sqlexec** executes. You have just used the first one.

- **ONEXIT** Execute when the extract or replicat ends gracefully. This is especially useful during your initial data load where you may have disabled a constraint and you want to enable it again after the load is complete.

- **EVERY <n> <interval>** Execute at the defined interval, which can be in units of seconds, minutes, hours, or days.

- **Default** Execute immediately, if the other two options are not used.

```
SQLEXEC " select sysdate from dual " EVERY 10 MINUTES
SQLEXEC " alter table HR.EMPLOYEES enable constraint EMP_DEPT_FK "
ONEXIT
END RUNTIME
```

The first **sqlexec** statement executes every 10 minutes. In this case the interval was chosen to bypass an idle session timeout requirement. The second **sqlexec** statement executes when the Replicat process terminates.

Configuring for RAC

GoldenGate supports RAC databases, but you will need to be aware of some requirements for RAC that you do not have to consider with single-instance databases. If you are using GoldenGate 11.2.1.0 or higher, you have even more options for configuring your replication on a clustered database. For more details for configuring GoldenGate for RAC, see the *Oracle GoldenGate Oracle Installation and Setup Guide* and *Oracle GoldenGate High Availability Using Oracle Clusterware*, which are available on the Oracle Technology Network.

Where to Install

GoldenGate can be installed and run from any node in your cluster, but it can be active on only one node at a time. You can install and run GoldenGate on local disk or shared storage that is available to all nodes in your cluster. The best practice is to install GoldenGate on shared storage.

Local Disk

Installing the GoldenGate software on a local disk involves the most effort. The software must be installed in the same directory on all nodes. The directories that contain trail files, checkpoints, and temporary files must be available to all nodes that may run GoldenGate. In short, unless you are planning to run GoldenGate from a single node in your cluster, this is the least desirable option.

Shared Storage

You can install GoldenGate on shared storage and have a single location from which any node can run GoldenGate. By doing this, you may choose to run your extract on a node that has a lighter workload than the others. If you encounter problems on the node where GoldenGate is running, you can stop processing on that node and start it on another node without any reconfiguration.

Next, you will need to decide if you want to perform your replication with Classic Capture mode or the newer Integrated Capture mode.

How to Capture Changes

As of GoldenGate 11.2.1.0, you have a choice for how you will capture changes. You can use Classic Capture or Integrated Capture.

Classic Capture

Classic Capture is the original method for doing GoldenGate replication. It supports most data types and features. When you run your replication in Classic Capture mode, data changes are captured from the redo logs or archive logs. If you are running GoldenGate from a physical standby database, data changes are captured in the archive logs, which were shipped from the primary database.

If some of your data is not supported, you may want to consider using Integrated Capture mode.

Integrated Capture

Integrated Capture is new for GoldenGate version 11.2.1.0. It provides support for features and data types that Classic Capture does not, such as compressed data and XMLType tables. Integrated Capture also handles RAC integration more efficiently than Classic Capture.

Integrated Capture works by interacting with a database log-mining server. The simplest method for setting up a mining database is local deployment, where the source database and the mining database are the same database. The other method for setting up a mining database is downstream deployment; the source and mining databases are different databases.

Synchronizing Nodes

It is important for the system date and time for each node in your cluster to be synchronized when you have a RAC database. It is especially important for the nodes to be synchronized when you are using GoldenGate for replication, since processing decisions are made based on the system clock. You may have replication issues if there is too much of a time difference.

In a RAC environment, the Extract process has a coordinator thread, which assembles the changes that are generated on each node into SCN order. The extract waits after the transaction has been written to the redo log, and if the node has been idle with no transactions, the coordinator thread will start to assemble the transactions. The wait time is controlled by the database parameter MAX_COMMIT_PROPAGATION_DELAY plus the internal GoldenGate padding (2 seconds). You can override the default with the MAXCOMMITPROPAGATIONDELAY option of the THREADOPTIONS parameter.

The IOLATENCY option of THREADOPTIONS allows you to compensate for differences in I/O latency between nodes. If it is set too low, the extract may abend with the message "encountered SCN XXXXX" too often. The default value for IOLATENCY is 1.5 seconds, but you can increase it to three minutes if necessary.

If you do get frequent abends, the best practice is to set MAXCOMMITPROPAGATIONDELAY and IOLATENCY to a high number to stop the abends, then lower them until the abends start again. This will give you a lower limit for your environment.

Threads

The number of threads you will define for your extract depends on the capture method you are using. If you are using Classic Capture, you will generally define one thread per active instance. If you are using Integrated Capture, you will define one thread. The number of threads is not dynamic. If you change the number of threads, you must drop and create a new extract with the updated number of threads.

This example defines an extract for a RAC database with four instances and four threads.

```
GGSCI (goldengate1) 1> dblogin userid ggadmin, password ggpwd
GGSCI (goldengate1) 2> add extract exrac01, tranlog, threads 4,
begin now
```

Connecting

Although you are connecting to a RAC database, the GoldenGate processes run on a single node at a time. You will want to configure a new service for GoldenGate that will allow you to start the service on a single instance and stop and start the service at any time without affecting other users. You can use the srvctl utility to configure the service, as shown here.

```
srvctl add service -d orcl -s goldengate -r orcl1 -a
orcl2,orcl3,orcl4 -P NONE
```

You just added a service named goldengate for the database orcl. The preferred instance is orcl1, and the service will start on that node when you start the database. Other available instances are orcl2, orcl3, and orcl4. Failover is set to NONE.

Now that you have defined the service, you will need to update your tnsnames .ora file.

```
GG =
(DESCRIPTION =
  (ADDRESS = (PROTOCOL = TCP)(HOST = goldengate1a-vip)(PORT = 1521))
  (ADDRESS = (PROTOCOL = TCP)(HOST = goldengate1b-vip)(PORT = 1521))
  (ADDRESS = (PROTOCOL = TCP)(HOST = goldengate1c-vip)(PORT = 1521))
  (ADDRESS = (PROTOCOL = TCP)(HOST = goldengate1d-vip)(PORT = 1521))
  (LOAD_BALANCE = NO)
  (CONNECT_DATA = (SERVER = DEDICATED)(SERVICE_NAME = goldengate))
)
```

The final step for connecting to the database is to configure your Extract or Replicat process to use the tns alias. By doing this, you will ensure that you are connecting to the same node every time.

Configuring for ASM

If you have chosen Classic Capture for your extract and your RAC database is using ASM, you can connect directly to the ASM instance to read the redo logs. To do this, you will need to configure the ASM listener and update the tnsnames.ora file. You must log in to ASM as the user SYS or another user with the SYSASM privilege, and you will need to update your extract parameter file.

Modify the Listener

Your Extract process will be logging in to the local ASM instance, and you need to make sure your listener is configured to listen for connections. Modify the listener file to include the ASM SID, if necessary.

```
(SID_DESC =
   (SID_NAME = +ASM1)
   (ORACLE_HOME = /u01/oracle/product/11.2.0/grid)
)
```

Update the listener on each node where you will be running the Extract process, and make sure you have the correct ASM instance name. Don't forget to recycle your listener for the changes to take effect.

Modify the tnsnames.ora File

Next, you need to update the tnsnames.ora file.

```
ASM =
(DESCRIPTION =
   (ADDRESS = (PROTOCOL = TCP)(HOST = goldengate1a-vip)(PORT = 1521))
   (ADDRESS = (PROTOCOL = TCP)(HOST = goldengate1b-vip)(PORT = 1521))
   (ADDRESS = (PROTOCOL = TCP)(HOST = goldengate1c-vip)(PORT = 1521))
   (ADDRESS = (PROTOCOL = TCP)(HOST = goldengate1d-vip)(PORT = 1521))
   (LOAD_BALANCE = NO)
   (CONNECT_DATA =
     (SERVER = DEDICATED)
     (SERVICE_NAME = +ASM1)
     (INSTANCE_NAME = +ASM1)
   )
)
```

Once again, remember to make the changes on each of the RAC nodes, changing the service name and instance name as appropriate.

Modify the Extract Parameter File

You will need to log in to ASM as SYS or another user with SYSDBA privilege, or SYSASM privilege if your database is Oracle 11.1 or higher. This is a good time to encrypt the password using a strong encryption algorithm, discussed earlier in this chapter.

```
-- Extract name.  Up to 8 characters
EXTRACT EXHR01

-- Optional - This ensures that the database environment is
-- configured correctly.  Using it is a best practice.
SETENV (NLS_LANG=AMERICAN_AMERICA.AL32UTF8)
SETENV (ORACLE_SID=orcl)

-- Login and password to the administrator account in the source
-- database.
USERID ggadmin, PASSWORD ggpwd

-- Set up connection to ASM instance
-- This does not remove the need to log into the database.
TRANLOGOPTIONS ASMUSER "SYS@ASM", ASMPASSWORD "<encrypted password>,
ENCRYPTKEY
key128_3

-- Defines the location and prefix of the trail files
EXTTRAIL ./dirdat/hr

-- This defines what we are replicating.
-- In this case, all tables in the HR schema.
-- Note the use of the wildcard character.
TABLE HR.*;

-- Note - there is no DDL capture in this extract, only DML.
```

The tns alias you use in the parameter file must match the entry you added to the tnsnames.ora file earlier. Setting up a connection to the ASM instance does not remove the need to log in to the database instance.

You are now ready to start your extract.

DBLOGREADER

If your source database is Oracle 10.2.0.5 and later 10*g* versions or 11.2.0.2 and later 11*g*R2 versions (but not 11*g*R1 versions), the previous steps in this section are unnecessary for communicating with ASM. You can specify TRANLOGOPTIONS DBLOGREADER, and the extract will use a newer ASM API, which was not available in the earlier releases. The API uses the database server to access the redo and archivelogs instead of connecting to the ASM instance. The Extract database user must have the SELECT ANY TRANSACTION privilege to use this feature.

To use DBLOGREADER, update your extract parameter file.

```
-- Extract name.  Up to 8 characters
EXTRACT EXHR01

-- Optional - This ensures that the database environment is
-- configured correctly.  Using it is a best practice.
SETENV (NLS_LANG=AMERICAN_AMERICA.AL32UTF8)

SETENV (ORACLE_SID=orcl)

-- Login and password to the administrator account in the source
-- database.
USERID ggadmin, PASSWORD ggpwd

-- Use the newer ASM API
TRANLOGOPTIONS DBLOGREADER

-- Defines the location and prefix of the trail files
EXTTRAIL ./dirdat/hr

-- This defines what we are replicating.
-- In this case, all tables in the HR schema.
-- Note the use of the wildcard character.
TABLE HR.*;

-- Note - there is no DDL capture in this extract, only DML.
```

You are now using DBLOGREADER instead of connecting to the ASM instance.

Error Handling

Let's face it. In a real-world replication, errors are likely to happen. Once you have the Extract, Data Pump, and Replicat processes configured correctly and they are running, the most common errors you will get are data errors. GoldenGate can log records it cannot process, but it must be configured first.

Discard File

A discard file will help identify why processing errors have occurred. Each operation that fails will be written to the discard file so the error can be reviewed and corrected. The discard file reports details about the error such as the database error message, the trail file sequence number, the trail file's relative byte address, and the details of the discarded operation. The best way to show this process is with a demonstration.

GoldenGate Workshop: *Configure Discard File*

Workshop Notes

In this workshop you will configure the Replicat process to use a discard file and force a primary key error to explore what is stored in the discard file.

Step 1. Modify the replicat parameter file rphr01.prm as follows:

```
-- Replicat name. Up to 8 characters
REPLICAT RPHR01

-- Optional - This ensures that the database environment is
-- configured correctly. Using it is a best practice.
SETENV (NLS_LANG=AMERICAN_AMERICA.AL32UTF8)

-- Login and password to the administrator account in the
-- source database.
USERID ggadmin, PASSWORD ggpwd

--We no longer want GoldenGate to handle duplicate records.
--Instead they will be discarded.
--HANDLECOLLISIONS

-- Add discardfile
DISCARDFILE /oracle/GoldenGate/dirdat/hr, PURGE

-- Log errors to the discard file and continue
REPERROR (DEFAULT, DISCARD)

-- Need to disable triggers.
DBOPTIONS SUPPRESSTRIGGERS

-- ASSUMETARGETDEFS is used here to indicate that the source
-- and target database schemas are basically the same.
ASSUMETARGETDEFS

-- The MAP clause essentially says that all HR.* tables on the
-- source database map to the same schema/object on the
-- target database
MAP HR.*, TARGET HR.*;

-- Note - there is no DDL capture in this extract. Only DML.
```

Normally the HANDLECOLLISIONS parameter will resolve primary key errors. Since you want to force a primary key (PK) error, the parameter needs to be disabled. The DISCARDFILE parameter specifies the name of the discard file, and PURGE directs the replicat to truncate the discard file each time the replicat restarts. Finally, the REPERROR controls how the replicat will handle errors. DISCARD directs the replicat to log the error to the discard file and continue, and DEFAULT directs the replicat to use the default error handler for all other errors.

Step 2. Start replicat RPHR01:

```
GGSCI (goldengate2) 1> start rphr01
```

Step 3. View the discard file:

```
GGSCI (goldengate2) 2> view report dirdat/h
Oracle GoldenGate Delivery for Oracle process started, group
RPHR01 discard file opened: 2012-08-18 23:22:43
```

Since the replicat was just started, the only entry in the discard file is the timestamp when it was started.

Step 4. Insert a row into the target database:

```
insert into hr.regions values (5, 'Ocean');
commit;
```

Step 5. Insert a row into the source database:

```
insert into hr.regions values (5, 'Ocean2');
commit;
```

The region_id column is unique in the source but because a row with the same region_id value was inserted into the target database, the record will be discarded.

Step 6. View the discard file:

```
GGSCI (goldengate2) 2> view report dirdat/h

OCI Error ORA-00001: unique constraint (HR.REG_ID_PK) violated
(status = 1).
INSERT INTO "HR"."REGIONS" ("REGION_ID","REGION_NAME") VALUES
(:a0,:a1)
Operation failed at seqno 1 rba 3291
Discarding record on action DISCARD on error 1
Problem replicating HR.REGIONS to HR.REGIONS
Mapping problem with insert record (target format)...
*
REGION_ID = 5
REGION_NAME = Ocean2
*
```

The row in the discard file shows the error number (ORA-00001), the constraint that was violated (HR.REG_ID_PK), the file name (seqno 1 means the file was hr000001), and the values for each column in the record.

Exceptions Table

You can choose to process errors as exceptions. Exception handling gives you more options than simply discarding a record, but it will also take more effort to set it up. Let's take a look at how to do it.

GoldenGate Workshop: *Process Errors as Exceptions*

Workshop Notes

In this workshop you will configure the replicat to process errors as exceptions. You will force a PK error using the same method as in the discardfile workshop.

Step 1. Create the exceptions table.

```
create table hr.regions_exception
(region_id number,
 optype varchar2(20),
 dberrnum number,
 dberrmsg varchar2(4000));
```

You can create the exceptions table to hold as much or as little detail as you wish. For this example, the only column of interest is the primary key column, region_id. The remaining columns contain data retrieved directly from GoldenGate—the operation type, database error number, and database error message. There is no need to add a primary key constraint—we want all rows to be inserted.

Step 2. Modify the replicat parameter file rphr01.prm.

```
-- Replicat name. Up to 8 characters
REPLICAT RPHR01

-- Optional - This ensures that the database environment is
-- configured correctly. Using it is a best practice.
SETENV (NLS_LANG=AMERICAN_AMERICA.AL32UTF8)
```

```
-- Login and password to the administrator account in the
-- source database.
USERID ggadmin, PASSWORD ggpwd

--We no longer want GoldenGate to handle duplicate records.
--Instead they will be discarded.
--HANDLECOLLISIONS

-- Add discardfile
DISCARDFILE /oracle/GoldenGate/dirdat/hr, purge

-- Handle errors as exceptions
REPERROR (DEFAULT, EXCEPTION)

-- Need to disable triggers.
DBOPTIONS SUPPRESSTRIGGERS

-- ASSUMETARGETDEFS is used here to indicate that the source
-- and target database schemas are basically the same.
ASSUMETARGETDEFS

-- The MAP clause essentially says that all HR.* tables on the
--  source database map to the same schema/object on the
-- target database
MAP HR.*, TARGET HR.*;

-- Map exception table
MAP hr.regions, TARGET hr.regions_exception,
  EXCEPTIONSONLY,
  COLMAP (USEDEFAULTS,
    OPTYPE = @GETENV("GGHEADER", "OPTYPE"),
    DBERRNUM = @GETENV("LASTERR", "DBERRNUM"),
    DBERRMSG = @GETENV("LASTERR", "DBERRMSG"));

-- Note - there is no DDL capture in this extract. Only DML.
```

Most of the parameters are the same as they were in the workshop for using discard files. The HANDLECOLLISIONS parameter is still disabled. The DISCARDFILE parameter was included in case you wish to switch back to using the discard file.

The main changes in this workshop are the use of the REPERROR parameter and the addition of the exception table. If there are any data errors, they will be handled as exceptions rather than discards. The new MAP/TARGET parameter tells the error handler how to process the exception.

The EXCEPTIONSONLY option specifies that the only rows that will get inserted into the table are those that are processed as exceptions. All columns that are present in both tables will be implicitly mapped (USEDEFAULTS), and the three new columns will be populated by reading GoldenGate's environment information.

Step 3. Stop Replicat rphr01.

```
GGSCI (goldengate2) 1> stop rphr01
```

Step 4. Start Replicat rphr01.

```
GGSCI (goldengate2) 2> start rphr01
```

Restarting allows the changed parameters to become active.

Step 5. Insert a row into the target database.

```
insert into hr.regions values (5, 'Ocean');
commit;
```

Step 6. Insert a row into the source database.

```
insert into hr.regions values (5, 'Ocean2');
commit;
```

Step 7. View the contents of the exceptions table.

```
SQL> select * from regions_exception;

 REGION_ID OPTYPE                          DBERRNUM
---------- -------------------- ----------
DBERRMSG
----------------------------------------------------------------------
------------
          5 INSERT                               1
OCI Error ORA-00001: unique constraint (HR.REG_ID_PK) violated
(status = 1).
INSERT INTO "HR"."REGIONS" ("REGION_ID","REGION_NAME") VALUES
(:a0,:a1)
```

The exceptions table shows that you received an ORA-00001 error when you were trying to insert a row into REGIONS where REGION_ID = 5. You can retrieve the whole row from the source and target tables and decide how to process the data contained in them.

You have just used two methods to configure GoldenGate to process data errors without stopping with an abend. Now let's look at maintaining your trail files so they do not fill up your storage.

Trail File Maintenance

During a normal replication the storage used by your trail files can grow quite large. You will want to delete unneeded trail files in order to control the growth. You already did this by adding the PURGEOLDEXTRACTS parameter to your manager parameter file in Chapter 5.

```
-- This is a Manager process file
PORT 7809
PURGEOLDEXTRACTS, USECHECKPOINTS
AUTOSTART ER *
AUTORESTART extract *, retries 10, WAITMINUTES 5, RESETMINUTES 60
```

In this manager parameter file, PURGEOLDEXTRACTS has one option: USECHECKPOINTS. You could have chosen NOUSECHECKPOINTS, but it is better to use checkpoints. If your Extract or Replicat process fails, but your Manager process keeps running, you are at risk of losing data. If you use checkpoints to determine when you will purge your trail files, you guarantee the files will not be deleted too early.

The parameters FREQUENCYMINUTES and FREQUENCYHOURS define how often the purging will occur. You can use MINKEEPHOURS or MINKEEPDAYS to define the minimum time a trail file will be available before purging or MINKEEPFILES to define the minimum number of files that will remain available. It's not a good idea to have multiple MINKEEP parameters for a single purge statement, though. Files that meet the criteria based on USECHECKPOINTS and MINKEEPHOURS will not be purged if they do not also meet the criteria for MINKEEPFILES.

Finally, even though the PURGEOLDEXTRACTS parameter is in the manager parameter file, that parameter is not necessarily global. You can customize purging by adding the trail name. You can have up to 500 PURGEOLDEXTRACTS statements in a single manager parameter file. The best practice is to include a default PURGEOLDEXTRACTS statement at the end to handle any trails that were not explicitly defined.

```
-- This is a Manager process file with additional purge options
PORT 7809
PURGEOLDEXTRACTS /oracle/GoldenGate/dirdat/hr*, USECHECKPOINTS, &
  MINKEEPHOURS 3, FREQUENCYMINUTES 30
AUTOSTART ER *
AUTORESTART extract *, retries 10, WAITMINUTES 5, RESETMINUTES 60
```

In this modified manager parameter file, additional purging options have been added for extract EXHR01. It will still use checkpoints, but it will run every 30 minutes instead of the default 10 minutes. It will not purge any files that have been modified in the past three hours. All other extracts will use the default options.

CHAPTER
9

Oracle GoldenGate
and Oracle Real
Application Clusters

ongratulations on making it this far! By now, you should have a good idea of what GoldenGate is and how replication is implemented by using GoldenGate. You should know the architecture, processes, and related parameter and log files within a GoldenGate environment. You should be able to take a blank sheet of paper and draw out the GoldenGate architectural components with some level of confidence. If not, you might want to review before continuing on with this chapter.

This chapter is different from previous chapters that have workshops. The emphasis will be placed on the planning, and the use of Oracle Clusterware as related to GoldenGate and Oracle Real Application Clusters (RAC). This chapter focuses on configuring GoldenGate with Oracle Clusterware and Oracle RAC. This chapter is not an introduction to or management aide for Oracle Clusterware or Oracle RAC. If you are not familiar with these features of Oracle, you should review the Oracle Press books on the subject. We recommend *Oracle Database 11g Oracle Real Application Clusters Handbook, Second Edition* from Oracle Press by K. Gopalakrishnan for a complete understanding of RAC, as well as the official documentation.

We will start with a quick overview of Oracle Maximum Availability Architecture (MAA). Once we have the big picture of what MAA is, we will focus on where GoldenGate fits into MAA. An explanation of the differences and similarities between disaster recovery, high availability, and replication is presented, just to make sure we are on the same page.

Oracle Maximum Availability Architecture (MAA)

One of the earliest case studies of MAA is "Oracle Maximum Availability Architecture Case Study," a paper written by Charles Kim. This paper covers MAA using a combination of Oracle Database 10g Release 2 technologies. They are

- Oracle Real Application Cluster
- Oracle Clusterware
- Automatic Storage Management (ASM)
- Oracle Data Guard
- Oracle Recovery Manager (RMAN)
- Flashback Database
- Enterprise Manager Grid Control

MAA has continued to evolve using Oracle Database 11g Release 2 (see Figure 9-1 for a high-level MAA layout of the relationships between RAC and Active Data Guard). This shows the primary and standby sites with Data Guard providing Disaster Recovery capabilities.

GoldenGate uses the standby site as the source of replication for one or more targets. Specifically, at the standby site, GoldenGate is configured to use the RAC database as the source. GoldenGate can be a managed application that Clusterware administers in case of node failure. For example, if Node 1 of a RAC fails where the GoldenGate Manager (GGM) is running, Clusterware can start the GGM on Node 2. See Figure 9-2, which focuses on a standby site.

In Figure 9-3, we see a RAC configuration made up of three nodes on the left and several single-node databases on the right. In Figure 9-4, we focus on just the RAC with three nodes and a single-node database. Once we cover these concepts, you should be able to configure the GoldenGate in various combinations of multinode RAC and non-RAC databases.

When configuring GoldenGate on RAC, make sure you have a clear understanding of the differences and similarities between disaster recovery, high availability, and replication. These terms are similar and can be a point of confusion. Take time here

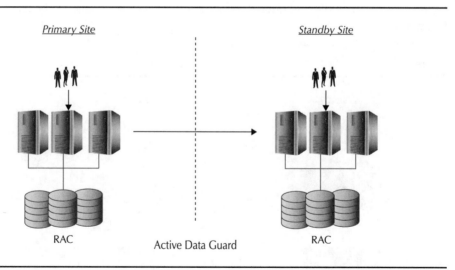

FIGURE 9-1.   *Maximum Availability Architecture layout*

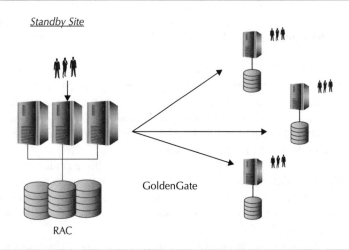

FIGURE 9-2. *MAA standby site*

to make sure that the solution you are building is solving the problem at hand. You should be matching the solution to the problem properly. Keep in mind that GoldenGate is a flexible and powerful tool, but like any tool it needs to be used appropriately.

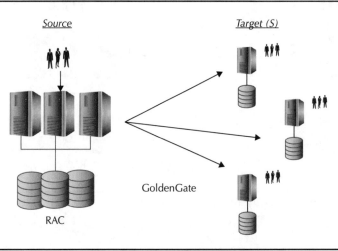

FIGURE 9-3. *RAC and GoldenGate configuration with multinode target*

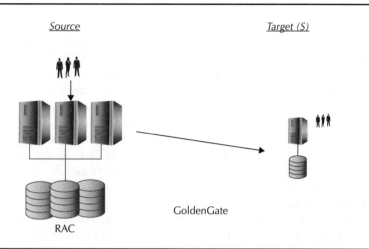

Source   _Target (S)_

GoldenGate

RAC

FIGURE 9-4.   *RAC and GoldenGate configuration with single-node target*

Disaster Recovery, High Availability, and Replication

Make sure you use the right tool for the right solution. You need a clear understanding of the differences and similarities between disaster recovery (DR), high availability (HA), and replication. Here are simple definitions of each term:

- **Disaster recovery**   Ability to survive a primary site disaster and continue to conduct business. This may involve one or more additional sites to take over if the primary site fails.

- **High availability**   Ability to conduct business if part of your system fails. This may involve redundant capabilities and automatic corrections to failures.

- **Replication**   Additional copies of data at alternative locations. This is done to create reporting environments.

Confusion related to these terms can occur when developing the requirements for an application or a system. Clients often know what they want, and you must identify the proper tools and their place in the overall solution. In MAA, RAC is used at both the primary and standby sites providing for site-level HA. Beyond HA, the RAC also provides site-level scalability and services to support each application. Furthermore, HA and application isolation can be accomplished at the storage level through the use of Automatic Storage Management (ASM). In our context, RAC does not provide for DR, because it is site-specific.

DR creates one or more standby sites in case a primary site (that should be using RAC) experiences a site failure. A site failure may be the result of a natural or man-made disaster. Regional power outages, network failure, acts of terrorism, and earthquakes can leave a primary site a "smoking hole."

DR and replication can be confusing terms. Remember this simple phrase: "Replication is not DR and should not be used as DR." To illustrate this point, compare GoldenGate and Data Guard. The main purpose of GoldenGate is for replication, while Data Guard is for DR. From the beginning, each tool provides a different solution respectively.

Data Guard provides for DR, not replication. Data Guard can be configured to provide a zero data loss environment. A partial list of Data Guard additional capabilities includes: failover, switchover, automated failover (Fast Start Failover), snapshot database, and Active Data Guard (ADG). The ADG capability can cause some confusion. It can appear that there is overlap with GoldenGate. ADG allows the standby database to be in an open read-only state. Depending on your requirements, ADG may fulfill the business needs.

Again let us emphasize that in a Data Guard configuration, the primary and standby databases are the same. For a DR environment this is a must, as the application(s) using the database does not and should not need to know if it is on the primary or if it is on the "new" primary (formerly the standby) once a failover/switchover happens.

Where Data Guard maintains a complete copy of the primary database to one or more standby(s), GoldenGate is often used to replicate only necessary schema(s) or table(s) from the source to the target. Notice here that even the terms are specific to the related product. When referring to Data Guard, the terms used to identify locations are primary and standby(s). GoldenGate uses different terms when identifying location, source, and target(s).

The bottom line is: Data Guard is for DR and GoldenGate is for replication. You must have a clear understanding of the differences. You can use GoldenGate for DR—but that does not mean you should. When a "smoking hole" does occur, you will find out the differences between DR and replication. We have covered the differences to convince you that "replication is not DR and should not be used for DR." If you're not convinced, we suggest further reading of *Oracle Active Data Guard and Oracle GoldenGate*, which can be found on the Oracle Technology Network.

Installing GoldenGate in a RAC Environment

When you're installing GoldenGate in a RAC environment, an early decision to make is where to install what. Pieces of GoldenGate can be installed on shared or nonshared storage. Deciding on where to install will determine how GoldenGate is managed and administered. At a minimum, the checkpoint and trail files must be accessible from each node in the cluster. The rest of GoldenGate can be installed on shared storage that each node can access. Also, an installation of GoldenGate can be installed on a nonshared disk. The nonshared method means GoldenGate is locally installed on each of the nodes in the RAC.

Once the installation is completed, we can focus on the HA aspect of configuring GoldenGate with Oracle Clusterware. We want to configure Clusterware to handle a node failure. For example, if Node 1 of a two-node RAC running GoldenGate Manager (GGM) should fail, then GGM will restart on Node 2 because Clusterware has been configured to handle such a situation. This configuration allows for the HA of GoldenGate.

GGM controls all other GoldenGate processes. The processes of Extract, Data Pump, Replicat, and Collector are run in the same ways as they would be in a noncluster environment. GGM would run the aforementioned process with the normal commands and parameter files.

Clusterware needs to be configured to make sure the GGM run properly. The node GGM is running on does not matter as the crucial checkpoint and trail files are accessible from all nodes in the cluster. This sounds simple at a distance, but now let's see how to configure GGM as an application that Clusterware manages.

Configuring the Application Virtual IP Address

An Application Virtual IP (A-VIP) address should be configured to support GGM. This A-VIP would be on the public subnet of the servers in the RAC configuration. The A-VIP would be a separate isolated VIP. This is done so as to not interfere with any other applications. If a node failure happens, the A-VIP would be migrated by Clusterware, and is faster than the failover function of the servers.

GGM uses the A-VIP to isolate itself from the physical server. Remote pumps must use the A-VIP to communicate with GGM. GGM uses the A-VIP to maintain HA if a node fails. Clusterware moves the A-VIP to a surviving node and restarts GGM. GGM is configured to autostart the other GoldenGate processes as normal based on the parameter file settings.

Now create an A-VIP using appvipcfg. This utility is recommend by Oracle to create or delete an A-VIP, and it is found at $GRID_HOME/bin/appvipcfg. Create an A-VIP with the following syntax:

```
appvipcfg create -network=network_number -ip=ip_address -vipname=vip_
name
-user=user_name [-group=group_name] [-failback=0 | 1]
```

- network_number is the number of the network

- ip_address is the IP address

- vip_name is the name of the A-VIP

- user_name is the name of the user who installed Oracle Database

- group_name is the name of the group

The default value of the -failback option is 0. If you set the option to 1, then the A-VIP (and therefore any resources that depend on A-VIP) fails back to the original node when it becomes available again. To obtain the ip_address, use Clusterware with the following command:

```
crsctl stat res -p |grep -ie .network -ie subnet |grep -ie name -ie
subnet
```

After running the command, look for the USR_ORA_SUBNET. The output of the command should appear similar to the following:

```
NAME=ora.net1.network
USR_ORA_SUBNET=10.1.41.93   <------ ip_address
```

To create our A-VIP for GGM, run the following as the root user:

```
$GRID_HOME/bin/appvipcfg create -network=1 \
-ip=10.1.41.93 \
-vipname=ggatevip \
-user=root \
-failback=1
```

We have chosen to name our A-VIP ggatevip and took the option of FAILBACK so that when the failed node recovers, it recovers to a "normal" state. After creating the A-VIP, proper permissions need to be set to allow the Oracle Grid infrastructure software owner (for example, Oracle) to run the script that starts the A-VIP.

```
$GRID_HOME/bin/crsctl setperm resource ggatevip -u user:oracle:r-x
```

Then, while logged in as the Oracle OS user, start the A-VIP:

```
$GRID_HOME/bin/crsctl start resource ggatevip
```

To validate the node the A-VIP is running on, execute:

```
$GRID_HOME/bin/crsctl status resource ggatevip
```

For example:

```
[oracle@gg01 ~]$ crsctl status resource ggatevip
NAME=ggatevip
TYPE=app.appvip.type
TARGET=ONLINE
STATE=ONLINE on gg01
```

Once the A-VIP is created and permission is set properly, the next step is to make GGM a registered application that can be managed by Oracle Clusterware. To do this, create an action script.

Creating an Action Script

The action script is used by Clusterware to control applications. We want Clusterware to control GGM. Our action script controls start, stop, and abort of GMM. The name of our script is ggaction.src and you will want to locate it in the directory $GRID_HOME/crs/public *on each node* of the RAC cluster. Here is the script that we will use:

```
#!/bin/sh
#############################################################################
####
# Script to Manage Golden Gate from Clusterware
# This needs to be installed in GRID_HOME//crs/public
#############################################################################
####
ORACLE_HOME=/u01/product/database/1120/db1
GGS_HOME=/u02/ggate
LD_LIBRARY_PATH=${LD_LIBRARY_PATH}:${GGS_HOME}
export GGS_HOME LD_LIBRARY_PATH ORACLE_HOME
# Function runCmd to run the Golden Gate Script Execution
runCmd()
{
ggCmd=$1
result=`${GGS_HOME}/ggsci << EOF
${ggCmd}
exit
EOF`
}
```

```
# Function CheckMgr to check the Golden Gate Manager process
checkMgr()
{
  if ( [ -f "${GGS_HOME}/dirpcs/MGR.pcm" ] )
    then
        pid='cut -f8 "${GGS_HOME}/dirpcs/MGR.pcm"'
        if [ ${pid} = 'ps -e |grep ${pid} |grep mgr |cut -d " " -f2' ]
        then
            exit 0
        else
            if [ ${pid} = 'ps -e |grep ${pid} |grep mgr |cut -d " " -f1' ]
            then
                exit 0
            else
                exit 1
            fi
        fi
    else
        exit 1
    fi
}
# Main Code to get the input and run it
case $1 in
'start') runCmd 'start manager'
sleep 5
checkMgr
;;
'stop') runCmd 'stop er *'
runCmd 'stop er *!'
runCmd 'stop manager!'
exit 0
;;
'check') checkMgr
;;
'clean') runCmd 'stop er *'
runCmd 'stop er *!'
runCmd 'kill er *'
runCmd 'stop manager!'
exit 0
;;
'abort') runCmd 'stop er *!'
runCmd 'kill er *'
runCmd 'stop manager!'
exit 0
;;
esac
# End of Script
```

Now that we have an action script on each of the nodes of our RAC, make sure that the permission to run the script is correct. The script must be executable by the Oracle GoldenGate software owner (CHMOD +X GGACTION.SRC) on each node. Now register the A-VIP and the action script with Clusterware to "bind" the two together. We will cover this in the next section.

Clusterware Registration

The registration of the A-VIP and action script is done using crsctl. This creates a resource that Oracle Clusterware controls. The registration makes sure that the dependencies are started in proper order. Oracle Clusterware ensures that the A-VIP is started first because GGM is dependent on the A-VIP. Connect as the Oracle user and issue the following commands to accomplish this task.

```
$GRID_HOME/bin/crsctl add resource ggapp \
 -type cluster_resource \
 -attr "ACTION_SCRIPT=$GRID_HOME/crs/public/ggaction.src,
 CHECK_INTERVAL=30,
 START_DEPENDENCIES='hard(ggatevip) pullup(ggatevip)',
 STOP_DEPENDENCIES='hard(ggatevip)'"
```

Let's look at some of the details in the previous code. First, we are creating a resource named ggapp. We used the START_DEPENDENCIES parameter to indicate that there is both a hard and a startup dependency on ggatevip. This indicates that the A-VIP and the ggapp application should always start together. We also used the STOP_DEPENDENCIES parameter to create a hard stop dependency on ggatevip. This indicates that the A-VIP and the ggapp application should always stop together.

If for some reason your installation of GoldenGate does not have the same owner as the Grid Infrastructure owner, then you will need to complete an additional step. Run the following as root:

```
$GRID_HOME/bin/crsctl setperm resource ggapp -o <ogg_software_owner>
```

where the <ogg_software_owner> would be the owner of the installation of GoldenGate.

Basic Administration of the GoldenGate Application

Now that GoldenGate is a registered application with Clusterware, the administration of GGM will be different. Use Clusterware commands to start, stop, migrate, and check the status of GGM.

From now on you should always use Clusterware to start GoldenGate. Log in as oracle and execute:

- To start Oracle GoldenGate, use (as oracle):

  ```
  $GRID_HOME/bin/crsctl start resource ggapp
  ```

- To stop Oracle GoldenGate, use (as oracle):

  ```
  GRID_HOME/bin/crsctl stop resource ggapp
  ```

At times you will need to migrate the GGM application to another node. For example, during server maintenance the GGM is on the node on which you need to take downtime. Use the following command to migrate the application.

```
$GRID_HOME/bin/crsctl relocate resource ggapp -f
```

At times, you might need to migrate the application to a specific server.

```
$GRID_HOME/bin/crsctl relocate resource ggapp [-n destination_server]  -f
```

- Where -n destination_server specifies the name of the server to which you want relocate resources.

- To check the status of the GoldenGate application, use (as oracle):

  ```
  $GRID_HOME/bin/crsctl status resource ggapp
  ```

For example:

```
[oracle@gg01 grid]$ crsctl status resource ggapp
NAME=ggapp
TYPE=cluster_resource
TARGET=ONLINE
STATE=ONLINE on gg01
```

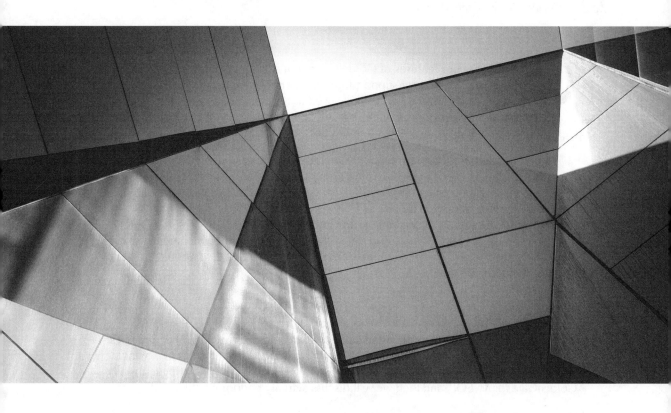

CHAPTER
10

GoldenGate for MySQL

O ne of the major features of GoldenGate that sets it above other replication products is its superior support for heterogeneous replication. In this chapter we will build on the skills used to replicate data from Oracle to Oracle to enable replication from Oracle to MySQL, and reverse the process by capturing data on MySQL and delivering the data to Oracle.

MySQL and GoldenGate are both actively developed, so which version you are using for GoldenGate and MySQL will determine which features are available. For this chapter we will be using versions 11.2 for GoldenGate and 5.5 for MySQL with the InnoDB storage engine option.

In this chapter we will cover setting up GoldenGate for MySQL. First, an Oracle database will be used as a source and the MySQL database will be the target. Next, we will reverse the process and capture transactions from MySQL and replicate the changes to an Oracle database.

Installing GoldenGate for MySQL

In this section we will discuss the installation of GoldenGate for MySQL. The process is not unlike installing GoldenGate for Oracle, so you should feel right at home, having read about that process in Chapter 3. In this section we will discuss preparing to install GoldenGate for MySQL, and then we will discuss actually performing the install.

Preparing for the Installation of GoldenGate on a MySQL Database Server

In this section GoldenGate binaries will be installed and initially configured. You will find the GoldenGate installation for MySQL the same as for other UNIX-like operating systems. Even before you start installing Oracle GoldenGate for MySQL, you should check the Oracle certification matrix for GoldenGate to ensure that the platform you are running MySQL on is certified. We have discussed this process in Chapter 2, so you should be familiar with how to check the certification.

At the time of this writing, the following requirements existed to run Oracle GoldenGate on MySQL:

- Oracle Linux 5.5 Server or higher
- MySQL 5.5 or higher database and client installed and running with the InnoDB storage engine
- Oracle 11.2 or higher database installed and running

After you have checked the compatibility requirements, you are ready to start installing GoldenGate and then begin to replicate data from Oracle to MySQL.

Installing GoldenGate for MySQL on a MySQL Database Server

You can find GoldenGate for MySQL on Oracle's E-Delivery web site, as discussed in Chapter 3. Instead of selecting GoldenGate for Oracle, you will select GoldenGate for your version of MySQL. Once you have downloaded the software, the install steps are the same as installing for Oracle, namely unzipping and untarring the file. This was all demonstrated earlier in this book in Chapter 3.

Once you have installed GoldenGate, you will want to test the install by starting the GGSCI interface and creating the subdirectories as shown in Chapter 3. As with the Oracle version of GoldenGate, the OS user that you will use to start GGSCI will need to have access to the MySQL client libraries. For this exercise, the GoldenGate processes will run as the same OS user as the MySQL database to ensure that GoldenGate has the correct file permissions for the MySQL client libraries and later to ensure access to the MySQL transaction log.

```
Oracle GoldenGate Command Interpreter for MySQL
   Version 11.2.1.0.1 OGGCORE_11.2.1.0.1_PLATFORMS_120423.0230
   Linux, x64, 64bit (optimized), MySQL Enterprise on Apr 23 2012 04:34:25

   Copyright (C) 1995, 2012, Oracle and/or its affiliates. All rights reserved.
   GGSCI (snode2.example.com) 1> create subdirs
   Creating subdirectories under current directory /var/lib/mysql/gg_mysql
   Parameter files              /var/lib/mysql/gg_mysql/dirprm: already exists
   Report files                 /var/lib/mysql/gg_mysql/dirrpt: created
   Checkpoint files             /var/lib/mysql/gg_mysql/dirchk: created
   Process status files         /var/lib/mysql/gg_mysql/dirpcs: created
   SQL script files             /var/lib/mysql/gg_mysql/dirsql: created
   Database definitions files   /var/lib/mysql/gg_mysql/dirdef: created
   Extract data files           /var/lib/mysql/gg_mysql/dirdat: created
   Temporary files              /var/lib/mysql/gg_mysql/dirtmp: created
   Stdout files                 /var/lib/mysql/gg_mysql/dirout: created
```

Next, we need to create a parameter file for the GoldenGate Manager process. This is similar to what we did in Chapter 5 when we configured the Manager process. Here is an example:

```
GGSCI (snode2.example.com) > edit params mgr
PORT 7802
GGSCI (snode2.example.com) > start manager
```

Oracle to MySQL GoldenGate Replication

With the GoldenGate software installed and a Manager process running, we are ready to continue to set up GoldenGate for our MySQL database. In this section we will be configuring an Oracle database as the source database and a MySQL database as the target database for GoldenGate replication. Before we can do any of that, we need to first get our MySQL database all set up. In this chapter we assume that you have some basic experience administering a MySQL database. Therefore we will skip basic processes such as installing MySQL, using MySQL utilities, and the like.

Setting Up the MySQL Database

Before we can start configuring replication between Oracle and MySQL, we will need to log in to the MySQL server and then create a database called MYDB for the destination tables.

```
bash> mysqladmin -u root -p
mysql> create database MYDB;
```

When replicating from similar databases, such as replicating from Oracle databases to Oracle databases, creating the destination schema can be trivial. However, in spite of the fact that both Oracle and MySQL are ANSI compliant, they are two different kinds of databases, and therefore we will often find DDL differences between the tables on the source and target servers. As a result, we need to translate the DDL between the two databases so Oracle GoldenGate will know what to do with the trail file information that it wants to apply.

The first thing we need to do is to translate Oracle DDL into MySQL. Between Oracle and MySQL there are some data type differences; for example, MySQL doesn't support Oracle syntax for defining numeric data types. We need to deal with these differences.

In our case, we have some tables that were created in Oracle, and now we need to create them in MySQL. The Oracle DDL is not compatible with MySQL, and therefore we will need to adjust the DDL in order to be able to re-create the table in MySQL. Here is our initial Oracle table DDL:

```
CREATE TABLE "SOE"."WAREHOUSES"
    (    "WAREHOUSE_ID" NUMBER(6,0),
         "WAREHOUSE_NAME" VARCHAR2(35),
         "LOCATION_ID" NUMBER(4,0),
          CONSTRAINT "WAREHOUSES_PK" PRIMARY KEY ("WAREHOUSE_ID")
    );
```

The equivalent MySQL DDL would look like this:

```
CREATE TABLE WAREHOUSES
    (    WAREHOUSE_ID INT,
         WAREHOUSE_NAME VARCHAR(35),
         LOCATION_ID INT,
      PRIMARY KEY(WAREHOUSE_ID)
    )
```

Note that the NUMBER data type in Oracle is replaced by an INT data type in MySQL. Also note that the DDL to define the primary key in MySQL is different than that for Oracle. As you might have guessed, this conversion of DDL can take some time and effort, as you will have to perform this conversion for each table that you want to replicate to. If you have a data modeling tool that you maintain your database schema DDL in, you may be able to get that tool to generate DDL for MySQL, rather than having to re-create the DDL on your own.

You can confirm that the tables are created in the MySQL database by using the MySQL command **show table status**, as seen here (note that we have adjusted the output—your display will provide quite a bit more information):

```
mysql> show table status IN mydb;
 | Name           | Engine | Version | Row_format | Rows | Avg_row_length |
 | WAREHOUSES     | InnoDB |      10 | Compact    |    0 |              0 |
```

Pay close attention to the Engine column. If you find that any of the tables in the schema show an engine listed as MyISAM, you will need to convert them to InnoDB or re-create them. GoldenGate does not support tables using the MyISAM engine. If you try to replicate to a table using the MyISAM engine, you will see the following error when replicating the table:

```
ERROR   OGG-00768  Oracle GoldenGate Delivery for MySQL, rp.prm:  The MyISAM
storage type tables are not supported for Replication. Please, create table
(mydb.ORDERS) with ENGINE=InnoDB. SQL error (0).
```

Once you have re-created the tables in the MySQL schema, you will not want to forget about the creation of other schema objects such as indexes and constraints.

Creating the GoldenGate Schema on MySQL

Recall that we created a GoldenGate administration schema in Oracle. We need to do the same thing with our MySQL database. We strongly recommend that you create this user as one that is dedicated to GoldenGate administrative operations, and nothing else.

When creating the MySQL GoldenGate schema, you will need to grant the following rights for a Replicat process:

- Insert, Update, and Delete privileges on all replicated tables

- Create Table privilege

- Execute privilege

To grant the required privileges, log on to the MySQL command prompt with an account that has the rights to create a new user, and assign privileges to the GoldenGate user. Here is an example:

```
mysql> CREATE USER 'ggs_user'@'localhost' IDENTIFIED BY 'welcome1';
mysql> use mydb;
mysql> grant select on mydb.* to 'ggs_user'@'localhost';
mysql> grant insert on mydb.* to 'ggs_user'@'localhost';
mysql> grant delete on mydb.* to 'ggs_user'@'localhost';
mysql> grant update on mydb.* to 'ggs_user'@'localhost';
mysql> grant execute on mydb.* to 'ggs_user'@'localhost';
mysql> grant create on mydb to 'ggs_user'@'localhost';
```

Performing the Initial Load from Oracle to MySQL

Next, we need to perform the initial load of data, populating the MySQL schema that we have created. We have covered how to configure GoldenGate on Oracle to replicate the contents of a given schema through the Extract process to the target database. Please refer to Chapter 5 for more information on this process.

There are some subtle differences we want to point out between what you do in Chapter 5 and what you will do when populating the MySQL target database. First, the parameter file that you will create will look like the parameter files created for replication on an Oracle GoldenGate database. The only thing you need to change will be to make sure that the RMTHOST parameter is pointing to the MySQL database server, and that the port address is correct. Recall from Chapter 5 that the RMTASK parameter will cause the replicat automatically, so we don't have to worry about that part of the process.

It is really kind of nice because the configuration of the Extract process when moving data to MySQL is pretty much the same as it is when moving it to Oracle. In these code examples, we have created the Extract process. We have also provided you with the content of the extract parameter file:

```
GGSCI (snode2.example.com)> add extract ex_load, sourceistable
EXTRACT added.

GGSCI (snode2.example.com)> edit params ex_load

EXTRACT  ex_load
USERID ggs_user, PASSWORD welcome1
RMTHOST snode, MGRPORT 7803
RMTTASK replicat, GROUP rp
TABLE SOE.*;
```

Creating the Definition File

One thing that is different from typical Oracle-to-Oracle replication is the conversion of the data types between Oracle and MySQL. Just as we had to convert the DDL with the **create table** command earlier, we will need to have GoldenGate convert the data in the trail files so that it will apply properly. As a result we need to create a definition file. We introduced you to the concept of the definition file and the defgen utility in Chapter 8. The definition file contains metadata about the tables being replicated, including column names and data types. The defgen utility is used to create the definition file.

The parameter file that we will create is like the other GoldenGate parameter files. It is simply an ASCII file that you create with your favorite editor like vi. We will create the parameter file in the dirprm directory under the Oracle GoldenGate Home directory. Here is an example of a definition file that we will call defgen.prm:

```
DEFSFILE ./dirsql/soeobject.sql
USERID ggs_user, PASSWORD ggs_user
TABLE SOE.*;
```

This parameter file has a few interesting and new parameters in it. First, there is the DEFSFILE parameter, which points to the definition file that will be created when we run the defgen utility, using this parameter file, to create our object definitions file. The USERID, PASSWORD, and TABLE parameters are the same as we have used in previous parameter files. We discussed these parameters extensively in Chapter 5, so refer to Chapter 5 if you want more information on them.

Now that we have created our parameter file, we are ready to run the defgen command-line utility to generate the definition file. See Chapter 8 for more detail on the defgen utility in general. To create the definition file, we call the defgen utility, passing to it the name of the parameter file we just created. Here is an example (note that we have somewhat edited this example for size and redundancy considerations—your output would be longer):

```
./defgen paramfile /home/oracle/gg_fix/dirprm/defgen.prm
***********************************************************************
         Oracle GoldenGate Table Definition Generator for Oracle
                      Version 11.2.1.0.1 14194540
       Linux, x64, 64bit (optimized), Oracle 11g on Jun 14 2012 05:07:21
   Copyright (C) 1995, 2012, Oracle and/or its affiliates. All rights reserved.
                      Starting at 2012-07-29 00:05:30
***********************************************************************
Operating System Version: Linux
Version #1 SMP Wed Mar 7 04:16:51 EST 2012, Release 2.6.18-308.1.1.el5
Node: snode2.example.com
Machine: x86_64
                        soft limit    hard limit
Address Space Size   :     unlimited     unlimited
Heap Size            :     unlimited     unlimited
File Size            :     unlimited     unlimited
CPU Time             :     unlimited     unlimited
Process id: 19386
```

```
************************************************************************
**              Running with the following parameters              **
************************************************************************
defsfile ./dirsql/soeobject.sql
userid ggs_user, password ********
table SOE.*;
Expanding wildcard SOE.*:

Retrieving definition for SOE.CUSTOMERS

2012-07-29 00:05:38  WARNING OGG-00869  No unique key is defined for table
'CUSTOMERS'. All viable columns will be used to represent the key, but may not
guarantee uniqueness.  KEYCOLS may be used to define the key.
Retrieving definition for SOE.INVENTORIES

2012-07-29 00:05:38  WARNING OGG-00869  No unique key is defined for table
'INVENTORIES'. All viable columns will be used to represent the key, but may not
guarantee uniqueness.  KEYCOLS may be used to define the key.
Retrieving definition for SOE.LOGON

2012-07-29 00:05:38  WARNING OGG-00869  No unique key is defined for table
'LOGON'. All viable columns will be used to represent the key, but may not
guarantee uniqueness.  KEYCOLS may be used to define the key.
Retrieving definition for SOE.ORDERENTRY_METADATA

-- Additional output removed for brevity

Definitions generated for 9 tables in ./dirsql/soeobject.sql
```

This file needs to be copied to the MySQL server to enable the replicat to be able to read the definition during replication. As a result we will move the soeobject.sql file from the Oracle GoldenGate installation dirsql directory to the MySQL Goldengate installation dirsql directory. Once the file has been copied over to the directory, we are ready to populate the tables. We will use the same process that we used in Chapter 5, allowing GoldenGate to do the initial population of data from the source Oracle database to the target MySQL database.

Initial Loading of the MySQL Schema

Before we can start normal replication, we need to populate the MySQL database schema with the data that is in the Oracle database schema. We did this in Chapter 5 using a special GoldenGate Replicat and Extract process, and we will do the same thing here as well.

To begin with, you will want to create a Manager process parameter file on both the Oracle server and the MySQL server. There are examples of this in Chapter 5. As we mention in Chapter 5, you should ensure that the manager port is the same as the MGRPORT defined in the extract parameter file. See Chapter 5 for an example of the creation of a Manager process parameter file.

Having created the Manager process parameter file, we will create a replicat parameter file (as covered in Chapter 5) for the Replicat process (on the MySQL node). The parameter file will look like this:

```
GGSCI (snode3.example.com)>edit params rp
REPLICAT rp
TARGETDB mydb@localhost, USERID ggs_user, PASSWORD welcome1
SOURCEDEFS ./dirprm/soeobject.sql
MAP SOE.*, TARGET mydb.*
```

This file should look familiar. First we name the Replicat process. The targetdb provides the connection string to the target database (a MySQL database). If you're connecting to a database on the localhost and the OS is Linux or UNIX, the directory used for the socket file must be in /tmp for GoldenGate to be able to connect to the MySQL database. Refer to the official documentation for your operating system and version of MySQL if this is not the case.

Our parameter file also contains the SOURCEDEFS parameter, which defines the location of the definition file we created earlier in this chapter. Finally, we have the MAP parameter, which you should be very familiar with by now. The MAP parameter specifies that all data received from the SOE schema tables should be replicated to the same table names in the MYDB database. This is one of the powerful features of GoldenGate, being able to replicate data between dissimilar schemas (though the heterogeneous replication features are also pretty powerful stuff!).

Having created the parameter file, we then add the Replicat process on the target node:

```
GGSCI (snode3.example.com)> add replicat rp, specialrun
REPLICAT added.
```

Recall that in Chapter 5, this special Replicat process runs only once, rather than all the time like a normal Replicat process. Also recall that there is no Extract process configured for this kind of Replicat process.

Let's review the steps we have completed so far. A Manager process has been defined on both the source and target systems, and an extract has been created for the initial load. We created the initial schema in MySQL and created a definition file to translate the objects in Oracle to those in MySQL, and a replicat has been created to populate data from the initial load.

We should now be ready to start the extract and load the initial data from Oracle into MySQL. To do this, ensure that the Manager process is running on both the target and source instance of GoldenGate and start the extract on the source. Do not start the replicat on the target. If you recall, the extract has an RMTTASK parameter, which will start the replicat on the target system. Here is an example of running this process:

```
GGSCI (snode2.example.com)>start mgr
GGSCI (snode2.example.com)>start ex_load
Sending START request to MANAGER ...
EXTRACT EX_LOAD starting
```

We can see the status of the conversion process during the data load by looking at the ggserr.log file (maybe using **tail –f** on the file) on the MySQL server, as seen in this example output:

```
2012-08-08 18:15:29  INFO    OGG-00996  Oracle GoldenGate Delivery for MySQL,
rp.prm:  REPLICAT RP started.
2012-08-08 18:15:29  INFO    OGG-03010  Oracle GoldenGate Delivery for MySQL,
rp.prm:  Performing implicit conversion of column data from character set windows-
1252 to ISO-8859-1.
```

We can see that the conversions are working just as we expected.

We know that the Extract process should have caused the Replicat process to start on the target server, and we know that the Extract and Replicat processes will automatically stop when the initial data has been copied over. We can check the progress by tailing the output files of the Extract and Replicat processes. We can also check the process by comparing row counts between the tables being loaded, or we can run the **stats** command from the GoldenGate command line to display the statistics associated with the runs (see Chapter 5 for more on all these techniques).

Since this data transfer is a one-time job, a normal GGSCI **info all** command will not show the extract or replicat. Instead, run the GGSCI command **info all** with the TASKS parameter (for example, **info all, tasks**) to see the status of the process as seen here:

```
GGSCI (snode2.example.com)> info all, tasks
Program     Status     Group       Lag at Chkpt   Time Since Chkpt
EXTRACT     RUNNING    EX_LOAD
```

Depending on how much data you are loading, we will want to check the status of the load process periodically. Again we can use the **info all, tasks** command to perform this check. Once we see a status of stopped for our extract, we know that the process has completed. Here is an example of the output of a completed process. Note we are running the command on both the source database node and the target database node:

```
GGSCI (snode2.example.com) > info all, tasks
Program     Status     Group       Lag at Chkpt   Time Since Chkpt
EXTRACT     STOPPED    EX_LOAD

GGSCI (snode3.example.com) > info all, tasks
Program     Status     Group       Lag at Chkpt   Time Since Chkpt
REPLICAT    STOPPED    RP
```

Creating the Oracle Extract Process and the MySQL Replicat Process

Now that we have populated the MySQL schema, we can create an extract on the Oracle database server, and a replicat on the MySQL server. These are the processes that will perform the ongoing replication between our two servers.

First, let's create the extract. As you might expect, we first create a parameter file and then add the extract—much as you have already seen in Chapter 5. First we create the parameter file:

```
EXTRACT ex_mysql
SETENV ("ORACLE_SID = gg2")
USERID ggs_user, password ggs_user
RMTHOST snode3, MGRPORT 7802
RMTTRAIL ./dirdat/rp
TABLE SOE.CUSTOMERS;
TABLE SOE.ORDERS;
TABLE SOE.ORDER_ITEMS;
TABLE SOE.PRODUCT_DESCRIPTIONS;
TABLE SOE.INVENTORIES;
TABLE SOE.PRODUCT_INFORMATION;
TABLE SOE.WAREHOUSES;
```

Next we add the extract just as we did in Chapter 5. Here is an example:

```
GGSCI (snode2.example.com) > add extract ex_mysql, tranlog, begin now
```

Even though the target is a MySQL database, the extract settings are the same as if the target were another Oracle database. For brevity, for this exercise we are not using a Data Pump process, but the creation process is just as you have already seen in Chapter 5.

We need to create the remote trail file for the Extract process to write to on the MySQL database server. Again, this looks quite like the same process we used when doing Oracle-to-Oracle replication in Chapter 5:

```
GGSCI (snode2.example.com) > add rmttrail ./dirdat/rp, extract ex_mysql
RMTTRAIL added.
```

Now, on the MySQL server we create the replicat parameter file, much like the one seen in this example:

```
GGSCI (snode3.example.com) > edit params rep
REPLICAT rep
TARGETDB mydb@localhost, USERID ggs_user, password welcome1
SOURCEDEFS ./dirsql/soeobject.sql
HANDLECOLLISIONS
MAP SOE.*, TARGET mydb.*;
```

The parameter file should look very familiar. Note that we used the HANDLECOLLISIONS parameter just as we did in Chapter 5. This way, the source data can continue to change while the initial load is being executed. Once we start the Replicat process, the HANDLECOLLISIONS parameter will cause GoldenGate to ignore primary key violations during the initial replication process where the changes that occurred during the instantiation of the database are applied (since some transactions might overlap and be duplicated during this time). As we mentioned in Chapter 5, once the initial load is complete and the delta changes sent to the target, you should not use HANDLECOLLISIONS for day-to-day replication.

We can now add the replicat in GGSCI on the MySQL side to process our day-to-day replication as seen here:

```
GGSCI (snode3.example.com) > add replicat rep, exttrail ./dirdat/rp,
checkpointtable checkpoint
REPLICAT added.
```

Now let's start the Replicat process we just defined:

```
GGSCI (snode3.example.com) > start replicat rep
Sending START request to MANAGER ...
REPLICAT REP starting
```

Of course, we also have to start the Extract process on the Oracle side:

```
GGSCI (snode2.example.com) > start ex_mysql
Sending START request to MANAGER ...
EXTRACT EX_MYSQL starting

GGSCI (snode2.example.com) > info all
Program     Status      Group       Lag at Chkpt  Time Since Chkpt
MANAGER     RUNNING
EXTRACT     RUNNING     EX_MYSQL    00:00:00      00:16:55
```

Now both the Extract and Replicat processes are running. We can monitor replication activity on both the source and target by running the **stats** command. Here is an example of the result of running the **stats** command on the Extract process (note that we have removed some of the output for the sake of brevity and to save a tree or two):

```
GGSCI (snode2.example.com) > stats ex_mysql
Sending STATS request to EXTRACT EX_MYSQL ...
Start of Statistics at 2012-08-21 08:35:45.
Output to ./dirdat/rp:
Extracting from SOE.CUSTOMERS to SOE.CUSTOMERS:
*** Total statistics since 2012-08-21 08:35:40 ***
        Total inserts                           9.00
        Total updates                           0.00
        Total deletes                           0.00
        Total discards                          0.00
        Total operations                        9.00

*** Daily statistics since 2012-08-21 08:35:40 ***
        Total inserts                           9.00
        Total updates                           0.00
        Total deletes                           0.00
        Total discards                          0.00
        Total operations                        9.00
```

```
*** Hourly statistics since 2012-08-21 08:35:40 ***
        Total inserts                                    9.00
        Total updates                                    0.00
        Total deletes                                    0.00
        Total discards                                   0.00
        Total operations                                 9.00

*** Latest statistics since 2012-08-21 08:35:40 ***
        Total inserts                                    9.00
        Total updates                                    0.00
        Total deletes                                    0.00
        Total discards                                   0.00
        Total operations                                 9.00
# Note that some of the output has been removed for brevity.

End of Statistics.
```

Here is an example of the statistics report on the Replicat process, again reformatted for brevity and tree preservation:

```
GGSCI (snode3.example.com)> stats replicat rep
Sending STATS request to REPLICAT REP ...
Start of Statistics at 2012-08-21 14:39:41.
Replicating from SOE.CUSTOMERS to mydb.CUSTOMERS:

*** Total statistics since 2012-08-21 14:34:40 ***
        Total inserts                               748666.00
        Total updates                                    0.00
        Total deletes                                    0.00
        Total discards                                   0.00
        Total operations                            748666.00
        Total insert collisions                     200000.00

*** Daily statistics since 2012-08-21 14:34:40 ***
        Total inserts                               748666.00
        Total updates                                    0.00
        Total deletes                                    0.00
        Total discards                                   0.00
        Total operations                            748666.00
        Total insert collisions                     200000.00

*** Hourly statistics since 2012-08-21 14:34:40 ***
        Total inserts                               748666.00
        Total updates                                    0.00
        Total deletes                                    0.00
        Total discards                                   0.00
        Total operations                            748666.00
        Total insert collisions                     200000.00
```

```
*** Latest statistics since 2012-08-21 14:34:40 ***
        Total inserts                       748666.00
        Total updates                            0.00
        Total deletes                            0.00
        Total discards                           0.00
        Total operations                    748666.00
        Total insert collisions             200000.00
```

```
End of Statistics.
```

From the **stats** output, you will see that more rows have been replicated than extracted. There are several possible reasons for this. The **stats** command only shows statistics since the Extract or Replicat process started. When a process is restarted, the statistics start again at zero. So if an Extract process is restarted but the Replicat process is left running, the replicat statistics will show more rows processed than the extract. Also, if the extract shows more rows being processed than a replicat, it could mean there are transactions in flight—transactions that have been extracted but haven't yet been processed by the replicat. Unless you are verifying replication and able to exactly control when a single transaction is replicated, using the **stats** command is not a good way of verifying whether all the data is being replicated.

So, we have created an extract and replicat to perform the initial load, and created a definition file since the source and target are different database platforms. We have also created another extract and replicat for ongoing replication. After the initial load was completed, we started the ongoing extract and replicat and viewed the statistics of the replication job. That was a lot of work, but still, there is more to do! Now, let's replicate from MySQL to Oracle!

Replicating from MySQL to Oracle

In this section we will reverse the process and send data from a table in a MySQL database to a table in an Oracle database. We will create a table to replicate, generate a definition file, verify that GoldenGate has the permissions to replication from MySQL, and create an extract and replicate.

Defining the Objects and Generating the Definitions

In this case we are just going to replicate one table in the MySQL database to our Oracle database. This table contains personal contact information and has the following definition:

```
CREATE TABLE DIRECTORY
    (    ENTRY_ID INT NOT NULL AUTO_INCREMENT,
```

```
       FIRST_NAME VARCHAR(25),
       LAST_NAME VARCHAR(35),
    EMAIL VARCHAR(50),
    PHONE INT,
     PRIMARY KEY(ENTRY_ID)
  ) ENGINE = INNODB;
```

Keeping in mind that there are differences between data types in Oracle and MySQL, it's no surprise that the definition of the table on the Oracle side is slightly different. For this exercise we will be using the same Oracle schema we used when replicating from Oracle. Here is the Oracle DDL for the object that we will be replicating:

```
CREATE TABLE DIRECTORY
    (    ENTRY_ID NUMBER(6,0),
         FIRST_NAME VARCHAR2(25),
         LAST_NAME VARCHAR2(35),
      EMAIL VARCHAR2(50),
      PHONE NUMBER(10,0),
       PRIMARY KEY(ENTRY_ID)
    );
```

There's a fly in the ointment here. The MySQL table is using an automatically incrementing column type (likely as a souragate key), which is not supported by Oracle. We want to make sure that the Oracle table will use the same value that GoldenGate replicates, so no sequence will be used. So, in this case we don't need a sequence on the Oracle side; we will simply replicate the value as is. Also, the user-name the Replicat process will be using will need to be able to log in to the database and have Select, Delete, Update and Insert privileges for the tables you are replicating, just as if you were performing Oracle-to-Oracle replication. See Chapter 5 for details.

Also, pay careful attention to the ENGINE clause for the MySQL table (we mentioned this earlier but thought it was important enough to mention again). In order to be able to replicate data from MySQL, the table must use InnoDB for the storage engine. Also, be aware that select permissions must be granted for the username GoldenGate is using for the extract. GoldenGate will also need to execute and read permissions for the directory that holds your MySQL configuration file, my.cnf, and read permission for the file itself. Check with your OS on where the default location is for the file. In addition, ensure that your LOG-BIN and LOG-BIN-INDEX parameters are set to a location where you want the log files to be written, and set BINLOG_FORMAT to row. The parameter LOG-BIN stores the location where MySQL should store the transaction log, and LOG-BIN-INDEX stores which log files have been used. GoldenGate needs to know where the logs are in order to read them. The BINLOG_FORMAT parameter affects how records are formatted in the transaction log file.

We have now created the table on both the Oracle and MySQL database. We also know that we need to create a definition file on the MySQL server and transfer it to the Oracle server. Here is an example of doing just that:

```
vi dirprm/defgen.prm

    defsfile ./dirsql/mysql_object.sql, PURGE
    SOURCEDB mydb@localhost, USERID ggs_user, PASSWORD welcome1
    table mydb.DIRECTORY;
```

As we did earlier in this chapter when we were moving data from Oracle to MySQL, we will use the defgen utility to create the definition file from the parameter file and copy the file to the Oracle server.

```
./defgen paramfile ./dirprm/defgen.prm
***********************************************************************
            Oracle GoldenGate Table Definition Generator for MySQL
        Version 11.2.1.0.1 OGGCORE_11.2.1.0.1_PLATFORMS_120423.0230
    Linux, x64, 64bit (optimized), MySQL Enterprise on Apr 23 2012 05:11:37
    Copyright (C) 1995, 2012, Oracle and/or its affiliates. All rights reserved.
                    Starting at 2012-08-21 16:30:07
***********************************************************************
Operating System Version:
Linux
Version #1 SMP Wed Jul 27 21:02:33 EDT 2011, Release 2.6.32-200.13.1.el5uek
Node: snode3.example.com
Machine: x86_64
                        soft limit    hard limit
Address Space Size   :    unlimited    unlimited
Heap Size            :    unlimited    unlimited
File Size            :    unlimited    unlimited
CPU Time             :    unlimited    unlimited

Process id: 11789
***********************************************************************
**              Running with the following parameters              **
***********************************************************************
defsfile ./dirsql/mysql_object.sql, PURGE
SOURCEDB mydb@localhost, USERID ggs_user, PASSWORD ********
table mydb.DIRECTORY;
Retrieving definition for mydb.DIRECTORY

Definitions generated for 1 table in ./dirsql/mysql_object.sql
```

Initial Population of the Oracle Table from MySQL Using GoldenGate

We have now created the table in Oracle that we will replicate to, and we have created the data definitions file that is needed by the Extract and Replicat processes. Now we need to create the Extract and Replicat processes to do the initial population of the table in Oracle from the data in MySQL.

We will be repeating the steps from the beginning of the chapter but switching the target and source. An extract for the initial load will be created, a definition file will be made on the MySQL server, and on the Oracle side a replicat will be created for the initial load.

First, let's create the extract and the parameter file on the MySQL server.

```
GGSCI (snode3.example.com) > add extract ex_load, sourceistable
EXTRACT added.

GGSCI (snode3.example.com) > edit params ex_load
extract ex_load
SOURCEDB mydb@localhost, USERID ggs_user, password welcome1
rmthost snode2, mgrport 7801
rmttask replicat, group rep3
TABLE mydb.DIRECTORY;
```

The commands and options are the same as in the first exercise. Only the connection string was changed to the MySQL database, as well as the table that will be initially loaded. Next, let's create the definitions parameter file. This is done by using the defgen utility to create the definitions file on the MySQL server. Then the resulting definitions file will be copied to the Oracle server which is the target server:

```
vi dirprm/mysql_objects.prm
defsfile ./dirsql/mysqlobject.sql
SOURCEDB mydb@localhost, USERID ggs_user, password ********
table mydb.DIRECTORY;
```

Run the defgen utility and copy the created file to the Oracle server.

```
[mysql@snode3 gg_mysql]$ ./defgen paramfile dirprm/mysql_objects.prm
**************************************************************************
          Oracle GoldenGate Table Definition Generator for MySQL
       Version 11.2.1.0.1 OGGCORE_11.2.1.0.1_PLATFORMS_120423.0230
Linux, x64, 64bit (optimized), MySQL Enterprise on Apr 23 2012 05:11:37
Copyright (C) 1995, 2012, Oracle and/or its affiliates. All rights reserved.

                    Starting at 2012-09-13 21:58:21
**************************************************************************
Operating System Version:
Linux
Version #1 SMP Wed Jul 27 21:02:33 EDT 2011, Release 2.6.32-200.13.1.el5uek
Node: snode3.example.com
Machine: x86_64
                       soft limit     hard limit
Address Space Size   :    unlimited     unlimited
Heap Size            :    unlimited     unlimited
File Size            :    unlimited     unlimited
CPU Time             :    unlimited     unlimited

Process id: 11058
```

```
**********************************************************************
**              Running with the following parameters             **
**********************************************************************
defsfile ./dirsql/mysqlobject.sql
SOURCEDB mydb@localhost, USERID ggs_user, password ********
table mydb.DIRECTORY;
Retrieving definition for mydb.DIRECTORY
Definitions generated for 1 table in ./dirsql/mysqlobject.sql
```

On the Oracle server, we will create a replicat and parameter and then we will
be ready to perform the initial load.

```
GGSCI (snode2.example.com) > add replicat rep3, specialrun
REPLICAT added
GGSCI (snode2.example.com) > edit params rep3
REPLICAT rep3
SETENV ("ORACLE_SID = gg2")
USERID ggs_user, password ggs_user
SOURCEDEFS ./dirsql/mysqlobject.sql
MAP mydb.*, TARGET SOE.*;
```

With the extract, replicat, and definition file created, all that is left is to start the
extract on the MySQL server and wait for the initial load to finish just as before.

```
GGSCI (snode2.example.com) > start extract ex_load
```

Configuring Replication Between MySQL and Oracle

Having populated the Oracle database table with the data from MySQL, we now
can create the regular Extract and Replicat processes. Recall that we will extract
from the MySQL database and then apply the trail file to the Oracle database.

First we will create the Extract process file on the MySQL database server side,
as seen here:

```
EXTRACT ex_orcl
SOURCEDB mydb@localhost, USERID ggs_user, PASSWORD welcome1
RMTHOST snode2, MGRPORT 7808
RMTTRAIL ./dirdat/rp
TRANLOGOPTIONS ALTLOGDEST /home/mysql/mysql_log/master-log-bin.index
table mydb.DIRECTORY;
```

A new parameter, ALTLOGDEST, is used for MySQL. This parameter states where
GoldenGate should find the log files created by MySQL.

We have now created the extract and we need to add the extract to GoldenGate
as seen here:

```
GGSCI (snode3.example.com) > add extract ex_orcl, tranlog, begin now
EXTRACT added.
```

Now we need to add the remote trail file to the process. Note that the remote trail file will reside on the Oracle Database server and that this command is executed on the MySQL server side:

```
GGSCI (snode3.example.com)> add rmttrail ./dirdat/rt, extract ex_orcl
RMTTRAIL added.
```

Now that the Extract process has been created, we will create the Replicat process on the Oracle server side. Here is the parameter file for the replicat:

```
GGSCI (snode2.example.com)> edit params rp_my

REPLICAT rp_my
SETENV ("ORACLE_SID = gg2")
USERID ggs_user, password ggs_user
SOURCEDEFS ./dirsql/mysql_object.sql
MAP mydb.DIRECTORY, TARGET SOE.DIRECTORY;
```

Of course, we need to add the replicat too:

```
GGSCI (snode2.example.com)> add replicat rp_my, exttrail ./dirdat/rt,
checkpointtable checkpoint
REPLICAT added.
```

And now we start the Replicat process on the Oracle side:

```
GGSCI (snode2.example.com)> start rp_my
Sending START request to MANAGER ...
REPLICAT RP_MY starting
```

Next, we can start the extract and insert data into the table and verify that the data is replicated to the Oracle database using both SQL*Plus and running the stats command from the GoldenGate command line. On the MySQL server, start the Extract process and insert a row in the table.

```
GGSCI (snode3.example.com)> start ex_orcl
mysql> insert into DIRECTORY(FIRST_NAME,LAST_NAME,EMAIL,PHONE)
VALUES('JOHN','DOE','john.doe@example.com',3433459874);
Query OK, 1 row affected, 1 warning (0.00 sec)
mysql> commit;
Query OK, 0 rows affected (0.00 sec)

SQL> SELECT * FROM DIRECTORY;
  ENTRY_ID FIRST_NAME                      LAST_NAME
---------- ------------------------------- -----------------------------------
EMAIL                                                   PHONE
------------------------------------------------------ ----------
         1 JOHN                            DOE
john.doe@example.com                                    2147483647
```

```
GGSCI (snode3.example.com) > stats ex_orcl
Sending STATS request to EXTRACT EX_ORCL ...
Start of Statistics at 2012-08-21 20:08:39.
Output to ./dirdat/rt:
Extracting from mydb.DIRECTORY to mydb.DIRECTORY:

*** Total statistics since 2012-08-21 20:08:23 ***
        Total inserts                                1.00
        Total updates                                0.00
        Total deletes                                0.00
        Total discards                               0.00
        Total operations                             1.00

*** Daily statistics since 2012-08-21 20:08:23 ***
        Total inserts                                1.00
        Total updates                                0.00
        Total deletes                                0.00
        Total discards                               0.00
        Total operations                             1.00

*** Hourly statistics since 2012-08-21 20:08:23 ***
        Total inserts                                1.00
        Total updates                                0.00
        Total deletes                                0.00
        Total discards                               0.00
        Total operations                             1.00

*** Latest statistics since 2012-08-21 20:08:23 ***
        Total inserts                                1.00
        Total updates                                0.00
        Total deletes                                0.00
        Total discards                               0.00
        Total operations                             1.00

End of Statistics.
GGSCI (snode2.example.com) > stats rp_my
Sending STATS request to REPLICAT RP_MY ...
Start of Statistics at 2012-08-21 14:08:49.
Replicating from mydb.DIRECTORY to SOE.DIRECTORY:

*** Total statistics since 2012-08-21 14:08:36 ***
        Total inserts                                1.00
        Total updates                                0.00
        Total deletes                                0.00
        Total discards                               0.00
        Total operations                             1.00

*** Daily statistics since 2012-08-21 14:08:36 ***
        Total inserts                                1.00
        Total updates                                0.00
        Total deletes                                0.00
```

```
        Total discards                              0.00
        Total operations                            1.00

*** Hourly statistics since 2012-08-21 14:08:36 ***
        Total inserts                               1.00
        Total updates                               0.00
        Total deletes                               0.00
        Total discards                              0.00
        Total operations                            1.00

*** Latest statistics since 2012-08-21 14:08:36 ***
        Total inserts                               1.00
        Total updates                               0.00
        Total deletes                               0.00
        Total discards                              0.00
        Total operations                            1.00

End of Statistics.
```

CHAPTER
11

Introducing Oracle
GoldenGate for
SQL Server

I n this chapter we are going to cover specific issues relating to Oracle GoldenGate and Microsoft SQL Server. As with other platforms, GoldenGate for MS SQL Server provides a heterogeneous transactional data replication solution allowing SQL Server to act as either the source or target database in a simple or multimaster homogenous or heterogeneous replication topology.

As you might expect from previous chapters, Oracle GoldenGate for SQL Server can capture committed transactions from *user* tables within a source SQL Server database and deliver them to a target SQL Server database or any GoldenGate-supported DBMS, flat file, message queue, and so on. Oracle GoldenGate for SQL Server is also used as an Apply component in a heterogeneous topology where captured data has been supplied from another installation of Oracle GoldenGate for a different DBMS. Data Manipulation Language (DML) operations for user tables are supported for Oracle GoldenGate for SQL Server, but replication of system tables, programming objects, logins, indexes, and Data Definition Language (DDL) are not supported.

In general, the architecture for Oracle GoldenGate for SQL Server is very similar to the other supported RDBMS platforms. However, there are some restrictions on GoldenGate support for objects and operations in Microsoft SQL Server. Only transactions on user tables are supported. Additionally, only DML is supported. There is no support for DDL with GoldenGate for MS SQL Server.

As we have already discussed in previous chapters, the general architecture for GoldenGate on Microsoft SQL Server includes the top-level Manager process (mgr .exe), which coordinates global activities of the child processes. Additionally we also have the same Extract (or Capture) process (extract.exe), which is responsible for reading committed transactions from the SQL Server transaction log and transaction log backups, and then writes those transactions to Oracle GoldenGate (OGG) trail files.

Positioning and checkpointing of an extract is maintained for a source database through timestamps and Log Sequence Numbers (LSNs) within the SQL Server transaction log. Although an extract uses an Open Database Connectivity (ODBC) data source to connect to the source database for table metadata information, the committed transactions are read from the physical transaction log through Windows file APIs and are not rebuilt by querying the database. An extract for SQL Server captures committed transactions from only one database to which it has been assigned. However, you can configure multiple extracts for a database, although in most cases this probably will not be necessary.

GoldenGate for MS SQL Server also supports the creation of GoldenGate Data Pump processes, which read a capture's Exttrail files and rewrite this data to a remote trail on the destination server(s).

Finally, GoldenGate for MS SQL Server includes the Server Collector process (server.exe) running on the target server, handling communication between the target server and a Pump process. We also have Replicat processes (replicat.exe), which process either the trail from the Capture component or the Pump component if used, against a target database.

As we have already described, the Oracle GoldenGate processes on MS SQL Server are configured with parameter files that contain specific parameter and option control settings. The parameter file for the Manager process is called the mgr.prm parameter file, and the parameter files for the Extract, Pump, and Replicat processes are given their own unique names, as we have already shown in previous chapters. You can configure Oracle GoldenGate parameter files using the GGSCI command-line interface, as already demonstrated in previous chapters.

Installing and Configuring Oracle GoldenGate for SQL Server

This section will focus on the requirements and concepts of implementing OGG for SQL Server, followed by a step-by-step guide to installing the Oracle GoldenGate software and configuring a Manager.

Later in this chapter we will walk through a setup of end-to-end replication using Oracle GoldenGate for SQL Server, capturing transactions from a source SQL Server 2008 R2 database and delivering to both a target SQL Server 2008 R2 database and an Oracle database.

Hardware Requirements

For the most current information regarding hardware requirements, we recommend that you review the *Oracle GoldenGate SQL Server Installation and Setup Guide* for your specific release of Oracle GoldenGate. Documentation is available on the Oracle GoldenGate Documentation site at the following link: http://www.oracle.com/technetwork/middleware/goldengate/documentation/index.html

Memory

Memory requirements for Oracle GoldenGate processes are documented as 25 to 55MB per Extract and Replicat process, but can be more depending on the size and number of the transactions being replicated at any given time. And in Oracle GoldenGate version 11gR1, a maximum of 300 concurrent Extract and Replicat processes can run under any given installation of GoldenGate. And with multiple installations of GoldenGate per source or target database server, this combination of 300 processes per installation can consume quite a lot of system resources. Plan accordingly with proper testing to ensure that you have enough available memory resources to service the Oracle GoldenGate processes for your configuration. In most cases a source database server will not need more than one extract and one pump per database; however, there may be a need for multiple replicats servicing a target database, as well as one server collector per pump attached to that target host, all requiring more memory for Oracle GoldenGate resources on the target database server.

NOTE
With Oracle GoldenGate 11gR2, the number of concurrent Extract and Replicat processes increases to 500.

Storage

Oracle GoldenGate installation binaries are included in a compressed zip file that is no more than 28MB in size depending on the specific platform build, and when uncompressed and installed is no more than 52MB, so at a minimum you will need approximately 80MB free disk space to install Oracle GoldenGate for SQL Server.

When you're using Oracle GoldenGate, storage allocation is more dynamic depending on the number and size of the data contained within trail files that are used to store the captured transactions by an extract or pushed by a Data Pump. An extract is configured to capture from one to all of the user tables in a database, and there can be multiple extracts per database if needed. Also DML operations that can be captured based on how you have configured the extract. This can add to the overall size of the trail files produced.

Oracle GoldenGate documentation suggests beginning with 1GB of available storage to be used by trail files, and includes a formula to produce a conservative estimate of how much of that disk space you should expect to be consumed by trails. That formula multiplies the size of the transaction log in an hour by the longest time in hours that the network could be down by a compression factor of 0.4.

Disseminating the components of the formula doesn't state whether the size of the transaction log in an hour is a possible maximum or an average over a period, but erring on the higher side and using the maximum size a transaction log could be in an hour is a safer stance, to ensure that you don't run out of storage space for OGG. However, transaction logs can grow quite impressive during index maintenance operations, but since Oracle GoldenGate cannot capture index operations from SQL Server, it would be safe to eliminate these sampling sizes from your calculation. Regarding network outage, typical production configurations of OGG include a Pump process to resend trail data produced by an extract to the target database server to be consumed by the Replicat process, and then allow the Manager process to purge those extract trails from the source database server at declared intervals using the PURGEOLDEXTRACTS and USECHECKPOINTS parameters, assuming that the Pump process has sent the data to the target server. Should a network outage occur for any given length, extract trail files marked for purging will not be purged and will queue up in the directory until the Pump process can resume delivery across the network. Only after checkpointing against the trails the Pump process has sent will Manager be able to purge those trails. For example, assume you have configured Manager to purge checkpointed trail files from the source database server every three days:

```
PURGEOLDEXTRACTS ./dirdat/et*, USECHECKPOINTS, MINKEEPDAYS 3
```

However, a network outage from the source to target server has been ongoing now for four days. Regardless of the MINKEEPDAYS rule in Manager, since the Pump process has not been able to resend data and therefore checkpoint against the source trails, Manager will not be able to purge these trails from the source system, which will indeed cause an increase in storage usage. And finally, what is the 0.4 multiplier in the equation? OGG documentation states that this is a multiplier representing 40 percent as that is the amount of data in a transaction log that Oracle GoldenGate needs.

Regardless of the estimates produced by using the formula, proper application and testing of your Oracle GoldenGate installation and configuration will produce a much more accurate metric for your storage needs.

Network

Oracle GoldenGate uses TCP/IP for internal connections as well as remote connections between a Pump process and the target server's Manager and Server Collector processes. The Manager port and port ranges for Server Collectors and local processes can be set to known values using the PORT and DYNAMICPORTLIST parameters of Manager. Ensure that your local network firewall is open for the port values that you designate.

Windows Server Requirements

Oracle GoldenGate for SQL Server runs only on the Microsoft Windows operating system, as does SQL Server, and the following lists some specific requirements and supported versions of Microsoft Windows needed to implement Oracle GoldenGate for SQL Server.

OS Version

Oracle GoldenGate for SQL Server is available for Windows Server 2003, Windows Server 2008, and Windows XP. In reality, you can also run the software on Windows 7, but both Windows XP and Windows 7 are not server-level operating systems, so I doubt this would be any customer's usage for a production environment. Stick with the supported server-level operating systems for production and use Windows XP or Windows 7 for testing purposes only.

Additional Software

Before you can use Oracle GoldenGate for Microsoft SQL Server, you must install the Microsoft Visual C++ 2005 SP1 Redistributable Package for your system based on its processor class: x86, x64, or IA64. In most cases the needed Visual C++ libraries are probably already installed; however, if they are not, you will not receive any proper error when executing some of the processes, and instead will find a failed component with no error report. Therefore, it is highly recommended to install the Visual C++ 2005 SP1 Redistributable Package, as the Oracle GoldenGate binaries are compiled against this specific release of Visual C++. Downloads to install the Microsoft Visual C++ 2005 SP1 Redistributable Package are available at the following Web sites, based on your processor class:

- For x86 systems: http://www.microsoft.com/en-us/download/details .aspx?id=5638

- For x64 systems: http://www.microsoft.com/en-us/download/details .aspx?id=18471

- For IA64 systems: http://www.microsoft.com/en-us/download/details .aspx?displaylang=en&id=13360

Follow the installation instructions available from Microsoft.

Windows Permissions

GoldenGate and required permissions on Microsoft Windows are somewhat different than on UNIX, as you might expect. On the Windows operating systems, Oracle GoldenGate processes run under the account that runs the Manager, and the Manager can run either as a Windows service or within a user's current Windows session. It is considered a best practice, and required when installing GoldenGate in a Windows cluster, to configure the Manager process as a Windows service. Not installing the Manager as a service would cause all GoldenGate processes to cease when the user logged off the server. Either way, the permission requirements of the account running the Manager are the same.

When the Oracle GoldenGate Manager process is configured as a Windows service, the Manager can use either the "local system" account or a local or domain Windows account, and requires membership in the server's Administrators group. The Manager requires Administrator group rights as it needs full access to the GoldenGate installation directories, trail files, report files, and so on; and for Capture, share-level read access against the SQL Server files that make up the transaction logs for a source Capture database. The specific share-level access to the transaction logs that Capture uses to read committed transactions from the log files must have Administrator rights, and therefore must be a member of the server's Administrator group.

ODBC System DSN

Oracle GoldenGate Capture and Apply connects to both source and target databases through a Windows system data source name (DSN). These connections provide metadata and other functionality for Capture, and metadata and DML operations for Apply. The client drivers needed to create these system DSNs are installed when installing SQL Server or the SQL Server tools.

Here are some details about the creation of the system DSN:

- For 32-bit versions of SQL Server running on 64-bit Windows servers, use the odbcad32.exe program in the %SystemRoot%/SysWOW64 directory to create the system DSN.

- Select the correct driver for the connection based on the source or target SQL Server version. You can select from the following:

  - SQL Server for SQL Server 2000

  - SQL Native Client for SQL Server 2005

  - SQL Server Native Client 10.0 for SQL Server 2008/2008 R2

- Using Integrated Windows authentication, Capture and Apply inherit the permissions of the account that runs Manager to connect to the database and to read from the transaction log in the case of Capture.

- If you're using a SQL Server–authenticated DSN, Capture and Apply will connect to the database with the supplied database credentials. However, the Capture process will still use the credentials of the Manager to read from the transaction log.

- Ensure that the option "Change the default database to" is checked and the correct source or target database is selected.

- Only one database per DSN is allowed. If you have multiple databases per instance or server that you will use GoldenGate to replicate to or from, you will need one DSN per each database.

SQL Server Requirements and Supported Features

In addition to certain Windows operating system requirements to run the Oracle GoldenGate software, there are also specific SQL Server requirements and features that are needed and supported.

Supported Versions and Editions

Oracle GoldenGate for SQL Server supports SQL Server Enterprise and Standard editions of SQL Server 2000, SQL Server 2005, and Enterprise editions of SQL Server 2008 and 2008 R2 for Capture, and both Enterprise and Standard editions for Apply to SQL Server 2008 and 2008 R2. The discrepancy between supported editions of SQL Server 2008 and 2008 R2 for Capture versus Apply is due to the way in which supplemental logging is enabled (this will be discussed in detail later), which requires that Change Data Capture (CDC) objects be created, which are only available in Enterprise editions.

There is no minimum service pack required for any of the versions of SQL Server, however, to support Capture from tables without primary keys in SQL Server 2005. Also, to avoid having to configure a distributor and distribution database, you must install Cumulative Update 6 for SQL Server 2005 Service Pack 2 (or greater). Therefore, it is highly recommended to go ahead and install the latest Service Pack for SQL Server 2005, which is Service Pack 4 and can be found at this link: http://www.microsoft.com/en-us/download/details.aspx?id=7218.

Finally, the Release Notes for OGG 11gR1 state that as of September 30 of 2012, OGG versions 11.1.1.x and 10.x will no longer support SQL Server 2000 and SQL Server 2005, and that customers should upgrade to SQL Server 2008 or later. If you are using these versions of SQL Server, you should determine what level of support that Oracle will continue to provide you.

Required SQL Server Installation Components

To use GoldenGate for SQL Server, you need to install SQL Server. This may seem self-explanatory, but it's important to list all of the requirements.

For GoldenGate Apply, it is not necessary to actually run the Apply process on the target database server, and a middle-tier server can be used instead to house the GoldenGate installation. However, this middle-tier server must still meet the Windows server requirements mentioned earlier, and the Client Tools Connectivity binaries must be installed on the server in order to create the necessary ODBC drivers needed for connectivity to the target database by Apply.

When installing SQL Server, ensure that the following are checked in the installer: the Database Engine Services, Client Tools Connectivity, Management Tools, and for SQL Server 2005 versions that will not be upgraded to Cumulative Update 6 for Service Pack 2 (or greater), you must install the SQL Server Replication components.

SQL Server Network Protocols

Oracle GoldenGate's Capture and Apply components connect through a system DSN, as mentioned earlier. The connection can be made over the available network protocols installed for SQL Server: TCP/IP, Shared Memory, or Named Pipes. TCP/IP is the preferred network protocol based on performance and consistency with the other communications needed for GoldenGate, and will be selected automatically by the ODBC connection if TCP/IP and any of the other protocols are enabled, which by default are all enabled after installing SQL Server. Network protocols for the SQL Server instance are enabled through the SQL Server Configuration Manager utility and may require a restart of the instance if changes are made.

Supported Data Types
(As of Oracle GoldenGate for SQL Server 11gR1)

Oracle GoldenGate for SQL Server 11gR1 supports most of the SQL Server data types, including some of the newer data types introduced with SQL Server 2008. The following is a list of those supported SQL Server data types that OGG can capture from and apply to.

BIGINT	BINARY	BIT	CHAR
DATE	DATETIME	DATETIME2	DATETIMEOFFSET
DECIMAL	FLOAT	IMAGE	INT
MONEY	NCHAR	NTEXT	NUMERIC
NVARCHAR	NVARCHAR (MAX)	REAL	SMALLDATETIME
SMALLINT	SMALLMONEY	TEXT	TIME
TIMESTAMP	TINYINT	UNIQUEIDENTIFIER	VARBINARY
VARBINARY (MAX)	VARCHAR	VARCHAR (MAX)	XML

Unsupported Data Types

While Oracle GoldenGate does support most of the data types available in SQL Server, there are some as of 11gR1 that are not supported. Those data types that are not supported are as follows:

- CLR data types such as Geometry, Geography, Hierarchyid
- CLR-based user-defined data types
- SQL_VARIANT
- VARBINARY (MAX) with the FILESTREAM attribute

NOTE
Oracle GoldenGate version 11gR2 supports the CLR and VARBINARY data types.

Supported Table Options

Oracle GoldenGate for SQL Server supports Capture and Apply of user tables enabled with PAGE and ROW compression, as well as from partitioned tables whose columns have the same leaf offset.

Limitations of Supported Data Types, Operations, and Configurations

There are also limitations to the previously mentioned supported features, operations, and configuration requirements. These limitations are mentioned in the following list.

- TIMESTAMP and persisted-computed columns cannot be part of the primary key.

- Extended XML enhancements introduced in SQL Server 2008 are not supported.

- DML performed by the TextCopy utility or the **updatetext** and **writetext** SQL statements is not supported.

- Encrypted databases enabled with Transparent Data Encryption (TDE) are not supported.

- SQL Server 2008 compressed transaction log backups are not supported.

- Table partitions with more than one physical layout across partitions are not supported.

- Partition switching is not supported.

- SQL Server 2008 MERGE operations are not supported.

- DDL operations are not supported.

Source Database SQL Server Instance Configuration

Oracle GoldenGate has certain specific requirements when it comes to enabling a source Capture component against a database for an instance of SQL Server. Namely, Oracle GoldenGate must be installed on the same database server where the SQL Server instance is installed. In a clustered environment, the Oracle GoldenGate Manager will need to be configured as a resource within the Cluster Group that contains the SQL Server instance resource and that will also require that the Disk Group where Oracle GoldenGate is installed be added as a resource to the Cluster Group containing the SQL Server instance as well.

And for SQL Server 2005, 2008, and 2008 R2, configuring tables for Capture that contain columns of data types TEXT, IMAGE, NTEXT, or any character data type with the (MAX) specification, such as VARCHAR (MAX) and NVARCHAR (MAX), may require adjusting the 'max text repl size (B)' server configuration setting from its default of 65MB to the maximum expected size that the database will receive from the user application for columns with these data types. Failure to adjust the size higher than its default when column data exceeds 65MB will produce the following SQL Server error:

```
Length of LOB data (#####) to be replicated exceeds configured maximum 65536
```

To adjust the 'max text repl size (B)' instance configuration option, connect to the source database instance of SQL Server and run the following against the master database:

```
EXE sp_configure 'max text repl size', {New Size in MB}
```

SQL Server instance security as needed by Capture requires use of either a SQL Server login if using SQL Server authenticated DSN settings, or a Windows login if using a Windows authenticated DSN. If you're using Windows authentication, the Windows account that will need to be added to the SQL Server instance is the account configured to run the Manager service. Regardless of the authentication method, the login has to be a member of the SQL Server server role, sysadmin. And when enabling supplemental logging for tables within a source database, the user information used to log in to the database within GGSCI must be a member of the sysadmin server role as well. Enabling supplemental logging requires logging in to the database with the GGSCI command:

```
DBLOGIN SOURCEDB {DSN Name} {USERID SQL Server Login} {PASSWORD Login Password}
```

If the DSN is configured with Windows authentication, then the credentials passed to SQL Server are the Windows login of the current user who is running GGSCI, and therefore that user must also be a member of the sysadmin role, even if only temporarily to enable supplemental logging. If the DSN uses a SQL Server–authenticated login and the USERID and PASSWORD options are completed with this information with the **dblogin** command, then there should be nothing extra to do regarding security, as that SQL Server login should already be a member of the sysadmin role, as mentioned in previous setup instructions.

Source SQL Server Database Requirements

Oracle GoldenGate's Capture process reads committed transactions from the database transaction log. To ensure that the information needed to replicate a transaction is fully written and persisted to the transaction log, a SQL Server source Capture database must be in FULL recovery mode and at least one full database backup must have been taken since the database was set to FULL recovery. Setting the database to BULK LOGGED does not guarantee that full records are written for all transactions, as it enables minimal logging for some bulk operations, and setting the database to SIMPLE automatically truncates committed transactions at periodic intervals.

Once the database has met these two conditions, do not set the database out of FULL recovery and do not break the log chain of the transaction log. The log chain of the transaction log is broken by setting the database from FULL to SIMPLE recovery or by backing up a SQL Server 2000 or 2005 database's transaction log with the NO_LOG or TRUNCATE_ONLY options.

If the source Capture database is installed on SQL Server 2005 versions below 9.00.3228 (which is Service Pack 2 with Cumulative Update 6), then you must also configure a Distributor instance and distribution database using SQL Server Replication configuration tools. This is a requirement that is needed in order for GoldenGate to enable supplemental logging (to be discussed later) for the database tables. GoldenGate enables supplemental logging differently for the different versions of SQL Server, and versions of SQL Server 2005 below 9.00.3228 are the only versions that require the SQL Server replication components when enabling supplemental logging. However, this has the undesirable effect of also requiring that the tables to be captured must have explicit primary keys created. For these reasons, it is highly recommended to update your SQL Server 2005 instance to Service Pack 2 with Cumulative Update 6, or greater, such as SP3 or SP4, if using GoldenGate Capture for a SQL Server 2005 database.

If the source SQL Server Capture database is running on a SQL Server 2008 or SQL Server 2008 R2 instance, then the edition is required to be Enterprise Edition. This requirement is due similarly to how GoldenGate enables supplemental logging for the Capture tables. In SQL Server 2008 and SQL Server 2008 R2, supplemental logging is enabled by the creation of placeholder Change Data Capture tables and therefore requires Enterprise Edition.

Source SQL Server Table Requirements

As mentioned earlier in this chapter, GoldenGate for SQL Server supports Capture and Apply of DML operations for user tables only. No other database objects are supported, nor is replication of DDL for SQL Server user tables. This is very important to keep in mind as you will definitely have to ensure that all necessary database objects, logins, and so on are kept up to date between source and target databases by means other than GoldenGate.

Having stated that boldly enough, there are also some exceptions to the user tables that are supported by GoldenGate. For example, table names with spaces in the name are not supported. You will need to either configure GoldenGate to ignore these tables or modify the names to meet the GoldenGate requirements.

The following is a list of unsupported table-naming conventions for source SQL Server tables:

- For SQL Server 2005 versions 9.00.3228 and higher, the maximum allowable table name length is reduced by the schema name length + 1, whose sum must be 128 or less. Table name length + schema name length + 1 <= 128. SQL Server allows a maximum of 128 characters in its table names; however, the call to the stored procedure that GoldenGate uses to enable supplemental logging for these versions of SQL Server appends the schema name and a "." to the table name when passing information to the stored procedure, and the stored procedure itself accepts no more than 128 characters for its input parameter.

■ Table names with spaces, single quotes, commas, and a list of other special characters are not supported. This is true for column names as well.

■ For a complete and up-to-date list of unsupported naming conventions, check the *Oracle GoldenGate for SQL Server Installation and Setup Guide*.

NOTE
Knowledge Document 1315720.1 (available at Oracle Support) provides an analysis script that can be run against a source or target SQL Server database to provide information about supported tables and other information relevant to OGG installation.

Source SQL Server Tables: Supplemental Logging

Supplemental logging must be enabled for all user tables to be configured for GoldenGate Capture. *Supplemental logging* is a GoldenGate term used to represent a method of instructing the DBMS to log extra information to the transaction log for a given transaction. This extra information is needed by GoldenGate Capture to reconstruct a full SQL DML statement to be delivered to any supported DBMS target database.

We will discuss the steps required to enable supplemental logging later in this chapter. Beyond supplemental logging you need to also understand that there are additional requirements that need to be met. These include settings associated with TRANLOGOPTIONS related settings.

For SQL Server 2000, supplemental logging is enabled by setting a flag on the record for the table in the SYSOBJECTS table of the database. This flag is also shared by DML triggers, and removing a DML trigger from a table that is also enabled with supplemental logging inadvertently disables supplemental logging for the table.

For SQL Server 2005 versions below 9.00.3228, supplemental logging is enabled for a table by adding the table as an article to a SQL Server publication for the database. Oracle GoldenGate creates this article automatically, and the first time supplemental logging is enabled for a table in the database, an Oracle GoldenGate publication is created and the table is added as an article to the publication.

The article properties do not include replicating any DML, however, and are used merely as a shell to achieve the goal required by supplemental logging. This does require that the SQL Server replication components have been installed and a Distributor and distribution database be configured for the instance. Once the publication is created, you can stop and disable any of the associated SQL Server Agent jobs that were created for this publication as long as there are not any other non-GoldenGate SQL Server transactional replication publications for the database. Since OGG is using a SQL Server publication and associated articles to enable supplemental logging, tables to be captured must have a primary key.

Supplemental logging for SQL Server 2005 versions equal to and above 9.00.3228 is enabled for a table by executing a Microsoft SQL Server system stored procedure called sys.sp_extended_logging. A Distributor and distribution database is not required and a primary key is not required for the table when only OGG replication is in use for the database. When coexisting with SQL Server Transactional Replication on the database, do not enable supplemental logging for any table that does not have a primary key, as this breaks the SQL Server Log Reader used by the native Transactional Replication.

Supplemental logging for SQL Server 2008 and SQL Server 2008 R2 is enabled for a table by creating a CDC (Change Data Capture) object for each table enabled with supplemental logging. This object is a system table having the naming convention of cdc.OracleGG_##########_CT.

A CDC Capture job (with naming convention cdc.DatabaseName_capture), a CDC Cleanup job (with naming convention cdc.DatabaseName_cleanup), and a per instance "syspolicy_purge_history" job are also created the first time a table in the database is enabled with supplemental logging, unless an existing SQL Server transactional replication publication or non-Oracle GoldenGate Change Data Capture configuration exists, in which case these CDC jobs or a SQL Server Log Reader job will already exist for the database, and then will be deleted by the extract the first time the extract is started after the CDC Capture Agent was created when using the MANAGESECONDARYTRUNCATIONPOINT option.

CAUTION
*Do not enable or disable supplemental logging for a table or tables through manual execution of any of the flag settings, stored procedures, and so on. Always use the Oracle GoldenGate commands **add** and **delete trandata** to add and disable supplemental logging for a table, as other activities are coordinated through these commands that are required for proper enabling/disabling of supplemental logging.*

Tables enabled with supplemental logging for SQL Server 2005 and SQL Server 2008/2008 R2 are set with the is_replicated flag within sys.tables and therefore follow some of the limitations of tables that would be configured with SQL Server Replication and Change Data Capture. Some restrictions include that TRUNCATE operations are not allowed and the 'max text repl size (B)' instance configuration option may need to be extended.

NOTE
Please review SQL Server Books Online for more
restrictions on replicated tables.

Target Database SQL Server Instance Configuration

For a SQL Server database to be used as a target for GoldenGate replication, there is no specific version or edition requirements as there are when the SQL Server database is to be configured as a source database for GoldenGate replication. Both Standard and Enterprise editions and all versions of SQL Server 2000, 2005, 2008, and 2008 R2 are supported. In fact, unlike the source database instance requirements, the Apply process for GoldenGate for SQL Server can even run on a separate server other than the target database instance server. As long as the SQL Server Client Tools Connectivity binaries have been installed on the server and the other Windows requirements for installing GoldenGate have been met, you can optionally run Apply for SQL Server on a middle-tier server. As the Apply process for GoldenGate is different than Capture in that it only needs a connection to the database to apply the captured transactions and is not reading from any transaction logs, only an ODBC DSN needs to be created for Apply, and no specific Windows operating system permissions are required for the Apply process. You still need to grant the Manager account membership in the server's Administrators group, however, since Manager needs full control over the GoldenGate installation directories regardless of what components will be configured for that installation of GoldenGate.

GoldenGate Apply requires either a SQL Server or Integrated Windows authenticated login that is at least a member of the target database's db_owner database role.

Target SQL Server Database Requirements

There are no specific SQL Server instance requirements for a database to be used as a target by Apply; however, there are some database requirements that must be addressed, namely for security. A target SQL Server database can be in SIMPLE recovery mode, for example, whereas a Capture SQL Server source database cannot. Keep in mind that if the target Apply database will also be used to either rebroadcast transactions or configured for an active-active topology, then the target Apply database will also act as a source Capture database and therefore must follow the requirements for source Capture SQL Server databases.

Apply will require that either a SQL Server or Integrated Windows authenticated login be used by the ODBC DSN connection to apply captured transactions, and that this login must be at least a member of the target SQL Server database's db_owner database role. It may be possible for implementations of GoldenGate used for

Apply to be configured with lesser permissions, but with operations like SET IDENTITY_INSERT ON and TRUNCATE (for SQL Server 2000 only), it is recommended in the Oracle GoldenGate documentation to assign the Apply login db_owner role membership within the target database. As well, the user executing the GGSCI **dblogin sourcedb** command with an Integrated Windows authenticated System DSN in order to create a checkpoint table must also be a member of the db_owner database role.

A target database must contain a copy of the source data at some point in time, unless of course insert operations will only be replicated and previous data is not required to exist in the target. The easiest method for instantiating a target SQL Server database from a source SQL Server database is to use SQL Server backup and restore, taking a current backup from the source and restoring it to the target. GoldenGate does have instantiation technology, however, if needed for heterogeneous environments, or any bulk load utility that is compatible between the source and target DBMSs can be used.

You can perform instantiation of the destination SQL Server database using backup and restore methodologies if you prefer. Oracle provides a Knowledge Document on Oracle Metalink that provides the instructions on how to do this operation. If you want to use this method of instantiating the destination database see Oracle Metalink Knowledge Document 1310946.1.

Target SQL Server Table Requirements

Allow me to repeat verbatim what has been stated in the previous section on source SQL Server table requirements: GoldenGate for SQL Server supports Capture and Apply of DML operations for user tables only. No other database objects are supported, nor is replication of DDL for SQL Server user tables. This is very important to keep in mind as you will definitely have to ensure that all necessary database objects, logins, and so on are kept up to date between source and target databases by means other than GoldenGate.

Having stated that boldly enough, there are also some exceptions to the user tables that are supported by GoldenGate. For example, table names with spaces in the name are not supported. You will need to either configure GoldenGate to ignore these tables or modify the names to meet the GoldenGate requirements.

The following is a list of unsupported table naming conventions for source SQL Server tables:

- Table names with spaces, single quotes, commas, and a list of other special characters are not supported. This is true for column names as well.

- For a complete and up-to-date list of unsupported naming conventions, check the *Oracle GoldenGate for SQL Server Installation and Setup Guide*.

■ Knowledge Document 1315720.1, available at Oracle Support, provides an analysis script that can be run against a source or target SQL Server database to provide information about supported tables and other information relevant to OGG installation.

Another very important consideration that applies to target SQL Server tables is whether or not to enable the NOT FOR REPLICATION option for certain SQL Server objects of the target tables to be replicated. Enabling the NOT FOR REPLICATION option for columns with the IDENTITY property, CHECK and FOREIGN KEY constraints, and table triggers provides some advantages when using the DBOPTIONS USEREPLICATIONUSER parameter for a Replicat process. The following is a list of those advantages:

■ **IDENTITY property** Enabling the NOT FOR REPLICATION clause on IDENTITY columns of tables to be replicated using GoldenGate provides the advantage that the replicat does not have to increment seed values on the target table in order to reserve the data value. For active-active configurations, IDENTITY seed and increment values must still be staggered (see the section "IDENTITY Property on Columns in Multimaster Configurations" for more information).

■ **Constraints** FOREIGN KEY and CHECK constraints enabled with the NOT FOR REPLICATION clause are not enforced against a GoldenGate replicat's delivered transactions to a SQL Server database. Cascade delete and update operations are also not executed against the target tables. One must ensure that any referenced tables that are enabled on the source SQL Server database to receive cascade operations are in fact configured by that source extract to capture data for those referenced tables in order to deliver those operations to a target SQL Server database with the NOT FOR REPLICATION clause enabled for cascade operations.

■ **DML triggers** DML triggers on the target SQL Server database fire just as they would on a source SQL Server database when using GoldenGate Apply. However, modifying the target DML triggers to include the NOT FOR REPLICATION option suppresses those target table DML triggers from firing. Again, just as with CASCADE operations, the source SQL Server extract must be configured to capture table data for any tables on the source database that are affected by another table's trigger, if the target SQL Server tables that fire the trigger are altered to include the NOT FOR REPLICATION clause.

Installing Oracle GoldenGate for SQL Server on Windows

Begin your installation by logging in to the Windows server where you plan to install GoldenGate, logging in with an account that is a member of the server's Administrators group. You can create a new account to be used by Oracle GoldenGate processes, or use an existing account, but installation and operation of Oracle GoldenGate should be performed by an account with Administrator rights.

Create an installation directory on the server to house the Oracle GoldenGate binaries and subdirectories. Remember, for a SQL Server database to be configured as a source Capture database, the GoldenGate installation must reside on the server where the database instance is installed. For SQL Server instances that are part of a Windows cluster, the GoldenGate installation for a source Capture database must be on a disk resource that is part of the group containing the SQL Server instance. And for installations of GoldenGate for SQL Server that will be used solely for target Apply databases, the installation does not have to be on the same server as the database instance. This might lead some of you to realize that you can conceivably install one instance of GoldenGate for SQL Server on the source database instance server and that installation can be used to set up the Apply process to a remote target SQL Server database instance. This is a correct assumption.

The installation directory must not contain any spaces in the full path name, and consideration should be given to the drive selection for Oracle GoldenGate, as there will be trail files that will be written here, and depending on the frequency and size of those captured transactions, this directory could see sizable growth and high read/write activity. You can, however, redirect trail file creation to another location other than the default software installation, but in general, for performance benefits, locate trail storage on a different storage device than your database and transaction log files if possible.

The following is an example of directory creation for Oracle GoldenGate for SQL Server on a Windows system.

```
Microsoft Windows [Version 6.0.6002]
Copyright (c) 2006 Microsoft Corporation.  All rights reserved.
C:\Users\ogg>mkdir C:\OGG\Software\SQLServer\OGGv11.1.1.1.2
```

Installing the Oracle GoldenGate for SQL Server software begins by downloading the correct build based on the bit-set of your SQL Server instance. After signing in to Oracle's Software Delivery Cloud (eDelivery), select the Oracle Fusion Middleware product pack from the drop-down menu of the Media Pack Search page, and select the correct platform for your environment.

NOTE
The builds for Oracle GoldenGate for SQL Server are not based on the operating system processor bit-set, but the bit-set of the SQL Server instance.

As seen in Figure 11-1, 32-bit instances of SQL Server are capable of running on x64 (64-bit) platforms, but you must select the "Microsoft Windows (32-bit)" platform for 32-bit instances of SQL Server, regardless of the bit-set of the operating system it is running on.

Sixty-four-bit instances of SQL Server can only run on either x64 or IA64 (Itanium) platforms, so select the appropriate download based on your processor class, either "Microsoft Windows x64 (64-bit)" or "Microsoft Windows Itanium (64-bit)."

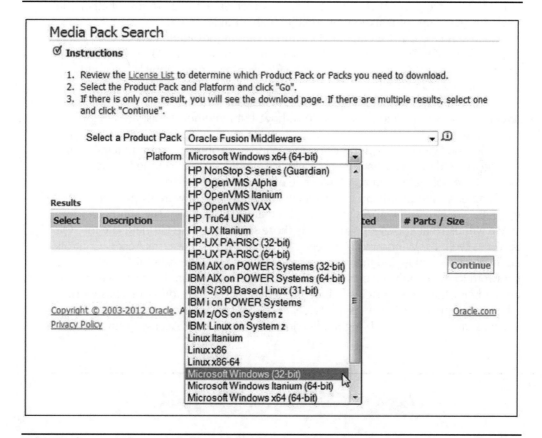

FIGURE 11-1.   *Software selection of GoldenGate for SQL Server*

	Oracle GoldenGate for Non Oracle Database v11.1.1.1.0 Media Pack for Microsoft Windows x64 (64-bit)	11.1.1.1.0	B63501-04	DEC-02-2011	7 / 190M

FIGURE 11-2. *GoldenGate build for non-Oracle databases*

After selecting the correct platform, click GO and search for the most recent software link with the following similar description: Oracle GoldenGate for Non Oracle Database v##.#.#.# Media Pack for Microsoft Windows (##-bit), as in Figure 11-2. There may be several builds listed, so you can choose to download either the most recent, or an older version depending on specific needs. It is recommended to check with Oracle Support or review Doc tickets should you decide to not use the most recent version of Oracle GoldenGate, to determine whether you might be giving up some fixed functionality with an older build.

Finally, in Figure 11-3, click the Download button for Oracle GoldenGate V##.#.#.# for SQL Server 2000, 2005, 2008 on Windows XP, 2003, 2008 (## bit) and save to a directory of your choice. The file-naming convention for the build will be similar to V#####-##.zip.

After the file has downloaded, extract it with your favorite unzip utility into the directory that you created earlier, or do so now, but remember, no spaces in the full path name.

Either use Windows Explorer or open a Windows command prompt (cmd.exe), change to the directory where you installed GoldenGate, and run the Oracle GoldenGate Software Command Interface executable, ggsci.exe.

Chapter 4 introduced you to the Oracle GoldenGate Software Command Interface (GGSCI) and walked you through creating the GoldenGate subdirectories, so we will use that knowledge and apply those steps to Oracle GoldenGate for SQL Server as well. For Windows 2008 Server environments where User Access Controls are in place, you may find that you are required to supply the Administrator password to run certain aspects of the GoldenGate installation. For example, a user with Administrator group rights will be prompted for the Administrator's password when installing the Manager as a service, even though that user is in the Administrators group. Disabling notifications within the User Access Controls

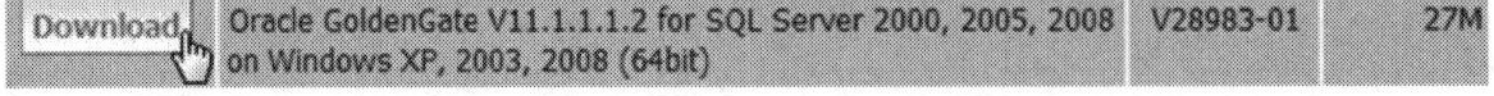

Download	Oracle GoldenGate V11.1.1.1.2 for SQL Server 2000, 2005, 2008 on Windows XP, 2003, 2008 (64bit)	V28983-01	27M

FIGURE 11-3. *GoldenGate build for SQL Server*

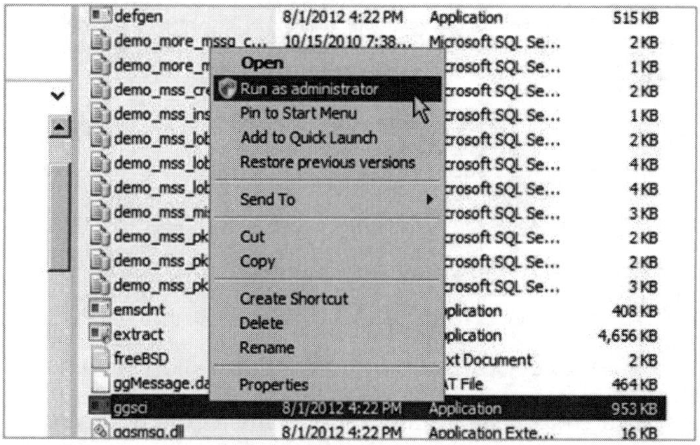

FIGURE 11-4. *Running GGSCI as Administrator*

settings or running GGSCI as the Administrator using the "Run as administrator" option for a program will remedy this situation. When running GGSCI as the Administrator, as seen in Figure 11-4, you will be prompted initially for the correct Administrator password but will not be prompted subsequently within that same session. Further, logging in to the server with the actual Administrator account and installing GoldenGate will negate the prompts for the Administrator's password.

The GGSCI interface looks similar to the Windows command prompt. It is your gateway to all things GoldenGate and is where most if not all commands to run GoldenGate originate from. In a Windows environment, the GoldenGate commands are not case sensitive.

Once the interface is initially opened, the first step is to set up some internal subdirectories for the GoldenGate installation. Type **create subdirs** at the prompt. This creates a set of predefined directories used by GoldenGate, as seen here:

```
Oracle GoldenGate Command Interpreter for ODBC
Version 11.1.1.1.2 OGGCORE_11.1.1.1.2_PLATFORMS_111004.2100
Windows x64 (optimized), Microsoft SQL Server on Oct  5 2011 00:28:20
Copyright (C) 1995, 2011, Oracle and/or its affiliates. All rights reserved.
GGSCI> CREATE SUBDIRS
Creating subdirectories under current directory C:\OGG\Software\SQLServer\OGGv11
.1.1.1.2
Parameter files C:\OGG\Software\SQLServer\OGGv11.1.1.1.2\dirprm: created
Report files C:\OGG\Software\SQLServer\OGGv11.1.1.1.2\dirrpt: created
Checkpoint files C:\OGG\Software\SQLServer\OGGv11.1.1.1.2\dirchk: created
Process status files C:\OGG\Software\SQLServer\OGGv11.1.1.1.2\dirpcs: created
SQL script files C:\OGG\Software\SQLServer\OGGv11.1.1.1.2\dirsql: created
Database definitions files C:\OGG\Software\SQLServer\OGGv11.1.1.1.2\dirdef:
created
```

```
Extract data files C:\OGG\Software\SQLServer\OGGv11.1.1.1.2\dirdat: created
Temporary files C:\OGG\Software\SQLServer\OGGv11.1.1.1.2\dirtmp: created
Veridata files C:\OGG\Software\SQLServer\OGGv11.1.1.1.2\dirver: created
Veridata Lock files C:\OGG\Software\SQLServer\OGGv11.1.1.1.2\dirver\lock: created
Veridata Out-Of-Sync files C:\OGG\Software\SQLServer\OGGv11.1.1.1.2\dirver\oos:
created
Veridata Out-Of-Sync XML files C:\OGG\Software\SQLServer\OGGv11.1.1.1.2\dirver\
oosxml: created
Veridata Parameter files C:\OGG\Software\SQLServer\OGGv11.1.1.1.2\dirver\
params: created
Veridata Report files C:\OGG\Software\SQLServer\OGGv11.1.1.1.2\dirver\
report: created
Veridata Status files C:\OGG\Software\SQLServer\OGGv11.1.1.1.2\dirver\
status: created
Veridata Trace files C:\OGG\Software\SQLServer\OGGv11.1.1.1.2\dirver\
trace: created
Stdout files C:\OGG\Software\SQLServer\OGGv11.1.1.1.2\dirout: created
```

That's it. The software has been installed and all the required directories have been created. Now it's time to configure some basic components of Oracle GoldenGate for a Windows server in preparation for setting up replication with GoldenGate later in the chapter.

Configuration

In this section we want to take a look at configuring Oracle GoldenGate for Microsoft SQL Server. First we will discuss configuring the Manager process. Then we will discuss the various parameters related to the Manager process.

Configuring the Manager Process

Begin by configuring the Manager to run as a service. This is optional for nonclustered configurations, but really there is no need to do this as the alternative is to run the Manager as a user process that would halt when the user logs out of the system. You can configure the Manager using the default service name GGSMGR, or you can use your own name by creating a GLOBALS file and adding the parameter MGRSERVNAME, and then set that parameter to whatever you desire, followed by adding the service within GGSCI.

If you're running multiple installations of Oracle GoldenGate on the same server, or if you're using an active-active Windows cluster environment wherein one or more installations of Oracle GoldenGate are owned by separate nodes but can at some point run on the same nodes, then you must use a GLOBALS file with the MGRSERVNAME parameter and use distinct Manager service names from each installation.

For example, create the GLOBALS file and add the following line:

```
MGRSERVNAME <yourservicenamehere>
```

For example:

```
MGRSERVNAME OGG MGR Service
```

Next, within GGSCI, issue **shell install addservice**:

```
GGSCI> SHELL INSTALL ADDSERVICE
  Service 'OGG MGR Service' created.
  Install program terminated normally.
```

The **shell** command within GGSCI just allows for calling external programs or commands, and in this case is calling the install.exe executable, which is part of the GoldenGate installation.

We have now created a Windows service named "OGG MGR Service," which runs under the Local System account and is set to start automatically at system boot. You can then edit the login information and autostart feature of the service as desired from the Services snap-in, services.msc. You could also have optionally issued the following command to add the service and override the defaults:

```
SHELL INSTALL ADDSERVICE MANUALSTART USER <domain\username>
```

However, I find it simple enough to modify this information within the Services snap-in and verify that everything I want is set correctly. Keep in mind, though, that where User Access Controls are in place for Windows 2008 servers, you'll need to run the Services snap-in as the Administrator in order to make these changes from the snap-in.

Another useful set of features to add next with the INSTALL program are the Windows events associated with GoldenGate. This is done with the INSTALL program and the parameter ADDEVENTS. Within GGSCI, type **shell install addevents**:

```
GGSCI> SHELL INSTALL ADDEVENTS
  Oracle GoldenGate messages installed successfully.
  Install program terminated normally.
```

Next, copy the category.dll and ggsmsg.dll files from the Oracle GoldenGate installation directory to the Windows SYSTEM32 directory. This will present more information to the Windows logs for GoldenGate events.

Now that the Manager is set to run as a service, configure a manager parameter file to provide startup parameters for the Manager process. At a minimum you need to tell the Manager process which TCP/IP port it will be running with. This is done with the PORT parameter and specifying an unused numerical value for the TCP/IP port, such as 7809. For installations of GoldenGate that are to act as a target environment, the Manager port will need to be open on the server's firewall to allow communications to that manager from remote GoldenGate servers.

```
GGSCI> EDIT PARAMS MGR
```

This command will open Windows Notepad for editing purposes (as seen in Figure 11-5). You will be prompted to create a new parameter file for the Manager called mgr.prm, if one does not already exist, located in the default GoldenGate parameters directory dirprm.

Alternatively, you can manually create the mgr.prm file using any text editor and save the file to the GoldenGate dirprm directory.

Add the line **PORT 7809** to the parameter file and save and close the file.

```
PORT 7809
```

In GGSCI, view the current status of the Manager by typing **info mgr** or **info all**. It will have a status of STOPPED and INFO MGR will report the Manager as DOWN!.

```
GGSCI> INFO MGR
Manager is DOWN!
GGSCI> INFO ALL
Program      Status       Group       Lag          Time Since Chkpt
MANAGER      STOPPED
```

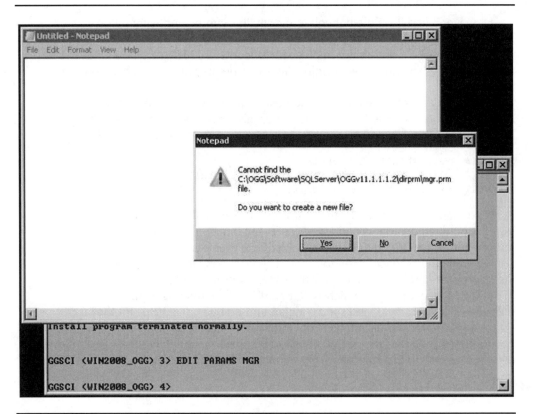

FIGURE 11-5. *Results of the **edit params mgr** command*

Using your knowledge about the Manager from previous chapters, start the Manager and verify that it is running.

```
GGSCI> START MGR
Starting Manager as service ('OGG MGR Service')...
Service started.
GGSCI> INFO ALL
Program      Status       Group       Lag            Time Since Chkpt
MANAGER      RUNNING
```

If the status is STOPPED, then you need to perform some investigation, and the best way do this is to view the Manager's report file located in the dirrpt directory, named mgr.rpt. If there is no report file at this point and Manager is still not running, you may have encountered one of the issues when the Microsoft Visual C++ 2005 SP1 Redistributable Package is not installed, so verify that it is installed at this point. There will be no other indication as to why the Manager is not running, but the fact that the report file for the Manager didn't get created means that the Manager couldn't even start to write out an error, so chances are you are missing some important binaries that are provided with the Visual C++ 2005 SP1 Redistributable Package.

We know that we have done our job correctly, as the Manager is up and running and Oracle GoldenGate is installed. This installation folder for GoldenGate can accommodate both source and target Capture and Apply components for any and all instances and supported versions of SQL Server on this server as long as the SQL Server instances are all of the same bit-set as the GoldenGate build.

You could also create multiple installations of GoldenGate on one server, all running separate Manager processes with unique service names and port numbers, allowing for separation of components like Capture from Apply.

There are no requirements or recommendations as to how many installations of GoldenGate one can have on a server. This is merely expressed here to draw attention to the flexibility of the software and decoupled approach that it can take.

Now, building on earlier chapters, let's dive a little deeper and get a better understanding of the usefulness and limitations of some useful Manager parameters to add to this configuration of GoldenGate for SQL Server on Windows.

Manager Parameters

It is highly recommended and practical that Manager runs as a Windows service. The default options for a Manager service are to start at system boot, but you can adjust this through the Control Panel's Services snap-in to be Manual or Automatic (Delayed Start). The timing of the start of Manager at system boot comes into play when considering the timing of the other GoldenGate components that Manager controls and the timing when the database comes online. Using available parameters for the Manager to start the other GoldenGate processes, the goal is to time the start of the Manager with the timing when SQL Server brings the databases online.

There is a restricted feature that allows creating a dependency on another service when installing the Manager as a service, but this option of the INSTALL program, called WAITFORSERVICE, only supports service names that have no spaces in the name, which makes it unusable for any named instance of SQL Server. In a Windows cluster, when Manager is added as a resource to the group that contains the SQL Server instance, you have the ability to bind the Manager as a dependency on the SQL Server instance.

Since it is the Manager that can automatically start the other GoldenGate components that it controls, it is important to ensure that the Manager starts after the last database that any GoldenGate component connects to has come online. For example, there is no GoldenGate setting that would allow an Apply component to keep retrying a database connection after the first attempt to start the Apply process on server boot. On server bootup, when the Manager starts, it will use the AUTOSTART parameter to start the specified GoldenGate process, and if the database to which a process connects is not online, that GoldenGate process will simply report a STOPPED status and there is no Manager parameter to retry the connection for that process.

BOOTDELAYMINUTES

The BOOTDELAYMINUTES parameter for the Manager can be set to a number in minutes that will delay other Manager parameter settings, like AUTOSTART. This does not coordinate starting the processes, such as an extract, with the opening of the source database upon system boot. However, you can get an average sample of time that it takes for the database to come online and then apply that to the BOOTDELAYMINUTES parameter, followed by the AUTOSTART parameter.

For example, you could use the following settings in your Manager parameter file:

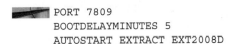

```
PORT 7809
BOOTDELAYMINUTES 5
AUTOSTART EXTRACT EXT2008D
```

This will delay starting the extract upon system boot by five minutes, allowing time for the source database to be brought online.

NOTE
Unfortunately, this parameter only works when a server initially boots up. The parameter will have no effect when a Cluster Group with a running manager process fails over to another node in the cluster. This is because the other node is already up and running.

AUTOSTART

As mentioned in Chapter 4, the AUTOSTART parameter can be used with process lists or wildcard lists for multiple processes within a GoldenGate installation. A big drawback for this parameter, as mentioned earlier, is that it does not retry attempts to start GoldenGate processes, such as in cases where the database that the process connects to is not yet online. When a GoldenGate process cannot connect to the database for which it has been configured, it returns a STOPPED status, and no attempt by AUTOSTART is made to retry the process.

To help remedy this, it is possible to write your own SQL Server Agent job that is set to start when SQL Server Agent starts up, and then queries the status of a database to determine when it's online, looping until that database comes online. and when it does, goes to the next step, which calls a Windows batch file that runs the GGSCI executable, calling in an obey file that starts up specific GoldenGate processes that connect to that database.

AUTORESTART

The AUTORESTART parameter was covered in Chapter 4, and there is nothing specific to this parameter working in Windows for SQL Server that necessitates a special write-up, other than to say it is a good practice to include it in your Manager parameter file.

SYSLOG

This parameter can be in either the Manager or GLOBALS file. It accepts options of WARN, ERROR, and INFO as well as a few others, and controls the types of events that are written to the Windows logs. Without this parameter, all information messages that OGG produces will be logged to the Windows logs, and this can be too numerous for a production environment. Familiarize yourself with the information logged by default and then consider using this parameter as desired.

Managing Oracle GoldenGate for SQL Server

Now we are going to really get into the nitty gritty of managing Oracle GoldenGate on Microsoft SQL Server. First we will look at managing the databases that will be benefiting from the GoldenGate Extract and Replicat processes. We will then look at configuring basic replication using GoldenGate on SQL Server.

Database Management Considerations with Oracle GoldenGate for SQL Server

In general, there are no special requirements for normal database management once Oracle GoldenGate is installed and the database is configured correctly as mentioned earlier in this chapter. A database that only receives replicated data from an Apply process has considerably fewer restrictions on its setup and management than a database configured for capture by an extract.

Database Management

Backup operations for the database can continue as normal through whatever tools or utilities you choose to use. Full and Differential database backups do not impact GoldenGate, nor does GoldenGate have any requirements for how those backups are taken. These types of backups can be done with any means available.

Other operations, such as database shrink operations and data file expansion, addition, and deletion, do not impact GoldenGate either. However, it has been seen with some versions of GoldenGate that when dropping existing files from the database, the GoldenGate Extract component may hold a file lock on the physical file, thus not allowing it to be dropped from the operating system's file storage. If you are performing data file drops for a database that is configured for GoldenGate Capture, be sure to verify that the file is actually deleted from the file system. If it has not been deleted after dropping the file from the database, stopping the extract and manually deleting the associated file from the system will be required.

The recovery model of the database is a very important factor for a source Capture SQL Server database. Alteration of the recovery mode out of FULL recovery to SIMPLE recovery will break the database's transaction log chain, invalidating Oracle GoldenGate Capture's ability to ensure complete data capture, and resulting in loss of data delivery to a target database. Therefore, do not change the recovery model of a source database out of FULL recovery when configured for GoldenGate Capture.

Transaction Log Management

The SQL Server transaction logs on the target database in a GoldenGate replication schema are a critical component and they need to be handled carefully. This is because the transaction logs can be used by the GoldenGate capture process at almost any time. That being said, there are some rules that you should follow with respect to the transaction log backups.

You should prepare for greater transaction log size due to enabling supplemental logging for tables in the database. The increase in size correlates to the frequency and width of update and delete operations for a table enabled with supplemental logging. There is no true formula to determine this in advance, so judicious application testing should vet this out. You will also notice that your transaction log backups will increase in size as well.

Do not break the log chain of the transaction log. The log chain is broken when the database is set to SIMPLE recovery or the transaction log is backed up with the deprecated NO_LOG and TRUNCATE_ONLY options. These last two options are available log backup options for SQL Server 2005 but have been deprecated in SQL Server 2008.

When using extract with the TRANLOGOPTIONS MANAGESECONDARYTRUNCATIONPOINT parameter, the Extract process must be running in order to mark committed transactions as distributed; otherwise, committed transactions would continue to queue in the transaction log and not be deleted as SQL Server sees fit upon completion of the next transaction log backup. The consequence of this is decreased log space, which could eventually lead to a full transaction log. See the following section for more information on how to maintain the truncation point when the Extract process is down for extended periods.

Finally, transaction log backups for a source database must be done in a specific manner in order for the MS SQL Server database to properly support GoldenGate replication.

The transaction log backups must be taken with SQL Server, not with a third-party backup utility. They must be uncompressed (available as of SQL Server 2008), unencrypted, not striped across multiple files, be written as one backup per file or device, and be written to disk, not tape. Basically, the log backups must be taken with a statement similar to the following:

```
Backup log <database name> to disk = 'path\uniquefilename'
```

UNC paths for log backups are supported if you are using a network share to back up your transaction logs, but the Windows account that is running the Manager process is the account that the Extract process uses at the operating system level to read the transaction log and log backups, so this account must have at least read access to that network share and its files. Also, a fast network connection between the local server and the network server where the log backups are being read from is a must as data replication latency could increase as a result of a slow connection to a network log backup directory. The best practice would be to use local disk storage for transaction log backups.

MSDB Historical Data and Transaction Log Backup Retention

GoldenGate needs transaction log backup information that is stored in the SQL Server MSDB system database in a few tables: BACKUPMEDIAFAMILY and BACKUPSET, which GoldenGate queries to determine the transaction log backups that are needed for an extract to read from based on a needed log sequence number (LSN).

To view the current required position that an extract would need to restart or recover from in case of a stop condition, use this command:

```
INFO EXTRACT <ExtractName> SHOWCH
```

and pay attention to the LSN of the recovery checkpoint.

```
GGSCI> INFO EXT2008D SHOWCH
   EXTRACT     EXT2008D  Last Started 2012-03-06 20:15    Status STOPPED
   Checkpoint Lag       00:00:00 (updated 3762:36:34 ago)
   VAM Read Checkpoint  2012-03-06 20:44:46.946666
     LSN: 0x00000021:00000101:0003
   Current Checkpoint Detail:
   Read Checkpoint #1
```

```
VAM External Interface
Startup Checkpoint (starting position in the data source):
   Timestamp: 2012-02-29 15:17:14.803333
   LSN: 0x00000021:00000040:0003
 Recovery Checkpoint (position of oldest unprocessed transaction in the data
source):
   Timestamp: 2012-03-06 20:44:46.946666
   LSN: 0x00000021:00000101:0003
 Current Checkpoint (position of last record read in the data source):
   Timestamp: 2012-03-06 20:44:46.946666
   LSN: 0x00000021:00000101:0003
```

In the preceding example, the time of the Recovery Checkpoint is 2012-03-06 20:44:46. When the extract starts, it may need to query the MSDB database for the transaction log backups that cover this time range up to the current system time, so ensure that the transaction log backups and corresponding log backup records still exist on the system.

The Cleanup History and Maintenance History tasks using the SQL Server Management Studio Maintenance Wizard are typically where the history and file retention for backups are controlled, so plan accordingly to store as much history and as many log backups as storage permits, coordinating with typical Recovery Checkpoint periods for your environment.

Table Management

Since Oracle GoldenGate for SQL Server does not support replication of DDL changes for tables configured for Capture or Apply, any changes to tables must occur in complete coordination with the completed processing by GoldenGate of that table's DML prior to the change, followed by a restart of the GoldenGate process just after the DDL change but before any new DML activities for that changed table occur. Further, consideration must be given for table changes that drop and re-create the table behind the scenes, which as a result may disable supplemental logging for that table. See Knowledge Document 1326044.1, available at Oracle's Support site, for information about which types of operations can disable supplemental logging for SQL Server tables.

In general, the steps to handle DDL changes are listed as the following: Step 1 would be to allow the GoldenGate process to finish processing all DML statements for a table that is about to undergo a DDL change. Step 2 would then be to stop the GoldenGate process that is configured to Capture or Apply against the table. Step 3 would be to make the required DDL change to the table and re-enable supplemental logging if required, and Step 4 would be to restart the GoldenGate process so that it can pick up the new table structure and store that structure in its metadata cache in memory. And to complicate this task, there can be no new DML activities for that table between Step 2 and Step 4.

Coordinating these steps is not as difficult if you have the ability to restrict user activity to the database during a maintenance window, for example, but in a 24×7 environment where there is no means to lock out DML for a given time, the process of ensuring that GoldenGate has processed all of the DML for a table prior to making any changes becomes just about impossible. Fortunately, GoldenGate does have a parameter to help out with such a need, and that parameter is called EVENTACTIONS. Using the EVENTACTIONS parameter in the Capture and Apply process combined with a database trigger (available beginning with SQL Server 2005 and higher) that fires on alter DDL statements, you can stop a GoldenGate process at the correct time in order to restart the process with the table's changed metadata. For more information on this procedure, see Knowledge Document 1326758.1, available at Oracle's support site.

Indexes and Index Maintenance

Indexes for source and target SQL Server databases utilizing Oracle GoldenGate can be created and are maintained separately for the different systems. Since Oracle GoldenGate does not replicate indexes, source and target index structures can be different based on utilization needs. For example, if you're using Oracle GoldenGate for offloading reports from a source OLTP database to a target reporting database, the indexes for reporting queries can be removed from the source database, reducing overhead, and be created only on the target database.

The caveat to index differences between source and target databases would of course be to ensure that the index on a primary key or a unique index is created identically across environments to avoid data conflicts.

Regarding index maintenance, these operations do not impact Oracle GoldenGate; however, there is a certain scenario in which an index rebuild for a clustered index on a table might actually alter the DDL for the table, causing a source Capture to error out. Specifics of when and why this might occur are obscured, so the support stance on index maintenance is to stop the OGG processes during index maintenance operations and restart them once completed.

It is highly recommended to load test index maintenance operations against a test system with Oracle GoldenGate Capture installed to help discover any potential issues.

Configuring Basic GoldenGate Replication for SQL Server

This sample configuration of Oracle GoldenGate for SQL Server will include creating new source and target SQL Server databases, configuring an extract for a source SQL Server 2008 R2 database, two data pumps, a target replicat to a SQL Server 2008 R2 database, and a target replicat using the same Exttrail data file from the source extract to deliver to an existing Oracle database running on Oracle Enterprise Linux.

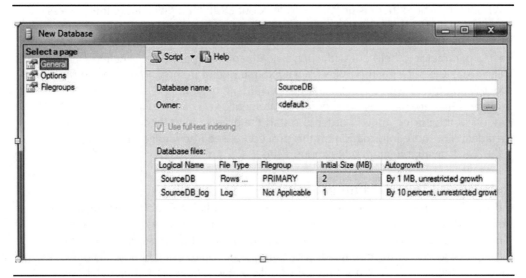

FIGURE 11-6. *Creating a source database*

Begin by connecting to your SQL Server instance with a login that is a member of the sysadmin SQL Server server role. Then create a new SQL Server database or configure an existing one to be used as a source database for GoldenGate Capture, ensure that the database is in FULL recovery mode, and make a full backup of the database. See Figures 11-6 through 11-8 for examples.

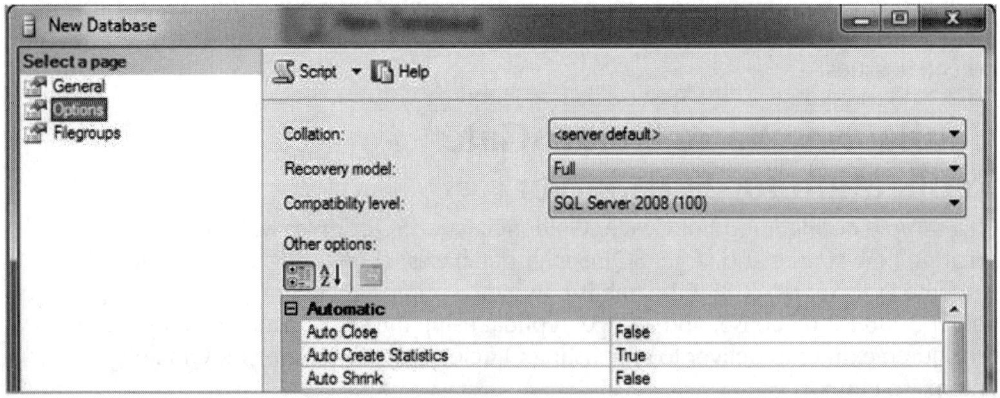

FIGURE 11-7. *Source database in full recovery*

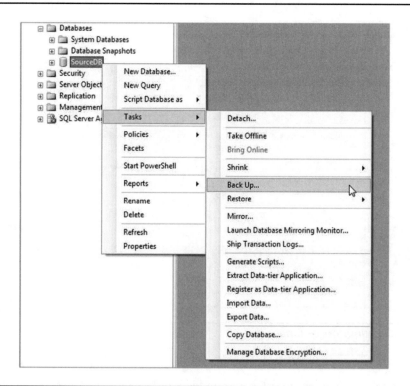

FIGURE 11-8. *Initial source database backup*

Once the source SQL Server database is created, we will add some tables to the database. The OGG installation includes a sample DDL script called demo_mss_create.sql located in the root OGG installation directory. This script can be used to create two tables: the tcustmer and tcustord tables. Open this script in SQL Server Management Studio, set the database connection to your newly created or existing source SQL Server database, and run the script to create the two sample tables, as in Figure 11-9.

We now have two tables in the source database: dbo.tcustmer and dbo.tcustord. Next, we need to enable supplemental logging for the two tables using the **add trandata** command in GGSCI, but first we will create a System DSN to allow us to connect to the source database from within GoldenGate and issue these commands.

As mentioned in the earlier section "ODBC System DSN," GoldenGate for SQL Server requires a DSN created for each database that an Extract or Replicat process will connect to. In this sample configuration, we create a new System DSN for the source GoldenGate extract, and we will use Integrated Windows authentication as

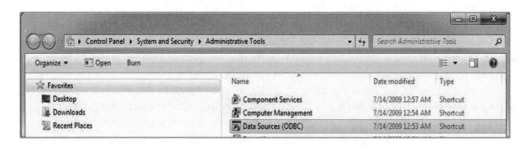

```
demo_mss_create.sql - ORACLE-WI...)
-- Copyright (C) 2002, 2010, Oracle and/or its affiliates. All rights reserved.
--
-- demo_mss_create.sql
--
-- Microsoft SQL Server Tutorial
--
-- Description:
-- Create the TCUSTMER and TCUSTORD tables.
--
-- Note: execute this script from the command line as "osql -U userid -P password -i demo_mss_create.sql"
--

if exists (select * from dbo.sysobjects where id = object_id(N'[tcustmer]') and OBJECTPROPERTY(id, N'IsUserTable') = 1)
 drop table [tcustmer]
 GO

if exists (select * from dbo.sysobjects where id = object_id(N'[tcustord]') and OBJECTPROPERTY(id, N'IsUserTable') = 1)
 drop table [tcustord]
 GO

CREATE TABLE tcustmer
(
    cust_code   VARCHAR(4)    NOT NULL,
    [name]      VARCHAR(30),
    city        VARCHAR(20),
    state       CHAR(2),
```

```
Messages
Command(s) completed successfully.
```

FIGURE 11-9.   *Creating source tables*

the security mechanism for the database connection. The Extract process will then run under the security account that is running the Manager service.

To begin, open the ODBC Data Source Administrator utility by running the odbcad32.exe program from the command line, or open the Data Sources (ODBC) utility from the Windows Control Panel as seen in Figure 11-10.

```
Start>Run>odbcad32.exe
```

	Name	Date modified	Type
	Component Services	7/14/2009 12:57 AM	Shortcut
	Computer Management	7/14/2009 12:54 AM	Shortcut
	Data Sources (ODBC)	7/14/2009 12:53 AM	Shortcut

Control Panel ▶ System and Security ▶ Administrative Tools

Organize ▼   Open   Burn

Favorites
Desktop
Downloads
Recent Places

FIGURE 11-10.   *Data Sources in Control Panel*

Next, using the ODBC Data Source Administrator, select the System DSN tab and click Add to create a new Data Source, and select the appropriate SQL Server driver based on the version of SQL Server that the database to connect to is installed under. In this example, the source and target SQL Server databases are SQL Server 2008 R2 instances, so the "SQL Server Native Client 10.0" driver will be used, as in Figure 11-11.

Continue with the creation of the new Data Source by supplying a unique name of your choosing, and be sure to reference the server and instance name (for named instances of SQL Server) in the Server field of the connection properties. A dot "." can be used to represent the local system name, as seen in Figure 11-12.

In Figure 11-13, we set the authentication method that the extract will use to connect to the source database for Metadata and other functional queries.

Next, ensure that the option to change the default database is checked and that the correct source database is selected from the drop-down menu as seen in Figure 11-14.

Accept the remaining default options and finish creating the System DSN.

Using the GGSCI interface, establish a connection to the source database using the newly created System DSN and the **dblogin sourcedb** commands.

dblogin and **sourcedb** are OGG commands (the term **sourcedb** seems redundant but is required for SQL Server, not for Oracle DB) and SourceSQLDB is the name of the system DSN that was created as an example.

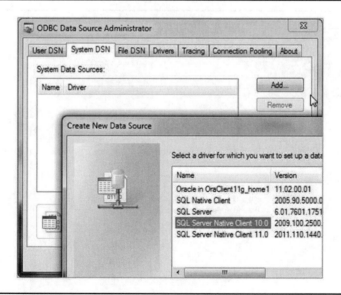

FIGURE 11-11.   *SQL Server driver selection*

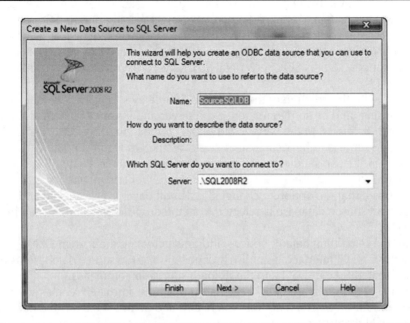

FIGURE 11-12. *Data source name*

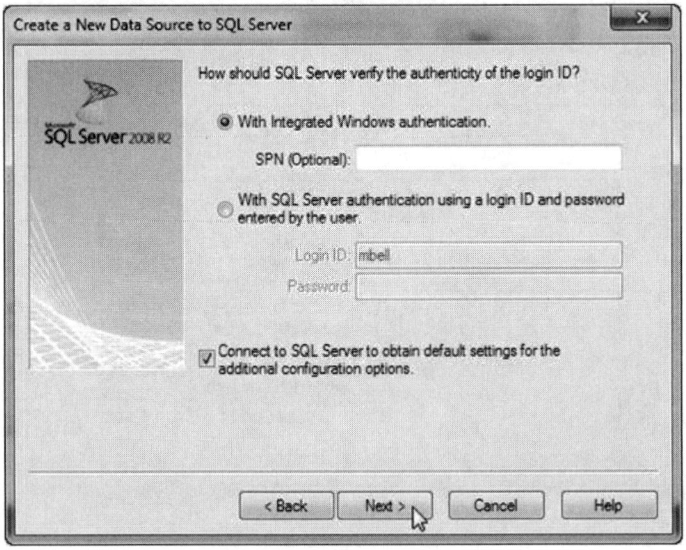

FIGURE 11-13. *Source data source authentication*

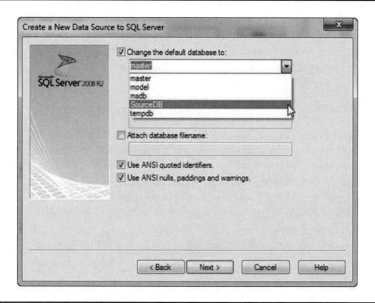

FIGURE 11-14. *Default source database*

Since this DSN connection is using Integrated Windows authentication, the login information passed through to the database is actually the current Windows user running GGSCI, so ensure that this user has sysadmin rights within the SQL Server instance, as it is required to set supplemental logging.

```
GGSCI> DBLOGIN SOURCEDB SourceSQLDB
```

Next, identify the tables to be configured for Capture and enable them with supplemental logging.

Issue **add trandata** for each of these tables.

add trandata is the command to enable supplemental logging for tables in the source database. The preceding example is enabling supplemental logging for all tables in the dbo schema using the optional wildcard symbol. One could have also stated each individual table name rather than using wildcard symbols, tedious as that may be for databases with large numbers of tables. Also, using the wildcard option on databases with large numbers of tables is actually slower than executing the individual add trandata statement per table. You could produce a SQL Server script to query the database for user tables, then append that information to the text add trandata, which outputs the individual statements to a text file (add trandata schema.tablename) and execute that as an obey file from GGSCI.

Be cautious when enabling supplemental logging for tables in a production environment, as this command does put certain share-level locks on the tables. Therefore, it would wait for an exclusive table lock, and conversely, would cause a wait for any database process needing an exclusive table lock. Here is an example of adding transactional data through the GGSCI interface:

```
GGSCI> ADD TRANDATA dbo.tcustmer
GGSCI> ADD TRANDATA dbo.tcustord
```

You'll notice in Figure 11-15 that a warning is issued when attempting to add tables. This occurs because the primary keys for these two tables include variable-length columns as stated in the warning. It is unlikely that this is a major issue of concern, but you should take the warning under advisement.

Now that supplemental logging is enabled for the two tables, move on to configure the Oracle GoldenGate components that will capture committed transactions from these tables.

Begin by checking the status of the Manager. If it is in a STOPPED state, start it up.

```
GGSCI> INFO ALL
     Program      Status      Group       Lag          Time Since Chkpt
     MANAGER      RUNNING
```

Next, create an extract that will capture the data for these two tables.

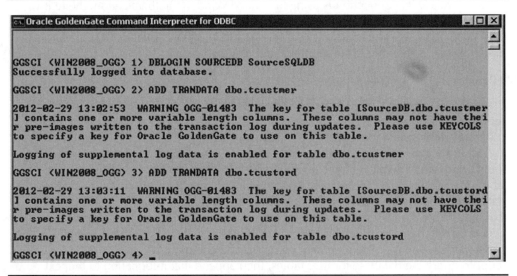

FIGURE 11-15. *Warning issued by* ***add trandata***

Use the **edit params** command in GGSCI to create the extract's parameter file:

```
EDIT PARAMS <ExtractName>
```

Choose an extract name of your liking. It must be less than or equal to eight characters in length.

```
GGSCI> EDIT PARAMS EXT2008D
```

This will open Windows Notepad as in Figure 11-16, and you can begin typing into a new Notepad document to create the extract parameter file. Click Yes to create the new file and when you save it, the correct file name and extension will already be set for you.

Configure the extract with a minimal set of options that include the extract name, Source DSN connection, required Tranlog option, Exttrail location and naming prefix, and tables to capture. These options have been discussed in previous chapters, but more details about SQL Server–specific options are listed after the following code.

```
EXTRACT EXT2008D
SOURCEDB SourceSQLDB
TRANLOGOPTIONS MANAGESECONDARYTRUNCATIONPOINT
EXTTRAIL ./dirdat/ET
TABLE dbo.tcustmer;
TABLE dbo.tcustord;
```

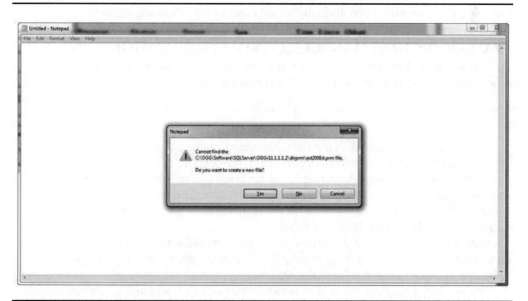

FIGURE 11-16. *Creating an extract parameter file*

Review the parameters used for this extract.

- **SOURCEDB <Source DB System DSN Name>**   This is the name of the system DSN that must be created for the source Capture database. If you're using a Windows authenticated connection for the DSN, no more information is needed; however, if you're using a SQL Server–authenticated connection, then the USERID and PASSWORD options must be specified with the correct information. Passwords can be encrypted using the ENCRYPT PASSWORD functions within the GGSCI options.

- **TRANLOGOPTIONS**   One of the important concepts to plan for and understand regarding GoldenGate for SQL Server involves a Capture parameter called TRANLOGOPTIONS. This parameter is used by other supported databases, but the parameter options MANAGESECONDARYTRUNCATIONPOINT and NOMANAGESECONDARYTRUNCATIONPOINT are unique to GoldenGate for SQL Server and require some careful planning and understanding.

To begin with, the TRANLOGOPTIONS parameter is only used for the Capture component and not for the Pump and Apply components. For a SQL Server extract, the TRANLOGOPTIONS parameter can accept several other options, but MANAGESECONDARYTRUNCATIONPOINT or NOMANAGESECONDARYTRUNCATIONPOINT is an absolute requirement for an extract for SQL Server 2005 and SQL Server 2008/2008 R2 and you must use one or the other. We'll explain when and why to use them in the following section.

TRANLOGOPTIONS MANAGESECONDARYTRUNCATIONPOINT

This parameter and option instruct Capture to execute the following system stored procedure against the database every 10 seconds during periods of database activity.

```
EXEC sp_repldone @xactid = NULL, @xact_segno = NULL, @numtrans = 0, @time = 0,
@reset = 1
```

If there are no transactions in the database, then Capture will pause this command and resume when database activity begins again. The purpose of issuing this stored procedure is to mark in the transaction log at the point in time when the procedure is executed, that all transactions up to that point in time are considered "distributed" and can be flushed from the transaction log at the completion of the next transaction log backup should SQL Server decide to do so.

Without the execution of the stored procedure, all transactions for tables configured for supplemental logging would queue in the transaction log as if waiting to be distributed and eventually fill the log.

This is a very important concept to understand, that as a result of the mechanisms used to enable supplemental logging for tables in SQL Server 2005 and SQL Server

2008/2008 R2, the tables are marked by SQL Server as "is_replicated" and therefore transactions for those tables must be marked as distributed in order to purge them from the transaction log as needed.

One can see the dependencies that are required to maintain a trim transaction log with supplemental logging added for at least one table in the database:

- Capture must be running and must be configured with MANAGESECONDARYTRUNCATIONPOINT.

- Routine transaction log backups must be taken.

This is similar to the requirements SQL Server would impose on itself if configured with SQL Server transactional replication. The log reader agent job must be running and transaction log backups must occur frequently enough to maintain free space in the transaction log.

One difference worth mentioning is that a log reader agent for a transactional replication publication issues sp_repldone with a specific transaction ID, whereas GoldenGate issues the blanket statement for that point in time. The reason for this is that neither SQL Server transactional replication nor the CDC Log Scan agent can read from the transaction log backups, so the agent must ensure that it truly has captured that transaction before marking it as distributed. However, GoldenGate Capture can read from transaction log backups, and therefore is not concerned whether or not it has captured those transactions at that point in time that it issued the blanket sp_repldone statement.

And since GoldenGate Capture can and must at times read from transaction log backups, the log backups need to be taken by SQL Server only (no vendor log backup utilities), be uncompressed, not striped across multiple devices, not stacked onto one device, and be saved to disk instead of tape.

In addition, for SQL Server 2008 and SQL Server 2008 R2, MANAGESECONDARYTRUNCATIONPOINT removes the CDC Log Scan job that gets created under SQL Server Agent. The CDC Log Scan job gets created soon after the first table of a database is enabled with supplemental logging and is a consequence of the means with which OGG implements supplemental logging in SQL Server 2008 and SQL Server 2008 R2. OGG utilizes SQL Server's Change Data Capture as a shell for logging the extra data needed by Capture but does not actually require any data to be stored in the shell CDC tables, so upon starting the extract after the first table is enabled with supplemental logging, the extract will stop and delete the CDC Log Scan job from SQL Server Agent.

Only use the MANAGESECONDARYTRUNCATIONPOINT option when a source Capture database is only running OGG replication. Do not use this option if either SQL Server transactional replication or a non-OGG configuration of Change Data Capture is in use.

TRANLOGOPTIONS NOMANAGESECONDARYTRUNCATIONPOINT

This option is the simplest to understand of the two as it is required when your current source database is already configured with either SQL Server transactional replication or Change Data Capture.

There is no requirement for GoldenGate Capture to mark transactions in the transaction log as distributed, as the SQL Server log reader or CDC Log Scan agent will do so instead.

A very important point to note here is that for a database in SQL Server 2005 versions 9.00.3228 or higher, running SQL Server transactional replication and GoldenGate Capture simultaneously does not enable supplemental logging for any table in the database that does not have a primary key. While it is true that GoldenGate Capture doesn't require primary keys on tables with SQL Server 2005 versions 9.00.3228 or higher, SQL Server transactional replication does, so when running these two replication technologies together, you must abide by SQL Server's limitation, as enabling supplemental logging on a table with no primary key in this specific situation will break the SQL Server Log Reader agent.

Continuing with the creation of the extract parameter file, save and close the file.

Now register the extract with GoldenGate. Instruct it to capture from the transaction log, and position it to start capturing data in the database from this point in time.

```
GGSCI> ADD EXTRACT EXT2008D, TRANLOG, BEGIN NOW
```

Next, register the Exttrail information that the extract will use to write out captured data.

```
GGSCI> ADD EXTTRAIL ./dirdat/ET, EXTRACT EXT2008D
```

Start the extract and check its status. See Figure 11-17 for an example.

```
GGSCI> START EXT2008D
GGSCI> INFO ALL
```

At this point, the extract was created 13 seconds ago, as can be seen in the Time Since Chkpt column of the readout. Checkpoints are updated every 10 seconds by default, and once the extract has positioned itself to read from the BEGIN NOW point in time in the transaction log, the Time Since Chkpt will drop to under 10 seconds, as shown in Figure 11-18.

```
GGSCI> INFO ALL
```

Now that the extract is positioned and reading from the transaction log of database SourceDB, let's configure two separate Pump processes to read, send, and rewrite the transactions that the Extract process is capturing.

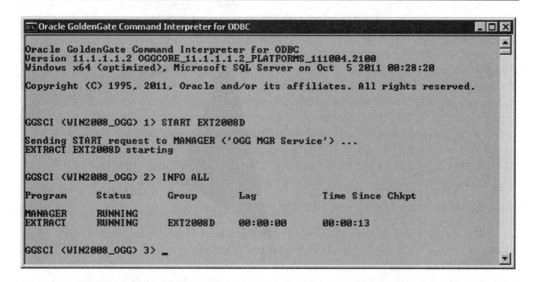

FIGURE 11-17. *Extract status*

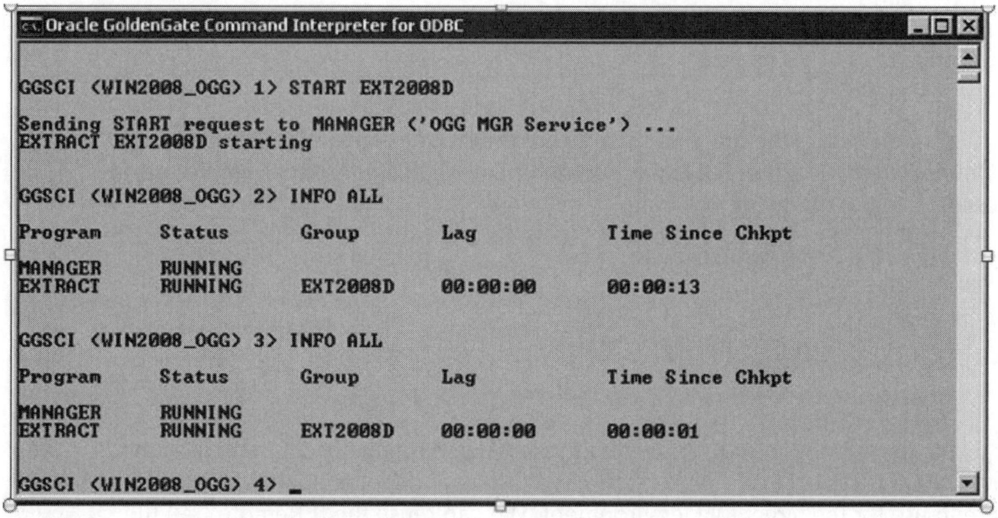

FIGURE 11-18. *Extract checkpointed*

A Pump process is used to send data that has been captured from the SQL Server database and written to a GoldenGate Exttrail file, to an RMTTRAIL or multiple remote trails, to be consumed by replicats. Although the Pump is an optional process, it is highly recommended in a production environment, as any network interruption only affects the Pump and would not affect an extract. If a Pump were not in use, network interruptions would cause the extract to abend and not be able to resume operations until network activity resumes. Depending on the length of such an outage, Extract may have to catch up by reading many transaction log backups, which is slower than reading from the transaction log itself.

Create one Pump to send to a SQL Server target installation of GoldenGate, and a second to an Oracle Enterprise Linux installation of GoldenGate to deliver to an Oracle database.

```
GGSCI> EDIT PARAMS PMP2008D
```

Add a set of base parameters to the Pump's parameter file including the Pump's name; the PASSTHRU parameter, which instructs the Pump not to parse the table definitions; the Remote Host information and RMTTRAIL locations; and the DML for the tables that we want to pump downstream to a target. In the source extract parameter, each table was listed separately, whereas for the Pump we use a wildcard designation. This means that any data that is in the trail with the dbo schema will get sent to the target RMTTRAIL.

```
EXTRACT PMP2008D
PASSTHRU
RMTHOST localhost MGRPORT 7809
RMTTRAIL ./dirdat/rt
TABLE dbo.*;
```

Save and close the file, and then repeat the steps to create the Pump to the Oracle Enterprise Linux (OEL) environment. Ensure that a distinct Pump name is used, as in the following example.

```
GGSCI> EDIT PARAMS PMPORCL
EXTRACT PMPORCL
PASSTHRU
RMTHOST remotehost MGRPORT 7810
RMTTRAIL ./dirdat/rt
TABLE dbo.*;
```

For this second pump, notice that the RMTHOST value is different, as is the MGRPORT value. This is the remote server name and GoldenGate Manager Port that are in use for the target OEL environment. We can reuse the rt Remote Trail file prefix since this target installation of GoldenGate is different than our installation on Windows.

Save and close the file.

Next, register the pumps with Oracle GoldenGate as in the following example.

```
GGSCI> ADD EXTRACT PMP2008D, EXTTRAILSOURCE ./dirdat/ET
GGSCI> ADD RMTTRAIL ./dirdat/rt, EXTRACT PMP2008D
GGSCI> ADD EXTRACT PMPORCL, EXTTRAILSOURCE ./dirdat/ET
GGSCI> ADD RMTTRAIL ./dirdat/rt, EXTRACT PMPORCL
```

These commands register Pump processes called PMP2008D and PMPORCL, which will be used as pumps for our sample configuration. The EXTTRAILSOURCE is the source data for the pumps, rather than a source database for an extract.

The RMTTRAIL must be registered as well and associated with its respective Pump process. The trail file location is a reference to a target installation of GoldenGate and will place the remote trail into the target installation's dirdat directory with a prefix of rt.

We've now configured the source Manager, Extract, and Pump processes, but we need to configure and start the target managers before starting the pumps, as the pump first communicates with the target manager, which then hands over communications between the pump and a target server collector.

Our SQL Server target installation of GoldenGate is the same as the source, so Manager is already running on port 7809.

Connect to the target OEL system and ensure that the Manager is configured and running on port 7810.

```
GGSCI > INFO MGR
Manager is running (IP port 7810)
```

Since both managers for the Windows and OEL installations of GoldenGate are up and running, start both pumps and verify their statuses, as seen in Figure 11-19.

```
GGSCI> START PMP*
GGSCI> INFO ALL
```

Now that the extract and both pumps are running, create the target SQL Server database and target tables for both SQL Server and Oracle.

In this sample configuration, we will use the same SQL Server instance and GoldenGate installation to house both source and target SQL Server databases and GoldenGate for SQL Server components. We will create a new target database, target System DSN, and replicat. We could just as easily create a new GoldenGate installation on the same server for the replicat only, but for simplicity's sake we will use the existing installation. If we had chosen to create a new GoldenGate installation on the same server, the Manager service name and port number would need to be different than the first installation.

Begin as in Figure 11-20 by creating a new target database.

The target database does not have to be set to FULL recovery, nor is a full database backup required. However, if the target database were to be used as a source in a multimaster configuration, then it would follow the same requirements as for a source database.

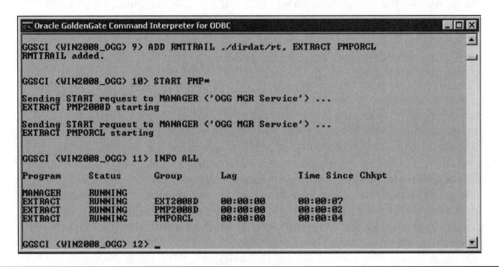

FIGURE 11-19. *Extract and Pump status*

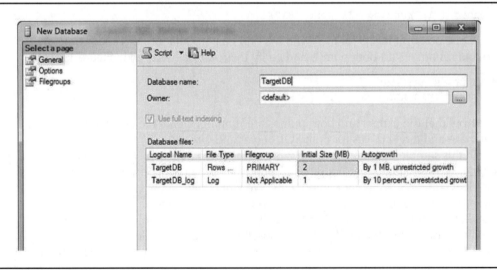

FIGURE 11-20. *Creating a target database*

Next, as in Figure 11-21, use Management Studio to execute the same demo_
mss_create.sql script against the target database as was run against the source. This
will create the exact same tables on the target as exist on the source.

Following the same steps that were used to create the source database System
DSN earlier, create a new System DSN for the target database, setting similar
options as you did for the source System DSN. In this example, the target database
is located on the same server and SQL Server instance as the source database, so
much of the configuration looks the same; however, note that the default database
to be used in the DSN will be the TargetDB.

Use the values in the following example to set in your new target database
data source.

```
Data Source Name: TargetSQLDB
  Server: .\SQL2008R2
  Authentication: Integrated Windows authentication
  Default Database: TargetDB
```

Now, create a minimally configured replicat to process the captured data as seen
in this example:

```
GGSCI> EDIT PARAMS REP2008D
```

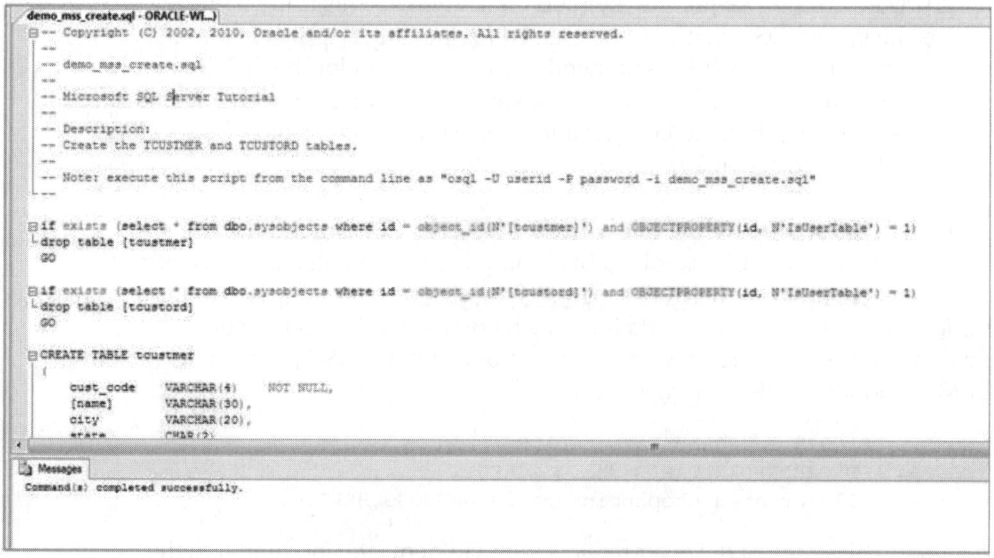

FIGURE 11-21. *Creating target tables*

Windows Notepad will open and prompt to save a new parameter file. Click Yes to accept, and type the following into the new Notepad document. When you are finished, save and close the document.

```
REPLICAT REP2008D
DBOPTIONS USEREPLICATIONUSER
TARGETDB TargetSQLDB
ASSUMETARGETDEFS
MAP dbo.*, TARGET dbo.*;
```

Let's review the parameters used for the replicat that are specific to GoldenGate for SQL Server.

- **DBOPTIONS USEREPLICATIONUSER**   This parameter is optional but must be placed above the TARGETDB parameter. By default, a replicat connects to SQL Server using ODBC over the System DSN created to the target database to retrieve table metadata and other information. Transaction delivery, however, utilizes OLE DB through the System DSN. This provides better performance over ODBC for transaction delivery.

  To complement the use of OLE DB, there is an option called DBOPTIONS USEREPLICATIONUSER that can be added to the replicat parameter file to take advantage of the NOT FOR REPLICATION option for certain SQL Server table objects.

- **TARGETDB <Target DB System DSN Name>**   This is the name of the system DSN that must be created for the target Apply database. If you're using a Windows authenticated connection for the DSN, no more information is needed; however, if you're using a SQL Server–authenticated connection, then the USERID and PASSWORD options must be specified with the correct information.

Each Replicat process, the one for SQL Server and for Oracle, will use a Checkpoint table. The Checkpoint table is an optional table that a replicat uses to update its activity in the delivery process of transactions. It's a backup to the replicat's CPE checkpoint file and is highly recommended for production environments. Create the Checkpoint table from within GGSCI, naming it with any DBMS-supported table-naming convention.

```
GGSCI> DBLOGIN SOURCEDB TargetSQLDB
GGSCI> ADD CHECKPOINTTABLE dbo.OGGCHKPT
Successfully created checkpoint table DBO.OGGCHKPT.
```

Now, register the SQL Server replicat with GoldenGate and bind it to the PMP2008D RMTTRAIL file, and to the newly created Checkpoint table.

```
GGSCI> ADD REPLICAT REP2008, EXTTRAIL ./dirdat/rt, CHECKPOINTTABLE dbo.OGGCHKPT
```

Start the replicat for SQL Server and check the status of the processes, as in Figure 11-22.

```
GGSCI> START REP2008D
GGSCI> INFO ALL
```

Now that the SQL Server extract, SQL Server replicat, and both pumps are running, create the target Oracle database tables and configure the Oracle database replicat on the OEL system.

Refer to Chapters 4 and 5 for installation instructions and configuration of GoldenGate for Oracle. You may use one of those installations of GoldenGate for Oracle as needed for the steps that follow.

The GoldenGate installation for Oracle also contains demo DDL scripts, and the demo_ora_create.sql script in the root GoldenGate directory will be used to create the same table structure on the target Oracle database as exists on the SQL Server source and target databases, with modifications to the data types that are needed for this DBMS.

Connect to your target Oracle database environment from the GoldenGate installation directory, and execute the demo_ora_create.sql script to create the target Oracle DB tables, as in the following example and in Figure 11-23.

```
$ sqlplus userid/password @demo_ora_create.sql
```

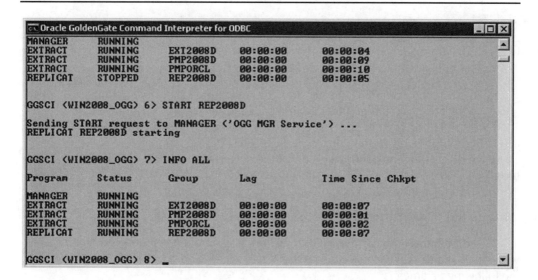

FIGURE 11-22. *Process status*

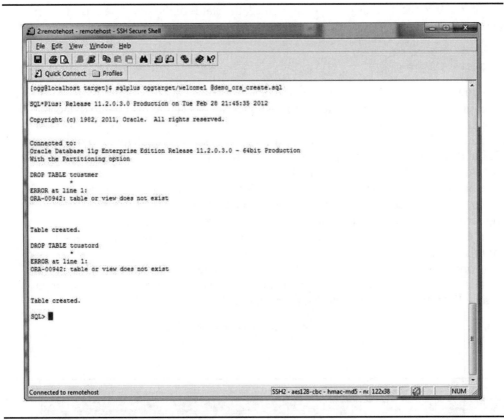

FIGURE 11-23. *Target Oracle database table creation script*

Next, create the SOURCEDEFS file from the source database table definitions
and copy the file to the dirdef directory in the OEL installation of GoldenGate.

Since this DBMS is a different one from the source database, we will use
a SOURCEDEFS file rather than the ASSUMETARGETDEFS parameter.

Begin by creating the parameter file that the defgen utility will use to produce
the SOURCEDEFS file.

On the source installation of GoldenGate, issue this command:

```
GGSCI> EDIT PARAMS SOURCESQLDEFS
```

The **edit params** command in GGSCI will once again open Windows Notepad
with the file name and extension set. Select Yes to accept and edit the file to include
the following parameters:

```
DEFSFILE <Full GoldenGate Source Installation Path>\dirdef\
sourcesqldefs.def
```

```
SOURCEDB SourceSQLDB
TABLE dbo.tcustmer;
TABLE dbo.tcustord;
```

The DEFGEN parameter file contains the full path which is required to write out the table definitions file. This file also contains the connection information to the source database, and the tables for which structure definitions are required.

Run the command to create the source table definitions file and view the output as in Figure 11-24.

GGSCI> SHELL DEFGEN PARAMFILE ./dirprm/sourcesqldefs.prm

Now copy or move this file to the target Oracle DB dirdef directory.

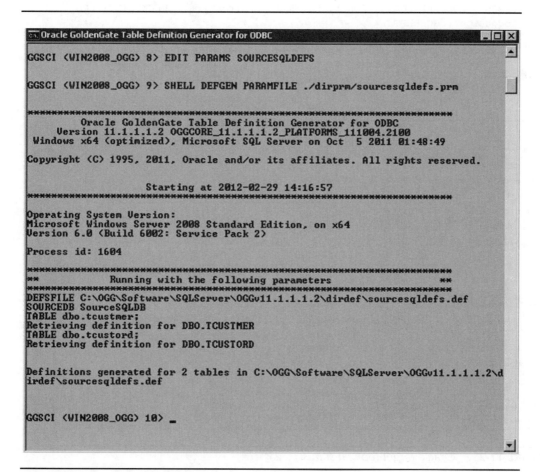

FIGURE 11-24. *DEFGEN output*

Configure the Oracle DB replicat with a minimal set of options that include the replicat name, database instance USERID and PASSWORD, Table Definition file location, and tables to replicate.

```
GGSCI> EDIT PARAMS REPORCL
REPLICAT REPORCL
USERID oggtarget, PASSWORD welcome1
SOURCEDEFS ./dirdef/sourcesqldefs.def
MAP dbo.*, TARGET oggtarget.*;
```

Save and close the REPORCL parameter file.
Create the Oracle DB Checkpoint table and register the replicat with the installation of GoldenGate.

```
GGSCI> DBLOGIN USERID oggtarget, PASSWORD welcome1
GGSCI> ADD CHECKPOINTTABLE oggtarget.OGGCHKPT
GGSCI> ADD REPLICAT REPORCL, EXTTRAIL ./dirdat/rt, CHECKPOINTTABLE
oggtarget.OGGCHKPT
```

Start the Oracle DB replicat and view the status as in Figure 11-25.

```
GGSCI> START REPORCL
GGSCI> INFO ALL
```

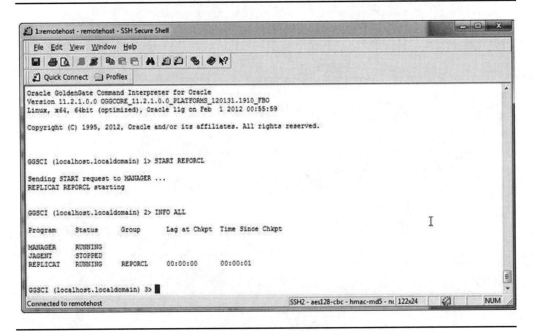

FIGURE 11-25. *Oracle target replicat status*

All replicats, pumps, and the extract for SQL Server are now running.

Apply some DML changes to the source SQL Server database and verify delivery to the target SQL Server and Oracle databases as seen in Figure 11-26. The GoldenGate installation directory for each DBMS also includes DML scripts to use against the demo tables that were created. In Management Studio, open the demo_mss_insert.sql script and run this against the source database.

Verify that the transaction was captured, and view the statistics for the SQL Server extract. See Figure 11-27 for report information from the **stats** command.

```
GGSCI> STATS EXT2008D TOTAL
```

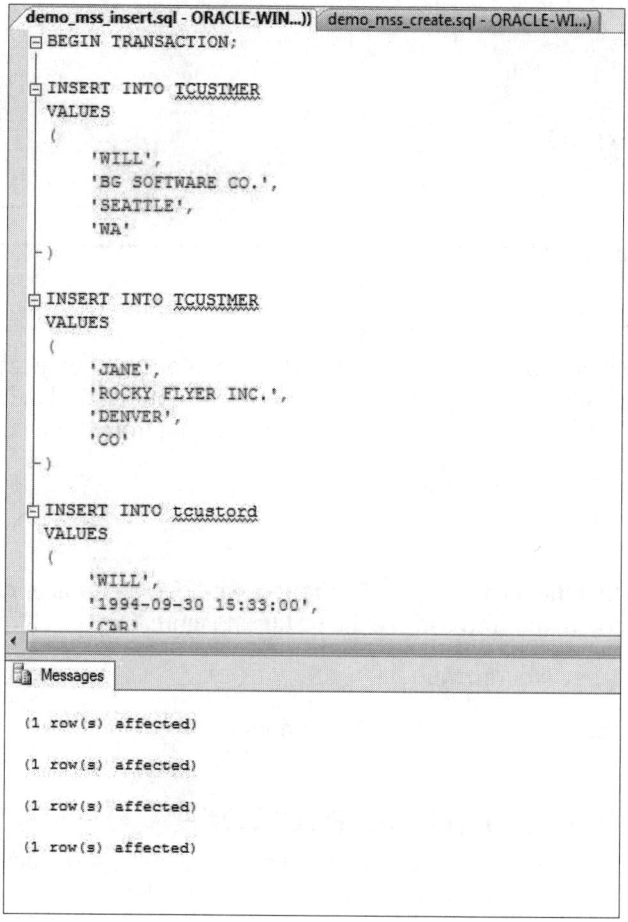

FIGURE 11-26. *Applying DML to source*

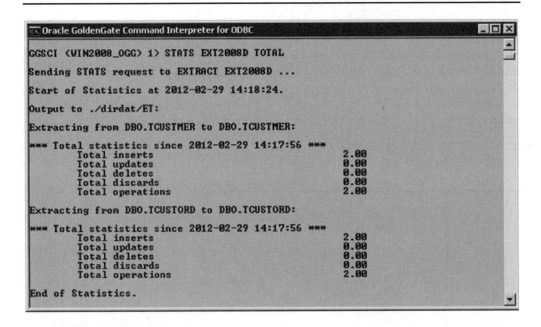

FIGURE 11-27. *Extract stats*

We can see that two inserts were captured for each of our source tables.

Verify that each OGG component in the topology captured and delivered the same data. See Figure 11-28 for an example of the output from these commands:

```
GGSCI> STATS PMP2008D TOTAL
GGSCI> STATS PMPORCL TOTAL
GGSCI> STATS REP2008D TOTAL
```

Now verify that the data was populated successfully to the Oracle database by using the **stats** command. You can see the results in Figure 11-29:

```
GGSCI> STATS REPORCL TOTAL
```

As you can see, the replication statistics show success.

Advanced GoldenGate for SQL Server

In the following section, we will go into detail on some of the more advanced configuration topics in using Oracle GoldenGate for SQL Server.

```
Oracle GoldenGate Command Interpreter for ODBC

GGSCI (WIN2008_OGG) 1> STATS PMP2008D TOTAL

Sending STATS request to EXTRACT PMP2008D ...

Start of Statistics at 2012-02-29 14:19:32.

Output to ./dirdat/rt:

Extracting from DBO.TCUSTMER to DBO.TCUSTMER:

*** Total statistics since 2012-02-29 14:17:57 ***
        Total inserts                          2.00
        Total updates                          0.00
        Total deletes                          0.00
        Total discards                         0.00
        Total operations                       2.00

Extracting from DBO.TCUSTORD to DBO.TCUSTORD:

*** Total statistics since 2012-02-29 14:17:57 ***
        Total inserts                          2.00
        Total updates                          0.00
        Total deletes                          0.00
        Total discards                         0.00
        Total operations                       2.00

End of Statistics.

GGSCI (WIN2008_OGG) 2> STATS PMPORCL TOTAL

Sending STATS request to EXTRACT PMPORCL ...

Start of Statistics at 2012-02-29 14:19:38.

Output to ./dirdat/rt:

Extracting from DBO.TCUSTMER to DBO.TCUSTMER:

*** Total statistics since 2012-02-29 14:17:57 ***
        Total inserts                          2.00
        Total updates                          0.00
        Total deletes                          0.00
        Total discards                         0.00
        Total operations                       2.00

Extracting from DBO.TCUSTORD to DBO.TCUSTORD:

*** Total statistics since 2012-02-29 14:17:57 ***
        Total inserts                          2.00
        Total updates                          0.00
        Total deletes                          0.00
        Total discards                         0.00
        Total operations                       2.00

End of Statistics.

GGSCI (WIN2008_OGG) 3> STATS REP2008D TOTAL

Sending STATS request to REPLICAT REP2008D ...

Start of Statistics at 2012-02-29 14:19:43.

Replicating from DBO.TCUSTMER to DBO.TCUSTMER:

*** Total statistics since 2012-02-29 14:18:01 ***
        Total inserts                          2.00
        Total updates                          0.00
        Total deletes                          0.00
        Total discards                         0.00
        Total operations                       2.00

Replicating from DBO.TCUSTORD to DBO.TCUSTORD:

*** Total statistics since 2012-02-29 14:18:01 ***
        Total inserts                          2.00
        Total updates                          0.00
```

FIGURE 11-28.   *Stats for Pump and Replicat*

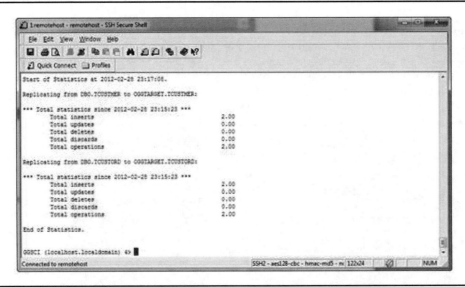

FIGURE 11-29. *Stats for Oracle Replicat*

Configuring Oracle GoldenGate in a Windows Clustering Environment

Oracle GoldenGate for SQL Server can be configured to work in a Windows clustered environment. The component of GoldenGate that gets added to the cluster is the Manager, which must be registered as a Generic Resource in the group that owns the SQL Server instance.

The disk device containing the installation folder for Oracle GoldenGate must also be in the same group as Manager.

Terminology differences exist between Windows 2003 Clustering and Windows 2008 Failover Clustering, but the concepts are similar.

Beginning on the node that currently owns the SQL Server instance group, install GoldenGate in a disk resource that is already a member of that group, or ensure that the disk resource gets added to the group that owns the SQL Server instance. Perform the installation of GoldenGate as if this were a standalone installation; create subdirectories, create the manager parameter file, install events, and so on.

Configure a GLOBALS file with the MGRSERVNAME option. Use of this parameter is optional for a single installation of GoldenGate that will be used within the cluster, but it is a must when multiple installations of GoldenGate will be in use, such as when one installation of GoldenGate runs under one cluster group on a node and a second instance of GoldenGate runs in another cluster group of a second node, such in an active-active configuration with multiple SQL Server instances.

Next, install Manager as is done in a nonclustered system, creating a service for the Manager:

```
SHELL INSTALL ADDSERVICE
```

Once the service is created, manually edit the service via the Windows Services applet and provide a Windows domain account for the Manager service to run under. Ensure that this domain account is in the Administrators group of all nodes in the cluster.

Next, create a Generic Service resource for the Manager within the group that contains the SQL Server instance. Configure this new Generic Service resource to run on all nodes available to the SQL Server instance and add dependencies for the SQL Server resource, and disk resources that house the database transaction logs and transaction log backups.

Ensure that the failover option "Affect the group" is not selected at this time, as you will need to move the group to the other nodes in the cluster later and install the Manager as a service on each.

Now, verify that the Manager can run on the node by starting the Manager service resource using the Cluster Administrator tool. If Manager starts successfully, stop it and manually move the group to the remaining nodes in the cluster. Once the group has been moved to each of the other nodes in the cluster, use GGSCI from the GoldenGate installation folder to install the Manager as a service on that node.

```
GGSCI> SHELL INSTALL ADDSERVICE
```

Edit the Manager service in the Services applet of each node to ensure that it is using the correct Windows domain account, and verify that the account is a member of the local Administrators group.

Next, bring the Manager resource online for each node via Cluster Administrator and confirm that the Manager service can run properly.

You can now move the group to the desired node and continue configuring the other components of GoldenGate.

Also, be sure that the System DSN that you create for the GoldenGate components on the first node is also created the exact same as on the other nodes in the cluster.

For environments that cannot afford to move groups from one node to another in order to configure GoldenGate, create a new group that will contain only the Manager Generic Service resource and the disk group that will contain the GoldenGate installation folder. This does require a separate disk group to be used, one that is not used by the SQL Server instance. Once this group exists, configure the Manager as a Generic Service resource as previously mentioned, add the disk resource to the group, and install GoldenGate on that disk. You can now move the group to the other nodes in the cluster and install the Manager as a service. When you have successes with all the nodes in the cluster, move this group back to the node that contains the SQL Server instance and move these resources into the group that contains the SQL Server instance. You can then delete this temporary group that was used to set up the Manager on the other nodes.

Maintaining the Transaction Log Secondary Truncation Point When Extract Is Stopped

When a Capture component is configured for a source database in SQL Server 2005 and SQL Server 2008/2008 R2 and there are no other SQL Server transactional publications or non–Oracle GoldenGate CDC configurations in use for that database, the Extract process must run with the TRANLOGOPTIONS MANAGESECONDARYTRUNCATIONPOINT parameter. The use of this parameter marks committed transactions as distributed (in other words, manages the secondary truncation point), as mentioned earlier, and therefore requires that the Extract process continue to run in order to maintain this truncation point.

Should the Extract process be stopped for an extended period of time, committed transactions in the transaction log will continue to queue up and not get rolled out by subsequent log backups. This could have the dire potential of eventually filling the transaction log and halting all new transactions.

Should an outage of extract occur for an extended period, you can manually create a SQL Server Agent job that performs the same task as the extract with the TRANLOGOPTIONS MANAGESECONDARYTRUNCATIONPOINT parameter.

To do so, create a SQL Server Agent job with an execution frequency of less than the interval between transaction log backups, such as every 15 minutes, and configure the job to start about a minute prior to the scheduled times for those transaction log backups.

The job needs to contain only one step, and that is to execute the following against the source Capture database:

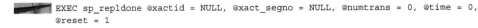

```
EXEC sp_repldone @xactid = NULL, @xact_segno = NULL, @numtrans = 0, @time = 0,
@reset = 1
```

IDENTITY Property on Columns in Multimaster Configurations

When columns exist in tables that use the IDENTITY property as a primary key or unique index, replication to another SQL Server target is handled by default without issue. However, if that SQL Server target also acts as another source database, such as in a multimaster configuration, then the IDENTITY seed and increment values must be staggered for each database.

For example, consider a two-node multimaster configuration of GoldenGate for SQL Server. Each database has the same table structure containing a column that uses the IDENTITY property, and each database acts as a source database to each other. Customers can perform DML against each database at the same time. In the case of a column enabled with the IDENTITY property, if two customers create a new record in the table on each of the separate databases, both records might contain the same value for the IDENTITY column. If TableA from DatabaseA is replicated to TableB on DatabaseB, and vice versa, then a constraint violation occurs because the primary key already exists on the replicated target. To remedy this, consideration must be given to the number of nodes in the topology that are configured as active-active to one another, and any column with the IDENTITY property enabled must be staggered accordingly to avoid such constraint violations.

For this two-node example, TableA from DatabaseA must have an Increment value of two (this is the number of nodes in the topology) and a seed value that will not occur through application DML on the other nodes(s).

Example:

```
TableA/DatabaseA: IDENTITY (0,2)
TableB/DatabaseB: IDENTITY (1,2)
```

Application DML on TableA will increment the IDENTITY column with values of 0,2,4,6, and so on, while application DML on TableB will increment the IDENTITY column with values of 1,3,5,7, and so on. Oracle GoldenGate will then be able to replicate this data from one database to the next without constraint violations.

For a three-node multimaster, seed and increment values would look like this example:

```
TableA/DatabaseA: IDENTITY (0,3)
TableB/DatabaseB: IDENTITY (1,3)
TableC/DatabaseC: IDENTITY (2,3)
```

Making DDL Changes to Existing Tables Configured for OGG

One of the more challenging aspects of database management when using Oracle GoldenGate for SQL Server is how to coordinate making table changes to a table currently configured for Capture or Apply, and timing these changes such that the GoldenGate process has already captured or delivered all of the current data that is using the existing structure of the table.

In an environment that has a maintenance window for the application, the situation is less problematic, as you can simply wait for GoldenGate to capture or deliver all of the current data in the transaction log or trail, stop the component, make the changes to the table, verify that supplemental logging is still enabled for a source table, and then restart the GoldenGate component and allow application data to continue.

For an environment that can't afford the luxury of application downtime, coordinating these events is crucial as you don't want an extract with an older cache of the table structure, capturing data from a table with an updated structure, and vice versa.

One means of coordinating when to stop an extract at the correct point in the transaction log prior to any table change is to use the EVENTACTIONS marker along with DDL triggers, which were introduced with SQL Server 2005. There is a knowledge document for this configuration available on the Oracle Support site, KM 1326758.1. We will list it here as reference for this configuration rather than repeating the setup verbatim.

The ALTARCHIVELOGDEST Extract Parameter

Oracle GoldenGate reference documentation unclearly defines this parameter as needed when transaction log backups are not written to their default location. This description adds confusion for readers who might have associated the data file default location with the database backup default locations, and the use of this option seems a requirement to some.

It has been my experience that this parameter, when needed, may not work as expected.

The option is supposed to be used if a DBA or operator, or whoever, manually moves the log backup from the location where it was taken by SQL Server, to a new folder, or changes the file name of the log backup. That's it. For example, suppose a database log is backed up with the following statement:

```
BACKUP LOG dbname TO DISK = 'C:\dbname_LogBackup.trn'
```

And now suppose once that database has completed, an operator either manually moves that log backup to a new folder, or even renames the file, before the extract has (if needed) had a chance to read from that log backup. The extract will report an error that it cannot find the required log backup.

If it is required that one must actually move or rename a log backup file for some reason before the extract has processed it, I would suggest moving it back to the original location and name.

If the use of this optional parameter does become required for the reasons stated, then thorough testing of its usage is recommended.

CHAPTER
12

Monitoring, Troubleshooting, and Performance Tuning GoldenGate

I n the earlier chapters you learned about GoldenGate installation, configuration, and the architecture. So now you should be able to perform all these activities and have a GoldenGate configuration up and running. The next important thing is the monitoring, troubleshooting, and tuning the performance of any GoldenGate process. Monitoring, troubleshooting, and performance tuning are very closely related topics. Many of the commands used in all of these activities are going to be the same. First we will talk about the monitoring part, covering how to monitor the status of various GoldenGate processes, and where to look if you need some detailed information about a process. Then we will move on to troubleshooting and talk about situations when some process is not getting started or is stopped with some error. Finally, we will discuss tuning the performance of various GoldenGate processes.

Monitoring Oracle GoldenGate

Like any other piece of enterprise software, GoldenGate also requires monitoring to ensure that everything is working fine. Oracle provides various tools to monitor GoldenGate. The purpose of monitoring could be to see if all the processes were working fine without any errors or to keep a check on the performance to see if it is meeting the required levels. Or the requirement could be as simple as finding the details of some GoldenGate process, for example, finding what tables are being replicated in an extract.

One of the most important aspects of monitoring is to ensure that all the processes are working fine and without any error. If any process has stopped with some error, the GoldenGate administrator needs to check that and take the corrective action.

In an environment with a large number of GoldenGate configurations, there has to be a strong monitoring strategy in place to take care of any errors or failures occurring in the environment. Any of the processes may stop working for a number of reasons. It could be related to some mistake made by some user, a tablespace getting full, no space left on disk, and so on. In many organizations, GoldenGate is used to send changes to various databases being used for management reporting purposes. In such cases it becomes even more critical to keep the data in sync with the production server. So there has to be an effective monitoring strategy in place to find or notice such scenarios and correct them as soon as they occur. There are many ways to achieve that goal. In this section first we will talk about the various options available for GoldenGate administration and monitoring.

GUI-Based Tools

There are two GUI-based tools available from Oracle that can be used to administer and monitor the GoldenGate configurations. The first product is Oracle GoldenGate Director, which was acquired by Oracle under the GoldenGate acquisition. It is a multitier configuration consisting of a database repository as back end, Oracle

GoldenGate Director Server running in a WebLogic domain, and various clients (Interface) that can be used for administration. The agents are installed on all the servers where GoldenGate is running and the Director Server pulls data through all these agents.

Another newer tool in the same line of products is Oracle GoldenGate Monitor. It is a separately licensed product and doesn't come included with the GG core product. It makes use of a very low-impact agent included with GoldenGate Version 11.1.1.1.1 and higher. The agent running on the server where GoldenGate runs collects the values for various metrics and sends the data to Oracle GoldenGate Monitor. You need to purchase a Management Pack license to use both these tools. Chapter 16 will cover these tools in detail.

NOTE
Both Oracle GoldenGate Monitor and Oracle GoldenGate Director are licensed separately from Oracle GoldenGate.

GGSCI

The second and the most commonly used option is the standard GoldenGate command-line interface, GGSCI. GGSCI provides various commands to perform the administration, monitoring, and troubleshooting of the GoldenGate processes. In this section first we will talk about the most commonly used commands to administer GoldenGate through the command line and then talk about how we can write some scripts and automate a task so that we are informed through an e-mail if any process ends or meets a failure. So let's get going and learn the most important of these commands.

The First Look

The most commonly used command to have a single look at all the GoldenGate processes is **info all**. It is probably the first command one fires after opening GGSCI. It shows all the GoldenGate processes running on the server where you are logged in. The basic information about lag and checkpoints is also displayed. Here is a sample output from our test machine:

```
GGSCI (goldengate1) 22> info allProgram
                  Status      Group        Lag             Time Since Chkpt
   MANAGER        RUNNING
   EXTRACT        RUNNING     DPHR01       00:00:00         00:00:01
   EXTRACT        RUNNING     EXHR01       00:00:00         00:00:01
   GGSCI (goldengate1) 23>
```

It shows a total of three GoldenGate processes running on this server: a Manager, an Extract process, and an Extract Pump.

To view more detailed information about a GoldenGate process, we can use the **info** command like this:

 `INFO {EXTRACT|REPLICAT} <group> [DETAIL]`

Let's use this command on an extract from the preceding output and check out the details.

```
GGSCI (goldengate1) 23> info extract EXHR01 detail
EXTRACT     EXHR01    Last Started 2012-04-03 09:41   Status RUNNING
Checkpoint Lag        00:00:00 (updated 00:00:03 ago)
Log Read Checkpoint   Oracle Redo Logs
                      2012-04-08 21:13:04  Seqno 564, RBA 13641216
  Target Extract Trails:
  Remote Trail Name                          Seqno       RBA     Max MB
  ./dirdat/hr                                  2        1043       100
  Extract Source                     Begin           End
  /home/oracle/app/oracle/oradata/orcl/redo03.log 2012-03-31 20:10 2012-04-08 21:13
  /home/oracle/app/oracle/oradata/orcl/redo03.log 2012-03-28 10:14 2012-03-31 20:10
  /home/oracle/app/oracle/oradata/orcl/redo02.log 2012-03-20 10:01 2012-03-28 10:14
  Not Available                      * Initialized *  2012-03-20 10:01

Current directory       /home/oracle/app/GoldenGate
Report file             /home/oracle/app/GoldenGate/dirrpt/EXHR01.rpt
Parameter file          /home/oracle/app/GoldenGate/dirprm/exhr01.prm
Checkpoint file         /home/oracle/app/GoldenGate/dirchk/EXHR01.cpe
Process file            /home/oracle/app/GoldenGate/dirpcs/EXHR01.pce
Stdout file             /home/oracle/app/GoldenGate/dirout/EXHR01.out
/* Note - the error log is very important to find the reasons for
the failures of extract or replicat processes */
Error log               /home/oracle/app/GoldenGate/ggserr.log
GGSCI (goldengate1) 24>
```

The detail shows us many pieces of information.

> **NOTE**
> *Extract and Pump both are basically Extract processes. The only difference is that the Extract process does the job of scanning the local redo log files (or the archive files, if required) and writing the committed changes to GoldenGate trail files, while the Extract Pump process is responsible for reading from these trail files and creating remote trail files on the target server.*

Another important use of the **info** command is to view the checkpoint information. The usage is like this:

 `INFO {EXTRACT|REPLICAT} <group> [SHOWCH]`

Let's run this command for the extract we created in the previous chapters:

```
GGSCI (goldengate1) 2> info extract exhr01 showch
EXTRACT     EXHR01     Last Started 2012-04-13 20:57    Status RUNNING
Checkpoint Lag         00:00:00 (updated 00:00:01 ago)
Log Read Checkpoint  Oracle Redo Logs
                       2012-04-13 21:26:01  Seqno 572, RBA 25759232
Current Checkpoint Detail:
Read Checkpoint #1
  Oracle Redo Log
  Startup Checkpoint (starting position in the data source):
    Sequence #: 571
    RBA: 22597136
    Timestamp: 2012-04-09 06:59:39.000000
    Redo File: /home/oracle/app/oracle/oradata/orcl/redo01.log
  Recovery Checkpoint (position of oldest unprocessed transaction in the
data source):
    Sequence #: 572
    RBA: 25758224
    Timestamp: 2012-04-13 21:26:01.000000
    Redo File: /home/oracle/app/oracle/oradata/orcl/redo02.log
  Current Checkpoint (position of last record read in the data source):
    Sequence #: 572
    RBA: 25759232
    Timestamp: 2012-04-13 21:26:01.000000
    Redo File: /home/oracle/app/oracle/oradata/orcl/redo02.log
  BR Previous Recovery Checkpoint:
    Sequence #: 0
    RBA: 0
    Timestamp: 2012-04-03 09:41:40.595712
    Redo File:
  BR Begin Recovery Checkpoint:
    Sequence #: 564
    RBA: 11696640
    Timestamp: 2012-04-03 20:26:54.000000
    Redo File:
  BR End Recovery Checkpoint:
    Sequence #: 564
    RBA: 11696640
    Timestamp: 2012-04-03 20:26:54.000000
    Redo File:
Write Checkpoint #1
  GGS Log Trail

  Current Checkpoint (current write position):
    Sequence #: 6
    RBA: 1043
    Timestamp: 2012-04-13 21:26:32.900214
    Extract Trail: ./dirdat/hr
Header:
  Version = 2
```

```
   Record Source = A
   Type = 4
   # Input Checkpoints = 1
   # Output Checkpoints = 1

File Information:
   Block Size = 2048
   Max Blocks = 100
   Record Length = 2048
   Current Offset = 0
Configuration:
   Data Source = 3
   Transaction Integrity = 1
   Task Type = 0
Status:
   Start Time = 2012-04-13 20:57:40
   Last Update Time = 2012-04-13 21:26:32
   Stop Status = A
   Last Result = 400
```

It tells us many details about this Extract process. In the beginning it shows the details about Startup, Recovery, and Current Checkpoints. The Startup Checkpoint is the position in the source redo logs where the Extract process started reading. The Recovery Checkpoint is the starting position of the oldest unprocessed transaction (in other words, the point from which the extract would start reading if restarted). The Current Checkpoint tells us about the position of the last record read (being currently read or was being read before the process stopped) by the Extract process. The Current Checkpoint also displays information on the current position of the write Checkpoint in the trail file.

Although the **info all** command shows the status of all the GoldenGate processes running on a server, there is another command called **status** that can be used to check the status of an individual GoldenGate process or a group of GoldenGate processes.

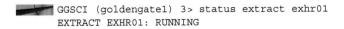

```
STATUS {MANAGER|MGR}
STATUS {EXTRACT|REPLICAT} <group>
```

```
GGSCI (goldengate1) 3> status extract exhr01
EXTRACT EXHR01: RUNNING
```

Process Reports and ggserr.log
Each GoldenGate process generates a log file called a *process report* where it records all the important messages like configuration details, environmental settings, and

runtime error messages. We can use the **view report** command to view the report for a particular GoldenGate process:

```
VIEW REPORT <group>
```

To view the report for a Manager process, we can use the **view report mgr** command as seen here:

```
VIEW REPORT MGR
```

Here is a sample report file for an extract.

```
GGSCI (goldengate1) 11> view report exhr01
**********************************************************************
                 Oracle GoldenGate Capture for Oracle
     Version 11.1.1.1.2 OGGCORE_11.1.1.1.2_PLATFORMS_111004.2100
   Linux, x86, 32bit (optimized), Oracle 11g on Oct  7 2011 15:32:42
Copyright (C) 1995, 2011, Oracle and/or its affiliates. All rights reserved.
                    Starting at 2012-04-13 21:49:11
**********************************************************************
Operating System Version:
Linux
Version #1 SMP Wed Sep 29 15:40:03 EDT 2010, Release 2.6.18-194.17.1.0.1.el5
Node: goldengate1
Machine: i686
                          soft limit    hard limit
Address Space Size    :    unlimited    unlimited
Heap Size             :    unlimited    unlimited
File Size             :    unlimited    unlimited
CPU Time              :    unlimited    unlimited
Process id: 3221
Description:
**********************************************************************
**              Running with the following parameters              **
**********************************************************************
EXTRACT EXHR01
USERID ggadmin, PASSWORD ******
EXTTRAIL ./dirdat/hr
TABLE HR.*;
Bounded Recovery Parameter:
BRINTERVAL = 4HOURS
BRDIR      = /home/oracle/app/GoldenGate
CACHEMGR virtual memory values (may have been adjusted)
CACHEBUFFERSIZE:                     64K
CACHESIZE:                            2G
CACHEBUFFERSIZE (soft max):           4M
CACHEPAGEOUTSIZE (normal):            4M
PROCESS VM AVAIL FROM OS (min):     2.79G
CACHESIZEMAX (strict force to disk): 2.58G
2012-04-13 21:49:11  INFO    OGG-01639  BOUNDED RECOVERY:  ACTIVE: for object pool
1: p14563_extr.
2012-04-13 21:49:11  INFO    OGG-01640  BOUNDED RECOVERY: recovery start XID:
0.0.0.
2012-04-13 21:49:11  INFO    OGG-01641  BOUNDED RECOVERY: recovery start position:
SeqNo: 564, RBA: 11692560, SCN: 0.12803
```

```
297 (12803297), Timestamp: 2012-04-03 20:26:54.000000.
2012-04-13 21:49:11  INFO    OGG-01642  BOUNDED RECOVERY: recovery end position:
SeqNo: 564, RBA: 11696640, SCN: 0.1280329
7 (12803297), Timestamp: 2012-04-03 20:26:54.000000.
2012-04-13 21:49:11  INFO    OGG-01643  BOUNDED RECOVERY: CANCELED: for object
pool 1: p14563_extr.
2012-04-13 21:49:11  INFO    OGG-01579  BOUNDED RECOVERY: VALID BCP:
CP.EXHR01.000000011.
2012-04-13 21:49:11  INFO    OGG-01629  BOUNDED RECOVERY: PERSISTED OBJECTS
RECOVERED: <<NONE TO RECOVER>>.
Database Version:
Oracle Database 11g Enterprise Edition Release 11.2.0.2.0 - Production
PL/SQL Release 11.2.0.2.0 - Production
CORE    11.2.0.2.0      Production
TNS for Linux: Version 11.2.0.2.0 - Production
NLSRTL Version 11.2.0.2.0 - Production

Database Language and Character Set:
NLS_LANG environment variable specified has invalid format, default value will be
used.
NLS_LANG environment variable not set, using default value AMERICAN_AMERICA.
US7ASCII.
NLS_LANGUAGE     = "AMERICAN"
NLS_TERRITORY    = "AMERICA"
NLS_CHARACTERSET = "AL32UTF8"

Warning: your NLS_LANG setting does not match database server language setting.
Please refer to user manual for more information.

2012-04-13 21:49:12  WARNING OGG-01423  No valid default archive log destination
directory found for thread 1.
2012-04-13 21:49:12  INFO    OGG-01513  Positioning to Sequence 572, RBA 27091984.
2012-04-13 21:49:12  INFO    OGG-01516  Positioned to Sequence 572, RBA 27091984,
Apr 13, 2012 9:48:59 PM.
2012-04-13 21:49:12  INFO    OGG-01055  Recovery initialization completed for
target file ./dirdat/hr000006, at RBA 1043.
2012-04-13 21:49:12  INFO    OGG-01478  Output file ./dirdat/hr is using format
RELEASE 10.4/11.1.
2012-04-13 21:49:12  INFO    OGG-01026  Rolling over remote file
./dirdat/hr000006.
2012-04-13 21:49:12  INFO    OGG-01053  Recovery completed for target file
./dirdat/hr000007, at RBA 1043.
2012-04-13 21:49:12  INFO    OGG-01057  Recovery completed for all targets.
*************************************************************************
**                    Run Time Messages                             **
*************************************************************************
2012-04-13 21:49:12  INFO    OGG-01517  Position of first record processed
Sequence 572, RBA 27091984, SCN 0.12864804, Apr
 13, 2012 9:48:59 PM.
GGSCI (goldengate1) 12>
```

There is a special command, **view ggsevt**, which can be used to view the contents from the ggserr.log file. The gsserr.log file is a special file that records messages related to various processes: startup, stops, exception conditions, and errors. The information about various commands run from GGSCI, rolling over the trail files, and so on is also recorded in this file.

```
GGSCI (goldengate1) 16> view ggsevt
2012-03-18 05:50:30  INFO    OGG-00987  Oracle GoldenGate Command Interpreter for
Oracle:  GGSCI command (oracle): edit params mgr.
2012-03-18 05:50:39  INFO    OGG-00987  Oracle GoldenGate Command Interpreter for
Oracle:  GGSCI command (oracle): start mgr.
2012-03-18 05:50:39  INFO    OGG-00983  Oracle GoldenGate Manager for Oracle,
mgr.prm:  Manager started (port 7809).
2012-03-18 05:51:41  INFO    OGG-00987  Oracle GoldenGate Command Interpreter for
Oracle:  GGSCI command (oracle): send mgr  status.
2012-03-19 10:25:50  INFO    OGG-00987  Oracle GoldenGate Command Interpreter for
Oracle:  GGSCI command (oracle): add trandata hr.*.
2012-03-19 10:34:32  INFO    OGG-00987  Oracle GoldenGate Command Interpreter for
Oracle:  GGSCI command (oracle): edit params mgr.
2012-03-19 10:34:41  INFO    OGG-00987  Oracle GoldenGate Command Interpreter for
Oracle:  GGSCI command (oracle): stop mgr.
2012-03-19 10:34:42  INFO    OGG-00963  Oracle GoldenGate Manager for Oracle,
mgr.prm:  Command received from GGSCI on host 192.168.0.109 (STOP).
2012-03-19 10:34:42  WARNING OGG-00938  Oracle GoldenGate Manager for Oracle,
mgr.prm:  Manager is stopping at user request.
2012-03-20 10:02:13  INFO    OGG-00992  Oracle GoldenGate Capture for Oracle,
exhr01.prm:  EXTRACT EXHR01 starting.
2012-03-20 10:02:13  ERROR   OGG-00303  Oracle GoldenGate Capture for Oracle,
exhr01.prm:  Unrecognized parameter (EXTRAIL).
2012-03-20 10:02:13  ERROR   OGG-01668  Oracle GoldenGate Capture for Oracle,
exhr01.prm:  PROCESS ABENDING.
2012-03-20 10:02:33  INFO    OGG-00987  Oracle GoldenGate Command Interpreter for
Oracle:  GGSCI command (oracle): edit params exhr01].
2012-03-20 10:02:42  INFO    OGG-00987  Oracle GoldenGate Command Interpreter for
Oracle:  GGSCI command (oracle): edit params exhr01.
2012-03-20 10:02:52  INFO    OGG-00987  Oracle GoldenGate Command Interpreter for
Oracle:  GGSCI command (oracle): start e*.
2012-03-20 10:02:52  INFO    OGG-00963  Oracle GoldenGate Manager for Oracle,
mgr.prm:  Command received from GGSCI on host 192.168.0.109 (START EXTRACT EXHR01 ).
--More--(5%)
```

NOTE
We can also use any OS-based text file editor (for example, Notepad on Windows and vi on UNIX/ Linux) to view the parameter and report file for any of the GoldenGate processes. The default location for storing the parameter files would be $GGHOME/ dirprm, and for report files it would be $GGHOME/ dirrpt. In fact, it will be a better option to view the ggserr.log file, especially as the size of this file becomes really large when GoldenGate has been running for a few days.

NOTE
GoldenGate maintains one file as a process report file for each of the Extract and Replicat processes. In total it maintains a total of 10 versions of the report files for each process. The latest report file is named <PROCESS NAME>.rpt and a number from 0 to 9 is appended to the names of the old report files, 9 being for the oldest one. Whenever any of the processes is restarted, the existing report file is renamed to <PROCESS NAME>0.rpt and a new report file is written that is named <PROCESS NAME>.rpt.

Monitoring Statistics

We can use the **stats** command to monitor the statistics related to Extract and Replicat processes. For the Extract process, it will show the number of records captured from redo logs or archive logs. For the Replicat process, it will show the number of records applied in the target database. It will also show the number of rejected records (for example, due to some database error), if any. The usage of the **stats** command is shown in the following example:

```
STATS {EXTRACT|REPLICAT},
{<STATISTIC>},
{<TABLE>},
{<TOTALSONLY>},
{<REPORTDETAIL | NOREPORTDETAIL>},
{REPORTRATE <HR|MIN|SEC}
```

The simplest use of the **stats** command could be like this:

```
stats replicat rphr01
```

That will show us the stats for all the tables for replicat RPHR01. Here is a trimmed output:

```
GGSCI (goldengate2) 21>stats rphr01

Sending STATS request to REPLICAT RPHR01 ...
Start of Statistics at 2012-05-29 10:09:07.
Replicating from HR.JOBS to HR.JOBS:
*** Total statistics since 2012-05-29 09:56:12 ***
        Total inserts                           1.00
        Total updates                           0.00
        Total deletes                           0.00
        Total discards                          0.00
        Total operations                        1.00
```

```
*** Daily statistics since 2012-05-29 09:56:12 ***
        Total inserts                           1.00
        Total updates                           0.00
        Total deletes                           0.00
        Total discards                          0.00
        Total operations                        1.00
*** Hourly statistics since 2012-05-29 10:00:00 ***
        No database operations have been performed.
*** Latest statistics since 2012-05-29 09:56:12 ***
        Total inserts                           1.00
        Total updates                           0.00
        Total deletes                           0.00
        Total discards                          0.00
        Total operations                        1.00
End of Statistics.
GGSCI (goldengate2) 22>
```

The output is self-explanatory and shows the statistics of operations on table HR.JOBS.

In an environment where a large number of tables are being replicated, such output may not be of much use. We would rather stick to checking the statistics of a particular table or the total statistics for all the tables in the replicat. Suppose we want to see how many records are being processed per minute for a specific replicat. The REPORTRATE option is there at our disposal.

```
stats replicat rphr01, totalsonly *, reportrate min
```

So here we are asking GoldenGate to give us the statistics for replicat RPHR01, display only the totals for all the tables, and it should display the number of operations happening per minute. Here is a sample output:

```
GGSCI (goldengate2) 23> stats replicat rphr01, totalsonly *, reportrate min
Sending STATS request to REPLICAT RPHR01 ...
Start of Statistics at 2012-05-29 10:14:44.
Cumulative totals for specified table(s):
*** Total statistics since 2012-05-29 09:56:12 ***
        Total inserts/minute:                   0.05
        Total updates/minute:                   0.05
        Total deletes/minute:                   0.05
        Total discards/minute:                  0.00
        Total operations/minute:                0.16
*** Daily statistics since 2012-05-29 09:56:12 ***
        Total inserts/minute:                   0.05
        Total updates/minute:                   0.05
        Total deletes/minute:                   0.05
        Total discards/minute:                  0.00
        Total operations/minute:                0.16
*** Hourly statistics since 2012-05-29 10:00:00 ***
        No database operations have been performed.
```

```
*** Latest statistics since 2012-05-29 09:56:12 ***
        Total inserts/minute:              0.05
        Total updates/minute:              0.05
        Total deletes/minute:              0.05
        Total discards/minute:             0.00
        Total operations/minute:           0.16
End of Statistics.
GGSCI (goldengate2) 24>
```

It didn't display anything in Hourly Statistics as it was only recently that we started this replicat. We can use the **latest** option to view the latest statistics for a process.

```
GGSCI (goldengate2) 9> stats replicat rphr01, latest
Sending STATS request to REPLICAT RPHR01 ...
Start of Statistics at 2012-05-29 18:32:50.
Replicating from HR.JOBS to HR.JOBS:
*** Latest statistics since 2012-05-29 09:56:12 ***
        Total inserts                      1.00
        Total updates                      0.00
        Total deletes                      0.00
        Total discards                     0.00
        Total operations                   1.00

Replicating from HR.REGIONS to HR.REGIONS:
*** Latest statistics since 2012-05-29 09:56:12 ***
        Total inserts                      0.00
        Total updates                      0.00
        Total deletes                      1.00
        Total discards                     0.00
        Total operations                   1.00
Replicating from HR.DEPARTMENTS to HR.DEPARTMENTS:
*** Latest statistics since 2012-05-29 09:56:12 ***
        Total inserts                      0.00
        Total updates                      1.00
        Total deletes                      0.00
        Total discards                     0.00
        Total operations                   1.00
End of Statistics.
GGSCI (goldengate2) 10>
```

This could be especially useful in a scenario where you have made some changes to improve the performance of the Replicat process and would like to check the new processing rate. Using the **reset** option, the statistics in the **latest** field can be reset.

```
stats replicat rphr01, reset
```

Similarly, using all the other available options, we can view the counters that interest us. To see all the available options with the **stats** command, issue the **help stats** command with either the **extract** or **replicat** options from the GGSCI prompt.

Monitoring Lag

Oracle GoldenGate provides the **lag** command to monitor the lag for different Extract or Replicat processes. The **info all** command also shows the lag, but that information is taken from the last record that was checkpointed. The **lag** command calculates lag on the basis of the current record being processed. So both of them could report a different value for lag for the same process. Here are examples of using the **lag** command:

```
GGSCI (goldengate1) 6> lag extract exhr01
  Sending GETLAG request to EXTRACT EXHR01 ...
  Last record lag: 2 seconds.
  At EOF, no more records to process.

GGSCI (goldengate1) 7> lag extract *
  Sending GETLAG request to EXTRACT DPHR01 ...
  No records yet processed.
  At EOF, no more records to process.

  Sending GETLAG request to EXTRACT EXHR01 ...
  Last record lag: 2 seconds.
  At EOF, no more records to process.
```

The output shows that there was a latency of two seconds between the time when GoldenGate processed the record and the time in the data source, and there are no more records to process. The process is idle, just waiting for the new transactions to happen.

There is another way to get the same output: using GETLAG with the **send** command. It can be used like this:

```
SEND {EXTRACT | REPLICAT} {GROUP | WILDCARD}, GETLAG
```

We will discuss more about lag and what to do when a process reports a lag in the "Performance Tuning" section of this chapter.

So far, we have covered two methods of monitoring GoldenGate processes. One uses the GUI and another one uses the GoldenGate command-line tool, GGSCI.

In environments with a large number of GoldenGate implementations, it becomes practically impossible to manually monitor each and every process. In such a scenario either we can rely on some GUI-based tool like Oracle GoldenGate Director or Oracle GoldenGate Monitor, or we can do some shell scripting work and make use of GGSCI to meet our requirements. Basically, what we want to see is whether all the processes are running fine and the lag is within acceptable limits. If there is some process that is stopped or abended, we should get an e-mail. Here is a sample shell script that does the basic task of informing us if any of the GoldenGate processes is abended or stopped. This script can be enhanced to capture more details as per your requirement.

Create a shell script called infoall.sh:

```
/home/oracle/app/GoldenGate/ggsci << EOF
info all
EOF
```

Now create another shell script (let's call it send_alert.sh) from which we are calling infoall.sh and sending an e-mail if any of the processes is abended or stopped.

```
cd /home/oracle/app/GoldenGate
a=`./info_all.sh |egrep -i 'STOPPED|ABENDED'|wc -l`
if [ $a -gt 0 ]
then
./info_all.sh |egrep -i 'STOPPED|ABENDED' > /tmp/infoall.log
#<mail logic goes here>
fi
```

When the e-mail is sent, the text from /tmp/infoall.log will be included in the body.

Monitoring and troubleshooting are very closely related topics. Some additional details about the commands discussed here and their use will be discussed in the "Troubleshooting" section.

Now that we have learned the about the **info all** command, perhaps the most important command used in monitoring GoldenGate, let's move on to the "Troubleshooting" section.

Troubleshooting

In the previous section about monitoring, we took a look at the various GoldenGate commands we can use to find detailed information about different processes. Some commands also help us in knowing the various statistics about Extract and Replicat processes. Now here we are, ready to take our journey into troubleshooting GoldenGate.

In this section we will first talk about a general troubleshooting methodology for GoldenGate, like what to do and where to look when someone comes and tells you that their data is not being replicated or is not in sync. Then we will move on to discuss some extract and replicat troubleshooting scenarios. Finally we will discuss how to use TRACE and LOGDUMP facilities to investigate GoldenGate issues or help Oracle Support with the investigation.

Common Methodology

As we discussed in the last section about monitoring, the most frequently used commands are **info**, **status**, **lag**, and **view report**. The very same commands are used while troubleshooting an issue with any of the GoldenGate processes. That's convenient, isn't it?!

In GoldenGate each process creates a report file where it writes the various pieces of information and also the error messages, if any. When we're trying to troubleshoot any GoldenGate process, the report file is our primary source of information. Most of the errors can be seen in report files, and then we can take the appropriate corrective action depending upon the nature of the error. Errors related to syntax, inclusion of nonexistent tables, invalid mapping in a replicat, issues with the network, and so on all can be seen logged in the report file of the respective process. A Manager process that experiences any errors while starting will write the error message in its report file. Similarly, the **info** and **lag** commands can be used to view the details of process and lag in processing respectively.

Now that we are aware of the basic methods used for troubleshooting, let's get our hands dirty and take a look at some of the most commonly occurring practical scenarios.

Commonly Used Diagnostic Tools

A number of different tools can be used by the Oracle GoldenGate administrator to diagnose problems with GoldenGate processes. These tools include GGSCI, the GoldenGate command-line interface, and STRACE. Let's look at each of these tools in a bit more detail next:

GGSCI

We have already introduced you to the GGSCI in several chapters of this book. GGSCI is the tool that is used to control Oracle GoldenGate operations and is used to start the various Extract, Replicat, and Manager processes. GGSCI is also used to produce various reports that will be used to diagnose problems with the GoldenGate replication infrastructure, as you will see throughout this chapter. Please see Chapters 3, 4, and 5 for more information on the Oracle GoldenGate GGSCI utility.

STRACE

STRACE is a UNIX utility that provides the ability to trace UNIX system calls and services called. We have provided some examples of using STRACE later in this chapter, but it is actually rare that you will experience a problem so bad that you need to use STRACE. Generally, if the problem is bad enough to use STRACE, you need to contact Oracle Support.

Common Extract Performance and Error Issues

In this section we will talk about some of the error scenarios with Extract and Extract Pump processes: The common errors you will see are access-related errors and network-related errors. Let's look at each of these types of errors in more detail next.

Access-Related Errors

Access-related errors occur if the GoldenGate Extract process tries to read an archive log file, but the Extract process does not have the proper permissions to do so. There can be many reasons for this error. The most likely reason is that there could be a user running an Extract process that is trying to access the directory where archive log files are stored, and they do not have permissions to access that directory. In some cases, the Extract process may report this error even in a case where the archive log it is searching for doesn't exist. In such a case, you need to restore the required archive log file and restart the Extract process.

Network-Related Errors

Network-related errors will also occur. Most of these network errors will be seen on the source (Extract) side. They may include an Extract Pump not being able to reach the target server, or the speed of transfer of trail files being really slow. The most common reason for the Connection Refused errors is some firewall (or some other obstruction in the connectivity) between the source and the target. In some of these cases, the Extract Pump process doesn't abend, but you will see Connection Timed Out (or other similar) messages being printed in the report file and ggserr.log. After a certain number of retries, finally the process will abend.

```
2012-04-08 21:51:19  WARNING OGG-01223  TCP/IP error 110 (Connection timed out).
2012-04-08 22:04:36  WARNING OGG-01223  TCP/IP error 110 (Connection timed out).
2012-04-08 22:07:55  WARNING OGG-01223  TCP/IP error 110 (Connection timed out).
2012-04-08 22:11:14  WARNING OGG-01223  TCP/IP error 110 (Connection timed out).
```

An OS-level trace of the Extract process could be really helpful in such a scenario. If we run STRACE on the Extract Pump process, it clearly shows the error:

```
[oracle@goldengate1 GoldenGate]$ ps -ef |grep dphr01
oracle   19057  2887  0 21:48 ?        00:00:00
/home/oracle/app/GoldenGate/extract PARAMFILE
/home/oracle/app/GoldenGate/dirprm/dphr01.prm REPORTFILE
/home/oracle/app/GoldenGate/dirrpt/DPHR01.rpt PROCESSID DPHR01 USESUBDIRS
oracle   20661 18686  0 22:16 pts/1    00:00:00 grep dphr01
[oracle@goldengate1 GoldenGate]$
[oracle@goldengate1 GoldenGate]$ strace -T -p 19057
Process 19057 attached - interrupt to quit
connect(17, {sa_family=AF_INET, sin_port=htons(7809), sin_addr=inet_
addr("192.168.0.110")}, 16) = -1 ETIMEDOUT (Connection timed out)
<77.226714>
<output trimmed>
```

Check with your network administrator to find out where the connection is being blocked. You can check it using telnet to connect to the correct IP and port as seen in this example:

```
[oracle@goldengate2 GoldenGate]$ telnet 192.168.0.110 7809
Trying 192.168.0.110...
Connected to goldengate2 (192.168.0.110).
Escape character is '^]'.
quit
^]
telnet> quit
Connection closed.
```

Here is an example of what you might see if the connections are being blocked:

```
[oracle@goldengate2 GoldenGate]$ telnet 192.168.0.110 7809
Trying 192.168.0.110...
telnet: connect to address 192.168.0.110: Connection timed out
telnet: Unable to connect to remote host: Connection timed out
```

What About Missing Archivelog Files?

If there are long-running transactions in a database and they involve the tables that GoldenGate is replicating, you may face an error of missing archivelog files if bounded recovery is disabled. Bounded recovery is a feature that was added in GoldenGate Version 11.1.1 to ensure an efficient recovery after the Extract process stops for any reason: error, planned or unplanned. It sets an upper boundary for the maximum amount of time it should take the extract to recover to the point where it was before. As per its normal behavior, the Extract process keeps the information about all the ongoing transactions in the cache. The moment it finds that some transaction has been committed, it writes that information to the trails and clears it from the cache. If some transaction is rolled back, the Extract process simply clears that information from the memory. Now in case the Extract process gets stopped for any reason, all this information in the cache would be lost, and on the next restart it has to be built again by scanning the old archive log files (beginning from the start time of the oldest transaction), resulting in a lot of redundant work. Bounded recovery solves this problem by making bounded recovery checkpoints at regular intervals (specified by the BRINTERVAL option of the BR parameter) and flushing the current state and data of the extract to disk. In case the Extract process stops, upon restart it doesn't need to scan all the old archive logs to recapture the information about all the open transactions because the information is already saved in the bounded recovery files. In this case, the Extract process needs to do minimal work to reach the position where it was before getting stopped.

But you may need the archive files if bounded recovery is disabled (not recommended). Let's assume that the Extract process was stopped and that there was a transaction running for five hours, and by the time the Extract process was restarted, the archive logs for this transaction duration were backed up to tape. So now to capture the changes made by this transaction, GoldenGate will need all the old archive log files for this duration. And if they aren't present at the default location, it is going to complain. If we check the report file of the Extract process, this is what we'll see:

```
2012-04-09 00:04:20  ERROR   OGG-00446  Could not find archived log for sequence
564 thread 1 under default destinations SQL <SELECT  name     FROM
v$archived_log   WHERE sequence# = :ora_seq_no AND         thread# = :ora_thread
AND          resetlogs_id = :ora_resetlog_id AND        archived =
 'YES' AND         deleted = 'NO>, error retrieving redo file name for sequence
564, archived = 1, use_alternate = 0Not able to establish initial p
osition for sequence 564, rba 29499920.
2012-04-09 00:04:20  ERROR   OGG-01668  PROCESS ABENDING.
```

Here GoldenGate is complaining about the missing archive sequence number 564. In such a case, you need to restore the archive log and restart the Extract process.

> **NOTE**
> *If you have some alternate directory where you move the archive logs from the default archive location for the database, then you can use the ALTARCHIVELOGDEST option of the TRANLOGOPTIONS parameter to make GoldenGate aware of it. GoldenGate will first check the default location and if it can't find the archive logs there, it will check in the directory pointed to by ALTARCHIVELOGDEST. Add the following line to the extract parameter file:*
> *TRANLOGOPTIONS ALTARCHIVELOGDEST /u01/ orcl/alternate_dest*

■ **Stuck in recovery**   An Extract process may appear to be stalled after you restart it after a failure. Only committed transactions are written in trails, so if there was any long-running transaction that is still open when you restart the Extract process, it has to scan the archive logs or bounded recovery files since the time when the oldest running (still open) transaction started. The Extract process keeps all the information about the uncommitted transactions in the cache, so it would be lost the moment it stops. So there could be a volume of archive logs to be processed before the Extract process starts scanning the current redo logs. It may appear to be stuck or stalled. You can verify the status by sending the **status** command. If it is doing the recovery, it should display a message similar to either of the following messages:

```
In recovery[1] - Extract is recovering to its input checkpoint.
In recovery[2] - Extract is recovering to its output checkpoint.
```

If you see one of these messages, it means the Extract process is recovering some old transactions and in some time it will resume scanning the current redo logs.

NOTE
If there are frequent long-running transactions in your database, you should ensure that enough space is available to keep the archive logs of that duration on the disk; otherwise, you may encounter frequent extract abend issues due to missing archive log files. Also you will want to make sure that the trail file sizes are large enough.

- **Manager process and DYNAMICPORTLIST** You may face a scenario where an Extract Data Pump process is not able to transfer any trail files to the target. One of the reasons for that could be that you are working in a secure environment where all the ports aren't open. You haven't used DYNAMICPORTLIST in the manager parameter file to define a range of ports on the target, so the Manager process assigns any random port to the Collector, which may be blocked in your environment. In such a case you can use the DYNAMICPORTLIST parameter to define a range of ports on the target side and get those ports opened at the firewall and restart the target Manager process.

NOTE
You can use OS utilities like TRUSS/STRACE to troubleshoot such issues. Run TRUSS or STRACE for the OS-level process of the Extract Pump process and see the log.

- **Trails not rolling over** Sometimes you may find that trail files aren't rolling over. One of the most common reasons for that could be that the trail file size hasn't reached the specified size. You can use the info **exttrail** * or info **rmttrail** * commands to see the specified size and then verify the actual size of the trail file.

If the trail size limit hasn't been reached yet you might want to change the trail file size. To do this you can use the **alter exttrail** or **alter rmttrail** commands with the MEGABYTES option:

```
alter exttrail ./dirdat/hr, extract exhr01, megabytes 20
```

You may face the opposite issue as well, where the trail files roll too fast. In such a case you may need to increase the trail file size to some larger value.

■ **Syntax errors** You may hit some syntax error in the beginning itself. You are trying to use some new parameter and it just doesn't work. The CHECKPARAMS parameter comes to the rescue in such scenarios. Whenever you want to check the syntax of a parameter file, put the CHECKPARAMS parameter in the parameter file for the extract and start it. It will check the syntax of the parameters and stop. The output can be seen using the **view report** command. Let's first use CHECKPARAMS on the very first extract parameter file we created in Chapter 5. Here are the minimum contents of the parameter file and CHECKPARAMS added at the top.

```
GGSCI (goldengate1) 17> view params EXHR01
CHECKPARAMS
EXTRACT EXHR01
USERID ggadmin, PASSWORD ggadmin
EXTTRAIL ./dirdat/hr
TABLE HR.*;
GGSCI (goldengate1) 18>
```

■ Now we start the extract EXHR01 and view the report.

```
GGSCI (goldengate1) 18> view report EXHR01
************************************************************************
                 Oracle GoldenGate Capture for Oracle
      Version 11.1.1.1.2 OGGCORE_11.1.1.1.2_PLATFORMS_111004.2100
   Linux, x86, 32bit (optimized), Oracle 11g on Oct  7 2011 15:32:42
<some output trimmed>
************************************************************************
**            Running with the following parameters             **
************************************************************************
CHECKPARAMS
EXTRACT EXHR01
USERID ggadmin, PASSWORD *******
EXTTRAIL ./dirdat/hr
TABLE HR.*;
Parameters processed successfully.
GGSCI (goldengate1) 19>
```

As you can see in the last part of the example, it has displayed the message "Parameters processed successfully." Now let's try introducing some syntax error and then running the extract with CHECKPARAMS parameters. So we make a change like the following:

```
EXTTRAIL ./dirdat/hr ^^
```

(Two "^" signs have been added at the end.)

Now let's start the extract with the CHECKPARAMS parameter enabled and view the report file.

```
<text truncated>
EXTTRAIL ./dirdat/hr   ^^
2012-04-01 10:31:43  ERROR   OGG-00435  Must be PURGE, APPEND, RESTART, MEGABYTES
or MAXFILES.
2012-04-01 10:31:43  ERROR   OGG-01668  PROCESS ABENDING.
```

So it stops at the line where there is a syntax error and prints some relevant error message.

Optionally, if you also want to validate the tables, you can include the NODYNAMICRESOLUTION parameter along with CHECKPARAMS. Let's add NODYNAMICRESOLUTION to our existing params file and start the extract.

```
GGSCI (goldengate1) 21> view params exhr01
CHECKPARAMS
NODYNAMICRESOLUTION
EXTRACT EXHR01
USERID ggadmin, PASSWORD ggadmin
EXTTRAIL ./dirdat/hr
TABLE HR.*;
GGSCI (goldengate1) 22>
```

Now if we view the report, you will notice that it has validated all the tables also. Here is the relevant part of the extract report file.

```
TABLE HR.*;
TABLEWildcard  resolved (entry HR.*):
  TABLE HR.COUNTRIES;

Using the following key columns for source table HR.COUNTRIES: COUNTRY_ID.
TABLEWildcard  resolved (entry HR.*):
  TABLE HR.DEPARTMENTS;
Using the following key columns for source table HR.DEPARTMENTS: DEPARTMENT_ID.
TABLEWildcard  resolved (entry HR.*):
  TABLE HR.EMPLOYEES;
Using the following key columns for source table HR.EMPLOYEES: EMPLOYEE_ID.
TABLEWildcard  resolved (entry HR.*):
  TABLE HR.JOBS;
Using the following key columns for source table HR.JOBS: JOB_ID.
TABLEWildcard  resolved (entry HR.*):
  TABLE HR.JOB_HISTORY;
Using the following key columns for source table HR.JOB_HISTORY: EMPLOYEE_ID,
START_DATE.
TABLEWildcard  resolved (entry HR.*):
```

```
   TABLE HR.LOCATIONS;
Using the following key columns for source table HR.LOCATIONS: LOCATION_ID.
TABLEWildcard  resolved (entry HR.*):
   TABLE HR.REGIONS;
Using the following key columns for source table HR.REGIONS: REGION_ID.
Parameters processed successfully.
```

But what if there is some table that actually doesn't exist in the database? No problem. It is going to complain about that, too. Let's try with some table name that actually doesn't exist in the HR schema and then see how the CHECKPARAMS parameter works. Here are the contents of our parameter file:

```
CHECKPARAMS
NODYNAMICRESOLUTION
EXTRACT EXHR01
USERID ggadmin, PASSWORD ggadmin
EXTTRAIL ./dirdat/hr
TABLE HR.NO_SUCH_TABLE;
```

Now let's start the Extract process and view the report. Here is the output from the relevant part of the report:

```
TABLE HR.NO_SUCH_TABLE;
  2012-04-01 10:44:27  ERROR   OGG-00901  Failed to lookup object ID for table
HR.NO_SUCH_TABLE.
  2012-04-01 10:44:27  ERROR   OGG-01668  PROCESS ABENDING.
```

So the CHECKPARAMS parameter can be used to check for all kind of syntax errors in extract parameter files. The same method can be used to check replicat parameter files as well.

NOTE
After you are done troubleshooting the syntax errors, remember to remove the CHECKPARAMS parameters; otherwise the Extract or Replicat process will keep on stopping after completing the syntax check.

Other Common Problems

There are a couple of issues that tend to show up from time to time when trying to replicate a table. One of the most common errors returned from GoldenGate is that it fails to look up the object ID for the table being replicated. This is typically a result of not having enabled supplemental logging on the database. A common error you might find if supplemental logging is not enabled is the following:

```
"Failed to lookup object ID for table HR.COUNTRIES."
```

Another error that occurs occasionally is that you will try to replicate a table that is set to NOLOGGING. While you can configure a table set to NOLOGGING for replication, errors might occur during the replication process due to the NOLOGGING configuration. So, make sure your tables are set to LOGGING. A common error you might encounter if a table is configured for NOLOGGING would be

```
"The table is created with the NOLOGGING option, which is not supported."
```

Common Replicat Issues

In this section we will talk about some of the issues that you may encounter with the GoldenGate Replicat process.

Database-Related Errors

The Replicat process simply runs the DML that was captured by the Extract process. It may encounter the same errors that a normal DML operation in a database can. We will discuss various database-related errors and the possible remedies for them:

- *ORA-01653: unable to extend table string.string by string in tablespace string.* In such a case you just need to add some free space to the tablespace and restart the Replicat process.

- To maintain data integrity the Replicat process may encounter errors like *ORA-00001: unique constraint (string.string) violated* or *ORA-01403: no data found*. In such cases the Replicat process prints this error message along with the sequence number and the redo byte address (RBA) and abends. The details of the rejected record(s) are printed in the discard file (it is always a recommended practice to use a discard file with a Replicat process). With the help from the error message and the details in the discard file, we can troubleshoot such errors. ORA-00001 will occur in case of an insert. It means that the record GoldenGate is trying to insert already exists in the database. So to maintain data integrity, the Replicat process abends. In such a scenario you need to investigate why the record already exists in the database. At the end of this section we will see some scenarios where you may face such errors. ORA-01403 can occur with an update or a delete operation. In case of a Replicat process, this error means that the record GoldenGate wants to update or delete doesn't exist in the target database or has already been modified, and using its specified criteria, GoldenGate can't locate that record. Let's first see an example of such a scenario and then we will move on to the possible reasons for such errors.

Our replicat RPHR01 is abended, and if we view the report file, it shows:

```
2012-04-09 03:26:53  WARNING OGG-01004  Aborted grouped transaction on 'HR.JOBS',
Database error 1403 ().
2012-04-09 03:26:53  WARNING OGG-01003  Repositioning to rba 1699 in seqno 3.
2012-04-09 03:26:53  WARNING OGG-01154  SQL error 1403 mapping HR.JOBS to HR.JOBS.
2012-04-09 03:26:53  WARNING OGG-01003  Repositioning to rba 1699 in seqno 3.
```

As we saw, this error is related to a missing record (indicated by "Database error 1403 ()"). Our next stop is the discard file. Let's view the contents of the discard file now:

```
Current time: 2012-04-09 03:26:53
Discarded record from action ABEND on error 1403
Aborting transaction on dirdat/hr beginning at seqno 3 rba 1699
                      error at seqno 3 rba 1699
Problem replicating HR.JOBS to HR.JOBS
Record not found
Mapping problem with delete record (target format)...
*
JOB_ID = PRES
*
Process Abending : 2012-04-09 03:26:53
```

So the discard file points us to a record with JOB_ID=PRES and this error is related to a delete statement. Now let's query the target database using the same condition.

```
SQL> select * from jobs where job_id='PRES';
no rows selected
SQL>
```

GoldenGate was right. There is actually no such record in the target database. Which record should the replicat delete? When it couldn't locate the record, it abended.

Let's see another example related to *ORA-00001: unique constraint (string.string) violated* before we move on to discuss the possible reasons of such errors. The contents of the report file are as follows:

```
2012-04-09 04:19:15  WARNING OGG-00869  OCI Error ORA-00001: unique constraint
(HR.JOB_ID_PK) violated (status
= 1), SQL <INSERT INTO "HR"."JOBS"
("JOB_ID","JOB_TITLE","MIN_SALARY","MAX_SALARY") VALUES (:a0,:a1,:a2,:a3)>.
2012-04-09 04:19:15  WARNING OGG-01004  Aborted grouped transaction on 'HR.JOBS',
Database error 1 (OCI Error O
RA-00001: unique constraint (HR.JOB_ID_PK) violated (status = 1), SQL <INSERT INTO
"HR"."JOBS" ("JOB_ID","JOB_T
ITLE","MIN_SALARY","MAX_SALARY") VALUES (:a0,:a1,:a2,:a3)>).
2012-04-09 04:19:15  WARNING OGG-01003  Repositioning to rba 1883 in seqno 3.
2012-04-09 04:19:15  WARNING OGG-01154  SQL error 1 mapping HR.JOBS to HR.JOBS OCI
Error ORA-00001: unique cons
traint (HR.JOB_ID_PK) violated (status = 1), SQL <INSERT INTO "HR"."JOBS"
("JOB_ID","JOB_TITLE","MIN_SALARY","MAX_SALARY") VALUES (:a0,:a1,:a2,:a3)>.
```

It clearly tells us that an insert has failed due to error ORA-00001. Now let's open the discard file and see some more details:

```
OCI Error ORA-00001: unique constraint (HR.JOB_ID_PK) violated (status = 1), SQL
<INSERT INTO "HR"."JOBS" ("JOB
_ID","JOB_TITLE","MIN_SALARY","MAX_SALARY") VALUES (:a0,:a1,:a2,:a3)>
Aborting transaction on dirdat/hr beginning at seqno 3 rba 1883
                         error at seqno 3 rba 1883
Problem replicating HR.JOBS to HR.JOBS
Mapping problem with insert record (target format)...
*
JOB_ID = PRES
JOB_TITLE = President
MIN_SALARY = 6000
MAX_SALARY = 10000
*
Process Abending : 2012-04-09 04:19:15
```

So it tells us that GoldenGate wanted to insert a row with JOB_ID=PRES but it got ORA-00001 while trying to do that. If we try to query the database to see if that record already exists, we will get this result:

```
SQL> select * from jobs where job_id='PRES';
    JOB_ID     JOB_TITLE                                      MIN_SALARY MAX_SALARY
    ---------- ----------------------------------------        ---------- ----------
    PRES       President                                            6000      10000
SQL>
```

Oh yes! GoldenGate is right again. That record it is trying to insert already exists in the database; hence the error!

NOTE
Here in both these cases these errors were generated by doing some manual DMLs on the target side.

Now let's move on to discuss the possible reasons that may cause these errors to happen:

■ You have some scheduled jobs on the target side that are modifying the data. In such a case, before the Replicat process tries to replicate the changes, the rows have already changed and the process can't locate the records it is interested in. At one of the customer sites we were replicating a complete schema from one database to another. We did the initial load multiple times, but every time we were hitting one or another error on start of the Replicat process. Finally, after spending a lot of time it was found that while taking expdp of the schema and then doing impdp on the target side, the scheduled jobs were getting created and they were changing the data before GoldenGate could start its work.

- Some users are connected to the database and they are manually making some changes by running ad hoc SQLs. If the target database is a reporting database and the users have the privileges to run the DML, they may change the data by running some ad hoc DMLs.

- You have some triggers enabled in the target database. As GoldenGate has already captured the DML being run from the trigger (on the source side), so you may run into various errors when the same statement is run for the second time.

- If you have a highly customized configuration, like not replicating all the columns or a table and you have missed defining KEYCOLS. The Extract and Replicat processes may be using a different set of columns to uniquely identify the rows. In some of such cases, the Replicat process may abend with 1403() errors. Always make sure that Extract and Replicat processes make use of the same columns as KEYCOLS on the source and target sides respectively.

- Another reason for such errors could be an improper initial load. It is recommended to use the SCN method (see Metalink note 1276058.1 for details) for doing the initial load because that avoids any overlapping of transactions, hence greatly reducing the likelihood of hitting such errors.

Hung Processes

Occasionally you may face the issue of some GoldenGate process getting hung. The most likely reasons for that to happen could be related to a break in network or some resource crunch on the OS level. In such a case it may appear to be running but actually won't be doing anything useful. You can view the OS-level trace of the process (TRUSS on Solaris and AIX, STRACE on Linux, and TUSC on HP-UX) to verify whether it is actually doing anything or not. In a scenario at one of the customer sites, none of the Extract Pump processes were able to send any files. In that case the Manager process was hung and was not able to start any Collector processes. Finally, killing the Manager process and restarting it resolved the issues.

Taking It Further

So far we have discussed the general troubleshooting methodology for various scenarios. In some cases you may need to dive even deeper. In this section we will discuss two more advanced options that GoldenGate provides. The first option is the TRACE option; using this option, we can generate various kind of traces for Extract or Replicat processes. The second option is the Logdump utility, which can be used to have a look at the information stored in the trail files. For example, when a Replicat process abends with the Database 1403(No Data Found) error, you may want to verify the same by looking at the values that are stored at that RBA. Logdump is what you need in such a case. Similarly, to find what exactly a process does before abending, you may need the GoldenGate TRACE option. It is equivalent to the similar options available in Oracle Database where we can generate trace at different levels to capture the different levels of detail. So let's talk about these two options.

Trace

Just like any other piece of software, GoldenGate also has the appropriate instrumentation built into it and we can see the details of the operations by enabling trace. There are two types of traces that GoldenGate provides: TRACE and TRACE2. Either of them can be enabled by using the **send** command. For example, to enable TRACE or TRACE2 for a Replicat process, we can use

```
SEND REPLICAT RPHR01, TRACE rphr01.trc
```

Similarly, to enable TRACE2, we can replace the keyword TRACE with TRACE2. To disable the trace for any process we can use

```
SEND REPLICAT RPHR01, TRACE/TRACE2 OFF
```

The TRACE option dumps the step-by-step processing information to the trace file whereas TRACE2 enables us to see where the Extract or Replicat process is spending its time. This could be especially useful while looking into the details, such as what exactly some process is doing, or when you are working on a support ticket with Oracle for some performance-related issue. They will request TRACE and TRACE2 files for diagnosing the issues related to performance.

Logdump

The Logdump utility helps us in viewing, filtering, searching, and saving the data that is stored in the trail files. As it directly plays with the data, it is recommended to use it under the guidance of Oracle Support or some experienced GoldenGate user. The interface provided by Logdump is similar to the GGSCI prompt. There are various commands that we can use to open the trail files and search, view, and save the data from them. To start the Logdump utility, go to the $GG_HOME directory and start Logdump:

```
[oracle@goldengate2 GoldenGate]$ ./logdump
Oracle GoldenGate Log File Dump Utility
Version 11.1.1.1.2 OGGCORE_11.1.1.1.2_PLATFORMS_111004.2100
Copyright (C) 1995, 2011, Oracle and/or its affiliates. All rights
reserved.
Logdump 1 >
```

The next step is to open the trail file we are interested in, but before that there are a few things we need to do. We need to configure the logdump utility so that it displays the details we want to see, the way we want to see them. To do so we configure logdump by using the commands **ghdr**, **detail**, and **usertoken**. Examples of the use of these commands and a quick description of their use is seen here:

```
Logdump 1 >ghdr on --Enables the display of record header that contains
information about the transaction
Logdump 2 >detail on -Enables the display of column information
Logdump 3 >detail data -Enables the display of data in Hex and ASCII format
Logdump 4 >usertoken on -Enables display of user defined custom information
```

To view the current values of various parameters in the current environment, you can use the **env** command:

```
Logdump 5 >env
  Version                 : Linux, x86, 32bit (optimized) on Oct  5 2011 00:04:52

  Current Directory       : /home/oracle/app/GoldenGate
  LogTrail                : *Not Open*
  Display RecLen          : 140
  Logtrail Filter         : On
  Show Ghdr               : On
  Detail                  : Data
  UserToken               : On
  Trans History           : 0 Transactions, Records 100, Bytes 100000
  LargeBlock I/O          : On, Blocksize 57344
  Local System            : LittleEndian
  Logtrail Data           : BigEndian/ASCII
  Logtrail Headers        : ASCII
  Dump                    : ASCII
  Savefile comments       : Off
  Timeoffset              : LOCAL
  Scan Notify Interval: 10000 records, Scrolling On
  Logdump 6 >
```

We are ready to open the trail file now. In most cases, you (or Oracle Support) will be interested in viewing a particular record at some specific RBA in some specific trail file.

We will use the **open** command to open a trail file and the **pos** command to position the pointer to the RBA we are interested in viewing. Pressing N (short for NEXT) displays the record details. Suppose we want to view the record at RBA 1412 in sequence 4. Let's follow these steps:

```
Logdump 24 >open /home/oracle/app/GoldenGate/dirdat/hr000004
Current LogTrail is /home/oracle/app/GoldenGate/dirdat/hr000004
Logdump 25 >pos 1412
Reading forward from RBA 1412
Logdump 26 >n

Hdr-Ind    :    E  (x45)    Partition  :   .  (x04)
UndoFlag   :    .  (x00)    BeforeAfter:   A  (x41)
```

```
RecLength   :     53   (x0035)    IO Time     : 2012/04/14 08:54:45.996.128
IOType      :      5   (x05)      OrigNode    :   255  (xff)
TransInd    :      .   (x03)      FormatType  :     R  (x52)
SyskeyLen   :      0   (x00)      Incomplete  :     .  (x00)
AuditRBA    :           573       AuditPos    : 12874768
Continued   :      N   (x00)      RecCount    :     1  (x01)

2012/04/14 08:54:45.996.128 Insert              Len     53 RBA 1412
Name: HR.DEPARTMENTS
After  Image:                                      Partition 4   G  s
 0000 000a 0000 0000 0000 0000 0118 0001 0007 0000 | ...................
 0003 4e45 5700 0200 0a00 0000 0000 0000 0000 cd00 | ..NEW..............
 0300 0a00 0000 0000 0000 0009 c4                   | ............
Column      0 (x0000), Len    10 (x000a)
 0000 0000 0000 0000 0118                           | ..........
Column      1 (x0001), Len     7 (x0007)
 0000 0003 4e45 57                                  | ....NEW
Column      2 (x0002), Len    10 (x000a)
 0000 0000 0000 0000 00cd                           | ..........
Column      3 (x0003), Len    10 (x000a)
 0000 0000 0000 0000 09c4                           | ..........
Logdump 27 >
```

The display tells us many details, for example, this is an **insert** statement. The time of the DML is also displayed. Also this operation was done on the HR.DEPARTMENTS table. We can see RBA 1412 being displayed; that means that this record is located at RBA 1412 in sequence 4 (the trail file we opened). It could be especially useful for Oracle Support personnel while troubleshooting some weird replicat abend errors. Details provided by Logdump help in checking the record details, hence helping us to know what information was written in the trail files.

Performance Tuning

As with any performance tuning endeavor, performance tuning in GoldenGate is part art, part science. This chapter covers GoldenGate settings to improve throughput, thus reducing the overall replication lag. However, there are many factors culminating in slow performance that are outside the control of GoldenGate. CPU, disk I/O, and network and database access are important items that should also be investigated and monitored during any GoldenGate performance tuning exercise. The real performance tuning should start right from the time when you are starting with the initial load. Depending on the volume of the data involved, a lot of time may be wasted in initial load itself if proper performance measures are not taken.

Tuning the Initial Load

A number of GoldenGate configurations involve Oracle as source and target databases. Given the fact that a large number of enterprises run Oracle Database 10g or 11g, Data Pump is the most common method used for initial load. There are a few things you can do to minimize the time taken for the initial load.

expdp and impdp

The Oracle Database Data Pump utilities (not to be confused with a GoldenGate Data Pump Extract process) expdp (Export Data Pump) and impdp (Import Data Pump) are logical backup and recovery tools that provide a way to instantiate the target database schemas that will be replicated to. These tools enable you to extract and import data into an Oracle database using a parallel option, which uses multiple workers for the export or import data pump job. This can significantly speed up your export or import process.

Depending on the resources available on the source and the target system, set the PARALLEL parameter to an appropriate value to take advantage of parallelism. Remember to use the same number of dump files as the value of the parallel parameter, as each worker process writes exclusively to a dump file. If the number of dump files specified is less than the value of PARALLEL, the number of active workers running at any time will be equal to the number of dump files specified, decreasing the overall throughput.

■ Oracle Database 11g provides an Advanced Compression option that can be used with expdp to compress the data before writing to the dump file. It can be useful in reducing the volume of data you need to transfer for initial load. In many of the scenarios, the source and target database are not on the same network and limited bandwidth is available for transferring of dump files. In such cases, Advanced Compression could be a really useful thing.

■ While importing the data on the target server for initial load, creating of indexes may need large sort area sizes; otherwise, it starts swapping to the TEMP tablespace, which slows down the index creation. If the circumstances allow, set PGA_AGGREGATE_TARGET to a higher value while importing the data for the initial load to speed up the index creation process and avoid swapping to the TEMP tablespace for sorting.

GoldenGate Lag

Understanding how GoldenGate reports lag is the key to uncovering performance bottlenecks. Examine Figure 12-1.

Each of the GoldenGate processes reports a different lag interval associated with transaction movement. All processes begin with a committed transaction timestamp in the source database. The Extract lag is the interval between the source record commitment and the timestamp of the record content placed in the source trail file.

You can observe lag readings with several different GGSCI commands. Submitting the command **info all** (sound familiar?) will give you general lag readings for all GoldenGate processes associated with a particular instance. More accurate lag readings can be obtained with the GoldenGate **lag** command. For example:

```
Lag extract Exhr01
```

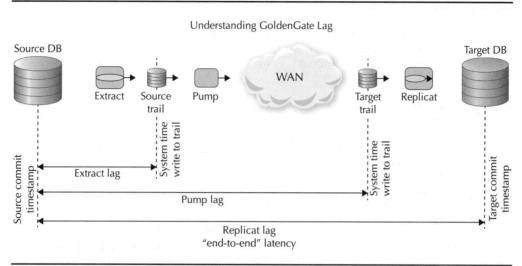

FIGURE 12-1.   *Understanding GoldenGate lag*

The **lag** command is a way to observe the current lag of the extract we created in Chapter 5. To get continuous lag readings automatically, you can add settings for the parameters LAGREPORT and LAGINFO in the Manager process. For example:

```
LAGREPORTMINUTES 5
LAGINFOMINUTES 0
```

LAGREPORTMINUTES is the interval at which the Manager checks for Extract and Replicat lag. LAGINFOMINUTES is the interval at which the Manager reports Extract and Replicat lag to the error log. Setting LAGINFOMINUTES to 0 forces the reporting interval to be the same as the LAGREPORTMINUTES.

The pump lag is the interval between the source record commitment and the timestamp of the record contents placed in the target trail file. The Replicat lag is the true overall lag. It is the interval between the source record commit and the commit to the target database. These different lag readings can be very useful to identify performance bottlenecks.

For example, if you have an Extract lag of 1 second, a Pump lag of 2 seconds, and a Replicat lag of 20 seconds, then the replication bottleneck is the Apply process to the target database within the replicat. If you have an Extract lag of 1 second, a Pump lag of 25 seconds, and a Replicat lag of 26 seconds, then you have a network issue associated with the pump.

Before You Begin

Observe lag readings over a period of time. Periodic fluxes in lag readings can be normal, especially if your application issues large transactions. Use the GoldenGate parameter REPORTCOUNT to observe processing rates in each of the GoldenGate process reports. For example:

```
Reportcount every 10000 records, rate
```

To view the REPORTCOUNT results, you use the **view report** command from the GGSCI command-line interface. Here's an example of viewing the REPORTCOUNT result:

```
Ggsci>view report reportcount
  12000 records processed as of 2011-01-01 12:27:40 (rate 203,delta 308)
```

The important parts of this output are the rate and delta statistics. The "rate" statistic represents the total number of records divided by the total time elapsed since the process started (in seconds). The "delta" statistic is the number of records since the last report divided by the time since the last report (in seconds).

You might want to determine specific GoldenGate statistics for one or more tables being processed by GoldenGate. Use the GGSCI **stats** command to report on the statistics of the operations performed for any table processed by GoldenGate since its last start. With the **stats** command, you can observe the tables receiving the highest use and highest level of DML. This can be a good place to start in your latency investigation. Here is an example of using the **stats** command to extract various information on the tables that GoldenGate has processed:

```
Ggsci> Stats extract Exhr01, total, table account reportrate sec
```

This statement will display the total statistics per second of the account table.

Usually, one Extract, Pump and Replicat process is sufficient for many replication scenarios. Tune these processes using the procedures described in the rest of the chapter. If these efforts still result in poor or increasing lag, then consider parallelization. Any GoldenGate process can be parallelized.

NOTE
Remember that if a table has a foreign key constraint to another table, both those tables have to be in the same Replicat group, and in these cases parallelism is not possible. In these cases you would need to disable the referential references between the tables, which might not be desirable.

Let's look at the more popular parameters you can use in each GoldenGate process to reduce latency.

Extract Lag

The largest part of the Extract process's work involves reading redo log files in a circular fashion to look for the transactions being committed. So one of the most important factors in the extract performance is that your redo logs should reside on the fastest disk available to you. Also, the recommended RAID configuration for placement of redo logs is RAID 1+0. Another important factor to focus on could be the number and size of the redo logs in the database. Ideally, you shouldn't see any significant Log File Sync wait events and any CHECKPOINT NOT COMPLETE messages in the alert log.

Remember, GoldenGate writes only committed transactions to the source trail file. Uncommitted transactions are placed into memory until the extract observes the commit. Very large transactions may reach the default memory limit for GoldenGate and spill to disk. Using the **send extract** command you can see if there is an issue with memory as seen here:

```
Send extract Exhr01 cachemgr cachestats
```

The result will be a report of the current usage of memory by that extract. If the GoldenGate default memory is not enough, then increase it by placing a CACHEMGR parameter into the extract. For example:

```
CACHEMGR CACHEBUFFERSIZE 64KB, CACHESIZE 500MB
```

The parameter EOFDELAYCSECS controls how often the Extract process checks for new data after it has reached the end of the current data in its data source. To reduce Extract lag, reduce the EOFDELAYCSECS value. However, reducing this value is not free. More I/O activity will occur on your system and database log sync times could increase. Make sure you monitor its impact.

FLUSHCSECS controls when the Extract process flushes its memory buffer. A fuller buffer will make a more efficient transport of data but can induce latency. Reducing this value can reduce your lag, but like EOFDELAYCSECS, it can incur additional I/O activity.

As we have discussed in previous chapters, tables without a primary key or unique indexes can cause unnecessary Extract lag. If GoldenGate cannot find a unique set of keys to identify a record, then the default behavior is to log all columns. This can be very costly with trail file space, especially if you have many large object data types associated with the record. For large tables with this condition, where you cannot add a unique index, consider using the GoldenGate KEYCOLS component in the TABLE parameter statement. KEYCOLS allows you to specify a set of columns to uniquely designate a record, thus reducing unnecessary column movement.

Pump Lag

Large lag values associated with a pump indicate network issues. Before you try to tune GoldenGate, examine your network for send and reply intervals and throughput capacity.

The GoldenGate parameter TCPBUFSIZE controls the size of the TCP socket buffer that the pump will try to maintain, allowing larger packet sizes to be sent to the target system. Increasing this value can reduce network lag. Work with your network administrator to ensure that the maximum socket buffer size for non-Windows systems is large enough to allow the TCPBUFSIZE parameter to work properly. TCPBUFSIZE is used in conjunction with the RMTHOST parameter. For example:

```
RMTHOST newyork, MGRPORT 7809, TCPBUFSIZE 100000, TCPFLUSHBYTES 100000
```

Activating GoldenGate network compression can improve performance but can also increase CPU consumption. GoldenGate compression is used in conjunction with the RMTHOST parameter. For example:

```
RMTHOST newyor, MGRPORT 7809, COMPRESS
```

If no filtering or data manipulation is required in the pump, then use the GoldenGate PASSTHRU parameter. PASSTHRU eliminates a database connection and table resolution, thus speeding up the trail movement process. If you are using the PASSTHRU parameter, be sure to remove any unnecessary USERID/PASSWORD parameter statements in the parameter file.

Replicat Lag

Increasing delay between the pump and Replicat lag is due to target database issues. Many factors will contribute to this outside GoldenGate. Check with your DBA for a properly sized and configured database. Check with your System Admin for disk I/O contention along with CPU availability and utilization.

Primary or Unique Key Issues   One culprit for large Replicat lag is a record commit resulting in a sequential update or delete because no index is present or utilized. This can be very costly if this is associated with a table with a large set of records. Remember, if GoldenGate cannot detect a primary key or unique index for a record, then all columns will be used to uniquely identify it. The Replicat report will list the action plan for each table it processes. It will tell you if GoldenGate is using an index for a table or it's defaulting to using all columns for the **update** or **delete** **where** clause. For example:

```
map OGGS.Customer, target oggt.Customer; Using following columns in default map
by name:   ID_NUM, S_NUM, FIRST_NAME, LAST_NAME  Using the following key columns
for target table OGGT.Customer: ID_NUM.
```

In this case the replicat found a unique key, ID_NUM, to update or delete the table Customer.

Examine this Replicat report statement:

```
MAP resolved (entry MySchema.LOAD_TRACKING):  MAP MySchema.LOAD_TRACKING, TARGET
MySchema.LOAD_TRACKING;  2011-07-21 13:28:46  WARNING OGG-00869  No unique key is
defined for table LOAD_TRACKING. All viable columns will be used to represent the
key, but may not  guarantee uniqueness.  KEYCOLS may be used to define the key.
Using following columns in default map by name:  TABLE_NAME, LAST_ADD_TS,
LAST_UPDT_TS, LAST_AUDT_TS  Using the following key columns for target table
MySchema.LOAD_TRACKING: TABLE_NAME, LAST_ADD_TS, LAST_UPDT_TS, LAST_AUDT_TS.
```

In the report output above, we see a warning that GoldenGate cannot find a unique key to apply to the target table LOAD_TRACKING. Because there is no unique key available, GoldenGate will use all of the columns of the table as the key when applying any update or delete's to the table.

Using the KEYCOLS qualifier to the mapping parameter, in association with an index associated with KEYCOLS columns, can improve performance significantly.

Using BATCHSQL in GoldenGate to Improve Throughput   The GoldenGate parameter BATCHSQL increases the throughput of Replicat processing by arranging similar SQL statements into arrays and applying them at an accelerated rate. This can be beneficial if you have transactions that are very similar and repetitive. For example, if you perform a large delete to a specific table, BATCHSQL can reduce costly target commits (and checkpoints) to the database.

Using GROUPTRANSOPS in GoldenGate to Improve Throughput   The GoldenGate parameter GROUPTRANSOPS can eliminate costly commits by grouping records into a singleton transaction. GROUPTRANSOPS works in conjunction with MAXTRANSOPS, which limits the number of transactions with a single commit. MAXTRANSOPS is not really necessary unless your target database is having difficulties handling large transactions. After activating these parameters, observe this behavior in the Replicat report to ensure that boundaries are not being broken for the original transaction.

Parallelization

Parallelizing a GoldenGate process can result in increased throughput but not without associated resource costs. When considering dividing data flows, ensure that you are not violating transaction or relational integrity. Use the same lag-reading technique described at the beginning of this chapter to determine which process requires parallelization.

Let's say you have a problem with a replicat not being able to apply records fast enough to the target database. You could create another replicat and divide the original map statements between the original and the new process. Both processes can continue to use the same target trail file, but they will work independently of each other and have separate pointer and checkpointing information.

Individual tables can be parallelized using the GoldenGate RANGE function. For example:

```
MAP sales.order_master, TARGET sales.order_master, FILTER (@RANGE (1, 2,
  order_ID));
```

In this mapping statement, the order_master table is being divided into two data sets based on a hash value of the Order_id column. The first data set (1 of 2) will be moved by the current replicat. Another replicat must be created with the complementary mapping:

```
MAP sales.order_master, TARGET sales.order_master, FILTER (@RANGE (2, 2,
  order_ID));
```

Parallelizing tables can be useful when large transaction volumes are applied, especially if a unique index cannot be utilized.

Fun stuff, isn't it? Remember, determining performance bottlenecks requires a thorough investigation. Making assumptions can waste many hours or days and lead to incorrect conclusions. Use both your system and GoldenGate tools to assist your investigation and correctly identify where adjustments are required to meet your throughput goal.

CHAPTER
13

Oracle GoldenGate
Monitor and Oracle
GoldenGate Director

Monitoring GoldenGate through commands and scripts can be effective and comprehensive. Sometimes, though, a nice tool to do the job is what is called for. The Management Pack for Oracle GoldenGate fills the bill. The Management Pack for Oracle GoldenGate improves and simplifies monitoring and reporting of GoldenGate. Additionally, the Management Pack for Oracle GoldenGate makes it easier to design, configure, and manage the entire replication environment. All of this is supported through an easy-to-use and intuitive GUI-based (graphical user interface) tool.

The Management Pack for Oracle GoldenGate license consists of two distinct products—a monitoring tool called Oracle GoldenGate Monitor and a configuration/ administration tool called Oracle GoldenGate Director. Let's look at Oracle GoldenGate Monitor first, and then we will look at Oracle GoldenGate Director.

Oracle GoldenGate Monitor

Oracle GoldenGate Monitor is the monitoring component of the Management Pack for Oracle GoldenGate. Starting with Oracle GoldenGate 11gR2, it is fully integrated with Oracle Enterprise Manager (OEM) 12c. It is essentially a plug-in for the OEM and can provide an end-to-end view of all the Oracle GoldenGate implementations in the organization. For earlier Oracle GoldenGate releases, the Oracle GoldenGate Monitor's interface is through a Web browser.

Oracle GoldenGate already comes with a low-impact agent that runs on both the source and the target. The way Oracle GoldenGate Monitor works is that it collects key measurable points such as status, lag, number of rows processed, and so on from the agents on source and target, through a server process. Using this data, the Oracle GoldenGate Monitor paints meaningful graphical representations of the state of the union in the replication world. Because the Oracle GoldenGate Monitor Server process is constantly in touch with all the processes or components of Oracle GoldenGate, it is able to provide an up-to-the-second view of the current state of replication. In addition to providing a complete visual representation, it also provides for a server-side alerting in case there is a status change on any of the key measurable components.

The alerting is through either SNMP or e-mail, which can be integrated with existing alerting mechanisms.

As shown in Figure 13-1, Oracle GoldenGate Monitor provides an in-depth complete flowchart-style visualization of all the replication components. It provides automatic solution discovery as and when new replications are implemented or when systems are shutdown/restarted, and so on. The views themselves are customizable to accommodate various dashboard/reporting/alerting needs of different organizations.

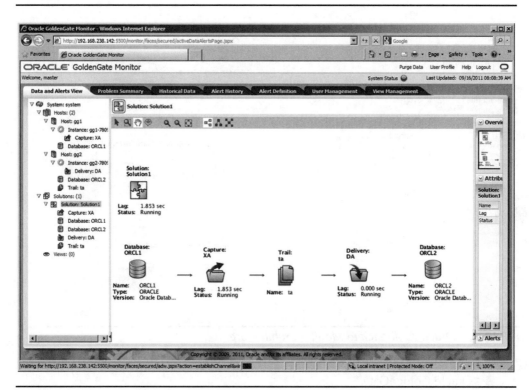

FIGURE 13-1. *A typical view of the Oracle GoldenGate Monitor*

It also provides for a drill-down of each monitoring point to get an in-depth real-time status, such as the current number of updates or checkpoint information, and so on— all without logging in to the server, without running the GGSCI commands.

Oracle GoldenGate Monitor Architecture

Oracle GoldenGate Monitor employs a Web-based GUI to monitor all Oracle GoldenGate components and installations, organization-wide. These components include:

- Oracle GoldenGate Monitor Server
- Oracle GoldenGate Monitor Repository

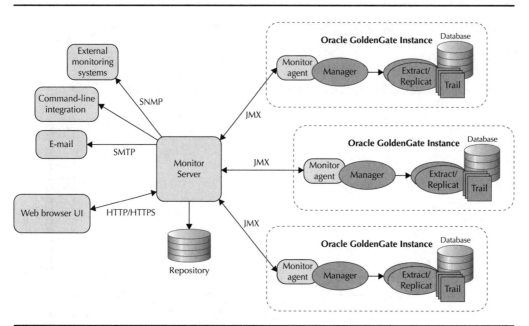

FIGURE 13-2. *Oracle GoldenGate Monitor architecture*

- Oracle GoldenGate
- Oracle GoldenGate Agent

Let's take a moment to look at each of these individual components in a little more detail. Also, Figure 13-2 provides an architecture diagram of these components for you to reference.

Oracle GoldenGate Monitor Server
Oracle GoldenGate Monitor Server, as the name implies, coordinates monitoring of multiple Oracle GoldenGate instances. It processes information collected from various Oracle GoldenGate agents and sends it to the Web browser for displaying. In addition, it also manages users, history, and event-triggered notifications.

Oracle GoldenGate Monitor Repository
Oracle GoldenGate Monitor Repository is a schema in an Oracle database that is used by the Oracle GoldenGate Monitor Server to store information regarding Oracle GoldenGate. Data that would be stored within the schema would include information on database instances, configurations, process statuses, events, users, groups, and so on.

Oracle GoldenGate Monitor

The Oracle GoldenGate Monitor communicates with the Oracle GoldenGate instance using the Java Management Extensions (JMX). The Oracle GoldenGate Monitor Server will communicate with multiple Oracle GoldenGate instances via the Oracle GoldenGate Manager process (in the GoldenGate instance home) and an associated Oracle GoldenGate Agent process.

Oracle GoldenGate Agent

The Oracle GoldenGate Agent is installed as a part of an Oracle GoldenGate instance. It collects information from Oracle GoldenGate instances and communicates it to the Oracle GoldenGate Monitor Server. Prior to Release 11.2, Oracle GoldenGate Agent is embedded with the Manager process. From Release 11.2 onward, it is a separate stand-alone Java agent (shown as JAGENT on Oracle GoldenGate).

Oracle GoldenGate Instance Prep

Each Oracle GoldenGate instance that needs to be monitored using Oracle GoldenGate Monitor should undergo some configuration and setup so that proper communication is established between the instance and the Oracle GoldenGate Monitor Server.

- *Step 1: Installation* The first step, of course, is installation of the software, which we will not go through in this book. It is recommended that the *Oracle GoldenGate Monitor Administrator's Guide* be referred to for detailed instructions on installing the binaries. Please pay specific attention to JDK/JRE prerequisites.

- *Step 2: Enabling Monitoring* To enable Oracle GoldenGate Agent, a parameter must be added in the GLOBALS parameter file. For Release 11.1 of Oracle GoldenGate software, the parameter to add is called ENABLEMONITORINGAGENT. For Release 11.2 and higher, the parameter to add is called ENABLEMONITORING. In situations where the Oracle GoldenGate version is getting upgraded from 11.1 to 11.2, then it is required that the old parameter ENABLEMONITORINGAGENT be replaced with the new parameter ENABLEMONITORING.

- *Step 3: Setting/Aligning Host Properties* You must ensure that the hostnames between the Oracle GoldenGate instances and the Oracle GoldenGate Monitor Server are aligned to allow Oracle GoldenGate Agent to communicate with Oracle GoldenGate Monitor Server. The name used for **monitor.host** in the config.properties file should be same as the name used for **monitor.jmx .server.host** in the monitor.properties file. Similarly, the RMTHOST extract parameter and **jagent.host** in the config.properties should match. Use resolvable hostnames or IP addresses, but do not mix and match.

■ *Step 4: Creating Oracle Wallet* Oracle Wallet is used to store monitoring credentials. Standard Oracle GoldenGate installation comes with a command-line utility called pw_agent_util.sh to create and manage Oracle Wallet. It can be invoked as shown here:

```
$> pw_agent_util.sh -create
```

This prompts the user to enter Oracle GoldenGate Agent's JMX password. The password is stored and passed to Oracle GoldenGate Monitor Server when the agent registers. The JMX password is first prompted for during the initial Oracle GoldenGate Monitor installation.

To update or change passwords, another similar utility, called pw_agent_util .sh, is used in the following fashion.

```
$> pw_agent_util.sh - {updateagentJMX | updateserverJMX}
```

The meanings of the two flags are as follows:

■ **updateagentJMX** To change Oracle GoldenGate Agent's JMX password

■ **updateserverJMX** To change Oracle GoldenGate Monitor Server's JMX password

■ *Step 5: Starting Oracle GoldenGate* Oracle GoldenGate and JAGENT must be restarted after configuration changes to make them effective.

Using Oracle GoldenGate Monitor Server

Once properly configured, Oracle GoldenGate Monitor Server process must be started on the command line using the utility monitor.sh. It can also be stopped using the same utility.

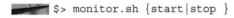
```
$> monitor.sh {start|stop }
```

Once the server process and agents are running, it is now time to begin using the tool. To do that, a browser window needs to be started to access the Oracle GoldenGate Monitor Server's interface. The following URL needs to be entered in the browser window.

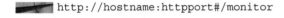
```
http://hostname:httpport#/monitor
```

NOTE
httpport# will have been decided during the installation process.

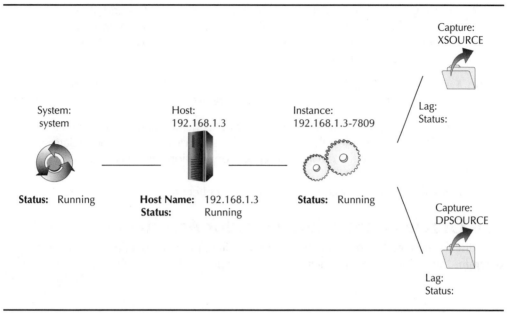

FIGURE 13-3.   *A typical view of a solution from Oracle GoldenGate Monitor*

Once logged in to the application, it will begin what is known as a "discovery process," which uses the information from all the registered Oracle GoldenGate Agents and presents all Oracle GoldenGate solutions available for display. A solution is a complete mapping from source to target, including Extract, Data Pump, and Replicat processes. Figure 13-3 shows a typical solution view, which graphically displays the status of all the components.

Oracle GoldenGate Director

Oracle GoldenGate Director is the second part of the monitoring pack, though it is a separate self-contained application. Oracle GoldenGate Director is used to set up, configure, and maintain Oracle GoldenGate installations and multiple replication components remotely through the client. Oracle GoldenGate Director provides a number of features and benefits including:

- Centralized management and control—starting and stopping of different Oracle GoldenGate modules from one centralized location. Oracle GoldenGate Director allows you to investigate the status of processes and also provides the ability to remotely access remote Oracle GoldenGate command-line interfaces.

■ Oracle GoldenGate Director provides for consolidated stats and alerts. This consolidation of events, logs, alerts, lag times, and so on provides for a much simpler and unified management of your enterprise GoldenGate replication architecture.

■ Oracle GoldenGate Director supplies features that allow for automatic population of relevant platform-specific parameters.

■ Oracle GoldenGate Director provides for quick deployment of GoldenGate solutions. From simple solutions to complex solutions, Oracle GoldenGate Director can make the creation of replication solutions much easier.

Let's look at the Oracle GoldenGate Director architecture in a bit more detail.

The Oracle GoldenGate Director Architecture

Let's discuss the Oracle GoldenGate Director architecture in this section. Figure 13-4 diagrams the various components involved in Oracle GoldenGate Director.

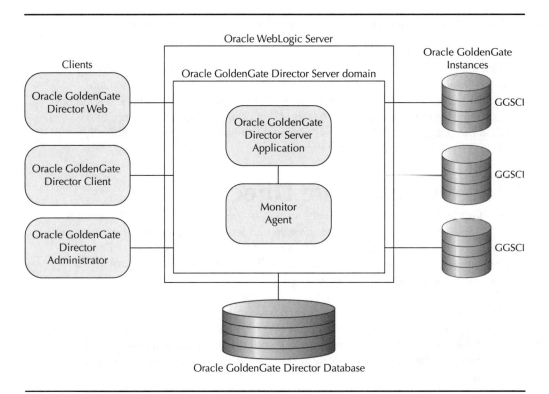

FIGURE 13-4. *Oracle GoldenGate Director architecture*

Let's look at some of these components in some additional detail. First we will look at the Oracle GoldenGate Director Domain components. We will then look at the Oracle GoldenGate Director Database, the Oracle GoldenGate Director Client, and the Oracle GoldenGate Director Web. Finally, we will look at the Oracle GoldenGate Director Administrator.

Oracle GoldenGate Directory Server

Oracle GoldenGate Director Server is installed as an Oracle WebLogic server domain. Within that domain, Oracle GoldenGate Director Server coordinates the management of all the Oracle GoldenGate instances in the desired realm. Applications that run within this domain include the following:

- **The Oracle GoldenGate Director Server application** This application is a collection of server processes that control items such as security, object modeling, diagramming, event logging, and alerting mechanisms.

- **The Oracle GoldenGate Director Monitoring Agent** This agent connects to each Oracle GoldenGate host through GGSCI and establishes a dedicated session. Once the connection is made, it is utilized for obtaining information about events, process statuses, and so on. The Oracle GoldenGate Director Server connects to the monitoring agent process via a manager port of each Oracle Golden Gate instance to be monitored.

Oracle GoldenGate Director Database

The Oracle GoldenGate Director Database acts as a repository for all the configuration information: diagrams, users, accounts, hosts, instances, events, and so on. A dedicated schema must be created in the database and provided with privileges to create, drop objects, unlimited quota on the schema's default tablespace, and so on (please refer to the Oracle GoldenGate Director documentation for specific permissions required for your version of Oracle GoldenGate Director).

Oracle GoldenGate Director Client

The Oracle GoldenGate Director Client is a GUI client that connects to the Oracle GoldenGate Director Server to manage the Oracle GoldenGate instances. The client is a typical desktop application that runs on any platform that supports Java. The client must be of the same version number as that of the server and is packaged along with the server.

The client can be installed on the same server as the database server or on separate machines running either the various supported operating systems including the various flavors of UNIX and the supported Windows operating systems (check the Oracle documentation for your version to determine what is supported). Each client environment needs its own Java Runtime Environment (check for the correct Java version that your client requires). At the time of the writing of this book, Java version 6.0 was required. If the client were to be installed on the same machine as the server, then the same Java environment could be used for both the server and the client.

Oracle GoldenGate Director Web

This is a Web application hosted within the Oracle GoldenGate server, which allows Web-based monitoring of the Oracle GoldenGate instances. Any Web browser can be used as an interface to connect to the Oracle GoldenGate Director Server, bypassing the Oracle GoldenGate Director Client.

Oracle GoldenGate Director Administrator

The Oracle GoldenGate Director Administrator is another client that is used to administer the Oracle GoldenGate Director Server itself. It can be used to add or remove Oracle GoldenGate instances, setup users, accounts, and so on.

Installing Oracle GoldenGate Director

In this section we want to discuss installing Oracle GoldenGate Director. Because the Oracle GoldenGate product is always being improved, it's possible that the information in this section could change or be incomplete. Because of this you should always refer to the detailed installation instructions before installing Oracle GoldenGate Director. Specifically, you will want to refer to the *Oracle GoldenGate Director Administrator's Guide*. First, we will discuss installing Oracle GoldenGate Director, and then we will discuss starting and managing Oracle GoldenGate Director.

Downloading Your Version of Oracle GoldenGate Director

Because the environment and details of the installation will vary, it's not possible to go into great detail with respect to installation of the product. What we do want to provide you, though, is a bit of a "gotcha list" and a checklist of items that you might want to be aware of as you install Oracle GoldenGate Director. Here is a list of items to be aware of:

1. Before you install Oracle GoldenGate Director, you will want to determine the installation directory that you will install Oracle GoldenGate Director files in during the install process.

2. You will also need to determine the location where the WebLogic components will be installed. This location is generally the directory above the path where

the WebLogic server is installed. For example, if you have installed WebLogic in the directory /var/opt/weblogic/wlserver_version, then the WebLogic Install location would be /var/opt/weblogic. Again, check with the install documentation for your specific hardware and operating system version and version of Oracle GoldenGate Director for any specific details.

NOTE
When you're installing WebLogic Server (WLS) separately or when installing on an existing WLS, the WLS has to be the full version and not the development version. If the WLS is a development version, you will get an error.

3. You will need to know which HTTP port you want to be used by the Oracle GoldenGate Director Server to communicate with Oracle GoldenGate Director Web. The default port is 7001. Ensure that there is no firewall blocking this port.

4. Determine the schema name that you will use in the repository database and create it according to the *Oracle GoldenGate Director Installation Guide*. When installing GoldenGate Director, you will need to know the database's Oracle system ID (SID) (or SCAN name if using RAC), hostname, user credentials, and other items that will be listed in the installation guide. Note that you can use either an Oracle, SQL Server, or MySQL Enterprise database to store this schema information in.

Once you have this information handy, you can install the Oracle GoldenGate Director Server according to the installation instructions for your specific hardware and operating system version.

The easiest way to find your version of Oracle GoldenGate Director is to find it on the Oracle GoldenGate home page, which can be found by searching for "Oracle GoldenGate Director Downloads" from your favorite search engine (the URL changes sometimes, so we figure it's better to just search for it). The most current and popular versions of Oracle GoldenGate Director can be found on that page. If you don't find a version of Oracle GoldenGate Director on the Oracle GoldenGate home page, you can use Oracle's Software Delivery Cloud at http://edelivery.oracle.com. Select the Oracle Fusion Middleware option there and the various options will appear.

As with other Oracle software, you download the install image and then load that image into a staging area. It is advisable to read the associated readme file and install guide before downloading the software. On a UNIX system, the following command can initiate the installation process. As an example, if you downloaded the UNIX version of Oracle GoldenGate Director from Edelivery, you would extract the downloaded zip file. You would then find the install code, which currently is called gg-director-serversetup_unix_version.sh. You would run the code like this (of course, this will differ based on different versions of Oracle GoldenGate Director):

```
gg-director-serversetup_unix_version.sh -c
```

This brings up the GUI installer, which asks for the input values from the checklist shown earlier. Once all values are put in, the installation process is begun and can be closed upon FINISH or successful completion.

Starting and Managing Oracle GoldenGate Director

Once Oracle GoldenGate Director is installed, the Oracle GoldenGate Director Server needs to be started. To do so you would use the following command.

```
directorcontrol.sh <-b> start <outfile>
```

where

- The option <-b> enables it to start in the background.

- The option <outfile> redirects the output to a file.

Once the Oracle GoldenGate Director Server is installed successfully and started, the next step is to install the client. To install the client, start a Web browser on the client machine and open the following address.

```
http://<hostname>:<port>
```

You would enter the hostname or IP address (the hostname should be fully qualified) to access the Oracle GoldenGate Director Server that is installed and running. The port is the port number that was picked during the installation of Oracle GoldenGate Director Server.

To start the Oracle GoldenGate Director Web, run a Web browser with the following address.

```
http://<hostname>:<port>/acon
```

These procedures will vary (sometimes significantly) based on the hardware system that you are installing Oracle GoldenGate Director on and the version of Oracle GoldenGate Director that you are using. Refer to the administration guide for detailed instructions.

Configuring Oracle GoldenGate Director Server

Once installed and started, the Oracle GoldenGate Director Server needs to be configured for managing the data sources, accounts, and so on. This needs to be done by running the Oracle GoldenGate Director Administrator program. The script will vary by operating system; for example, with a UNIX install you would run the script

```
run-admin.sh
```

This script will prompt for the userid and password for the admin user. It also prompts for the machine and port on which the Oracle GoldenGate Director Server is running. The admin account's initial credentials are "admin" with the password "admin". The password must be changed after the first login.

The Oracle GoldenGate Director Administrator program is a simple program that is fairly intuitive and is used to set up

- **User Accounts** All users of Oracle GoldenGate Director need individual accounts, which need to be set up using the Administrator program.

- **Manage Data Sources** Add or remove Oracle Golden Gate instances to be managed.

Individual users can log in with their respective credentials to Oracle GoldenGate Director Server via the Oracle GoldenGate Director Client or Oracle GoldenGate Director Web. Once logged in, users can create, manage, and monitor Oracle GoldenGate configurations.

CHAPTER
14

Zero-Downtime Upgrades and Migrations Using Oracle GoldenGate

A s the application requirements for database management keep getting more and more complex, the availability requirements also keep increasing, thereby shrinking the maintenance window. It is almost impossible to obtain downtime these days for performing routine maintenance activities on a database. Major upgrades like database versions from 10g to 11g will need a significant amount of downtime for successful accomplishment of intended upgrades that are subject to stringent user acceptance requirements. A typical database upgrade project will need an enormous amount of planning, testing, and application certification, which can run into weeks or months, depending on the complexity of the application. In addition to database upgrades, migrations or "re-hosts" also call for extensive downtime in order to achieve the end result. For example, an enterprise may choose to replace legacy hardware and consolidate multiple databases on a single Exadata database machine. Or it may choose to move from AIX-based servers to Linux-based commodity hardware. The process of migration of the data from legacy to new environment can take from a few hours to probably days depending on the size of the data. In this modern Internet/online world, can any business afford that kind of downtime, which directly leads to loss of revenue? Can an online retailer or an airline reservation site be down during a database upgrade or re-host activity?

Traditionally, Oracle database upgrades have been "in-place," meaning that the application and the database are brought down and the prescribed procedures to upgrade the database are followed on the production database. This procedure is "invasive." In case a failback is required, there is no option other than extending downtime and restoring the database to its previous state. As discussed in the introduction, this option is more and more likely to be hit with severe resistance from the business owners.

With the advent of Real Application Clusters (RAC) and Oracle Data Guard Technologies, rolling upgrades have been possible, meaning upgrading each node at a time without bringing down the entire cluster. Oracle Maximum Availability Architecture prescribes this, and it is a major step up from the options available before now.

Oracle GoldenGate can reinforce the rolling upgrade methodology in significant ways. By deploying Oracle GoldenGate and taking advantage of its real-time heterogeneous data movement capabilities, complex database environment upgrades and cross-platform database migrations can be achieved with near-zero downtime, making the transition transparent to the business and end users. The only downtime that will be experienced by the users will be during the application switchover.

Zero-Downtime Methodology

This section describes, at a high level, the overall approach to achieving a successful environment migration and/or upgrades with zero downtime using Oracle GoldenGate.

Let's call the database to be upgraded and/or migrated the "source" and the environment where the database is migrated to the "target." The basic architecture behind achieving a zero-downtime migration is nothing but setting up a one-way replication between the source and the target. The steps required to achieve that have been explained in the earlier chapters. Once the target is in sync with the source and ready, the application needs to be switched over to connecting to the target database. This will guarantee that the only downtime that needs to be scheduled is the time it takes to switch over the application to the new database.

If an upgrade is in the plan, the target database can be upgraded to the desired version and then the data resynchronized before cutting over to the target.

If a failback option is desired, which it often is, this concept can be extended and a reverse one-way replication can be set up after the cutover to the target. Now, the target becomes the source and vice versa. This role reversal ensures that changes made in the new database after cutover are applied to the old or the original source database, in case the business decides to fail back to it. The reasons for that can be any; for example, if some new bugs are discovered that were not in the test environment, or if there was a problem in the cutover for some reason. Once the business is satisfied with the new environment, the reverse replication can be discontinued.

Also, if Oracle GoldenGate is set up for bidirectional replication between the old and new environments and both systems support the application for transaction processing, then the application migration to the new environment can be achieved in a phased manner. This helps in eliminating the downtime related to application switchover too, and the transition to the new environment can be completely transparent to the end users.

As Figure 14-1 shows, the steps are self-explanatory, but they are summarized in the following list for clarification. Notice the difference between the database connections of the application server pre- and post-migration.

- Set up a one-way replication between the source and the target. The steps for setting this up are no different than described in earlier chapters. The source server will have the Extract and the Data Pump processes running with access to the source trail file.

- The target server will have the Replicat process running with access to the destination trail file.

- The initial load decisions can be similar to the ones to be made during a plain-vanilla forward replication setup. Export/import or direct load insert, backup/restore may also be possible provided endian compatibility exists.

- The target database can be a brand new database on the desired version or platform. For example, the source is on Oracle 9i/SCO and the target is on Exadata/Linux/11gR2.

■ Oracle GoldenGate Veridata can be employed to verify that the data between the source and target are synchronized. It is optional, but recommended.

■ Shut down the application and restart it to point to the new database. If the application is a client/server application, the switch can be affected by switching to a prestaged new tnsnames.ora file. For applications using JDBC, the data source would have to be changed, meaning that a new jar file may have to be deployed. All these steps can be staged ahead of time to minimize the cutover time.

Failback Option

This is the best advantage of employing Oracle GoldenGate: the ability to go back to an old or the original state. But why would anybody want to do that? There can be many reasons. New application bugs may be uncovered in the new environment, or the environment could be encountering unforeseen stability problems. Since the original environment wasn't altered in any way, the application can be just as easily pointed back to the original source database. But, if business wants to have all the

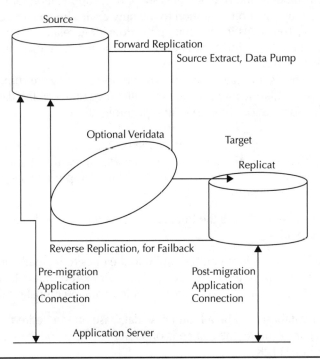

FIGURE 14-1. *GoldenGate architecture supporting zero downtime*

transactions since the cutover back in the original database after failing back, then GoldenGate will come to our rescue.

In the migration project design, it is best to keep in mind the possibility of failback. This high-level process needs to be slightly tweaked to achieve that.

- A new Extract process should be configured and started on the target server, which will act as the new source. The original source will now act as the new target with the Replicat process running on it.

- Essentially, it is a new one-way replication in the reverse direction. This should be done and verified before the application is restarted, during the original cutover process.

- With Oracle GoldenGate Veridata, it can be verified if the data is in sync.

- In the event of stability issues in the new environment, a reverse switchover of the application connection needs to be performed, very similar to the original process.

- Bidirectional data replication can also be used, to make the failback even simpler, but the design of the overall process can get a bit more complicated.

In addition to minimizing the downtime required for such migration/upgrade projects, we can see that we have simplified the whole process by eliminating a large number of steps and associated risks with each of them. Executing of upgrade scripts such as u***.sql—gone. Restore from backup for failback—gone. Downtime—nearly eliminated. Legacy character set conversions—accomplished. Endian conversion—accomplished. Cross-platform migration—easily achieved. Again, all of this has been accomplished with very little downtime.

CHAPTER
15

Oracle GoldenGate
Veridata

When doing Oracle GoldenGate replication, there are times when you find yourself wondering if the various replicated data sets are in or out of synchronization with each other. You might want to check data sets after initial instantiation of the target database, for example, making sure that the two data sets are equivalent. Perhaps you have had to deal with some errors that occurred during replication and you want to make sure that your data sets are in synchronization with each other.

While Oracle GoldenGate only does replication (and it also does things like checking for missing updates, dealing with correctly synchronizing updates, and conflict resolution), it can't really detect if two schemas, and the data in those schemas, are different. Enter Oracle GoldenGate Veridata. It is the job of GoldenGate Veridata to compare two data sets and determine if one is out of sync with the other. This functionality of the Oracle GoldenGate Veridata product really enhances Oracle GoldenGate's value, and thus Veridata becomes the topic of this chapter.

Once Oracle GoldenGate Veridata is deployed, it can compare data values during replication, thereby ensuring the quality of data. This is especially useful in round-the-clock replication environments, where replication cannot be stopped to run a custom tool to check for any data discrepancies.

Veridata Functionality

How does Oracle GoldenGate Veridata actually compare the data between source and target? The comparison is achieved in two steps: the initial step, which produces the May Be Out of Sync (MOOS) queue, and then the confirmation step, which moves the record from the MOOS queue to a Confirm Out of Sync (COOS) status.

In the initial step, rows are retrieved from source and target via a SQL query. All columns of the primary key are compared value to value while a hash key is used to compare the rest of the columns. The hash key is arrived at by a unique digital signature that also reduces the data transfer across the network for comparison. If desired, Oracle GoldenGate Veridata can also be configured to compare literal values of each nonkey column, too. But it does increase the network usage and introduce possible performance issues.

In the confirmation step, rows are extracted from the MOOS queue and are evaluated for one of the following status settings:

- **In-sync** The target row values have since been updated via replication and are in synchronization with the source row values.

- **In-flight** The target row value was out of sync in the initial step, but that row has now been updated. It is in-flight, though, because Oracle GoldenGate Veridata is unable to confirm the change yet. The row should become in-sync eventually.

■ **Persistently out of sync** Also known as Confirm Out of Sync or the COOS step, this status setting confirms that the row hasn't changed since the initial comparison step and is therefore definitely out of sync. This confirmation step waits until a specified replication latency threshold has been reached or expired. This allows the replication mechanism to post any in-flight changes. Confirmed out-of-sync rows are then stored in a comparison report.

The Veridata architecture is made up of a number of different components. Let's look at each of these components in a bit more detail. You can also examine these components in Figure 15-1:

■ **The Oracle GoldenGate Veridata Server** This coordinates execution of all the Oracle GoldenGate Veridata tasks, compares data, confirms out-of-sync values, and produces a report.

■ **The Oracle GoldenGate Veridata Web Client** A thin Web client for the Oracle GoldenGate Veridata server with which a user can configure and initiate comparison jobs, view the output, and review the out-of-sync data.

■ **The Oracle GoldenGate Veridata Repository** Contains the user configurations on disk.

■ **The Oracle GoldenGate Veridata Agent** Performs the fetching of the blocks of rows to compare and returns column-level details of the out-of-sync rows. Agent is Java-based code and is used on all non-Oracle databases. For Oracle

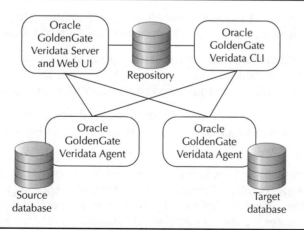

FIGURE 15-1. *Oracle GoldenGate Veridata architecture*

databases, however, a C-code-based agent is required. The C-code-based agent is controlled by a Manager process. Veridata Agent is installed on both source and target machines. A dedicated agent is required for each instance on a database server. One agent cannot work with multiple database instances.

■ **The Oracle GoldenGate Veridata CLI or Command-Line Interface**
A text/command-based client, called vericom, which enables running of comparisons, specifying overrides, and stopping Oracle GoldenGate Veridata Server. The actual configuring and monitoring can be done only through Oracle GoldenGate Veridata Web.

Configuring and Using Oracle GoldenGate Veridata

As Veridata configuration and implementation will differ slightly depending on the system it's running on, this chapter can really only serve as a general introduction to Oracle GoldenGate Veridata with respect to details of installation, configuration, usage, and performance tuning. For further details with respect to your operating system, please refer to the appropriate administration guide.

The general steps that you would follow to set up and configure GoldenGate Veridata are shown in the following list:

Step 1. Set up database connections for each Oracle GoldenGate Veridata Agent, on the source and target database servers. A connection is achieved by the inputs—host, port number, and data source or the instance name that the Agent needs to read the data from.

Step 2. Set up groups. A group or compare group is a logical entity that pairs a source database connection and its corresponding target database connection.

Step 3. Set up compare pairs under a compare group. A compare pair is a set of source and target tables/files or views to compare. It is set up by mapping corresponding columns of source and target tables, files, or views to compare.

Step 4. Set up jobs. A job is the actual task or a unit of work, which consists of one or more Compare Groups. A job is executed to run the compares as defined in the associated groups.

Step 5. Set up profiles (optional). A profile is a set of runtime parameters, like memory usage, number of threads, sorting methods, reporting output, and so on. A profile can be applied globally for a job or to specific compare pairs. Defining profiles is optional because a default profile exists, which should suffice for most of the jobs.

The completion of a job produces an Out of Sync or OOS report in binary format, which can be viewed from Oracle GoldenGate Veridata Web. In addition to source and target data values, the report also consists of general statistics of the operation, like the number of rows compared, time taken, and so on. Optionally, the OOS report can also be produced in an XML format, the data from which can be read and tabulated by external programs for producing executive summaries, and so on.

Oracle GoldenGate Veridata Web

Oracle GoldenGate Veridata Web is a thin Web-based GUI client with which all the operations of Oracle GoldenGate are performed. It can be accessed from a browser with the following address.

```
http://<hostname>:<port>/veridata
```

Note that the hostname in this example is the name of the server where the Oracle GoldenGate server is installed and the port defaults to 8830, where the JDBC connection can be made. This port might be different depending on how you have configured GoldenGate.

Let's quickly discuss the steps required to configure and use Oracle GoldenGate Veridata as described in the previous section. First, you will use the Oracle GoldenGate Veridata Web client to perform this configuration.

First, you will log in to the Web client. Then you will configure the database connections using the Oracle GoldenGate Veridata Web client. That includes configuring the source database connection and the target database connection. This includes the configuration of the hostname, port number, and data source type for both the source and target databases.

Once all the information is entered, there is a Verify button you can click to test the connections you have created. Now that we have created the connections, it's time to create our groups. Groups are used to define the source and destination targets of a Veridata comparison. You will give the group a name and then you would add the source and target databases we just created to a group, in the expectation that we will be comparing those databases.

Having added the group, and added the source and target databases to the group, we will be given the option to compare the source and target pairs. To do so, look for a box titled "Go To Compare Pair Configuration."

You will now need to add the source and target tables that you want Veridata to compare. For example, you might compare a table named PLAYERS that exists on both the source and target databases. You might want to know if the tables on the source and target database and the data in those tables are the same. Having added the PLAYERS table to the group that we created, we can now start the compare process.

First, you will be presented with a screen that asks you to validate the column mapping. An option will be presented to you to validate the column mappings. You select the option and the validation of the mappings will begin. After the column mapping is validated, the validation status will turn green.

Having validated the mappings, we can create the actual comparison job. You will find a Job Configuration link on the Web page that provides that functionality. When configuring the compare job, you can apply filters to the job, and do a final review of the compare job and the tables and columns assigned to it. Finally, after having created the job, you will want to run the job. From the main menu of the client, you will click on the Run/Execute job option. Then you will see the menu that gives you an option to run the jobs you have created. You simply select the job and click the Run button to execute the job.

Once the job is run, you can review the results. To see the results, click the View hyperlink under the column that is titled "Rows Out of Sync" to view the output. You may find that some rows are out of sync. In this case you can select the View link to get more details on the issue. Of course, there can be a number of reasons why the data may be out of sync.

You can always rerun the compare jobs again. For example, you might have corrected the data differences and want to determine if all the data in the tables is not in sync.

Running Comparisons on the Command Line

The Oracle GoldenGate Vericom command-line interface tool can be used to run most of the comparison tasks. The following can be achieved using the **vericom** command:

- Shut down Oracle GoldenGate Veridata Server.

- Run a job for comparison.

- Generate Out of Sync reports—text and XML.

- Set tracing for debugging, if necessary.

Vericom is invoked from the command line of the operating system as follows.

```
<bin>/vericom - < input parameters> - < optional input parameters >
```

<bin> is the bin directory under veridata_loc or the location of Veridata's software home.

The most common input arguments are listed in the following table.

Option	Description
shutdown	Shuts down the Oracle GoldenGate Veridata Server processes
help	Displays Vericom syntax components

Option	Description
helprun	Displays run-related syntax components
version or v	Displays the version of Oracle GoldenGate Veridata CLI
job or j <jobname>	Specifies the job with the jobname to be run
g <groupname>	Specifies the group
c < comparepair>	Specifies the compare pair
	If -g, -c are used, then -j (job) must also be used.
rp < profile>	Overrides the profile that is defined for a job
	If -rp is used, -j should also be used.

Optional input parameters are many, listed in total, in the *Oracle GoldenGate Veridata AdministrationGuide*.

The **vericom** command can complete or abort with one of the following exit statuses.

Status	Description
0	The command executed successfully.
1	Invalid vericom syntax was used.
2	Vericom could not find connection information. Connection parameters were not specified with command arguments.
3	Provides more granularity for input errors.
4	The job ran successfully, but there were rows that had a comparison status of something other than in-sync.
5	Communication error with Oracle GoldenGate Veridata Server.

Here's an example of an output after the completion of a comparison job, when run by vericom. The display shows a successful run of group ogg_group, which is a part of the job ogg_job, set up to compare data from table PLAYERS between source and the target. Shows a successfully completed execution (with exit status 0), along with runtime statistics like number of rows compared, IN-SYNC, location of the report file, and so on.

```
<bin>vericom -j ogg_job -g ogg_group -c PLAYERS=PLAYERS -w
Connecting to: localhost:8126
Run ID: (4900, 0, 0)
Job Start Time: 2012-08-28 00:45:52
Job Stop Time: 2012-08-28 00:46:20
Job Report Filename: $<veridata_loc>/data/rpt/4900/ogg_job.rpt
Number of Compare Pairs: 1
Number of Compare Pairs With Errors: 0
```

```
Number of Compare Pairs With OOS: 0
Number of Compare Pairs With No OOS: 1
Number of Compare Pairs Cancelled: 0
Compare Pair Report Filename:
$<veridata_loc>/data/rpt/4900/ogg_group/CP_ players=players.rpt
Number of Rows Compared: 1000000
Number of Rows In Sync: 1000000
Number of Rows With Errors: 0
Number of Rows Out Of Sync: 0
Number of Inserts Out Of Sync: 0
Number of Deletes Out Of Sync: 0
Number of Updates Out Of Sync: 0
Compare Pair OOSXML Directory:
$<veridata_loc>/data/4900/oosxml/ogg_job/4900/ogg_group
Compare Pair OOSXML Filename:
Job Completion Status: IN SYNC
$<bin> if errorlevel 0 echo EXITED 0 STATUS
EXITED 0 STATUS
```

As you can see, Vericom is a very powerful tool that can be used in automation scripts, startup routines, and so on. Each exit status can be coded for and be fed to alerting and monitoring tools like Oracle Enterprise Manager.

CHAPTER
16

Oracle GoldenGate
Integration Options

I n previous chapters we have shown how Oracle GoldenGate supports transactional replication between various databases. Databases are not the whole universe, though. We need GoldenGate to do other things. Can we use Oracle GoldenGate to apply transactions to targets that are not databases? Yes, we can! Oracle GoldenGate provides these options to enhance integration options:

- Using GoldenGate to create a Oracle SQL*Loader compatible file
- Oracle GoldenGate for Flat File
- Other API interfaces into GoldenGate

This chapter is about these various GoldenGate integration options. Each of these options is implemented by creating extensions to the core GoldenGate product. Oracle GoldenGate provides an API called the Oracle GoldenGate User Exit interface, which can be written to. So, let's look at our nondatabase integration options in a bit more detail.

Using GoldenGate to Create a File for a Database Utility to Use

GoldenGate provides the ability to create flat files that can be used by Oracle Database utilities such as SQL*Loader and SQL*Plus. These files can be used to instantiate a target database, or even update the target database with DML commands that represent the changes to be made. Configuring GoldenGate to create these external files for use by database utilities is pretty straightforward. You essentially need to just create a single extract, much as we did in Chapter 5. There is no Replicat process required since you will be using a utility like SQL*Loader to import the data into the target database.

The extract parameter file looks much like the parameter files you have seen already, with a couple of differences. First the **rmtfile** command will reference the file that you are going to create. You will also use parameters to indicate that the file should be an ASCII-formatted flat file and that the format should be one of the following:

Parameter	Format Output Style
SQLLOADER	Oracle SQL*Loader Utility output file and command file will be created.
FORMATXML	Output should be in XML format.
FORMATSQL	Output should be in the form of SQL statements.

Here is an example of a parameter file that you might create:

```
EXTRACT EXSQLDR1
SETENV (NLS_LANG=AMERICAN_AMERICA.AL32UTF8)
USERID ggadmin@orcl_one, PASSWORD ggadmin
FORMATASCII, SQLLOADER
EXTFILE ./dirdat/mysqlldr.dat, PURGE
TABLE HR.*;
```

Once you have created the parameter file, simply add the extract and then start the Manager and the Extract process. The output will be the SQL*Loader output file and an associated SQL*Loader control file that contains the appropriate SQL*Loader parameters.

Oracle GoldenGate for Flat File

As we mentioned, the Oracle GoldenGate product provides a user exit interface. Using this interface, you can write C programs to interface with Oracle GoldenGate. If you want to write the output to flat files, Oracle GoldenGate has simplified your job by providing the Oracle GoldenGate for Flat File utility. This utility is a set of program libraries that can be linked into the Oracle GoldenGate Extract processes. They are easy to use; no programming is required and they can be customized using a properties file.

Installing Oracle GoldenGate Flat File

Before we can use all this cool stuff, we have to first download and install the Oracle GoldenGate Application Adapters 11.1.1.0.0 for JMS and Flat File Media Pack. See Chapter 3 for instructions on how to use Oracle's Software Delivery Cloud to find and download the Oracle GoldenGate Application Adapters 11.1.1.0.0 for JMS and Flat File Media Pack. Each version of the media pack is unique to a given operating system, so make sure you download the correct version.

After downloading the pack from the Software Delivery Cloud, you will find that the file downloaded is either a .zip file (for Windows environments) or a .tar.gz file for UNIX platforms. Simply copy the file into the GoldenGate home directory that you wish to use and unzip or uncompress/untar the file into the GoldenGate home directory. The file will contain the .dll (Windows) or the .so (Linux) shared library required by Oracle GoldenGate to provide the flat file-writing capabilities that will be described here. The shared library that is installed is an Oracle GoldenGate user exit program (mentioned earlier) created by Oracle to provide the services required to support the creation of flat files by Oracle GoldenGate.

The Oracle GoldenGate Flat File Infrastructure

Generally the process for using Oracle GoldenGate for Flat File (or any of the other integration options) works something like this. First, GoldenGate extracts transactions from the source database in the normal way. You will create Extract processes, trail files, and Data Pump processes on the source system. It's where the trail file data is sent, and what happens to it later in the process, that changes with the integration options.

When using the Flat File processing options, the trail file will be subsequently read by the Oracle GoldenGate Data Integration Server (we will call it the DIS). This is a fancy name for a machine (the same machine or another machine) that had an Oracle GoldenGate directory installed on it, with the Flat File Media Pack installed. On the DIS you will create a new Extract process (not a Replicat process) that will process the trail file and create the expected output. The output is in the form of either a file with the data that is delimited in some form, or a file where the data is stored in fixed, predefined lengths. Additionally, an optional control file might also be created to assist the integrations programs with processing the flat-file output.

To configure Oracle GoldenGate Flat File, you will create a properties file, which will define how the flat file Extract process works. This file defines a number of metadata properties associated with the individual flat file processes you will create. In the rest of this chapter we will dive further into the details of how to configure and use Oracle GoldenGate Flat File.

When creating the flat files, GoldenGate will append to an existing flat file, or it will create a new flat file if one does not already exist. GoldenGate will also optionally create a control file for each flat file that is created. Summary information on the write process can also be written to the GoldenGate report file or to a separate summary file.

Types of Flat Files That Can Be Created

Two different kinds of output files can be created by the flat file process. The first is a file with the information delimited (by a character defined in the properties file). This first kind of output is known as a DSV or Delimiter Separated Values file. The second kind of flat file is the LDV or Length Delimited Values file. Also, both kinds of flat files can contain various metadata that can be helpful when processing the data within the flat files. Let's look at each of these file types in a bit more detail.

DSV Files

DSV files are output files that contain the data from the source database, in a text output file, that is delimited in some manner (for example, by using a comma). For example, if you had a table called PEOPLE, and you wanted GoldenGate Flat

File to process the columns EMP_ID, LAST_NAME, and FIRST_NAME, you might configure GoldenGate Flat File to create output files that contained a column, and then a comma, then the next column, and a comma, and so on. This is what is known as a *comma-delimited file*. In such a case, you would want to create a DSV output file, in which the output data was comma-delimited. The resulting output might be something like this:

 `001,Freeman, Robert,002,Johnson,Carrie`

And so on. We will show you, later in this chapter, how to create a properties file that will create a DSV as the output file type.

LDV Files

LDV files are output files that produce the data in fixed-length format. For example, if you had a table called PEOPLE, and you wanted GoldenGate Flat File to process the columns EMP_ID, LAST_NAME, and FIRST_NAME, you might configure GoldenGate Flat File to create output files that contained each of these columns in a fixed length (say, 10 characters). The resulting output might look something like this:

```
001    Freeman    Robert      002    Johnson    Carrie
```

The User Exit Properties File

The Oracle GoldenGate Flat File product is built on the Oracle GoldenGate User Exit APIs that Oracle GoldenGate supplies for product integration into GoldenGate. These user exits are written in C. To configure the GoldenGate Flat File product, you will use the Oracle GoldenGate user exit properties file, which is used to configure the GoldenGate Flat File user interface.

The user exit properties file is used to provide specific configuration metadata associated with the user exit associated with a GoldenGate process. Within the properties file you will define various settings for Oracle GoldenGate Flat File to use, such as the definition of the writers to be used (we discuss writers later in this chapter). The Oracle GoldenGate user exit properties file is typically called ffwriter .properties by default. This name can be changed using the GoldenGate parameter CUSEREXIT PARAMS.

The format of the parameters in the property file takes the form of a fully qualified property name and then the resulting value for that property. For example, one parameter in the user property file might look like this:

```
goldengate.log.logname=mywriter
goldengate.log.level=info
goldengate.log.tostdout=false
goldengate.log.tofile=true
```

This would define the prefix for the logfile name for the GoldenGate writer process being defined. The logfile name would be prefixed with the name mywriter. Also we have defined the level of logging as "info". In this case, we used the Goldengate.log .level parameter, which will cause all modules to globally log at the setting chosen (info in this case). We could add another level of logging to indicate the module that the logging level is defined for. This kind of logging is typically only done for advanced debugging issues, often with the recommendation of Oracle Support.

For the level of logging we can choose from the following levels:

Logging Level	Description
ERROR	Messages are only written in the event an error occurs.
WARN	Messages are written if errors or warning events occur.
INFO (Default)	This default setting will cause messages to be written if errors or warnings occur. Also, informational messages will be written.
DEBUG	This is the highest level of information regarding the process. All messages, including debugging ones, will be written.

Finally, we have indicated that logging should not be through the stdout device, and that logging should be written to a file (the name of which we have already defined).

The Writer Process

Writers are configured in the GoldenGate properties file. The definition of a writer will result in the creation of the output data file and, optionally, a control file. A writer can create a single rolling flat file for all the tables processed, or it can create individual flat files for each individual table, whichever you prefer. Oracle GoldenGate Flat File will create the output file with a temporary extension. Once the file writing has been complete (called a rollover), then the temporary extension is renamed, indicating the file is ready for processing.

The optional control file contains information that is created when the output files are ready for processing. Thus, the control file can be used by the integration programs reading the flat files associated with the control file to determine which flat files have been created and are ready for processing.

The control file and flat file are typically used together then. In practice, your data integration process might look something like this:

■   Oracle GoldenGate Flat File creates the control file.

■   Your data integration program detects the creation of the control file.

- Your data integration program renames the extension of the control file, indicating that it is the control file that is currently being processed.

- Your data integration program parses through the control file, determining which flat files have been created and are ready for processing.

- Your program opens the flat files in the order listed in the control file and processes the data records within those flat files.

- When each individual data file is processed, the data file is deleted.

- When all data files in the renamed control file are processed, then the control file is deleted.

This summary of actions does not include addressing issues such as what happens if the data integration program fails when it's in the middle of reading a data file, and of course, you also want to include error-handling routines in your data integration programs. These are all normal programming kinds of things, but you would be surprised how many dirty little programs I've seen over the years that don't include such things.

Defining the Writers

You define writers in the properties file using the goldengate.flatfilewriter.writers attribute. You can define one or more writers within this attribute as seen here:

```
Goldengate.flatfilewriter.writers=mywriter,yourwriter,overwriter
```

In this case, we have defined three different writers in our properties file. They are called mywriter, yourwriter, and overwriter. Note that we did not put any spaces between the equal sign or the commas. This is important! Within the properties file for these writers, we will prefix many of the remaining attributes with the name of the writer that the attribute applies to. For example, if we wanted to configure the mywriter process to be a DSV process, we would set the mode attribute for the mywriter process like this:

```
mywriter.mode=dsv
```

We have prefixed the attribute with the name of the writer (mywriter), and then used the mode attribute. We then used the equals sign and indicated that it should be a DSV file by using the parameter DSV.

Defining the Writer Mode

We mentioned earlier that there were two different format output types, DSV and LDV. You use the mode attribute, prefixed with the name of the writer, to define which type of output you wish your writer to produce. For example, if we wanted the mywriter process to create a DSV file, we would use the mywriter.mode attribute with the DSV setting as seen here:

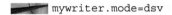 `mywriter.mode=dsv`

If we wanted to use the LDV mode, then the setting would be

 `mywriter.mode=ldv`

Defining the Output File Name

You use the files.formatstring attribute in the property file to define the naming format for the output files associated with the writer. An example of the use of this parameter is seen here:

 `mywriter.files.formatstring=myext_%d_%010n_%s_%`

You will notice that we used substitution variables in the formatting of the output file. The following are valid substitution variables.

Substitution Variable	Description
%d	This is the date/time timestamp.
%n	This is a sequence number. You can indicate that the sequence should be zero filled by including a number between the % sign and the n symbol. For example, %5n would indicate that the sequence number should be zero filled to five digits.
%s	This is the schema name for the table in the output file.
%t	This is the table name for the transactions in the output file.

Text and substitution variables can be intermingled when setting the property. Here is an example:

`mywriter.files.formatstring=mywriter_%d_%05n_%s_%`

Defining Rollover Attributes

When GoldenGate is finished with a file, and closes it, this is called *rolling over* the file. There are several attributes associated with rolling over the file that you can set in the properties file, including the following:

- **Files.data.rollover.time** The number of seconds that should elapse from the first record write until the file is rolled over. This parameter is a numeric value.

- **Files.data.rollover.size** The size of the file, in bytes, until the file is rolled over.

■ **Files.data.norecords.timeout**   The amount of idle time that would pass, when no records have been written, that will cause a rollover of an empty file. This parameter is a numeric value and is defined in seconds.

■ **Files.rolloveronshutdown**   Indicates whether a rollover should occur if the Extract process writing to the file is shut down. This parameter is a true or false value.

■ **Writebuffer.size**   This is the size of the write buffer in bytes.

Here are some examples:

```
mywriter.files.data.rollover.time=120
mywriter.files.data.rollover.size=10000
mywriter.files.data.norecords.timeout=120
mywriter.files.rolloveronshutdown=true
```

Other Writer Output File Property Settings

There are a number of properties that can be set with respect to the format of the output files that are created by GoldenGate Flat File. The following table lists the most commonly used parameters and their usage.

Parameter Name	Description	Example
Files.onepertable	Indicates if there should be one file per table being processed, or if there should be one single output for the defined writer process. Valid values are TRUE and FALSE.	`Mywriter.files.onepertable=true`
Files.prefix	Indicates the prefix that should be added to the physical files that are being created for the process.	`Mywriter.files.prefix=u01db01`
Files.data.rootdir Files.control .rootdir	This indicates the root directory where the flat files (data) and control files (control) should be written. This is a global setting.	`Files.data.rootdir= /u01/GG/flatfiles Files.control .rootdir= /u01/GG/controlfiles`
Files.data.ext Files.control.ext	This indicates the file extension that should be given to the flat files (data) and control files (control) after writing has been completed (also known as rollover).	`Files.data.ext=_ data.don Files.control.ext= _control.ctrl`

Parameter Name	Description	Example

Files.data.tmpext
Files.control
.tmpext
	This indicates the file extension that should be given to the flat files (data) and control files (control) as writing is occurring. This is a temporary extension and the files will be renamed with the permanent extension once they are rolled over.	`Files.data.ext=_`
		`data.tmp`
		`Files.control.ext=`
		`_control.ctmp`

Configuring File Data Content Properties

It probably makes sense that you would want to configure what data is actually written to the output file. There are properties you can set that will let you do this. These properties include:

- **Rawchars**   Binary value (True or False) determines if raw characters are to be written to the data file. The default value is False for this parameter.

- **Includebeforces**   Binary value (True or False; False is the default) indicating if the data to be written to the flat file should include both before and after images of the data to be written.

- **Includecolnames**   Binary value (True or False; False is the default) indicating if the data to be written to the flat file should include the column names along with the data values.

- **Omitvalues**   Binary value (True or False; False is the default) indicating if the data to be written to the flat file should include or omit the values of the data written.

- **Diffsonly**   Binary value (True or False; False is the default) indicating if the data should be written to the flat file if the before and after values are not different.

- **Omitplaceholders**   Binary value (True or False; False is the default) indicating if delimiters should be included for missing columns.

Here are some examples:

```
mywriter.includecolnames=TRUE
mywriter.includebefores=TRUE
```

Including Meta File in Your Datafile Output

The GoldenGate output to a flat file can also include various kinds of metadata (for example, you might want each individual record in the flat file to indicate if the transaction was an update, delete, or insert operation) with the output. These are called Meta columns. Table 16-1 lists the Meta columns supported by Oracle GoldenGate for Flat File.

An example of the use of a Meta column might look like this:

```
mywriter.metacols=timestamp,opcode,txind,position,schema,table
```

For LDV output, the columns can be variable or fixed length. Additionally, position data can be written in hex or decimal and a Meta column can display the internal value, or it can be read from a column from the original data. For example, if we wanted to include the timestamp column but make it a fixed length, we could set the property as follows:

```
mywriter.metacols.timestamp.fixedlength=10
```

The result would be to truncate a timedate stamp of 2012-01-01 10:00:00.123456 to a value of 2012-01-01 10:00:00 in the output file. If you wanted to output the value of a given column, rather than take the default format, you might do something like this:

```
mywriter.metacols.timestamp.column=app_timestamp
```

Meta Column Name	Description
POSITION	A unique position indicator of records in a trail
OPCODE	I, U, or D for insert, update, or delete records
TXIND	Kind of record in a transaction (0 - begin, 1 - middle, 2 - end, 3 - whole)
TXOPPOS	Position of record in a transaction, starting from 0
SCHEMA	The schema (owner) name of the changed record
TABLE	The table name of the changed record
SCHEMAANDTABLE	Both the schema and table name concatenated as schema.table
TIMESTAMP	The commit timestamp of the record
@<token name>	A token value defined in the Extract param file
GETENV	A GETENV value as documented in the *Oracle GoldenGate Reference Guide*; for example $GGHEADER.OPCODE

TABLE 16-1. *Meta Columns Supported by Oracle GoldenGate for Flat File*

In this case, we will pull the timestamp value from the APP_TIMESTAMP column, rather than have the tool insert the value from the internal metadata that was captured.

You might want to right- or left-justify your data, and this is provided for through the fixedjustify attribute. Note that by default all columns are left-justified, so if you wanted to right-justify, you might want to do the following:

```
mywriter.metacols.timestamp.fixedjustify=right
```

There are many other Meta options that you can take advantage of when using GoldenGate for Flat File. There are also properties specific to the type of flat file you are writing (LDV and DSV). Check the documentation for the options available to you in the version of the product you are using.

NOTE
Make sure when you create the parameter files that no spaces exist between the individual values being defined and the equal sign or commas.

Including Statistics in Your Datafile Output

You might have a need to include statistics in your datafile output. Information such as when the rollover actions occurred, what the interval of time between rollovers was, total number of records by schema or table that were written, and what kinds of records they were (insert, update, or delete). To include statistics in your output, you would set the statistics property in the parameter file as seen in this example:

```
mywriter.statistics.statistics.tosummaryfile=TRUE

mywriter.statistics.summary.fileformat=
schema,table,total,totaldetail,gctimestamp,ctimestamp
```

In this example we first indicate that we want statistics generated for the mywriter writer process, and then we indicate what information the writer process should produce in a statistics output. We want summary statistics as well as detailed statistics, so we use the summary property to indicate this. We have indicated we want statistics by schema and table as well as total statistics and details about the total statistics written as well as timestamp information.

The following table provides a list of the information that can be configured in the properties file to indicate what information should be recorded with respect to statistics:

Option	Meaning
Schema	Report the schema or owner of the table that the statistics relate to.
table	Report the table that the statistics relate to.
schemaandtable	Report the schema and table in one column. The two values will be separated by a period in the output.
Gtotal	Report the total number of records output for the specified table since the user exit was started.
gtotaldetail	Report the total number of inserts, updates, and deletes separated by the delimiter since the user exit was started.
gctimestamp	Report the minimum and maximum commit timestamp for the specified table since user exit was started.
ctimestamp	Report the minimum and maximum values for the commit timestamps for the specified table in the related data file.
Total	Report the total number of records output for the specified table in the related data file.
Totaldetail	Report the total number of inserts, updates, and deletes output for the specified table in the related data file.
rate	Report the average rate of output of data for the specified table in the related data file in records per second.
ratedetail	Report the average rate of inserts, updates, and deletes for the specified table in the related data file in records per second.

Including Statistics in Your Datafile Output

The process to create the output flat files from GoldenGate is similar to what you would do in any GoldenGate configuration in most cases. To create the process, you would do the following:

1. You might have to run the defgen utility if the schema definitions are different between the source and target systems. We will call our defs file flatdefs.def.

2. Create the GoldenGate Extract process as outlined in Chapter 5. You may need to use functions, such as the @date functions, to properly format the output data. Here is an example:

```
EXTRACT myflatextract
EXTTRAIL dirdat\fl
TARGETDEFS dirdef\flatfile.def
```

```
MAP sh.my_table, TARGET <owner>.my_table,COLMAP (USEDEFAULTS,
my_timestamp=@DATE ("YYYY-MM-DD HH:MI:SS.FFFFFF",
"YYYY-MM-DD:HH:MI:SS.FFFFFF",my_timestamp));
```

In this case, the @DATE function is used to format the MY_TIMESTAMP column data as it's written to the output file.

3. Create a primary GoldenGate Data Pump Extract process to move the trail file data to the location where it will be processed. This is also outlined in Chapter 5.

4. Configure the file writer properties file. A typical file writer properties file might look like this:

```
# true/false flag to determine whether to output all data to one
# file, or to create one file per table
mywriter.files.onepertable=true
# number of seconds before rolling over
mywriter.files.data.rollover.time=100
# max file size in KB before rolling over
mywriter.files.data.rollover.size=100000
# additional timeout to rollover in case no records for a period
# of time
# Other parameters of interest.
mywriter.files.data.norecords.timeout=10000
goldengate.log.logname=uelog
goldengate.log.level=INFO
goldengate.log.tostdout=false
goldengate.log.tofile=true
goldengate.log.modules=UEUTIL,LOGMALLOC,TXSTORE,UTILS,DSUSEREXIT,
FILEWRITER,CSVFILEWRITER,BINFILEWRITER
goldengate.flatfilewriter.writers=dsvwriter
goldengate.userexit.chkptprefix=shpump_
mywriter.mode=DSV
mywriter.rawchars=false
mywriter.includebefores=false
mywriter.includecolnames=false
mywriter.omitvalues=false
mywriter.diffsonly=false
mywriter.omitplaceholders=false
mywriter.files.onepertable=true
mywriter.files.data.rootdir=C:\datafiles
mywriter.files.data.ext=_data.dsv
mywriter.files.data.tmpext=_data.dsv.temp
mywriter.files.data.rollover.time=100
mywriter.files.data.rollover.size=100000
```

```
mywriter.files.data.norecords.timeout=10000
mywriter.files.control.use=true
mywriter.files.control.ext=_data.control
mywriter.files.control.rootdir=C:\datafiles\control
mywriter.dsv.nullindicator.chars=
mywriter.dsv.fielddelim.chars=;
```

5. Configure the file writer Extract process.

```
EXTRACT mywrit
CUSEREXIT C:\ggora\flatfilewriter.dll CUSEREXIT PASSTHRU
INCLUDEUPDATEBEFORES
SOURCEDEFS dirdef\flatdefs.def
TABLE <owner>.MY_TABLE;
```

6. Create the table sh.my_table (or make sure it exists) and ensure it matches the data in the extract trail file.

7. Now, as shown in Chapter 5, use the GGSCI program to add each of the three extracts that have just been created. Start the extracts and watch the external flat file being created.

Other API Interfaces into GoldenGate

Oracle GoldenGate supports JMS and MQ Series messaging services, among others. As with Oracle GoldenGate for Flat File, these different services are supported by supplied Oracle plug-in adapters that use the GoldenGate-supplied API interface to provide these services. GoldenGate is adding support for many different types of vendor products, and of course provides support for you writing your own interface code through its set of C API interfaces. The Oracle Technology Network (OTN) provides a number of examples that you can follow for the many different kinds of interfaces into GoldenGate that Oracle provides. If you have a need for these kinds of specialized use cases, please look at OTN for more information.

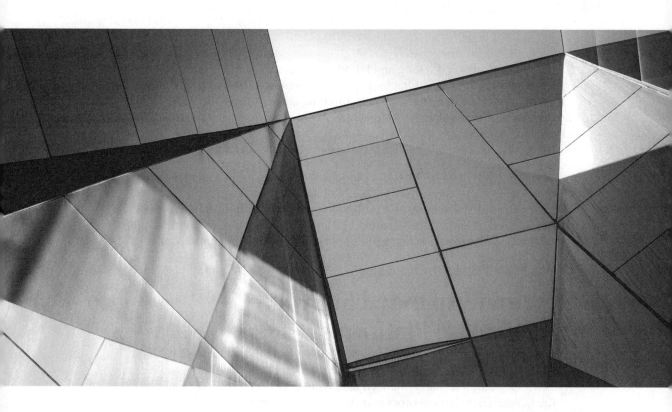

CHAPTER
17

GoldenGate 11.2
New Features

Writing a book is a long and laborious process. While the authors were writing this book, Oracle released GoldenGate Version 11.2. We decided to provide this chapter as a last-minute update to provide you with information on the new updates to Oracle GoldenGate. The latest release of 11.2 of GoldenGate provides a number of new features, and in this chapter we will cover a few of the new features that are likely to have the largest impact on you.

As with other versions of Oracle GoldenGate, Oracle GoldenGate Version 11.2 provides some new features that only apply to specific database vendors, while other enhancements will apply to all supported platforms. Improvements and new features in Oracle GoldenGate Versions 11.2 include such things as improvements in globalization, security, conflict resolution, general performance improvements, and expanded platform support.

New and Expanded Support for Database Platforms

New platform support is always of interest. Oracle GoldenGate Version 11.2 has added support for new database platforms for both capture and delivery. Additionally, Oracle GoldenGate 11.2 has enhanced data type support for different platforms.

The GoldenGate Capture process is now supported on the IBM AS/400 (iSeries) platform. While capture is supported on the AS/400, delivery is not supported. Conversely, Oracle GoldenGate 11.2 now supports delivery (and not capture) on Postgres databases. So now you should be able to replicate changes from AS/400 to Postgres! Wild, eh?

Finally, GoldenGate version 11.2 has expanded support for data types for both MySQL and Microsoft SQL Server databases.

Globalization

Globalization is probably one of the bigger new features of GoldenGate 11.2 and it's also one that is mostly an under-the-hood improvement. Character set conversion issues are now less of a problem in GoldenGate 11.2. For example, GoldenGate will now process table and column names, schema, and catalog data in the character set of the source and target databases.

The ability to process native character sets extends to support of non-ASCII character sets, which really helps to make the implementation of GoldenGate easier in various parts of the world. The use of the native character set is also extended to GoldenGate parameter files.

Security

In this day and age, securing your data is right at the top of most organizations' priorities. Often security is considered even more important than performance, and even on par with recoverability. While significant resources and time are often spent to secure data within a database, securing that same data when it leaves the database is often overlooked. GoldenGate has always provided features related to security, and Oracle GoldenGate 11.2 adds to this feature set.

Oracle GoldenGate has supported encrypting the trail files for several releases, and now the encryption capabilities have been enhanced. On Oracle GoldenGate Version 11.2, Advanced Encryption Security (AES) support has been added to trail and parameter files as well as the TCP connection between the extract and collector. This provides more secure encryption of the data being processed by GoldenGate.

The Oracle GoldenGate keygen program has been updated in Oracle GoldenGate 11.2 so that it can now generate AES type keys. In the following example we will create five keys using AES 256-bit encryption. Changing 256 to 128 would create 128-bit keys. As in past releases, the output can be saved to the ENCKEYS file to be used for encrypting passwords and trail files by redirecting the output to a text file.

```
keygen 256 5 > ENCKEYS
cat ENCKEYS
0x4B213511DE66310950530D400B1CDD48F38D6A38335C590D41BB527ACECA221C
0xF3270C7B919D901332F25F55BAC25322514DB912F6D2C2290A25296B339D2C31
0x9C2EE36444D4EF1D1491B26A6869CA7BAE0C086DB9492C46D38EFF5B986F3646
0x4535BA4EF70A4F28F72F0500171041550CCC56477CC095629CF8D54CFD41405B
0xEE3B9138AA41AE32D9CE5715C6B6B72E6A8BA5213F37FF7E6562AC3D62144A70
```

Having set up the ENCKEYS files with encrypting passwords, you can configure trail files and network traffic as you normally would. Using the encrypted form of any sensitive text compared to plain text is considered best practice. You wouldn't want someone to see a password simply by viewing a text file. In the following example, we get the encrypted value for a password.

```
ggsci>encrypt password ggs_user encryptkey securekey1
Encrypted password:
 AADAAAAAAAAAAAIARGHAJHZEPJMGSEXGSDDJDDEEVDDGSCDGVDWEGIIDLBUGMBYAGCH
DLHUAGAHBQIHH
Algorithm used:  AES128
```

Intelligent Conflict Resolution

Conflict resolution is a major issue when implementing a GoldenGate bidirectional and multimaster node replication scheme (see Chapter 6 for more on multimaster replication). A conflict occurs when similar changes occur on more than one node that conflict with each other (for example, two different birth dates are entered for the same employee on different master nodes). In these cases, where data that is entered is conflicting, we need to have a way to resolve the issue. This is known as conflict resolution, and conflict resolution can be the hardest thing to deal with when configuring multimaster replication.

Oracle GoldenGate 11.2 tries to make conflict resolution easier for the DBA to set up and administer. The new conflict resolution framework works in conjunction with the error reporting used in earlier releases of GoldenGate. In the event that a conflict resolution rule and an error-reporting condition exist for the same error condition, the conflict rule takes precedence. Additionally, an exception table can also be created for conflict resolution. Any time a conflict occurs, regardless of whether the conflict is resolved or not, the data that generated the error can be logged to an exception table.

There are many different types of conflict that could happen during active-to-active replication. Some of these conditions might include:

- A unique constraint error is generated during an **insert** statement.

- A data mismatch for an **update** or **delete** statement. For example, the row to be changed exists, but a column(s) does not match in the WHERE clause.

- No rows are found when performing an **update** or **delete** statement.

With the new release, the RESOLVECONFLICT option has been added to the **map** statement that is part of a replicat file. The RESOLVECONFLICT option is used to instruct GoldenGate on how to resolve conflicts for the particular **map** statement. When you have used the RESOLVECONFLICT option in a replicat parameter file, you will need the GETBEFORECOLS option in the associated extract file. This will allow you to compare the before values for the full row in the source against values in the target row, allowing for more flexibility in writing conflict rules.

In Oracle GoldenGate, column types used for conflict resolution must have before images. The result of this is that columns containing data types of CLOB, BLOB, abstract data types, or user-defined data types can't be used to determine conflict resolution because before images of these data types are not available to the Replicat process. This doesn't mean you can't perform replication with tables that contain these data types, but you cannot use columns that contain these kinds of data types when writing conflict resolution rules.

Sometimes the data types that you need to support conflict resolution are not supported by GoldenGate for conflict resolution purposes. In this case, there are other options that you might consider using as the "tie-breaker" to determine which change should be applied on all nodes. For example, you might consider using a column with a timestamp such that the change with the most current timestamp is the one that is used. Another option might be to use a derived (virtual) data column that contains some part of the unsupported data that could be used as the tie-breaker that would determine which conflicting operation is the one to be processed. The bottom line is: if you are using unsupported data, you might have to get a bit imaginative with respect to figuring out which change is the one to be applied.

We have talked about these new conflict resolution features in some detail. Now let's take a look at a few examples of using these conflict resolution features. In the examples, required information for the replicat parameter files that are not related to conflict resolution, such as login information and trail file, are omitted. Here is our first example:

```
REPERROR (DEFAULT, DISCARD)
DISCARDFILE ./dirrpt/discard.txt, APPEND
MAP hr.employees, TARGET people.people, &
COMPARECOLS (ON UPDATE ALL, ON DELETE ALL), &
RESOLVECONFLICT (UPDATEROWEXISTS, (DEFAULT, USEMAX (last_mod_time))), &
RESOLVECONFLICT (DELETEROWEXISTS, (DEFAULT, OVERWRITE)), &
RESOLVECONFLICT (UPDATEROWMISSING, (DEFAULT, OVERWRITE)), &
RESOLVECONFLICT (DELETEROWMISSING, (DEFAULT, DISCARD));
```

Let's look at this replicat file in a bit more detail. Note in this replicat file that we use the REPERROR and DISCARDFILE parameters (we have reprinted these two lines again after this paragraph) to handle replication problems not covered by the resolution rules. In the cases where we have not provided rules, GoldenGate will discard unhandled records and put them in the GoldenGate discard file.

```
REPERROR (DEFAULT, DISCARD)
DISCARDFILE ./dirrpt/discard.txt, APPEND
```

Next, we use the MAP parameter to map the source and target tables. Note that in our example the source and target schema and table are different. We are replicating from HR.EMPLOYEES to the PEOPLE.PEOPLE target table.

```
MAP hr.employees, TARGET people.people, &
```

Now, we need to tell GoldenGate that we want to do some conflict resolution and when we want to perform conflict resolution. To do so we use the COMPARECOLS keyword. We use the UPDATE ALL and DELETE ALL options to indicate that we want GoldenGate to detect conflicts for **update** and **delete** statements. Additionally, this statement will cause GoldenGate to compare all columns.

```
COMPARECOLS (ON UPDATE ALL, ON DELETE ALL), &
```

The next four lines use the RESOLVECONFLICT parameter, which defines what we want GoldenGate to do to resolve a conflict when it is detected. The first **resolveconflict** statement defines how GoldenGate will handle cases where column values don't match when an **update** statement has been executed. Also, in this example we have used the DEFAULT keyword to indicate that the column names will match in both source and target databases. In this case, the LAST_MOD_TIME column will be used as the tie-breaker and the column with the most recent date/time stamp value will be used.

```
RESOLVECONFLICT (UPDATEROWEXISTS, (DEFAULT, USEMAX (last_mod_time))), &
```

The next line is for cases when columns being deleted don't match. In this case we overwrite the values from the source. The result is that the row is deleted:

```
RESOLVECONFLICT (DELETEROWEXISTS, (DEFAULT, OVERWRITE)), &
```

The third line executes in the case of an **update** statement where there are no rows to be updated. In this case the **update** statement is turned into an **insert** statement and the row is added to the target database.

```
RESOLVECONFLICT (UPDATEROWMISSING, (DEFAULT, OVERWRITE)), &
```

The last line is for **delete** statements where the delete operation affects zero rows. In this case the **delete** statement is simply ignored.

```
RESOLVECONFLICT (DELETEROWMISSING, (DEFAULT, DISCARD));
```

Let's look at another example. This example is for a table that tracks the quantity of stock for products. In addition to using the PRODUCT_ID column as the key, we will include the IN_STOCK and PRICE columns to detect and process conflicts occurring with replication to the table STORE.ITEMS. In this example we model a situation where two different databases contain a table that tracks stock levels that are both active. Since both databases could change the number of an in-stock item, both databases could contain the wrong value for the stock. Since the value from both the source and target are incorrect, we need a way to compute the correct value for the stock of the particular item. To resolve this potential conflict situation, we use the **usedelta** method to add the delta value from the source to the target for the stock column. The result is that the delta in stock value will be added to the value in the target source. The next line handles conflicts for all other columns included in the KEYINCLUDING clause. In this case the values that are part of the data set with the most recent change time are used.

```
MAP store.items, TARGET store.items,
COMPARECOLS
(ON UPDATE KEYINCLUDING (in_stock, price)),
RESOLVECONFLICT (
UPDATEROWEXISTS,
(delta_res_method, USEDELTA, COLS (In_stock)),
(DEFAULT, USEMAX (last_change_time)));
```

Using these new GoldenGate features and the new (and simple) conflict resolution features that have been added, it is possible to quickly set up powerful resolution rules.

Network Performance Improvements

GoldenGate has the ability to replicate data over long distances very efficiently via TCP/IP connections. One consistent performance problem is that over longer distances, replication is more and more subject to the inefficiencies of the WAN being used, which results in latency and increasing overall lag times with respect to replication.

In order to try to increase network performance, Oracle GoldenGate 11.2 now will asynchronously stream packets to the collector by default. The STREAMING option has been added to the RMTHOST and RMTHOSTOPTIONS parameters.

Since asynchronous streams are now the default option, you do not have to add anything special to your parameter files to take advantage of this new feature. In some cases the platforms that are being used will not support asynchronous operations. In these cases GoldenGate will fall back to synchronous transmission.

The benefit of asynchronous streaming is that the Extract process will stream network packets to the collector without waiting for a response for each packet. Since the extract continues sending packets without waiting for individual responses, performance is increased. This can be very helpful when you are using slow or high-latency networks. GoldenGate has added additional checks to ensure that data has been transmitted and applied correctly. For example, the Extract process embeds a flag requesting an acknowledgment from the target that is later processed.

Integrated Capture

Oracle GoldenGate Version 11.2 has introduced a new capture method called Integrated Capture. Integrated Capture is the integration of the GoldenGate Capture process with the Oracle Database kernel (only with Oracle databases). Oracle GoldenGate still supported the old method of capturing data, and they have renamed the old method "Classic Capture." In integrating the Capture process with the core log parsing code of Oracle Database, Oracle can provide additional enhancements to the GoldenGate product, such as the ability to process compressed data streams, expanded data type support, better control memory allocations of the Extract process, and also support for Downstream Capture from an Oracle Data Guard database. Let's look at each of these new features next.

GoldenGate and Compressed Data

Oracle GoldenGate Version 11.2 can now capture compressed data (when using Oracle Database Version 11.2.0.3 database and higher).

NOTE
*If you choose to use the old Classic Capture method,
you will still not be able to process compressed data.*

This is a nice new feature because businesses and organizations are storing and processing more data than ever before. This has resulted in huge storage requirements, and as anyone who has dealt with enterprise-level storage will tell you, storage is not cheap. To try to deal with these storage challenges, Oracle has developed several data compression technologies. These compression technologies include database features such as advanced compression, and if you are running Exadata or Oracle ZFS Storage Appliances, you can also use Hybrid Columnar Compression (HCC).

These compression technologies have helped many organizations reduce their storage requirements, but they have caused problems with users trying to use Oracle GoldenGate, since previous releases of Oracle GoldenGate did not support replication of compressed data.

GoldenGate and Extract Memory

Oracle GoldenGate now allows you to configure the amount of memory available to the log mining process. This is helpful for high-activity databases where you may need to increase the amount of memory due to the rate of new data that needs to be processed from the redo logs. In this next example we will create a classic extract and upgrade it to an integrated extract.

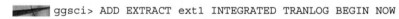
```
ggsci> ADD EXTRACT ext1 INTEGRATED TRANLOG BEGIN NOW
```

This example uses TRANLOGOPTIONS in an extract parameter file to set a maximum of 164 megabytes of memory. For brevity, only the line dealing with Integrated Capture is shown.

```
TRANLOGOPTIONS INTEGRATEDPARAMS (MAX_SGA_SIZE 164)
```

Next, it is a simple one-line command to upgrade the extract:

```
ggsci>ALTER EXTRACT ext1, UPGRADE INTEGRATED TRANLOG
```

Downstream Capture

In addition to capturing compressed data with Integrated Capture, the mining of data can now be done from a secondary server of the same platform as the source. This process is known as Downstream Capture. When using Downstream Capture, an Oracle Data Guard database is used as the mining database for GoldenGate. In this configuration the mining database receives the redo information from the primary database. The database redo information is recorded in the Data Guard database standby redo logs when the data is applied to the database. GoldenGate is able to capture this redo using the Integrated Capture method just as if it were running on the primary database. This configuration is very helpful when you want to ensure that Oracle GoldenGate extract operations do not interfere with the performance of your production database.

Finally: A RAC-Related Change

Last but not least, another major new enhancement with Integrated Capture applies when the source database is RAC. Previously, when creating an Extract process, you had to set the number of threads to match the number of instances for the database, but with Integrated Capture, this is no longer necessary.

Index

A

Abended state, 29
@ABSENT function, 194, 196
access-related errors, 328
action scripts, 227–229
active-active replication. *See* bidirectional
replication
Active Data Guard (ADG), 13, 221, 224
add checkpointtable command, 181
add extract command
    Data Pump process, 132
    extract memory, 400
    Extract process, 124, 138
    target database, 136
add exttrail command, 125
add replicat command
    checkpoint tables, 181
    Replicat process, 140, 148
    target database, 136
add rmttrail command, 132
add schematrandata command, 94–95
add trandata command
    object-level logging, 94–96
    SQL Server, 285, 289–290
ADDEVENTS parameter, 275
ADG (Active Data Guard), 13, 221, 224

Advanced Compression option, 342
Advanced Encryption Security (AES)
    algorithm, 181–183, 395
Advanced Workload Repository (AWR)
    reports, 75
ALO (Archive Log Only) mode, 25
ALTARCHIVELOGDEST option, 312, 330
alter database add supplemental log data
    command, 94
alter database archivelog command, 88
alter database open command, 88
alter exttrail command, 332
alter replicat command, 181
alter rmttrail command, 332
alter session command, 92
alter system command, 81, 88
alter table command, 95
ALTLOGDEST parameter, 248
API interfaces, 391
Appliance Import Settings screen, 50, 54
Appliance Import Wizard screen, 49
Application Virtual IP (A-VIP) addresses,
    225–227
Apply process, 10
    lag, 343
    SQL Server, 267–268
appvipcfg utility, 226

architecture
    Data Pump process, 33
    database support, 19–20
    documentation and
       information, 19
    Extract process. *See* Extract
       process
    GGSCI, 34
    latency, 34–35
    Manager process, 22
    overview, 18
    parameter files, 34
    processes, 21–22
    Replicat process, 34
    Server Collector, 33–34
    trail files, 30–33
    versions, 35
Archive Log Only (ALO) mode, 25
archived redo logs, 25–26
archivelog files, missing, 329–334
ARCHIVELOG Mode, 87–89
ASM. *See* Automatic Storage
   Management (ASM)
ASSUMETARGETDEFS parameter
    GoldenGate configuration for
      SQL Server, 302
    Replicat process, 139
    table-level column mapping,
      197–198
authentication in SQL Server, 263
Automatic Storage Management
   (ASM), 210
    DBLOGREADER, 211–212
    extract parameter file, 211
    high availability, 224
    listeners, 210
    RAC databases, 210–212
    tnsnames.ora file, 210
automating startup, 103
    Linux, 105–108
    Windows, 103–105
AUTORESTART parameter, 279
AUTOSTART parameter, 100, 104–105,
   278–279
AWR (Advanced Workload Repository)
   reports, 75

B

BACKUPMEDIAFAMILY table, 281
backups
    RMAN, 25
    SQL Server, 280–281
BACKUPSET table, 281
BATCHSQL parameter, 347
BEFOREFILTER clause, 167
begin command for Extract process, 124
bidirectional replication, 6–7, 162
    applications, 163
    cascaded deletes, 164
    conflict detection and resolution,
      165–168, 172–174
    Data Pump Extract process,
      170–171
    Extract process, 169–170
    issues, 168–169
    keys, 164
    loops, 165
    preparation, 162
    Replicat process, 171–172
    schema instantiation, 172
    starting, 174
    triggers, 164
    trusted source, 164
BINLOG_FORMAT parameter, 245
Blowfish encryption algorithm, 181
BOOTDELAYMINUTES parameter, 278
bounded recovery, 329–330
BRINTERVAL option, 329
broadcast replication, 6–7
bug reports, 19
bulk load mode, 28–29
BULK LOGGED mode, 263
bulk run mode, 23

C

CACHEMGR parameter, 345
capture changes in RAC databases,
   207–208
capture data loads, Extract process, 28

Capture process, 9–11. *See also* Extract process
cascaded deletes, 164
cascading replication, 6–7, 9, 159–160
@CASE function, 204
category.dll file, 275
Change Data Capture (CDC) objects, 260, 266
changes in trail files, 32–33
CHECK constraint, 269
CHECKPARAMS parameter, 332–334
checkpoint information
tables, 180–185, 300
viewing, 316–318
CHECKPOINT NOT COMPLETE messages, 345
chkconfig command, 108
chmod command, 106–108
Classic Capture method, 207–208
Cleanup History task, 282
Cleanup jobs in CDC, 266
clones, disk, 3, 61
Cloning Configuration screen, 61
clusters. *See* Real Application Clusters (RAC)
Clusterware
action script, 227–228
for administration, 229–230
for node failures, 221, 225–226
registering, 229
CMDSEC file, 185
Collector process, 22
COLMAP parameter, 197–198, 205
COLMATCH statement, 202
COLS option, 193–194
COLSEXCEPT option, 193–194
columns
avoiding errors, 195–196
filtering, 193–194
IDENTITY property, 310–311
table-level mapping, 197–202
command security, 185
Commit Sequence Numbers (CSNs), 32–33

committed transactions in Extract process, 26–27
COMPARECOLS keyword, 397
comparisons in Vericom, 372–376
compression
exported data, 342
network, 346
new features, 400
@COMPUTE function, 203
configuring
Data Pump process, 130–136
Extract process, 121–129, 137–138
file data content properties, 386
Manager process, 96–108, 117–121, 274–277
multitarget replication, 154–155
Oracle GoldenGate. *See* configuring Oracle GoldenGate
Oracle GoldenGate Director Server, 361
Replicat process, 138–140, 145, 150–152
configuring Oracle GoldenGate
checklists, 84–86
database configuration, 87–89
DDL replication, 80–82
deferred constraints, 91–92
directories, 83–84
flashback queries, 89–90
GLOBALS file, 96
after initial install, 73–76
Manager process, 96–108
memory, 75–76
operating system, 74–76
overview, 72–73
primary keys, 90–91
sequences, 82–83
supplemental logging, 92–96
systems preparation, 86–87
users, 76–80

configuring Oracle GoldenGate for
    SQL Server
        basic, 283–292
        MANAGESECONDARYTRUNCA-
            TIONPOINT option, 292–293
        NOMANAGESECONDARYTRUN-
            CATIONPOINT option,
            294–306
        Pump process, 296–298
Confirm Out of Sync (COOS) status,
    370–371
conflict detection and resolution
        bidirectional replication, 165–168
        conflict handlers, 172–174
        new features, 395–399
Connection Refused errors, 328
Connection Timed Out errors, 328
connections
        network-related errors, 328
        RAC databases, 209
        SQL Server, 289, 291
        Veridata, 372
consolidation replication, 6–7
constraints, deferred, 91–92
COOS (Confirm Out of Sync) status,
    370–371
copy on write method, 4
create directory command, 158
Create New Virtual Disk screen, 57
Create New Virtual Machine Wizard
    screen, 55–57
create sequence command, 163
create snapshot command, 8
create subdirs command, 83, 273
create user command, 76
crsctl command, 226
CSNs (Commit Sequence Numbers),
    32–33
ctimestamp statistic, 389
Current Checkpoint, 318
CUSEREXIT PARAMS parameter, 381
Custom Setup screen, 45

D

data cleansing method, 5
Data Definition Language (DDL)
        database data replication, 5
        replication configuration, 80–82
        SQL Server, 311–312
Data Integration Server (DIS), 380
Data Pump process
        administering, 132–134
        bidirectional replication, 170–171
        configuring, 130, 134–136
        with encrypted trails, 183
        extract parameter file, 130–131
        overview, 33
        registering, 131–132
Data Source in ODBC, 287–289
data source names (DSNs), 258–259,
    289, 291, 299, 309
data transformation, 5
data types
        MySQL, 234–235
        SQL Server, 261
Database Configuration Assistant
    (DBCA), 61
databases and database platforms
        configured processes, 140–141
        Data Pump process, 157–158
        Data Pump Extract process,
            155–159
        data replication features, 4–6
        errors with, 335–338
        Extract process, 137–138, 156
        instantiation, 136–141
        Manager process, 154–155
        MySQL, 234–235
        new features, 394
        object replication, 7
        one-way replication, 114–117
        RAC, 207–209
        Replicat process, 138–140, 158
        SQL Server, 267–269, 279–283
        support, 19–20, 39–40
        upgrades and migrations, 365
        Veridata connections, 372

datafile output
meta file, 387–388
statistics, 388–391
DBCA (Database Configuration
Assistant), 61
dblogin command
Data Pump process, 131
Extract process, 124
SQL Server, 263
supplemental logging, 95
dblogin sourcedb command, 268, 287
DBLOGREADER, 211–212
DBOPTIONS DEFRERRCONST
parameter, 92
DBOPTIONS LIMITROW parameter, 91
DBOPTIONS SUPPRESSTRIGGERS
parameter, 139–140
DBOPTIONS USEREPLICATIONUSER
parameter, 300
DDL (Data Definition Language)
database data replication, 5
replication configuration, 80–82
SQL Server, 311–312
ddl_setup.sql script, 82
DDLOPTIONS parameter, 82
DEBUG logging level, 382
decrypttrail command, 183
DEFAULT keyword for conflicts,
397–398
deferred constraints, 91–92
DEFERRCONST option, 92
DEFGEN parameter file, 303
defgen utility
MySQL, 237, 246–247
source definition files, 198
definition files
creating, 198–202
MySQL, 237–238
DEFSFILE parameter, 237
DELETE ALL option, 397
deletes
cascaded, 164
conflict resolution, 165

Delimiter Separated Values (DSV)
file, 380
Delivery Cloud, 63, 68–69, 359
demo_mss_create.sql script, 285, 299
demo_mss_insert.sql script, 305
demo_ora_create.sql script, 301
demonstration environments, 42
detail command, 340
DETAIL parameter
Data Pump process, 133
Extract process, 127
Replicat process, 149
diagnostic tools, 327
Diffsonly property, 386
directorcontrol.sh script, 360
directories
configuring, 83–84
download, 63
DIS (Data Integration Server), 380
disaster recovery (DR), 223–224
discard files, 212–215
DISCARDFILE parameter, 397
discovery process, 355
disk-based replication, 3–4
disk cloning method, 3
disk space requirements, 40–41
Distributor instances in SQL Server, 264
DML triggers, 269
documentation and information, 19
double quotes ("") for literal strings, 194
downstream capture, 9, 400–401
downtime in upgrades and migration,
364–366
DSNs (data source names), 258–259,
289, 291, 299, 309
DSV (Delimiter Separated Values)
file, 380
DYNAMICPORTLIST parameter
Manager process, 99, 331
SQL Server, 257
DYNAMICPORTREASSIGNDELAY
parameter, 99

E

edit params command
Data Pump process, 130
Data Pump Extract process, 155
Extract process, 121
GLOBALS file, 96, 98, 103
Manager process, 97
Replicat parameter file, 146
SQL Server, 291, 302
edit params mgr command, 276
ENABLEMONITORING parameter, 353
ENABLEMONITORINGAGENT
parameter, 353
ENCKEYS files, 182–183, 395
encryption
new features, 395
passwords, 181–183
trail files, 183–185
encrypttrail command, 183–184
END RUNTIME parameter, 139–140
ENGINE clause, 245
env command, 340
Environment Variables window, 75
EOFDELAYCSECS value, 345
error handling, 212
discard files, 212–215
exceptions table, 215–218
trail file maintenance, 218
error issues
access-related, 328
archivelog files, 329–334
column filtering, 195–196
networks-related, 328–329
ERROR logging level, 382
EVENTACTIONS parameter, 283
EVERY setting in sqlexec, 206
exceptions table, 215–218
exit properties file, 381–382
expdp utility, 157, 342
exporting source schema, 157–158
extract memory, 400
EXTRACT parameter
Data Pump process, 133
Replicat process, 149

Extract process, 23
administering, 125–126
bidirectional replication, 169–170
bulk loads, 28–29
bulk run mode, 23
configuring, 121, 128–129
extract files, 29
initial-load, 137–138
lag, 345
memory for, 76
in migrations, 367
MySQL Replicat process, 240–244
online mode, 24–27
overview, 21
parallel, 29–30
parameter files, 121–124,
130–131, 211
performance issues, 328–334
problems, 27–28
purpose, 23–24
RAC clustered databases, 30
registering, 124
SQL Server, 263–264
stalled, 330–331
states, 29
statistics, 322–325
target database, 156
trail files, 30–33, 125
exttrail command, 331
EXTTRAIL parameter, 184
EXTTRAILSOURCE parameter, 297

F

failback option, 366–367
FAILBACK parameter, 226
Fast Recovery Area (FRA), 88
fast refresh method, 8
FETCHBEFOREFILTER option, 194
FETCHCOLS option, 194, 196
FETCHCOLSEXCEPT option, 194, 196
ffwriter.properties file, 381
file data content properties for
writers, 386

Files.control.ext parameter, 385
Files.data.ext parameter, 385
Files.data.norecords.timeout
    attribute, 385
Files.data.rollover.size attribute, 384
Files.data.rollover.time attribute, 384
Files.data.rootdir parameter, 385
Files.onepertable parameter, 385
Files.prefix parameter, 385
Files.rolloveronshutdown attribute, 385
FILTER option
        conflict resolution, 165, 168
        rows, 195
filter statement, 167
filters, 191
        conflict resolution, 167–168
        data replication, 5
        rows, 194–197
        tables, 191–194
First Run Wizard, 58–59
flashback queries, 89–90
flat files. *See* Oracle GoldenGate for
    Flat File utility
flush sequence command, 83
FLUSHCSECS parameter, 345
FOREIGN KEY constraint, 269
FORMATSQL parameter, 378
FORMATXML parameter, 378
FRA (Fast Recovery Area), 88
FREQUENCYHOURS parameter, 218
FREQUENCYMINUTES parameter, 218
FULL recovery mode in SQL Server, 263

G

gctimestamp statistic, 389
Generic Service resource, 309
GETBEFORECOLS option, 396
GETLAG parameter, 325
@GETVAL function, 205
gg-director-serversetup_unix_version.sh
    script, 360
GGADMIN user, 81
GGHOME parameter, 74

GGS_DDL_HIST table, 81
GGSCI. *See* GoldenGate Software
    Command Interface
    (GGSCI) program
ggserr.log file, 240, 318–321
ggsmsg.dll file, 275
GGTBS tablespace, 81
ghdr command, 340
global mapping, 202–206
globalization as new features, 394
GLOBALS file
        for Agent, 353
        auto startup, 103–105
        checkpoint tables, 177
        configuring, 96
        double quotes, 194
        GSSSCHEMA parameter, 81
        for Manager, 308
        purpose, 98
        SQL Server, 274, 279
GoldenGate Agent, 353
GoldenGate Data Pump process. *See*
    Data Pump process
GoldenGate Director. *See* Oracle
    GoldenGate Director
GoldenGate Extract process. *See*
    Extract process
GoldenGate for Flat File utility.
    See Oracle GoldenGate for Flat
    File utility
GoldenGate Management Pack for
    Oracle, 350
GoldenGate Manager (GGM), 104
        action scripts, 227–229
        Clusterware for, 229–230
GoldenGate Manager process. *See*
    Manager process
GoldenGate Monitor component, 315
        architecture, 351–353
        instance prep, 353–354
        overview, 350–351
        server, 354–355
GoldenGate Replicat process. *See*
    Replicat process

GoldenGate Server Collector process
  overview, 33–34
  SQL Server, 254–255, 257
GoldenGate Software Command
  Interface (GGSCI) program
  bidirectional replication, 174
  checkpoint tables, 176–181
  configuration for SQL Server,
    294–306
  Data Pump Extract process,
    130–136, 155
  description, 34
  Director Server, 357
  directory configuration, 83–84
  encryption, 182, 186,
    188–190, 395
  Extract process, 24, 121,
    124–128, 137
  initial data loads, 140
  installation tests, 64–65
  lag, 325–326, 342–344
  Manager process, 97, 102–105,
    118, 154
  memory, 400
  MySQL, 233, 240–243, 247–251
  overview, 315–318
  path variables for, 75
  process reports and ggserr.log,
    318–321
  process status, 29
  Replicat process, 138,
    146–150, 159
  for SQL Server, 272–279,
    285–292, 294–306, 309
  statistics, 322–325
  supplemental logging, 95–96, 263
  swap space, 40
  troubleshooting with, 327,
    332–333
  Windows installations, 65–68
GoldenGate User Exit APIs, 381
GoldenGate Veridata, 366–367
  comparisons, 374–376
  configuring and using, 372–373
    functionality, 370–372
    web, 373–374
grant command, 82
Group name parameter, 98
groups in Veridata, 372
GROUPTRANSOPS parameter, 347
GSSMGR process, 99
GSSSCHEMA parameter, 81
Gtotal statistic, 389
gtotaldetail statistic, 389
Guest Additions, 59
GUI-based tools for monitoring,
  314–315

H

HANDLECOLLISIONS parameter
  bidirectional replication, 172–174
  discard files, 213, 216
  MySQL, 241–242
  Replicat parameter file, 147
  Replicat process initial-load, 140
hardware requirements for SQL Server,
  255–257
HCC (Hybrid Columnar
  Compression), 400
help stats command, 325
heterogeneous replication, 2, 9–11
high availability (HA), 223–224
Home environment variable, 74
host properties for Monitor, 353
HR schema, 110–112
hung processes, 338
Hybrid Columnar Compression
  (HCC), 400

I

IDENTITY property
  multimaster columns, 310–311
  SQL Server target databases, 269
@IF function, 204
images
  install, 40
  VirtualBox, 46–48

impdp utility, 158, 342
In-flight status for MOOS queue, 370
in-place upgrades, 364
In-sync status for MOOS queue, 370
Includebeforces property, 386
Includecolnames property, 386
indexes for SQL Server, 283
info command
  checkpoint information, 180,
    316–318
  Data Pump Extract process, 133
  Extract process, 127
  Replicat process, 149
info all command
  Data Pump Extract process, 132
  Extract process, 29, 126
  lag, 325–326, 342
  Manager process, 102–105,
    118, 276
  MySQL schema, 240
  overview, 315–316
  Replicat process, 149
INFO logging level, 382
info mgr command, 276
initial load
  Extract process, 137–138
  in filtering, 196
  MySQL, 236, 238–240
  performance tuning, 341–342
  Replicat process, 138–140
insert statement, 91–92
install adsservice command, 104
install images, 40
installing
  GoldenGate for MySQL, 232–233
  Oracle GoldenGate. *See*
    installing Oracle GoldenGate
  Oracle GoldenGate Director, 358
  Oracle GoldenGate for Flat
    File, 379
  SQL Server, 260
  VirtualBox, 43–46
installing Oracle GoldenGate
  database platforms supported, 39

database versions supported,
    39–40
disk space requirements, 40–41
downloading, 62–63
on Linux, 64–68
memory requirements, 40
network requirements, 42
Oracle VirtualBox. *See* Oracle
  VirtualBox
overview, 38
for RAC, 207
requirements, 39
on Windows, 65, 69–70
instances
  description, 40
  Monitor, 353–354
instantiating
  schema in bidirectional
    replication, 172
  target database in multitarget
    replication, 157–158
  target database in one-way
    replication, 136
INT data type, 235
Integrated Capture
  as new feature, 399
  RAC, 207–209
integration options, 378
  API interfaces, 391
  exit properties files, 381–382
  flat files. *See* Oracle GoldenGate
    for Flat File utility
  writers. *See* writers
invasive upgrades, 364
IOLATENCY option, 208

J

JAGENT, 354
JMS messaging service, 391
JMX password, 354
job setup for Veridata, 372

K

KEYCOLS parameter, 91, 193, 345, 347
keygen utility, 182
KEYINCLUDING clause, 398
keys
 bidirectional replication, 164
 password, 182
 primary, 90–91
 Replicat lag issues, 346–347

L

lag, 342–343
 Extract process, 345
 monitoring, 325–326
 overview, 344
 Pump process, 345–346
 Replicat process, 346–347
lag command, 325, 342–343
LAGINFO parameter, 343
LAGINFOMINUTES parameter, 343
LAGREPORT parameter, 343
LAGREPORTMINUTES parameter, 343
latency
 networks, 42
 overview, 34–35
LATEST option, 324
LCRs (logical change records), 9
LD_LIBRARY_PATH variable, 64, 75
Length Delimited Values (LDV) files
 description, 381
 meta columns, 387
LIBPATH path, 75
licenses, 63
 OTN, 66, 69
 virtual machines, 50
LIMITROWS option, 91
Linux
 auto startup in, 105–108
 installation on, 64–68
 virtual machines, 46–54
listeners in ASM, 210
literal strings, double quotes for, 194
local disks for RAC databases, 207

local trail files, 22, 27, 30, 32
LOG-BIN parameter, 245
LOG-BIN-INDEX parameter, 245
log sequence number (LSN), 281
Logdump utility, 339–341
logging
 SQL Server. *See* transaction logs
  for SQL Server
 supplemental, 92–96, 265–266
logging levels for user exit, 382
LOGGING setting, 335
logical change records (LCRs), 9
loops in bidirectional replication, 165
LSN (log sequence number), 281

M

MAA (Maximum Availability
 Architecture), 220–223
MAC addresses for virtual machines, 54
Maintenance History task, 282
Manager process
 administering, 101–103
 configuring, 96–101, 117–121,
  274–277
 DYNAMICPORTLIST, 331
 overview, 22
 SQL Server, 274–279, 308–310
 on target server, 154–155
MANAGESECONDARYTRUNCATION-
 POINT option, 266, 280,
 292–293, 310
many-to-many replication, 6–7
many-to-one replication, 6–7
MAP parameter and mapping
 column data, 197–202
 conflict resolution, 165–167
 filters, 192–193
 global, 202–206
 MySQL schema, 239
 parallelization, 348
 Replicat process, 139–140
 SQLEXEC, 204–206
map statements, 165–166
MAPEXCLUDE parameter, 192–193
marker_setup.sql script, 82

master-to-master replication, 6–7

materialized views, 8

MAX_COMMIT_PROPAGATION_
DELAY parameter, 208

MAXCOMMITPROPAGATIONDELAY
option, 208

Maximum Availability Architecture
(MAA), 220–223

MAXTRANSOPS parameter, 347

May Be Out of Sync (MOOS)
queue, 370

Media Pack, 63

Media Pack Search screen, 66–67,
69, 270

memory
configuring, 75–76
requirements, 40
SQL Server, 255
virtual machines, 56

Memory screen, 56

metadata, 387–388

Metalink, 19, 35

mgr command, 101–102, 106

Mgr parameter, 98

MGRPORT parameter, 296

MGRSERVNAME parameter,
274–275, 308

Microsoft Visual C++ 2005 SP1
Redistributable Package, 277

migration
failback option, 366–367
zero-downtime methodology,
364–366

minimal database supplemental
logging, 93–94

MINKEEP parameter, 101

MINKEEPDAYS parameter, 218, 257

MINKEEPFILES parameter, 218

MINKEEPHOURS parameter, 218

missing archivelog files, 329–334

Monitor component, 315
architecture, 351–353
instance prep, 353–354
overview, 350–351
server, 354–355

monitor.sh utility, 354

monitoring, 314
Data Pump process, 132–134
Extract process, 126–128
GGSCI for, 315–326
GUI-based tools for, 314–315
Monitor. *See* Monitor component
Replicat process, 149–150

MOOS (May Be Out of Sync)
queue, 370

MQ Series messaging service, 391

MSDB historical data, 281–282

multimaster replication, 8–9
bidirectional. *See* bidirectional
replication
IDENTITY property, 310–311

multitarget replication
Manager process configuration on
target server, 154–155
target database on Data Pump
Extract process, 155–159

MySQL, 232
database setup, 234–235
definition files, 237–238
GoldenGate installation for,
232–233
initial load, 236
Replicat process, 240–244
replication configuration,
248–249
replication to Oracle, 233–234,
244–251
schema creation, 235–236
schema initial loading, 238–240

N

names
Data Pump processes, 33, 122,
130–131
DSNs, 258–259, 289, 291, 299
Extract processes, 23, 122
output files, 384
Replicat processes, 122, 146
SQL Server, 264–266, 268, 272
trail files, 31

NAMES option in global mapping, 202
Natural Language Support (NLS)
    language, 123
networks
    connectivity checking, 86
    errors related to, 328–329
    new features, 399
    requirements, 42
    SQL Server protocols, 260
    SQL Server requirements, 257
    virtual machines, 50, 54
new features
    compressed data, 399–400
    conflict resolution, 395–399
    database platforms, 394
    downstream capture, 400–401
    globalization, 394
    integrated capture, 399
    network performance, 399
    RAC, 401
    security, 395
NLS (Natural Language Support)
    language, 123
NLS_LANG parameter
    Extract process, 123
    Replicat parameter file, 147
NO_LOG parameter, 263, 280
NOARCHIVELOG mode, 88
node synchronization in RAC, 208
NODYNAMICRESOLUTION
    parameter, 336
NOENCRYPTTRAIL parameter, 184
NOLOGGING setting, 335
NOMANAGESECONDARYTRUNCA-
    TIONPOINT option, 292, 294–306
NOT FOR REPLICATION option, 269
NOUSECHECKPOINTS option, 218
NUMBER data type, 235

O

object definitions in MySQL, 244–246
object-level supplemental logging, 94
ODBC Data Source Administrator
    utility, 286–287

ODBC System DSN, 258–259
odbcad32.exe program, 286
OEL (Oracle Enterprise Linux)
    environment, 296
Omitplaceholders property, 386
Omitvalues property, 386
one-to-many replication, 6–7
one-to-one replication, 6–7
one-way replication, 110
    checklist, 113–114
    Data Pump process configuration,
        130–136
    Extract process configuration,
        121–129
    HR schema, 110–112
    Manager process configuration,
        117–121
    Replicat process configuration,
        145–152
    target database, 114–117, 136
    topology, 112–115
ONEXIT option, 206
online mode in Extract process, 24–27
OOS (Out of Sync) reports, 373
open command, 340
operating system configuration, 74–76
ORA-00001: unique constraint (string
    .string) violated message, 335–337
ORA-01403: no data found
    message, 335
ORA-01653: unable to extend table
    string.string by string in tablespace
    string message, 335
Oracle Active Data Guard, 13, 221, 224
Oracle Advanced Replication, 8
Oracle Data Guard, 221, 224
Oracle Database, 7–8, 87–89
Oracle Database Data Pump utility,
    114–117
    expdp and impdp, 342
    target database on, 157–159
Oracle Enterprise Linux (OEL)
    environment, 296
Oracle Fusion Middleware option, 360

Oracle GoldenGate, overview
  background, 11–13
  best practices, 14
  in Oracle Stack, 13–14
Oracle GoldenGate Agent, 353
Oracle GoldenGate Data Integration
  Server (DIS), 380
Oracle GoldenGate Data Pump
  process. *See* Data Pump process
Oracle GoldenGate Director, 355–356
  architecture, 356–361
  client, 357–358
  downloading, 358–360
  installing, 358
  server, 361
  starting and managing, 360
Oracle GoldenGate Director
  Administrator, 358
Oracle GoldenGate Director Client,
  357–358
Oracle GoldenGate Director
  Database, 357
Oracle GoldenGate Director
  Monitoring Agent, 357
Oracle GoldenGate Director Server,
  357, 361
Oracle GoldenGate Director Web, 358
Oracle GoldenGate Extract process.
  See Extract process
Oracle GoldenGate for Flat File utility,
  378–379
  exit properties file, 381–382
  flat file types, 380–381
  infrastructure, 380
  installing, 379
  meta columns, 387
  overview, 379
Oracle GoldenGate Manager process.
  See Manager process
Oracle GoldenGate Monitor
  component, 315
  architecture, 351–353
  instance prep, 353–354
  overview, 350–351
  server, 354–355

Oracle GoldenGate Monitor
  Repository, 352
*Oracle GoldenGate Oracle Installation
  and Setup Guide*, 40
Oracle GoldenGate Replicat process.
  See Replicat process
Oracle GoldenGate Server
  Collector process
    overview, 33–34
    SQL Server, 254–255, 257
Oracle GoldenGate Software
  Command Interface. *See*
  GoldenGate Software Command
  Interface (GGSCI) program
"Oracle GoldenGate Statement of
  Direction", 12
Oracle GoldenGate User Exit APIs, 381
Oracle GoldenGate Vericom interface,
  374–376
Oracle GoldenGate Veridata, 366–367
  comparisons, 374–376
  configuring and using, 372–373
  functionality, 370–372
  web, 373–374
Oracle GoldenGate Veridata
  Agent, 371
Oracle GoldenGate Veridata CLI, 372
Oracle GoldenGate Veridata
  Repository, 371
Oracle GoldenGate Veridata
  Server, 371
Oracle GoldenGate Veridata Web
  Client, 371, 373–374
Oracle Heterogeneous Replication
  Services, 9–11
Oracle Maximum Availability
  Architecture, 220–223
Oracle Metalink, 19, 35
ORACLE_SID parameter, 122
Oracle Software Delivery Cloud, 63,
  68–69
Oracle Streams, 8–11
Oracle Supplemental Logging Log
  Groups, 94
Oracle Technology Network (OTN), 391

Oracle VirtualBox, 42–43
    downloading, 42–44
    images, 46–48
    installing, 43–46
    overview, 43
Oracle Wallet, 354
OS PATH environment variable, 74–75
OS version for SQL Server, 257
OTN (Oracle Technology Network), 391
OTN License Agreement, 66, 69
Out of Sync (OOS) reports, 373
output file for writers
    names, 384
    property settings, 385–386

P

PARALLEL parameter, 342
parallelization
    Extract processes, 29–30
    performance tuning, 347–348
parameter files, 34
    DEFGEN, 303
    Extract process, 121–124,
        130–131, 211
    Replicat process, 146–147
    REPORCL, 304
PASSTHRU parameter
    buffers, 346
    Pump process, 296
PASSWORD parameter, 237
passwords
    definition files, 237
    encrypting, 181–183
    JMX, 354
PATH environment variable, 74–75
peer-to-peer replication, 6–7
performance tuning, 341
    initial load, 341–342
    lag. See lag
    new network features, 399
    parallelization, 347–348
permissions for SQL Server, 258

Persistently out of sync status, 371
PGA (program global area) memory
    allocations, 75
PGA_AGGREGATE_TARGET, 342
PORT parameter
    Manager process, 98, 118
    SQL Server, 257, 275–276
ports, checking, 86
pos command, 340
PREFIX option in global mapping, 202
@PRESENT function, 194, 196
primary keys
    overview, 90–91
    Replicat lag, 346–347
privileges, user, 76–80
PROCESS VM AVAIL FROM OS (min)
    setting, 76
processes
    hung, 338
    reports, 318–321
profiles in Veridata, 372
program global area (PGA) memory
    allocations, 75
propagation in Capture process, 9
Pump process. See also Data
    Pump process
    lag, 345–346
    SQL Server, 256–257, 296–298
PURGEOLDEXTRACTS parameter
    Manager process, 100–101, 118
    for SQL Server, 256
    trail files, 218
pw_agent_util.sh utility, 354

R

RAC. See Real Application
    Clusters (RAC)
RANGE function, 348
rate statistic, 389
ratedetail statistic, 389
Rawchars property, 386
RBA (redo byte address), 335

Real Application Clusters (RAC),
    207, 220
    A-VIP addresses, 225–227
    action scripts, 227–229
    capture changes, 207–208
    Clusterware registration, 229
    connections, 209
    disaster recovery, high availability,
        and replication, 223–224
    Extract process, 26, 30
    GoldenGate installation in, 225
    installation location, 207
    Maximum Availability
        Architecture, 220–223
    new features, 401
    synchronizing nodes, 208
    threads, 209
Recovery Checkpoint, 318
RECYCLEBIN parameter, 81
redo byte address (RBA), 335
redo log files, 31
redo streams, 25–26
register extract command
    Extract process, 124
    Replicat process, 148
registering
    Clusterware, 229
    Data Pump process, 131–132
    Extract process, 124, 137–138
    Replicat process, 138–140, 148
remote trail files, 22, 30, 32
REPERROR parameter
    conflict resolution, 165–166
    replicat file, 397
reperror statement, 166–168
REPLICAT parameter, 149
Replicat process
    administering, 148–150
    bidirectional replication, 171–172
    configuring, 138–140, 145,
        150–152
    initial-load, 138–140
    lag, 346–347
    memory for, 76

MySQL, 239–244, 249
    overview, 22, 34
    parameter file, 146–147
    registering, 148
    statistics, 322–325
    on target database server, 158
    troubleshooting, 335–338
replication overview, 2
    database data, 4–6
    database objects, 7
    disk-based, 3–4
    forms of, 6–7
    history, 7–11
    purpose, 3
    types, 3
REPORCL parameter file, 304
REPORTCOUNT parameter, 344
REPORTRATE parameter, 323
reports
    AWR, 75
    OOS, 373
    processes, 318–321
RESET option in global mapping, 202
RESOLVECONFLICT parameter,
    396–398
resolveconflict statement, 397
restricted session privilege, 82
RMAN backup operations, 25
RMTASK parameter, 236
rmtfile command, 378
RMTHOST parameter
    buffers, 346
    Data Pump process, 131
    Extract process, 125, 156
    Monitor, 353
    MySQL, 236
    Pump process, 296
    STREAMING option, 399
RMTHOSTOPTIONS parameter, 399
RMTTASK parameter
    Extract process, 138
    MySQL schema, 239
rmttrail command, 331

RMTTRAIL parameter
    Data Pump process, 131
    Extract process, 125, 156
    Pump process, 296–297
role_setup.sql script, 82
rolling upgrades, 364
rollover attributes for writers, 384–385
ROWIDs in supplemental logging, 92
rows, filtering, 194–197
run-admin.sh script, 361
Run/Execute job option, 374
Running state in Extract process, 29

S

scalability in RAC, 224
scheduling sqlexec, 206
schema
    bidirectional replication, 172
    MySQL, 235–236, 238–240
    statistics, 389
schema-level supplemental logging,
    94–96
Schema statistic, 389
schemaandtable statistic, 389
schematrandata, 94–95
scp command, 158
secondary truncation point in
    transaction logs, 310
security, 181
    commands, 185
    networks, 42
    new features, 395
    password encryption, 181–183
    SQL Server, 263
    steps, 186–191
    trail file encryption, 183–185
Select an Appliance to Import
    window, 49
select count statement, 167
Select Installation Media window, 58
send extract command
    lag, 345
    transaction memory status, 40

send replicat command, 147
sequence configuration, 82–83
sequence.sql script, 83
Server Collector process
    overview, 33–34
    SQL Server, 254–255, 257
Services applet, 309
SETENV parameter, 122–123
SGA (system global area) memory
    allocations, 75
shared library environment variable, 75
shared storage for RAC databases, 207
shell command for SQL Server, 275
show parameter command, 88
show table status command, 235
SHOWCH option, 180
shutdown abort command, 88
shutdown immediate command, 88
size of trail files, 40–41
snapshot clones, 3
snapshot copies, 4
snapshot replication, 8
Software Delivery Cloud, 63,
    68–69, 359
source database
    Capture process, 9
    SQL Server, 262–264, 284–285,
        302–303
    upgrades and migrations, 365
source definition files, 198–202
Source DSN connections, 291
source schema, exporting, 157–158
source tables
    filtering tables, 192
    for SQL Server, 264–266, 285–286
sourcedb command, 287
SOURCEDB PARAMETER, 292
SOURCEDEFS parameter
    MySQL schema, 239
    SQL Server, 302
    table-level column mapping,
        197–198
SOURCEISTABLE parameter, 138

SPECIALRUN option, 140
SQL Server
    ALTARCHIVELOGDEST
      parameter, 312
    backups, 280–281
    data type support, 261
    database management, 279–283
    DDL changes, 311–312
    GoldenGate configuration. *See*
      configuring Oracle
      GoldenGate for SQL Server
    hardware requirements, 255–257
    IDENTITY property on columns,
      310–311
    indexes, 283
    installation components, 260
    limitations, 262
    Manager process configuration,
      274–277
    Manager process parameters,
      277–279
    MSDB historical data, 281–282
    network protocols, 260
    overview, 254–255
    source databases, 262–264
    source tables, 264–266
    supported versions and editions,
      259–260
    table management, 282–283
    table options, 261
    target database, 267–269
    target tables, 268–269
    transaction log management,
      280–282
    transaction log secondary
      truncation point, 292–306, 310
    Windows clustering environment,
      308–310
    Windows Server requirements,
      257–259
    on Windows systems, 270–274
SQL Server Management Studio
  Maintenance Wizard, 282

sqlexec command
    conflict resolution, 167
    deferred constraints, 92
    foreign keys, 140
    scheduling, 206
    as standalone statement, 206
SQLEXEC parameter, 204
    conflict resolution, 165
    Replicat process initial-load, 139
    for TABLE and MAP, 204–206
SQLLOADER parameter, 378
SQLPREDICATE option, 196
srvctl utility, 209
stages in Capture process, 9
stalled Extract processes, 330–331
standby sites, 224
START_DEPENDENCIES parameter, 229
start extract command
    Data Pump process, 132
    Extract process, 29, 126
    target database, 140
start manager command, 118
start now parameter, 126
start Replicat command, 149, 159
starting
    bidirectional replication, 174
    Data Pump process, 132
    Extract process, 29, 126
    Manager process, 101–102, 118
    Oracle GoldenGate Director, 360
    Oracle GoldenGate with
      Clusterware, 230
    Replicat process, 149, 159
Starting state for Extract process, 29
startup, automating, 103
    Linux, 105–108
    Windows, 103–105
Startup Checkpoint, 318
startup mount command, 88
startup restrict command, 88
states for Extract process, 29
static clones, 3

statistics and stats command
configuration for SQL Server,
305–308
datafile output, 388–391
Extract and Replicat processes,
322–325
lag, 344
monitoring, 322–325
MySQL Replicat process, 242–244
MySQL schema, 240
status and status command
Extract process, 331
Manager process, 102–103
processes, 318
Vericom, 375
STOP_DEPENDENCIES parameter, 229
stop extract command, 29, 126, 132
stop manager command, 102
stop replicat command, 149
Stopped state for Extract process, 29
stopping
Data Pump process, 132
Extract process, 29, 126
Manager process, 102
Oracle GoldenGate with
Clusterware, 230
Replicat process, 149
storage requirements for SQL Server,
256–257
STRACE utility, 327–328
STREAMING option, 399
@STRFIND function, 195
strings in filtering, 194
@STRNUM function, 203
substitution variables, 384
SUFFIX option for global mapping,
202–203
SUPPLEMENTAL_LOG_DATA_MIN
column, 93
supplemental logging
enabled, 92–96
SQL Server, 265–266
swap space, 40, 76

synchronizing nodes for RAC
databases, 208
syntax errors, 332
sys.sp_extended_logging procedure, 266
SYSLOG parameter, 279
SYSOBJECTS table, 265
System DSN tab, 287
System DSNs, 299, 309
system global area (SGA) memory
allocations, 75
System Properties window, 74–75

T

TABLE parameter
Data Pump process, 131
definition files, 237
Extract process, 156
filters, 192–193
lag, 345
SQLEXEC, 204–206
table statistic, 389
TABLEEXCLUDE parameter, 192–193
tables
checkpoint, 180–185
column mapping, 197–202
filtering, 191–194
SQL Server management, 282–283
SQL Server options, 261
TABLES parameter for primary keys, 91
tar files, 64
target databases
configured processes, 140–141
Data Pump Extract process,
155–159
Extract process, 137–138, 156
filtering tables at, 192–193
instantiation, 136–141
Manager process, 154–155
one-way replication, 114–117
Replicat process, 138–140, 158
SQL Server, 267–269
upgrades and migrations, 365

target table requirements for SQL Server, 268–269
TARGETDB parameter, 300
TCP/IP for SQL Server, 260, 275
TCPBUFSIZE parameter, 346
Technology Network GoldenGate forum, 19
TEMP tablespace, 342
testing data, 203–204
THREADOPTIONS parameter, 208
threads in RAC databases, 209
timestamps, 342
tnsnames.ora file, 210
topology in one-way replication, 112–115
Total statistic, 389
Totaldetail statistic, 389
TRACE option, 338–339
tracking changes in trail files, 32–33
trail files
    change tracking, 32–33
    contents, 31–32, 184–185
    encrypting, 183–185
    Extract process, 27, 125
    location, 32
    maintenance, 218
    overview, 22, 30–31
    rolling over problems, 331–332
    size, 40–41
    for SQL Server, 256
TRANLOGOPTIONS parameter, 310
    archive logs, 330
    DBLOGREADER option, 211–212
    GoldenGate configuration for SQL Server, 292
    SQL Server, 265
transaction logs for SQL Server, 256
    backup retention, 281–282
    extract memory, 400
    management, 280–281
    secondary truncation point, 310
    supplemental logging, 265–266
transforming data, 5, 203–204

triggers
    bidirectional replication, 164
    SQL Server, 269
troubleshooting, 326
    common problems, 334–335
    diagnostic tools, 327
    Extract process performance and errors, 328–334
    hung processes, 338
    Logdump utility for, 339–341
    methodology, 327
    missing archivelog files, 329–334
    Replicat process, 335–338
    TRACE option, 338–339
truncate command, 168
TRUNCATE_ONLY parameter, 263, 280
TRUSS utility, 331
trusted source in bidirectional replication, 164

U

UDTs (user-defined types), 91
uncompress command, 64
UNDO_RETENTION parameter, 89–90
UNDO tablespace, 90
unidirectional replication, 6–7
unique keys in Replicat lag, 346–347
UPDATE ALL option, 397
update statement in conflicts, 397
updateagentJMX flag, 354
updateserverJMX flag, 354
upgrades, 364
    failback option, 366–367
    zero-downtime methodology, 364–366
USEANSISQLQUOTES parameter, 194
USECHECKPOINTS parameter
    Manager process, 100–101, 118
    SQL Server, 256
    trail files, 218
USEDEFAULTS parameter, 197–198
usedelta method, 398
user-defined types (UDTs), 91

user exit properties file, 381–382
USERID parameter
    definition files, 237
    Extract process, 122–123
    Manager process, 99
users
    configuring, 76–80
    Oracle GoldenGate Director
        Server, 361
usertoken command, 340
USR_ORA_SUBNET, 226

V

@VALONEOF function, 204
VB. *See* VirtualBox (VB)
vericom command, 374–375
Veridata, 366–367
    comparisons, 374–376
    configuring and using, 372–373
    functionality, 370–372
    web, 373–374
versions in replication, 35
view ggsevt command, 320
view report command, 319
    bidirectional replication, 174
    Data Pump process, 134
    Extract process, 127
    lag, 344
    Replicat process, 150
    syntax errors, 332
    target database, 141
view report mgr command, 319
Virtual Disk Creation Wizard screen, 56
Virtual Disk File Location and Size
    screen, 57
Virtual Disk Storage Details screen, 57
Virtual Hard Disk screen, 56
virtual machines
    Linux, 46–54
    Windows, 54–62

VirtualBox (VB), 42–43
    downloading, 42–44
    images, 46–48
    installing, 43–46
    overview, 43
VirtualBox Setup Wizard, 45
Visual C++ 2005 SP1 Redistributable
    Package, 277
Visual C++ for SQL Server, 257–258
VM Name and OS Type screen, 55

W

WAITFORSERVICE option, 278
Wallet, 354
WARN logging level, 382
WebLogic components, 358–359
WebLogic Server (WLS), 359
WHERE option, 194, 196–197
Windows
    auto startup in, 103–105
    installation on, 65, 69–70
    SQL Server on, 257–259, 270–274
    virtual machines, 54–62
Windows Clustering environment,
    308–310
WLS (WebLogic Server), 359
Writebuffer.size attribute, 385
Writer mode, 383–384
Writer process, 382–384
writers
    datafile output statistics, 388–391
    defining, 383
    file data content properties, 386
    meta files, 387–388
    output file property settings,
        385–386

Z

zero-downtime methodology, 364–366
zip files, 65